TRANSITIONS

Studies in Critical Social Sciences Book Series

Haymarket Books is proud to be working with Brill Academic Publishers (www.brill.nl) to republish the *Studies in Critical Social Sciences* book series in paperback editions. This peer-reviewed book series offers insights into our current reality by exploring the content and consequences of power relationships under capitalism, and by considering the spaces of opposition and resistance to these changes that have been defining our new age. Our full catalog of *SCSS* volumes can be viewed at https://www.haymarketbooks .org/series_collections/4-studies-in-critical-social-sciences.

TRANSITIONS

Methods, Theory, Politics

TOM BRASS

Haymarket Books
Chicago, IL

First published in 2022 by Brill Academic Publishers, The Netherlands
© 2022 Koninklijke Brill NV, Leiden, The Netherlands

Published in paperback in 2023 by
Haymarket Books
P.O. Box 180165
Chicago, IL 60618
773-583-7884
www.haymarketbooks.org

ISBN: 979-8-88890-010-9

Distributed to the trade in the US through Consortium Book Sales and
Distribution (www.cbsd.com) and internationally through Ingram Publisher
Services International (www.ingramcontent.com).

This book was published with the generous support of Lannan Foundation,
Wallace Action Fund, and the Marguerite Casey Foundation.

Special discounts are available for bulk purchases by organizations and
institutions. Please call 773-583-7884 or email info@haymarketbooks.org for more
information.

Cover design by Jamie Kerry and Ragina Johnson.

Printed in the United States.

Library of Congress Cataloging-in-Publication data is available.

For Amanda,
Anna, Ned, and Miles;
and in memory of my parents

⋰

Contents

Acknowledgements

The focus of this volume is on political discourse about the pattern and desirability of economic development, and how/why historical interpretations of social phenomena connected to this systemic process alter. It is a trajectory pursued here with reference to the materialism of Marx, Lenin and Trotsky (among others), via the mid-nineteenth century ideas about race held by Gobineau, Wagner, and those in the antebellum American South, through the 1960s development decade. the 1980s 'cultural turn', debates about modes of production and their respective labour regimes, culminating in the role played by immigration before and after the Brexit referendum of 2016. The object is to account for the way concepts informing this trajectory – among them different forms and effects of 'otherness' – do or do not alter, what this implies for the way capitalism itself develops, and how this in turn feeds into interpretations both of prefiguring structures and of future changes.

This entails drawing a contrast between on the one hand non- and anti-Marxist notions informing this trajectory, and on the other Marxist theory, which in the main has argued that the driver of any such trajectory is class, its formation, consciousness, and struggle, and that consequently the process and its participants, together with their respective economic and political interests must be differentiated in terms of their economic position. Furthermore, this is an approach which, in all respects, is not merely different from but the antithesis of other historical and current variants of non- Marxist (and even anti-Marxist) approaches. The trajectory follows a path extending from concepts and causes of racist ideology, via debates in the social sciences about labour regime change, modes of production, the desirability (or otherwise) of labour-power that is unfree, to the ideological content of narratives about travel and tourism.

This is not to say that a paradigm shift is undesirable or unnecessary, only to point out the dangers of not asking why this happens when it does, by whom it is done and for what reason, and with what political consequences. Where and when change is affected simply as a result of institutional pressure (encouraging conformity) or intellectual fashion (uncritical acceptance of the 'new'), such causes require foregrounding and interrogation, notwithstanding the discomfort and unpopularity of what is then revealed. For those on the left drilling down like this is especially important, not least because the aim of transition – now as in the past – is all too frequently to eject Marxist analysis from debates in the social sciences, on the grounds that either it no longer adequately explains material reality (= 'the world has moved on' trope), or that it should be replaced with a more in vogue theoretical approach (= 'old issues reassessed' trope). That the same economic and social problems stubbornly continue to surface in much the same form as before, even after having been redefined in this manner, suggests that surviving attempts at epistemological recasting is, if nothing else, evidence for the enduring political relevance of Marxist theory.

Special thanks are due to the following people. To Professor David Fasenfest, the Series Editor, for encouragement; to Athina Dimitriou of Brill publishers, who guided the book through production; and to my daughter Anna Luisa Brass, who provided the drawing for the front cover. She drew the cover for six of my previous books – *New Farmers' Movements in India* (1995), *Labour Regime Change in the Twenty-First Century* (2011), *Class, Culture and the Agrarian Myth* (2014), *Labour Markets, Identities, and Controversies* (2017), *Revolution and Its Alternatives* (2018), and *Marxism Missing, Missing Marxism* (2021) – as well as the drawings which have appeared at the start of each section in past volumes, and do so also in the present one. Here the front cover drawing of knives, forks, and spoons, indicates (to me) that bread-and-butter issues are at the root of the analysis, while images associated with Venice appearing throughout (Figures 1–6) are connected to the city featuring in a number of chapters.[1]

Like all my previous monographs, this one is dedicated to two sets of kin. To my family: Amanda, and Anna, Ned and Miles. Also, to the memory of my parents: my father, Denis Brass (1913–2006), and my mother, Gloria Brass (1916–2012).

Richmond-upon-Thames
February 2022

---

1   Anna Brass writes: the Knife Fork Spoon drawing is from c. 2006 – I was about 18 when I drew it. It's been sitting quietly in my parents' house for fifteen years. The Venice monoprint drawings are from 2016; the ship (Fig. 2) is from the de' Barbari Map, and Fig. 5 is a lock or a key from the Last Judgement mosaic on the west wall of Santa Maria Assunta in Torcello.

Figures and Tables

Figures

Tables

FIGURE 1   Wall (Arsenale)
           © ANNA LUISA BRASS

Introduction

Steps Forward or Backwards?

> It is now almost impossible ... to remember a time when people were *not* talking about a crisis in representation ... To represent someone or even something has now become an endeavour as complex and as problematic as an asymptote, with consequences for certainty and decidability as fraught with difficulties as can be imagined.
>
>> An observation by EDWARD SAID about how aporia has trumped writing and speech.[1]

∴

Transition refers to a process of change that, once in train, is difficult to halt, let alone reverse. Like the dialectic, it results in a synthesis whereby elements of a previous form are retained but altered to the extent that the substance (and perhaps also the form) of the earlier configuration is no longer recognizable. In epistemological terms, the capacity of what is transformed to establish itself depends in turn on the effectiveness (or otherwise) either of the intellectual challenge to its politics, or to the support it receives. Academia is an important site where views about the nature of transition are constructed/deconstructed, in the course of which concepts, ideas, and – more broadly – what becomes recognized as dominant interpretations about the issue in question are formulated and reproduced. In the course of this process, what constitutes transition, and why, together with theory and debate about it can be declared 'normal', and circulates widely, becoming accepted as such (= 'hegemonic'). Alternatively, a hitherto dominant interpretation can equally be declared banished, as a result of which it ceases to circulate as the topic for debate, not long after vanishing from the intellectual and political agenda.

---

1   Said (2002: 293, 294, original emphasis).

Unsurprisingly, in terms of political debate the theoretical approach most affected negatively by the process of intellectual transition has been Marxism. Where academia is concerned, therefore, transition refers to the process whereby many of those who, as Marxists, obtained university posts, and from the 1960s onwards used this platform to dismantle this discourse from within. Faced with having to make a space for themselves intellectually, in an increasingly hostile political environment, they did this either by 'improving' Marxism, combining it with anti-Marxist concepts and theory, or – much the same thing –discarding it altogether. Fairly predictable, therefore, was the twofold outcome of this transition. On the one hand, it entailed deprivileging Marxist approaches to political economy across many different historical periods and places, not least interpretations based on class analysis, modernity, and progress, along with the desirability/possibility of further industrial development in metropolitan and so-called Third World contexts. And on the other, this was accompanied by the essentializing and privileging of 'otherness'/'difference', peasant economy, traditional culture, non-class identities, populism, and the agrarian myth.

As applied to the issue of labour regime change, for example, transition involves what appears to be attempts to expel the concept of unfree labour from the development debate.[2] This can be done in a number of ways, but an emerging one currently is the claim that abolitionism in general amounts to a Tory plot, the object of the latter being to exculpate free labour by joining condemnations of unfreedom and insisting – implausibly – that such production relations do not exist (they do) or will shortly be rooted out (they aren't). Recent exponents of this view fail to address the much earlier objections to unfreedom, including that by Marxism, and so miss the fact that there is a different and more radical case opposing the employment of unfree labour. In the case of Marxism, this is unconnected with 'saving' capitalism, or as has been argued by me, returning to a 'kinder'/'nicer' form of accumulation, but much rather entails going beyond capitalism altogether, to socialism. Against non-Marxist forms of contemporary abolitionism, together with those who perceive it as a Tory plot, all of which regard capitalism as the solution, therefore, Marxism argues that unfreedom enables capitalism to reproduce itself, on which grounds it should be opposed.

---

2 A number of attempts to expel the concept of unfree labour from debate are considered in Chapters 2, 3, and 4 (this volume).

Reified Notions, Fantasmic Representations?

Central to much of the debate considered here is the tension between two distinct forms of identity, together with their respective political and ideological consequences. Psychologistic interpretations of racism correspond to an approach whereby its presence in working class ideology is decontextualized economically: examined in ahistorical terms, racism is consequently deemed innate and ineradicable, to be condemned as such. However, that working class perceptions of ethnic/national 'otherness' is not a static (= innate) discourse, but one both the terms and incidence of which are reproduced by the wider economic context, is self-evident. In the case of France, for example, racist attitudes expressed by workers changed in their intensity from the late 1970s onwards, from being views that were apologized for – that is, acknowledged as being wrong – to 'a hegemonic way of perceiving the social world', or what its subjects felt to be an entirely legitimate *weltanschauung*.[3] That the desire by workers for a better life necessarily entailed a transcendence of their existing social conditions poses questions about the oft-heard postmodern claim that all from below resistance is designed to do nothing more than protect the status quo.[4]

How and why racism emerged among the French working class when it did are issues addressed recently by Didier Eribon. Hostility towards forms of 'otherness' – not just racism but also homophobia and sexism – are regarded by him simply as innately pathological, a kind of psychosis that amounts to a social disease having no explanation beyond the realm of neurosis.[5] Given that it refuses to probe beneath the surface appearance of these pathologies, and thus precludes contextualizing opposition to these forms of 'otherness' in

---

3   According to Eribon (2018: 137–38), during the 1970s racism already existed in his kind of working class community, a response to the arrival of Maghrebi families. However, these 'racist feelings never became established as the kernel of a set of political preoccupations ... it took time for the daily expressions of ordinary racism to join up with more directly ideological elements and become transformed into a hegemonic way of perceiving the social world', adding (Eribon, 2018: 140): 'My family could stand as a representative case of the ordinary racism found in working class milieus in the 1960s and of the way it increased in harshness throughout the 1970s and 1980s.'

4   Hence the view (Eribon, 2018: 39): 'In working class environments, a leftist politics meant first and foremost a pragmatic rejection of the experience of one's own daily life'.

5   'Why is it that a certain number of people seem committed to the hatred of others,' asks Eribon (2018: 211–12), 'Why is it that certain categories of the population – gay men, lesbians, transsexuals, Jews, blacks, and so [on are hated]?' He continues: 'This was a question I found myself asking over and over again: Why? And also: What did we do to deserve this? There is no answer to these questions other than the absurdity and arbitrariness of social verdicts ...'

terms of an economic dimension, such a seemingly uncurious view cannot be anything but odd coming as it does from a sociologist like Eribon. No attempt is made by him to place antagonism to these sorts of 'otherness' within an economic context, despite the fact that, in at least some instances, the presence of a specific economic background enables a better understanding (but not a justification) of why this form of animosity occurs. Racism can on occasion be the outcome of labour market competition between workers belonging to different ethnic groups, a clash of identities frequently encouraged by employers so as to undermine, prevent or pre-empt the construction of solidarity based on class.

Having condemned those leftists who turned to neoconservatism as betraying the working class, responsible in a large part for the loss of grassroots support on the part of labour, many of whom abandoned communism and shifted their support to the far right, Eribon then is equally critical of those who remained leftists.[6] The latter, in his eyes, were equally culpable of misconstruing working class politics, by imagining – wrongly – that labour was, and would always remain, the 'natural' supporter of the left. Not only was this not the case now, maintains Eribon, but perhaps in a fundamental sense it had never ever been so. He recounts how, when Marxism dominated political discourse during the 1960s and 1970s, all identities or struggles unconnected with class were considered subordinate to the struggle of working class as workers. Movements the focus of which were on cultural issues or non-class identities (gender/sexual/race) were 'set aside' by Marxism, as a result of which they found 'other avenues' of expression, frequently in direct and antagonistic opposition to Marxist politics.[7] In view of this negative assessment, it is

---

6 'I'm afraid', cautions Eribon (2018: 145), 'it's the case that there are some cruel disappointments – along with some rather scathing refutations of their ideas – in store for those [leftist] intellectuals [whose] enthusiasm is enabled by the fact that they have never in their life encountered anyone who belongs to these classes, except perhaps while reading writings from the nineteenth century.' His a-plague-on-both-your-houses approach is summed up thus: 'It is precisely these kinds of mythologies and mystifications [workers = 'natural' supporters of the left] that the left needs to shake off – along with the neoconservative currents ... – if it wishes to understand the phenomena that are leading to its downfall ...'

7 See Eribon (2018: 235), who indicts Marxism for maintaining 'the only "true" struggle, the only struggle worthy of interest [was] that of the working class.' He continues: 'Movements that came to be labelled as "cultural" were focusing their attention on various dimensions that Marxism had set aside: gendered, sexual, and racial forms of subjectivation ... Because Marxism's attention was so exclusively concentrated on class oppression, these other movements were required to find other avenues for problematizing lived experience, and they often ended up to a great extent neglecting class oppression.'

unsurprising that Eribon also takes issue with two interrelated issues: the conceptual efficacy of class struggle, and the call for a return to Marxist theory.[8]

To term such non-class mobilizations as having been 'set aside' – that is to say, ignored – by Marxism is problematic. In some instances – for example, ideology which insisted that ethnic or national difference within the ranks of labour were more important politically and thus overrode class distinctions – they were perceived as part of the armoury of conservatism and the far-right. In these situations, it was not so much a case of 'neglecting class oppression' on the part of those advocating mobilization on the basis of non-class identities, as Eribon claims, as attacking Marxism head-on, and categorizing it as no longer having anything valid to say about the nature of society. He concludes by asking whether Marxism had to die so that these forms of cultural 'otherness', their politics and discourse, might live. His answer, a revealing one, is in the affirmative.[9]

The description of the transfer by the working class in France of its support from communism to the far-right as a vindication of 'populism' is rejected by Eribon, on the grounds that it implies workers are acting irrationally, whereas in his view it is evidence of their rationality.[10] Such an interpretation overlooks the fact that, in terms of class position, such workers can indeed be said – when espousing a politics that is populist – to be acting contrary to their interests (= 'irrationally'). This is because populist far-right parties cannot – and will never – represent working class interests: that is to say, of workers *as workers*, instead offering them what Marxist theory terms false consciousness, or varieties of empowerment based on non-class identities.[11] An instance of this

---

8   Hence the view (Eribon, 2018: 147) that 'we might ask how one is to take into account the practical existence of "social classes" and of the conflictual nature of society … without falling into the magical or mythical invocation of the "Class Struggle" extolled these days by those who call for a "return to Marxism"…Such invocations rely blindly on … reified notions and fantasmic representations …'

9   'Was it the case,' asks Eribon (2018: 236), 'that the disappearance of Marxism, or at least the way it was expunged as a hegemonic discourse on the left, was a necessary condition for the possibility of thinking politically about the mechanism of sexual, racial and other forms of subjection, about the production of minoritarian subjectivities?' To his own question he replies: 'The answer is probably yes'.

10   See Eribon (2018: 133ff.).

11   Equating populism with *false* consciousness where the class interests of labour is concerned is different from the position held by Eribon (2018: 126), who almost comes close to arguing that, by voting for the populist far right, workers in France were expressing their consciousness of *class* ('However paradoxical it might seem to some people, I am convinced that voting for the National Front must be interpreted, at least in part, as the final recourse of people of the working classes attempting to defend their collective identity …').

would be the contrast in the UK between on the one hand a political undertaking by conservatives/populists to regulate immigration so as to restrict access to the labour market, and thus the negative impact of job competition, while on the other permitting exemptions which in effect negate much of the original undertaking. The latter option is followed because conservatives/populists ultimately represent the interests not of labour but of capitalists, who – since they rely on continued access to cheap migrant labour-power, want a deregulated labour market.

In an attempt to understand why the left in France has lost ground to the far right, Eribon returned to his working-class roots in the northern city of Reims, where many of his family members who used to support the communists now vote for the far right. In accounting for this change, he expresses his bewilderment thus: 'It is impossible for me to understand how and why the issue of harsh working conditions and all the slogans denouncing them ... have disappeared from discourse on the left, and even from its perception of the social world.'[12] Rightly, he attributes this change in working class politics in a large measure to the ideological shift in what Eribon terms 'the official left wing'.[13] The latter, composed for the most part of academics and/or intellectuals who in the late 1960s had declared themselves to be socialists, were now to be found in the ranks of neoconservativism, advocating not working class empowerment but rather the economic austerity of *laissez-faire* policies.[14] It

12   Eribon (2018: 81). '[D]uring my childhood', he writes (Eribon, 2016: 119), 'my entire family was "communist" in the sense that the Communist Party was the organizing principle and the uncontested horizon of our relation to politics. How could my family have turned into one in which it seemed possible, even natural sometimes, to vote either for the right or for the extreme right?'.

13   Asking 'What heavy measure of responsibility for this process must be borne by the official left wing?', Eribon (2018: 120–21) continues: 'What is the responsibility of those people who, having set aside the political commitments they held in the 1960s and 1970s as youthful follies of a bygone moment, having risen to positions of power and importance, would do all they could to encourage the spread of right wing thinking, would consign to the dustbin of history anything associated with what had once been one of the essential preoccupations of the left (even, since the middle of the nineteenth century, one of its fundamental characteristics), which is to say the attention paid to oppression, to social conflict ... Look at what has become of all those who back then had been advocating civil war ... These days ... their vehemence is focused on opposing the slightest hint of protest arising from the working classes. They have returned [and] turned themselves into the enemies of all those people whose vanguard they used to claim to represent ...'

14   This transformation is delineated by Eribon (2018: 122–23) thus: 'The socialist left set out on a major project of transformation, one that became more and more marked as the years went by. With a suspicious degree of enthusiasm, they started to turn to neoconservative intellectuals for guidance. Those intellectuals, pretending to offer a way to renovate leftist thought, in fact set out to eliminate all that was leftist from the left ... Gone was

was this twofold process – desertion by the leftist parties/intellectuals, cou-pled with the espousal by the latter of views contrary to the interests of people such as themselves – that turned workers away from the left and towards the far right.[15]

Having written extensively about his own sexuality, and the necessity of its being 'hidden' socially, Eribon wonders why he never had the courage to write about shame linked to his working class family background, observing that – comparatively speaking – it had been much easier for him to discuss shame connected to sexuality.[16] Significantly, this confession underlines the veracity of a political claim made repeatedly over the years by those who remain Marxists: namely, that in the humanities generally, and social scien-tific discourse in particular, talking about non-class identity is currently seen as politically 'safe', whereas raising the spectre of class is now regarded as taboo, amounting in effect to an ideological reversal of the ways in which these issues were treated not so long ago. This sort of transition, whereby a paradigm seemingly vanishes from debate, can be explained in terms of its locus and its dynamic: in academia, where there is a dialectic between apostasy, critique, and silence.

Transition, Critique, Silence

The fact of apostasy can be traced in part to the epistemological transition accompanying the 1960s expansion of higher education: once inside the acad-emy, therefore, many of those who started out as leftists replaced Marxism with postmodern theory. For the latter approach, the central epistemological problem is to construct a model that subsumes all kinds/forms of narrative, a

---

any talk of exploitation ... gone the references to relations between the classes ... gone any mention of unequal social opportunities ... The notion of domination, the very idea of a structuring opposition between those in positions of dominance and those who were dominated disappeared from the official political landscape of the left.'

15   As Eribon (2018: 125) puts it, '[w]hole sectors of the most severely disadvantaged would thus, in what almost seemed like an automatic reshuffling of the cards in the political deck, shift over to the only party that seemed to care about them, the only one, in any case, that offered them a discourse that seemed intended to provide meaning to the expe-riences that made up their daily lives.'

16   See Eribon (2018: 19–20), who explains how 'making an "avowal" of who one is [has] become these days valorized and valorizing [so] that it was even strongly encouraged in the contemporary political context – when it was sexuality that was in question. Yet the same kind of project was extremely difficult, and received no support from prevailing categories of social discourse, when it was a question of working class social origins.'

framework that accounts merely for the fact of narrative, not its purpose. No significance is attached to the link between language and the material conditions that give rise to or sustain a particular narrative. Indeed, it is a link the very existence – let alone the efficacy – of which postmodern theory denies. This means that there is no longer a necessary relation between ideological practice and infrastructure, a non-determinate view that postmodernism inherited from structuralism. Nor is there any form of consciousness that – from the point of view of a particular class – can be categorized as false.

For anyone not placing this transition in its 1960s academic context, quite why postmodernism ought not to be viewed sympathetically remains a mystery.[17] In the case of development studies, for example, the impact of postmodern theory has been negative, in that the 'cultural turn' set out to deprivilege socialism, materialism and class as illegitimate Enlightenment/Eurocentric forms of 'foundationalism' inapplicable to the Third World.[18] In sharp contrast to Marxism, postmodern theory re-essentializes national/ethnic identity, recasting this as empowering for 'those below'. Consequently, quotidian resistance by (undifferentiated) peasants in defence of indigenous culture and tradition is seen as a legitimate part of the struggle against capitalism, a result being that rural struggle is no longer about class but identity politics. This recuperation by postmodernism of an essentialist peasant culture/economy leaves intact the existing class structure, and reproduces the populist mobilizing discourse of the political right. It is, in short, a conservative form of anti-capitalism.[19]

This is because grass-roots resistance as envisioned by the 'new' populist postmodernism is deemed to be simply about cultural empowerment, with little or no reference to the political economy. Viewed through the lens of the

---

17   See Brass (2017: Chapter 18) on how and why this academic context is important.

18   The replacement by many leftist academics of Marxism with postmodernism brings to mind the reasons given by Trotsky as to why the pre-revolutionary Russian intelligentsia discarded Marxism, in the process of becoming a liberal bourgeois intelligentsia. 'In spite of the large perspectives held out by the new doctrines [in the 1880s],' he writes (Trotsky, 1930: 88, 113), 'the Marxists in reality remained imprisoned by the conservative mood of the eighties, displaying an inability to take bold initiatives, remaining inactive when confronted by obstacles, shoving the revolution into an indefinite future, and inclining generally to regard socialism as a task for centuries of evolution … Its dialects were convenient for demonstrating the progress of capitalist methods of development, but finding that it led to a revolutionary rejection of the whole capitalist system, they [= intelligentsia] adjudged it an impediment and declared it out of date … In this roundabout way the old Populist intelligentsia, with its archaic sympathies, was slowly being transformed into a liberal bourgeois intelligentsia.'

19   This issue is examined in Chapter 2 (this volume).

latter, an expanding industrial reserve army is disempowering, and as such can be blamed by workers on capital: the struggle accordingly becomes one of class. Viewed through a postmodern lens, however, the same process alters in meaning and agency. Struggle becomes about non-class identity, with workers seeing the impact on them of the industrial reserve army of labour as the fault not of capital but of migrants belonging to a different ethnicity, gender or nationality. Not the least worrying effect of the 'cultural turn' is that it licenses a particular kind of silence, extending from not engaging with debate when it occurs to shutting it down.

Among other things, this takes the form of claiming that only the subaltern can speak about what it means to be a subaltern. Perhaps one of the most problematic concepts inserted into discussion about racism, therefore, is the term 'white saviour'. The latter is currently a trope that remains undifferentiated, applied as it is invariably to any attempts by whites to establish solidarity with an 'other' in countering racism. To apply the term 'white saviour' to 'celebrities' whose 'solidarity' is nothing more than a self-serving process of virtue-signalling, the thinly disguised object of which is to boost a media career, is of course uncontroversial. However, to apply the same term to principled acts of solidarity on the part of those who – although themselves not 'other' – nevertheless participate in struggles against colonialism, is politically far more controversial. It ignores the long history of backing for the anti-colonial and anti-imperial struggles, not to mention particular causes such as disinvestment from banks supporting the apartheid system in South Africa, and opposition to continued forms of unfree labour. Moreover, into this same frame, as yet another kind of 'white saviour' intervention, it is possible to place Marxist theory about the desirability of development, dismissed by subaltern studies as an inappropriate foundational ideology emanating from the Eurocentric discourse of the Enlightenment, which is precisely what postmodern/postcolonial theory does.

Marxist Methodology?

Noting that '[i]ntellectual life isn't always very pretty when you look at it up close,' Eribon concludes that 'its reality bears little resemblance to the idealized image you might have looking in from the outside'.[20] This is borne out

---

20   Hence the following observation (Eribon, 2016: 226): 'A certain little clique of academics considered the literary pages of this magazine [for which Eribon wrote] to be their private reserve. They used these pages shamelessly to advance their own agendas, attempting to

by Lévi-Strauss, who observed of French academics undertaking research in 1930s Brazil that 'we all attempted to surround ourselves with an exclusive court, more important than our neighbours.'[21] The situation back in France was no better, since '[u]nfortunately, in French anthropology there reigns an atmosphere we have inherited from our forebears, a climate of mutual suspicion. Each one jealously stakes out what he considers to be his own domain.'[22] This much was obvious even to outsiders such as Trotsky, who described Paris at that conjuncture as 'the petty and envious little universe of scholars'.[23] Responding to criticism is pointless, averred Lévi-Strauss, but a response is necessary to correct 'obvious errors or bad faith'; even this results in nothing.[24] Not considered by Lévi-Strauss, however, is another kind of academic reaction to criticism, which takes the form of silence.[25] That is, not referring to a criticism made, even when this is relevant to the matter discussed. It could be argued that silence is the worst of the two, in that a response to criticism is at least recognition of an alternative position taken, whereas silence amounts to a denial that any such criticism was ever made.

A case in point concerns a recent attempt to construct a fieldwork approach that, it is claimed, provides researchers with a methodology that is specifically

---

impose their power and their drift towards reactionary thought on the whole politico-intellectual scene. At every turn they would fight against anything ... that threatened to leave them in the shadows, against anything that was leftist and intended to remain so.'

21   Lévi-Strauss and Eribon (1991: 23).

22   See Lévi-Strauss (Lévi-Strauss and Eribon, 1991: 66, 70–71, 72, 84–5, 102, 106–7, 116, 120), who also refers to numerous academic quarrels (with, among others, Gurvitch, Foucault, Caillois, and Sartre) in which he has participated over the years.

23   This observation by Trotsky is contained in a 1935 essay about Céline, included in the volume edited by Howe (1964: 344).

24   'When [a review] is hostile, I'm irritated', he concedes (Lévi-Strauss & Eribon, 1991: 69), 'because I tell myself I ought to clear up factual errors, dispel misunderstandings. However, I resent the author of such remarks less than the temptation he inspires in me to drop my work to respond. And then [I know] that I wouldn't change his mind.' As to whether a response manages to shift perceptions, his view is that 'I believe so less and less'.

25   Silence about politically critical interpretation – explicit or implied – has long been a stock bourgeois academic response. In a 1952 article discussing a 1946 book by Dobb that made an important contribution to the debate about a transition from feudalism to capitalism, Hilton (1985: 278–79) noted the absence of reviews in 'historical journals nearer to the centre of what one might call the British "historical establishment"', a silence he explained in the following manner: 'The reasons for the general neglect of Dobb's book are fairly obvious. British academic historians do not like Marxism [and] the decade after the end of the war was hardly propitious for the unprejudiced discussion of a Marxist interpretation of capitalism'.

Marxist.[26] Not only does the volume in question fall well short of this objective, but the reasons for its shortcomings are revealing in terms of what these days passes for Marxism. In a compilation such as this it is helpful to have some familiarity with Marxism, the issues to which it is applied methodologically, and pre-figuring debates about all the latter. Unfortunately, a number of contributions display scant knowledge about either the theory, the methods, or indeed the debates. Not the least problematic aspect is the frequent citation as authoritative Marxist analyses that are nothing of the sort.[27] Among the things lost sight of are that Marxism is not just about what is, but also about its link with what ought to be. Socialism as an objective, and how this might be achieved, is nowhere to be seen in the analyses; practice, it is inferred, is confined to study. Consequently, even when addressed, talk of a specifically Marxist approach seems teleologically pointless. In the midst of present-day *laissez-faire* capitalism, with its attendant economic and social crises, the decoupling of Marxism and its revolutionary politics is lamentable.

In terms of a guide not just to fieldwork but to how this might incorporate a Marxist approach, this volume fares poorly when compared with earlier counterparts. Far superior, therefore, is a collection indicating methods used by anthropologists in furtherance of specifically Marxist ethnographic research.[28] Subsequent volumes, edited and contributed to by social scientists with experience of development studies research, have essays that not only cover geographical areas, economic issues, and fieldwork accounts relevant to Marxism, but also provide valuable methodological insights.[29] It seems odd that at least one contributor to the volume admits to not having done any fieldwork, a

---

26   The collection of essays, according to its editor (Mezzadri, 2021: 2), has as its 'primary scope ... becoming a far more practical guide on how to carry out concrete, meaningful Marxian analysis in specific contemporary setting'. A worthy aim, but the volume in question fails to live up to this aspiration.

27   For example, Jairus Banaji, cited endorsingly throughout the volume (Mezzadri, 2021: IX, 4, 9, 18, 20, 32, 36, 55, 57, 64, 70, 71, 73, 121, 158, 203, 205, 207), despite the fact that his claim to be a Marxist has been strongly disputed, on which see Chapter 3 below. It is difficult not to agree with Lévi-Strauss when he states (Lévi-Strauss & Eribon, 1991: 69) that although 'I tell myself that I ought to clear up factual errors, dispel the misunderstandings ... I resent [having] to drop my work to respond [particularly when I know] that wouldn't change his [or her] mind'.

28   The volume in question was edited by Bloch (1975); it contained important analyses by Godelier, Feuchtwang, Terray, Kahn, and Friedman outlining in some detail the shape that a Marxist approach to fieldwork might adopt.

29   Edited volumes that would have undoubtedly repaid consideration, methodologically speaking, are those by Epstein (1967), by Srinivas, Shah, and Ramaswamy (1979), by Ellen (1984), by Bardhan (1989), and by Long and Long (1992).

lacuna that raises the issue of what credence is to be attached to his views.[30] Significantly, one manifestation of this methodological absence surfaces in the problem he has with theory about class (see below). As odd is a failure on the part of the volume as a whole to consider what Marx and other Marxists have had to say about fieldwork methodology, the questions to ask, and of whom.

In the mid-1860s Marx himself drew up a comprehensive questionnaire schedule ('an enquiry into the condition of the working classes') covering issues such as age/gender of the workforce, hiring practices, wages, hours of labour in the factory or homework, meal times, conditions of work, their impact on health, educational levels, together with seasonal and economic issues affecting employment.[31] Again, in the 1880s Marx compiled a list of a hundred questions, noting that '[w]e also rely upon socialists of all schools who, being wishful for social reform, must wish for an *exact* and *positive* knowledge of the conditions in which the working class – the class to whom the future belongs – works and moves', adding that '[t]hese statements of labour's grievances are the first act which socialist democracy must perform in order to prepare the way for social regeneration.'[32] During the early 1930s a series of *Marxist Study Courses*, covering many of the same issues (wages and accumulation of capital, the distribution of surplus value, economic crises) were accompanied by questions that all Marxists should ask and attempt to answer. Their age notwithstanding, these methodological interventions underline not just the kind of fieldwork a Marxist should undertake, but also – and as importantly – the political end to which such practice is geared.

The methodological shortcomings of the current attempt to construct a specifically Marxist methodology can be traced to theoretical problems of two kinds: issues not addressed, or addressed inadequately, and concepts not understood. Accordingly, some terms central to a Marxist analysis are ignored, rejected as irrelevant, or – when addressed – misinterpreted. This absence is itself linked to problematic interpretations of class. Rejecting the Marxist approach that differentiates the peasantry along class lines, a contributor pronounces Lenin mistaken about this process, arguing instead the replacement of Marxist concepts such as 'proletariat'/'proletarianization' with his own term 'classes of labour'.[33] However, this case against Lenin and in support of 'classes

30   The contributor in question is Bernstein (2021: 18).
31   See Marx (1985).
32   'A Workers' Inquiry', by Marx, was published in *La Revue socialiste*, April 20, 1880.
33   On 'classes of labour', see Bernstein (2021: 26–27). The term not only pops up regularly throughout the volume (Mezzadri, 2021: 26, 28, 37, 139, 179, 180, 186), but also features centrally in Mezzadri and Fan (2018).

of labour' – a category which includes undifferentiated peasants – is based on an article every claim of which turns out to be wrong.[34] Why these Marxist concepts and processes are discarded, and why smallholding is retained within his all-inclusive sociological category ('classes of labour'), is not difficult to explain: it is because the contributor in question is himself an agrarian populist, not a Marxist.[35] More broadly, the many debatable claims made and, equally problematic, unreferenced critiques of arguments presented in this attempt to formulate a specifically Marxist approach to methodology, illustrate the contention that unmentioned criticisms which go to the heart of what is – or what is not – to be considered Marxism amount in the end to one kind of silence.

A Lesser Status and a Distant Place?

Another and different kind of silence, not linked to the above, concerns who it is that is permitted to speak, and why. The role of the social sciences in formulating theory about systemic transition is well understood, but the reasons for this, and why the concept of development used in academic debate changes the way it does is perhaps less so. Attempts to address the latter question include that by Edward Said, who sought to portray it generally as the outcome of a crisis of representation following decolonization, and in particular as 'a genuine malaise about the sociopolitical status of anthropology as a whole'.[36] According to Said, therefore, 'today's anthropologists can no longer go to the postcolonial field with quite the same ease as in former times.' Because of the resulting crisis of representation, the issue is seen by Said as one involving two kinds of interlocutor – s/he who is permitted to speak/write about the

---

34   The article is Bernstein (2018), the critique is Brass (2020). At issue was precisely methodology, since Bernstein attempted to construct a case about rural Russia without consulting any of the early materialist analyses on the subject. The latter, needless to say, presented a picture of the agrarian sector completely at odds with its idealized depiction by Bernstein. Sad to relate, a problematic analysis of Russia such as this, one that would never have been accepted for publication by *The Journal of Peasant Studies* before 2009, nowadays seems to pass muster unchallenged.

35   Outside SOAS, it seems, this apparent contradiction has long been recognized, by – among others – Gibbon & Neocosmos (1985) and Brass (2007, 2015, 2022a).

36   Said (2002: 296), who regards anthropologists as his most vigorous critics (Said, 2002: 300) because 'it is anthropology above all that has been historically constituted and constructed in its point of origin during an ethnographic encounter between a sovereign European observer and a non-European native occupying, so to speak, a lesser status and a distant place ...'

'other' – and the difference between them. It becomes a question of who is to tell that story, and consequently what that story is to be.

One form, termed interlocutor-as-internal-subject, emerges when those spoken about decide to take the matter into their own hands, and insist that any/every interpretation of who/what they are, think and do, together with what they want, can only be undertaken by someone like themselves. That is, by someone belonging to the same social category, the same ethnicity, or the same nationality. Interpretations by anyone falling outside these categories are henceforth deemed inauthentic and thus inappropriate. The second form, or interlocutor-as-external-subject, is composed of those 'from almost entirely academic' origin, who despite not sharing the identity of the 'other' spoken about are nevertheless sympathetic towards the plight/interests of the latter. Referred to as 'philosophers discoursing animatedly in a handsomely appointed salon', those in the category of interlocutor-as-external-subject are perceived by Said as lacking the authenticity and thus the same commitment as their counterpart, the interlocutor-as-internal-subject.[37]

The difficulty with this approach is that it assumes a specificity which no longer exists: that the first and second categories are wholly separate, and consequently the academy contains none of those from the 'other' identity, or interlocutor-as-internal-subject among its number, which of course is not the case. Contrary to what Said imagined, therefore, it is now not possible to speak of the 'other' as if s/he is still excluded from places and posts in the university system of metropolitan capitalist nations. In short, the original distinction as envisaged by Said, which could be viewed as one between *speaking about* and *speaking as*, has changed. These two forms have now been combined in the same interlocutor, him/herself an 'other', now an academic who, in effect, challenges – and on occasion forbids – any interpretation of the 'other' selfhood by someone who does not share this 'subaltern' identity. Since s/he has become the purveyor of 'authentic' and thus legitimate explanation of what it means to be a 'subaltern', this kind of interlocutor is, unsurprisingly, successful in the academic labour market when it comes to jobs linked to the study of this form of alterity.

When viewed politically, however, this transition is less successful: it begets a populist or nationalist version of 'otherness', and not – as in the past – a

---

37   The external form is described by Said (2002: 298) as 'this kind of scrubbed, disinfected interlocutor [who] is a laboratory creation, and therefore falsified, connections to the urgent situation of crisis and conflict that brought him or her to attention in the first place. It was only when subaltern figures [= the internal interlocutor] like women, Orientals, blacks, and other "natives" made enough noise that they were paid attention to ...'

Marxist one. It is perhaps significant, therefore, that in the vanguard of the attack on socialist theory have been academics who form part of the current global diaspora. Now established in the university system of metropolitan capitalist nations, they have aimed what are unambiguously nationalist critiques at Marxist internationalism, dismissing this as 'Eurocentric' and 'foundationalist', and as such of no use in explaining the development trajectory followed by Third World countries. Not the least problematic aspect of these nationalist critiques is that, unlike earlier ones that insisted socialism would necessarily be preceded by what was thought to be a benign nationalist/bourgeois/democratic stage, current variants tend to halt at the latter and proceed no further in systemic terms.

A Distant Place as a Greater Status

As will be seen in the chapters that follow, there has been a discernible transformation, broadly speaking, in the way the ethnicity is perceived, a contrast nowhere more apparent in the distinction between academic discourse on the one hand, and on the other views expressed in the public domain. Over the past century, travel writing and ethnography have to a large degree shared as positive an idealized image of the 'primitive other', plus its accompanying conceptual apparatus (the purity of nature, the 'natural', the rural; the undesirability of urban 'civilization') but also its corollary. Stay as you are, the 'other' is advised, you are spared thereby becoming and being like us (= 'civilized', Western, urban, alienated). Now, however, a noticeable change has occurred. What used to be regarded as the 'primitive other' is increasingly becoming like us, and instead of being viewed as a positive 'other', to be cherished as such, s/he is currently more often than not regarded with fear, as a negative 'other' that cannot be prevented from coming our way, threatening not just to occupy our space but there to displace us.

The subtext is clear. As long as the 'other' continues to be just that, in his or her own rural context, s/he is to be esteemed; however, once this subject not only takes on the economic characteristics of and ideologically subscribes to Western 'civilization', but also travels to and enters the central domain of metropolitan capitalism, this esteem vanishes. What remains the same is the initial view of 'otherness' as rooted physically (in its 'natural' place) and ideologically (as 'childlike' or 'primitive'): they are not, and never can become modern, like us, so why do they try to do this. As will be seen in Part 2 of this volume, it is a subtext that has informed not just travel writing and ethnographic accounts, but also current social science theory about the rural 'other' in so-called Third World nations.

Broadly speaking, writers who travel, and write about their experiences, tend to regard this as secondary to their main literary activity, whereas for travel writers voyaging and accounts about this is their raison d'être. It is a difference that is not absolute, as is clear from travel writers considered in the second part of this volume and those who, although not travel writers, nevertheless write about travel.[38] What they all have in common is a desire not to be seen as mere tourists; this is ironic, since writers who travel and travel writers also share with tourists the same aspirations and concerns. Each category wants to visit what remains still an 'untouched land', a place devoid of people like themselves; that is, to undertake a voyage to a hitherto undiscovered (or hidden) location, there to gaze upon – and ideologically appropriate – its cultural resources.

Just as capitalism has become over time more dependent on an enhanced industrial reserve, with the object of generating yet more competition among workers for existing jobs, so the same process has fuelled tensions among those who write about travel. Consequently, those who generate most concern in these quests are rival selves: for anthropologists, other anthropologists; for travel writers, other travel writers; and for tourists, other tourists.[39] In keeping with this fear, and its logical extension, is the lament by anthropologists and travel writers alike that the kind of fieldwork or journey undertaken in the past – by, for example, Graham Greene, Lévi-Strauss, and Peter Keenagh during the 1930s – is no longer possible.[40] Nowadays many anthropologists conduct research in their own societies, while travel writers recount as an 'adventure'

---

38   Included in the category of travel writers are Norman Lewis and Paul Theroux; among those who, although not travel writers, nevertheless write about travel, are Claude Lévi-Strauss, Peter Keenagh, Paul Bowles, Graham Greene, Giuseppe Tomasi di Lampedusa, John Mortimer, Peter Green, John Addington Symonds, Margaret Symonds, L.P. Hartley, Rose Macaulay, and Ethel Mannin. What each has to say about travel, and why, is outlined in Chapters 5–7 below.

39   Lévi-Strauss describes the rivalry between anthropologists in the following manner (Lévi-Strauss & Eribon, 1991: 39): 'I knew Ralph Linton and Ruth Benedict well. Each one used to invite me to dinner to criticize the other ... they hated one another.' About those who have written about journey they have undertaken, Theroux (2018: 58, 59) dismisses Greene because '[h]e knew nothing of Africa', and complains further that 'the travels and writings of Greene's contemporaries – Evelyn Waugh, Robert Byron, Peter Fleming, and others whose works over the past decades have been much praised, even (to my mind) overpraised.' On the issue of tourist disdain for other tourists, see Chapter 5 below.

40   Hence the confession by one travel writer (Hamilton-Paterson, 2006: 223–24) looking back on his earlier trips abroad that 'I am suddenly overtaken with nostalgia for a lifetime of uncomfortable journeys [that] would no longer be possible today.'

nothing more exotic than a railway journey between European capital cities or coach trips within their own nation.[41] And what tourists everywhere fear is encountering only more like themselves, visiting places that increasingly resemble home.

On the connection between tourism/travel and film, it is a cliché that in the UK (and probably elsewhere) part of the popular appeal of the early James Bond films was due to their supplementary role as travelogues.[42] The film locations in which the plots and narrative were set during the 1960s, therefore, showed cinema audiences the kinds of context – the Caribbean, southern Europe, the Balkans, the Middle East, and Asia – which at the time were still only places of the imagination, and not ones that a plebeian was able to visit.[43] While the foreign locations used in these films have stayed the same, their exotic nature has declined as hitherto inaccessible places have been absorbed into routine holiday destinations. What remains of the attractions offered by the franchise no longer includes forms of 'otherness' not found at home.

This change in externalities, or the meaning of places de-exoticized by mass tourism, has been accompanied by a less obvious – but no less significant – internal transformation. Over the years a discernible break has occurred between the way Bond is portrayed in the books by Ian Fleming and the films based on them.[44] As depicted by Fleming in the published versions, Bond

---

41 See, for example, the accounts by Chesshyre (2020) and Aitken (2021).

42 In a newspaper article marking the most recent contribution to the franchise, its author recounts how he saw the early Bond films in the cinema at the time, in company with his parents, noting that amongst the attractions of these films for individual family members was that '[m]y mother swooned for the locations'. See 'A life-long bond with Bond', *Financial Times* (London), 25–26 September 2021.

43 Watching spy/thriller films of the 1960s and 1970s – such as *The Ipcress File* (1965), directed by Sidney J. Furie, *The Quiller Memorandum* (1966), directed by Michael Anderson, *Funeral in Berlin* (1966), directed by Guy Hamilton, *Billion Dollar Brain* (1967), directed by Ken Russell, and *The Tamarind Seed* (1974), directed by Blake Edwards – is now an oddly comforting experience, in that they address issues that do not seem insuperable, and do so in a low-tech, personal manner. This contrasts with the large, impersonal, powerful (and therefore daunting) forces and/or issues one faces currently (among them state capture by corporate power, high-tech surveillance, climate change). It is easy to understand, therefore, how things seemed much simpler then as portrayed on film (the relative ease of travel, banal activities such as getting a hotel room, etc.) compared to what has to be done these days.

44 The main books on which films were based – *Casino Royale, Live and Let Die, Moonraker, Diamonds Are Forever, From Russia with Love, Dr No,* and *Goldfinger* – all appeared throughout the 1950s, followed in the early 1960s by *Thunderball, The Spy Who Loved Me, On Her Majesty's Secret Service, You Only Live Twice,* and *The Man with the Golden Gun.* For this chronology see Amis (1965: 156–58).

came from an upper class background and had tastes to match (his car was originally a Bentley, not the Aston Martin); moreover, he was an assassin not a spy, and his role in the immediate post-war era was to protect the British ruling class against the 'from below' challenge by eliminating socialistically-inclined enemies.[45] In the course of the franchise, therefore, the class position of Bond has undergone a change: from upper-class to plebeian hit-man, the character becoming in effect just one more superhero.[46] Just as the plebeian from home arrives in places frequented by Bond as portrayed by Fleming, so the cinematic depiction of Bond moves away from the character Fleming envisaged.[47]

Themes

In Part 1 (*Travelling On*) of this volume (Chapters 1–4), transition encompasses debates not just about the nature of development a variety of contexts and conjunctures, but also the methods, theory, and politics supporting the claims made in these discussions. Extending from the way ethnicity and nationalism have been recast in terms of ideology and cause, via the dynamics structuring modes of production, their distinctiveness (or otherwise) and logics, to – more broadly – the way free/unfree production relations are said to define

---

45   The social background is outlined (Amis, 1965: 38–39) thus: 'Mr Fleming is able to smuggle in a good deal of semi-aristocraticness by the back door ... Bond is an Old Etonian [and his] social standing ... is distantly and deviously related to the youth of noble birth in Byron's poem'.

46   The principal challenge to the Bond series has come from films in the Bourne franchise, consisting of *The Bourne Identity* (2002), directed by Doug Liman, and *The Bourne Supremacy* (2004), *The Bourne Ultimatum* (2004), and *Jason Bourne* (2016), all directed by Paul Greengrass. The eponymous Bourne is in many respects indistinguishable from Bond: nowadays like Bond, the Bourne films situate its main character in different locations, undertaking travel and sexual adventures; but the antagonists are no longer the Soviet Union, the People's Republic of China, or communism, but rather a politically nonspecific State apparatus. Like Bond, Bourne is a trained assassin; unlike Bond, however, he is depicted as having a guilty conscience about this role. Both are chivalrous towards their women, and in the course of combatting opponents experience the loss of a lover, killed by a villain. Each is in a fundamental sense the superhero of their respective eras.

47   Attuned as ever to the niceties of class distinctions, Amis (1965: 39) commented on the question of accents that 'Sean Connery's total wrongness for the film part of Bond is nowhere better demonstrated [than in the fact that] Connery could put up a show as a Scottish businessman all right, but a Scottish baronet never.' In short, the pronounced Scots accent of Connery was appropriate for a bourgeois but not an aristocrat. It could be argued that the closest the film characterization comes to that of Fleming is by Timothy Dalton in *The Living Daylights* (1987) and *Licence to Kill* (1989), both directed by John Glen.

the capitalist labour regime. Part 2 (*On Travel*) of the volume (Chapters 5–8) looks at the trajectory followed by travel writing, and how many of its core assumptions overlap with those made in the social sciences and development studies, not least calls for the preservation/conservation of an earlier 'pristine/ primitive' selfhood redolent of the agrarian myth. The latter discourse, both in travel writing and the social sciences, advocates resistance to economic development, a position that slides imperceptibly into the conservative politics of the 'new' populist postmodernism.

Chapter 1 considers the different forms, causes and meanings of racism, a discourse that follows an historical trajectory from mere alterity, via 'otherness'-as-inferiority, to the 'other' as equal competitor in the global labour market. Foregrounded in the mid-nineteenth century racism of Gobineau and Wagner is the hierarchical concept of race as a culturally innate and exclusionary marker of national belonging, diminished only by a process of 'blood-mixing'. This reactionary view was opposed by Marxists such as Lenin, Trotsky, and Deutscher, whose materialist approach not only emphasized the socio-economic heterogeneity of the 'other', but also underlined the way capitalists used ethnic identity to undermine the consciousness, solidarity and struggle based on class.

The latter tactic currently fuels populist anti-immigration discourse among the European working class, the exclusionary position of which vis-à-vis the 'other' is informed principally by livelihood considerations. The mid-nineteenth century definition of the problem as a psychologistic issue is an approach which to some degree overlaps with that of the 'new' populist postmodernism, which not only re-ethnicizes anti-capitalist discourse, but also sees racism as an epiphenomenon of imperial nostalgia. Unlike the culturally 'not-us' ideology of Gobineau and Wagner, the present concept of 'not-belonging' is linked more closely to the economy, where the plebeian self now regards the 'other' as an equal competitor in the capitalist labour market. Post-Brexit labour shortages in the UK have improved the bargaining power of workers, generating in turn employer calls for resumed access to the industrial reserve.

Illustrated with reference to the way antebellum Southern pro-slavery discourse opposed Northern capitalism in the period leading to the American Civil War, Chapter 2 compares what links pro-slavery discourse to contemporary postmodern theory, and how a shared antagonism towards capitalism and support for 'those below' constitutes a populist anti-capitalism of the right. Unlike the anti-capitalism of the left, that of the right mobilizes on the basis of categories outside the working class. An idealized perception of traditional culture as empowering, plus a mutual dislike of *laissez-faire* underwrites the emergence and consolidation of the (non-class) identity politics endorsed by pro-slavery discourse and postmodernism, but against which Marxism warned. A consequence of this failure politically to differentiate opposition to capitalism is the current misunderstanding by postmodern theory of the deleterious impact of a globally burgeoning industrial reserve army on working class solidarity/organization in metropolitan capitalist nations.

The focus of Chapter 3 in on revision, or transition as conceptualized by Jairus Banaji with reference to modes of production encompassing the process of historical transformation extending from late antiquity, via feudalism, to capitalism in the present day. Among the problematic claims informing this systemic trajectory are the following: the reappearance of feudalism, a mode initially absent; the insertion of a space between late antiquity and feudalism; neither the latter nor late antiquity seem to undergo a process of decline (= catastrophist theory); and, ultimately, the assertion that all modes can be reduced to a single form, capitalism, a pan-historical systemic variant that is merchant capital. In keeping with this, every production relation encountered throughout this trajectory – whether slavery, bonded labour, *coloni*, tenant, smallholder, or 'peasant tenures' – is similarly reduced to a single relational varian: 'disguised wage-labour' that is contractually 'free'. This in turn provides his model with the 'proletariat' required for his claim about the ubiquity of the capitalist mode.

Difficulties faced by these claims include the following: defining feudal 'peasant tenures' as wage payments rather than rent-taking; and presenting as a hired labour that is free what turns out to be an unfree worker or peasant bonded by debt. Nor were the subjects of these production relations landless, since rural estates leased them holdings in exchange for which they provided landlords with labour-service. In short, such labour was that of tenants who, as part of the colonate, formed an unbroken link between antiquity and feudalism, or the element of relational and historical continuity that Banaji is at such pains to deny. However, it is necessary for him to claim that such labour was not unfree, since – along with money and merchant capitalists – a free worker is crucial to his broader claim that capitalism was ever-present from late antiquity onwards.

The kind of production relations which signal the presence of capital accumulation, whether they are indeed free or unfree, and why the debate about this issue has not only featured centrally in the study of development but also undergone epistemological twists and turns from the mid-twentieth century to the present, are questions examined in Chapter 4. Because unfree production relations and accumulation were regarded as incompatible, the paradigms dominant in the immediate post-1945 era categorized unfree labour as a pre-capitalist obstacle to economic development. Maintaining consequently that in Third World nations these kinds of relational forms should be eradicated, much development theory – including that by some Marxists – concluded that transition in these countries would be not to socialism but rather to capitalism.

From the 1980s, however, it became increasingly clear that in many contexts unfree labour-power was not an obstacle to accumulation but the relation of choice where capitalists were concerned. Since unfree labour-power enhanced profitability, such production relations were used by capitalists to restructure their workforce, replacing free workers with unfree equivalents. This more radical Marxist interpretation repositioned unfreedom within capitalism *per se*, not as an outlier found only in the periphery but present also in the metropolitan contexts of the core. Although a number of those who criticized this view now changed their mind, and adopted the interpretation which initially they had dismissed, its link to a socialist transition was discarded; instead, they opted for amelioration within the existing capitalist system.

Chapter 5 examines a recent history by D'Eramo of travel and tourism which encompasses all forms of motion, from which no kind of movement or physical relocation appears to be excluded. In this all-embracing approach, every and any sort of journey – whether temporary (holidays) or permanent (migration) – contributes to the construction of a broadly anti-tourist interpretation. Claiming that tourism is a form of 'ambulatory determinism' (= the need to travel), and an industry not a service economy, he overlooks how and why travel/tourism narratives reproduce the heritage/tradition/nostalgia that structure identity politics and the agrarian myth. Similarly unnoticed is the extent to which travel involves a quest for sameness abroad, a validation of selfhood, either 'from above' in the case of the Grand Tour, or 'from below' where the plebeian mass tourist is concerned. Like anthropology, travel writing tends to essentialize 'otherness' as pristine and largely unchanging. Much like postmodernism subsequently, narratives about journeys outside Europe over the 1930–50 period opposed modernity and romanticized 'otherness', rejecting progress and development as the imposition of alien and inappropriate systemic models, dismissed as 'civilization', 'Westernization', or 'Europeanization'.

Because of their importance as destinations in the era of mass tourism, accounts of journeys within Europe, particularly to Italy, are examined in Chapter 6. The period following the 1939–45 war was marked by a transformation in the tourist gaze, whereby traveller condescension at the lack of amenities provided in places visited was replaced by enthusiasm for signs of 'backwardness'. Hence the underdeveloped and impoverished condition of tourist locations were recast as evidence for 'authentic' cultural alterity, to be contrasted favourably with the home context of visitor. Accordingly, many of the tropes informing travel writing about contexts outside Europe during the pre-war era surface in post-war narratives about voyages within Europe. These include the different variants of the agrarian myth (pastoral/Darwinian, aristocratic/plebeian), an idealization of the countryside, the rural community and its inhabitants, the traditional hierarchy and its ancient institutions, together with a corresponding a dislike of urbanization/industrialization. Traveller opprobrium was itself transferred: from the local inhabitants of the place visited to the arrival there of a different and alien 'other': the plebeian mass tourist from home.

The extent to which travel narratives and agrarian myth discourse coincide is evident in the way they combine in accounts of journeys to Venice, a fusion outlined in Chapter 7. Pastoral images which inform the aristocratic variant reveal the presence of economic links between the city and the surrounding countryside, and in particular the ownership by Venetian noble families of large rural estates, formed as a result of profits from trade being reinvested in land. Depicting it as a beleaguered city, Venice symbolizes the tension between an external but encroaching modernity, in the form of mass tourism, and the desire to protect its aristocratic hierarchy, culture, and traditions. Across the different contexts and conjunctures, the element of transition entails the following shift: whereas travel accounts of journeys outside Europe defend the 'other' against the intrusion of 'civilization' emanating from Europe itself, narratives about travel within Europe defend its civilization from the plebeian mass tourist, whose requirements abroad are characterized negatively as reproducing what is found at home. In this way, such changes act as the harbinger of modernity, a process that erodes the cultural 'authenticity' of places visited.

Venice also features in Chapter 8, where the city is a locus in the non-economic writings of A.V. Chayanov, an important Russian neopopulist. His political significance transcends his own time and space, influencing as it has done – and continues to do – both the debate about rural development in Third World countries and – more broadly – resurgent agrarian populist interpretations in academia and elsewhere. Less well known, but epistemologically as revealing of his politics, are his non-economic writings, particularly his contributions to the Gothic literary genre. Examined in this chapter are three stories written pseudonymously by Chayanov, each of which is structured by the same discourse. All were composed over a short period just after the Bolsheviks took power in Russia and reveal as a sub-text the political divergence and concomitant struggle between neo-populist and Bolshevik versions of societal development.

PART 1

Travelling On

∴

Racisms (Home and Away)

In art, our [= European] inferiority to India, as well as to Egypt, Greece, and America, is very marked. Neither in sublimity nor beauty have we anything to compare with the masterpieces of antiquity. When our day has drawn to its close, and the ruins of our towns and monuments cover the face of the land, the traveller will discover nothing, in the forests and marshes that will skirt the Thames, the Seine, and the Rhine, to rival the gorgeous ruins of Philae, Nineveh, Athens, Salsette, and the valley of Tenochtitlan. If future ages have something to learn from us in the way of positive science, this is not the case with poetry, as is clearly proved by the despairing admiration that we so justly feel for the intellectual wonders of foreign civilizations.

> A somewhat deceptively progressive observation made in the mid-nineteenth century by ARTHUR DE GOBINEAU, who formulated the idea of racial inequality.[1]

•••

Introduction: A Place in the World

Explored in this chapter is the view that the discourse loosely subsumed under the single term 'racism' encompasses two distinct phenomena, each different in terms of historical origin, systemic circulation/reproduction, and political object. One invokes the presence of what is presented as an innate and enduring hierarchy based on racial/ethnic 'otherness' and derives mainly from the era of colonialism (= away). It purports to define ethnic/national identity in terms of a hierarchy of instances, corresponding to cultural and economic

---

1 See Gobineau (1915: 104). Although he conveys a respect for the achievements of 'other' cultures – ancient and modern – in support of their claims to civilization, to the extent of comparing them favourably with their European counterparts, the reason for doing so derives from his view that Europe is irretrievably on a path of historical decline, a process attributed by him to its decadence/degeneracy, an effect as Gobineau sees it of 'race-mixing'.

subordination or superiority. Although ideologically similar, the other – at home – derives from and addresses a different set of circumstances. At issue, therefore, is what for an existing workforce constitutes a form of double jeopardy; an expanding industrial reserve army combined with (and licensing) yet more acute labour market competition. The latter processes are viewed by those already in – or seeking – employment as an attempt by capitalists to roll back any gains achieved hitherto as a result of class struggles, such as livelihood prospects, income levels, the social wage, job security, and employment conditions generally.

Whereas historically this ability to conduct struggle 'from above' – one favouring capital over labour – has been restricted to particular national contexts, with the onset of globalization, and a concomitant decrease in skill levels required of workers coupled with an increase in the source and quantity of the industrial reserve in a context where capitalism itself is deregulated, employers are now able to access labour world-wide. In such circumstances, racism can and does arise where capital draws on this enhanced reserve army, generating acute competition for jobs between workers of different ethnic/national identity. This sort of rivalry is itself fostered by employers for two reasons: to maintain or enhance profitability when competing with other producers in the market; and in order to pre-empt or prevent the emergence or consolidation of consciousness based on class, a solidarity which might threaten the ownership/control of the means of production/distribution/exchange currently enjoyed by capital.

Such a process can in turn be related to shifts in the perception of race. Historically, colonialism licensed a superior/inferior structure corresponding to the way in which the white/colonizer regarded the non-white colonized. This type of gaze was linked to and overlapped with the ruler/ruled dichotomy informing colonialism. Significantly, in this variant racist discourse did not connect the subordination of non-whites to a perception of this ethnically 'other' subject as a competitor in the same labour market: that is to say, the colonized 'other' was not deemed to be a rival for the same jobs held or sought by the colonizer.[2] Currently, however, this pattern has changed somewhat: although

---

2 As Lenin (1968: 520) recognized, over time economic rivalry emerged between European settlers, already established in the colonies, and aspiring European emigrants wishing to join them. In his *Notebooks on Imperialism*, therefore, a heavily emphasized section of the text annotated goes as follows: 'In earlier overseas expansion, there was always a margin of elbow-room left; all Western nations had adequate place for development in their respective "New Europes" and rivalry gave rise only to fruitful competition. But now North America will not hear of more immigrants, Australia is already closing its doors ... while South Africa is revealing, with horrible clarity, the grim fact that emigration can no longer help, as it has

perceptions based on superior/subordinate locations in a racial hierarchy have not of course vanished, they are accompanied now by an economic dimension. Unlike in the past, the actual/potential appearance of the 'other' in the domestic labour market is now regarded by those already in it as a rival.

Invariably, a distinction between these variants of racist ideology is not made, and the two forms are often conflated.[3] The result is that the presence currently of racism in the UK and Europe tends to be viewed in one particular way: since racism is rooted in colonialism, so the argument goes. it is an ideology attributed to a backwards-looking nostalgia for Empire and its form of domination on the part of its holders. As such, this sort of argument continues, racism cannot be other than a pervasive and enduring ideology that has always been – and will always be – the same. This despite the fact that those who now hold racist views can have no experience – and in many cases, little knowledge – of Empire. Constituted as an undifferentiated and ever-present phenomenon, therefore, racism metamorphoses into an essentialist or intrinsic belief, an internal or quasi-psychologistic form that cannot be explained by reference to any process or systemic element currently existing outside and beyond itself. The latter interpretation is common among many of those who subscribe to the 'cultural turn'.

Rather than the Althusserian term 'overdetermination', this process of epistemological break (or a transition in the meaning of the concept) corresponds more accurately to the model of 'combined and uneven development' applied by Trotsky initially to the co-existence of economic linkages and subsequently more generally to all elements contributing to the development process.[4] Following this usage, therefore, here the term is applied to the process whereby a concept or an ideological component which is part of a larger discourse persists, despite the dynamics and/or structure – and thus the meaning – of the process in question having altered. In this sense, it describes the way racism

---

hitherto, to obtain a place in a world which has shrunk; one European will have to strangle another.'

3   It is important to be clear what is, and what is not, being said here. To argue for the presence of these two variants is not to say that there is a 'good' and a 'bad' variant – where racism is concerned, there are no 'good' variants – only that racism as an ideology can be the outcome of different kinds of determination, and thus on occasion is a product of different causes, and hence a discourse 'about' distinct phenomena. Rather obviously, where the objective – desirable, it goes without saying – is to combat racism, then it is crucial to identify its cause, an objective the attainment of which is hindered by any misrecognition of the reason for its presence.

4   For 'over-determination' see Althusser & Balibar (1970), and on 'combined and uneven development' see Trotsky (1962).

has changed, becoming in effect a concern about the 'other' based on the acceptance that those in the latter category are *equals*, and as such rivals to be reckoned with when they enter the same labour market. This shift in focus contrasts with that of the earlier meaning, whereby the 'other' is deemed to be innately an *inferior*, whose ability to compete in any capacity (let alone the same labour market) is unthinkable, and thus cannot be taken seriously.[5]

This chapter consists of four sections, the first of which considers the way in which 'otherness' informs the discourse of the political right (Gobineau, Wagner) while the second looks at how the same identity is viewed by those on the political left (Lenin, Trotsky, Deutscher). That warnings about privileging non-class 'otherness' remain unheeded is considered in the third, and the fourth examines the way in which identity politics are interpreted by those at the grassroots.

I

Instances of the view that dismisses even the possibility of economic competition from rivals deemed inferior are found in the ideas of Arthur de Gobineau and Richard Wagner, each of whom contributed to the theoretical formulation of race as an historically foundational identity.[6] For them, ethnicity is not merely a non-transcendent characteristic, and thus innate, but also and therefore an ever-present determinant that overrides all other aspects and issues structuring economic and social existence. Their racism was part of the 'from above' ideological reaction – mainly aristocratic – to events and processes that

---

5   Informed by different political approaches, these perceptions give rise to the following distinctions:

Politics	Theoretical approach	Otherness perceived as:	Mobilizing discourse	Exponents
The Right	psychology	inferior	ethnicity, nationalism	Gobineau, Wagner
The Left	political economy	equal	class, class struggle	Lenin, Trotsky, Deutscher

6   Not only was Gobineau friends with Wagner, whose ideas on race he influenced, but also and via the latter Gobineau shaped the subsequent racist ideas resulting in the *völkisch* fusion over the late nineteenth and early twentieth centuries of racism and nationalism espoused by Houston Stewart Chamberlain, Alfred Rosenberg, and Hitler himself. This reactionary political lineage underlines the way in which identity politics combines ideologically with the agrarian myth to generate populist mobilizations.

coalesced around the mid-nineteenth century, signalling the unfolding of systemic transitions. On the one hand, 'from above' optimism linked to progress, the development of capitalism, the emergence of nationalism, colonialism and imperialism, together with the consolidation of a European bourgeoisie. On the other, 'from above' pessimism concerning accompanying 'from below' responses to these same developments: working class organization, struggles, and political movements throughout Europe, all designed to further their own interests. Discourse about race necessarily encompassed – for Gobineau and Wagner alike – two contrasting identities: that of the self ('who are we?') and that of the other ('who are they?'), with particular reference to the kind of characteristics associated with a specific culture or nationality, and consequently with claims on their part to be a civilization.[7]

Blood of the Founders

For Gobineau, race – a concept he regarded as synonymous with 'blood' – is an identity permanently inscribed on every society and all history, one that rests on what for him is a fusion of social characteristics (history, morality, culture, politics, law), all of which combine over time to form a civilization. Generated as a result is the relay-in-statement at the centre of his discourse: blood = race = nation = people = civilization. To understand how national character and history are determined by race, argues Gobineau, one has to turn to ethnology, and the identification by the latter of what he terms 'racial types'.[8] The overlap between race with nation is due, he explains, to the fact that 'racial elements impose their modes of existence on nations, circumscribing them ... [t]hey dictate their laws, inspire their wishes, control their sympathies and stir up their hatreds and contempt.'[9] Consequently, the sole

---

7 These concerns inform the attempts from the latter half of the nineteenth century onwards at broad synthesis, by – among others – ethnologists such as Latham (1859), Westermark (1906/ 1908), and Risley (1908), comparing and evaluating so-called primitive societies in relation to ones categorized as more advanced, so as then to place them all in an ascending hierarchy of economic/political/ideological/moral achievement (= 'civilization'). At the beginning of the twentieth century, however, Risley (1908: 26) thought it necessary to qualify his research into anthropometry by pointing out that '[t]he intermixture of races with different head-forms ... especially when combined with other characters, is a good test of racial affinity. It may be added that neither the shape nor the size of the head seems to bear any direct relation to intellectual capacity. People with long heads cannot be said to be cleverer or more advanced in culture that people with short heads.'
8 See Gobineau (Biddiss, 1970: 165).
9 Gobineau (Biddiss, 1970: 164).

cause of national decline is racial degeneration, and as such cannot be attributed to other issues, among them fanaticism, luxury, moral corruption, irreli-
gion, geography, climate, and soil.[10]

Guided by what he terms 'instinctual currents', Gobineau maintains that
strong racial elements are realized politically in the form of an assemblage of
people, leading to a 'civilizational impulse' composed in turn of material and
intellectual components.[11] Although these characteristics are for him intrinsic markers of the innateness of racial identity, they nevertheless dissipate,
due to a process he terms 'blood-mixing', the inevitable result as he sees it of
a merger between those at the top and bottom of his racial hierarchy.[12] This
gives rise to a situation which for Gobineau is one whereby 'racial types ... lose
their distinctive characteristics only by intermixture with completely different ethnic types.'[13] The outcome is a decline of 'pure' blood = decline of racial
'purity' = decline of the nation, and with it the people, a process leading to a
situation Gobineau labels 'decadence' or 'degeneration'.[14]

Gobineau opens his attempt to define race by considering it physiologically,
only to dismiss explanations based on this.[15] In keeping with such an approach,

---

10   Gobineau (1915: 18, 56, 61).

11   In the words of Gobineau (1915: 86, original emphasis), 'those in which the racial elements
        are so strong that they grip fast everything that comes within their reach ... for the first
        time we have reached what can be called a *civilization* ... From the moment when an
        assemblage of men, which began as a mere tribe, has so widened the horizon of its social
        relations as to merit the name of a *people*, we see one of the two currents of instinct, the
        material and the intellectual, flowing with greater force than before ...'

12   Gobineau (Biddiss, 1970: 170) allocates the top position in this racial hierarchy to the
        'Germanic race' which in his opinion is because it is 'endowed with all the vitality of the
        Aryan vitality [needed] in order to fulfil the role to which it was destined ... the finest
        human species, of the whole white race'.

13   See Gobineau (Biddiss, 1970: 167, 172). He elaborates (Gobineau, 1915: 26) on this theme,
        maintaining that 'great peoples, at the moment of their death, have only a very small and
        insignificant share in the blood of the founders, into whosed inheritance they come: [this]
        is how it is possible for civilizations to fall – the reason being that they are no longer in the
        same hands.'

14   For an analogous view, equating national decline with 'degeneracy', see Balfour (1908).
        According to Gobineau (1915: 25, original emphases), '[t]he word *degenerate*, when
        applied to people, means ... that the people has no longer the same intrinsic value as it
        had before, because it has no longer the same blood in its veins, continuous adulterations
        having gradually affected the quality of that blood. In other words, though the nation
        bears the name given by its founders, the name no longer connotes the same race; in fact,
        the man of a decadent time, the *degenerate* man ... is a different being, from the racial
        point of view ... the heterogenous elements that henceforth prevail in him give him quite
        a different nationality [whereby he] is only a very distant kinsman of those he still calls
        his ancestors ... It is at this point that all the results of degeneration will appear.'

15   Gobineau (1915: 106).

he takes issue with arguments that denigrate tribal and/or indigenous groups, seeming to defend the latter by noting that '[m]ost scientific observers up to now have been very prone to make out the lowest type as worse than they really are.'[16] However, the reason for his disagreement with such views is far from progressive: thus he opposes those who, on the basis of such explanations, 'say that the separation of races is merely apparent', and that consequently '[a]ll mankind is, for them, capable of the same improvement', which in his opinion is a theory that 'cannot be accepted'.[17] What Gobineau objects to, therefore, is the idea that all races are the same, and any differences between them are an effect of 'deviations' from the norm, due to 'habits, climate, and locality', an interpretation with which in his opinion 'it is impossible to agree'.[18]

Against the sameness/improvement point of view, Gobineau advances an a-historical and essentialist concept of race as a permanent, innate and unchanging identity, bound up with ideas about nationality, civilization, and progress.[19] For him, different races are fundamentally the same over time and space: changes in the latter do not alter the basic characteristics forming 'otherness'.[20] It is a fixity of identity that Gobineau believes constitutes 'a permanence that can only be lost by a crossing of blood'.[21] Even when they inhabit different contexts and environments, contends Gobineau, races 'have remained relatively pure'. The apogee of this 'purity' is civilization, a state when reached that is marked by peace, political stability, co-operation, sociability,

---

16   Gobineau (1915: 154). Elsewhere the same kind of point is made (Gobineau, 1915: 73) as forcefully: 'I know that some learned men [have asserted] that between some human races and the larger apes there is a slight difference of degree, and none of kind ... I absolutely reject such an insult to humanity ... I believe, of course, that human races are unequal; but I do not think that any of them are like the brute, or to be classed with it.'

17   Gobineau (1915: 117).

18   Gobineau (1915: 119–120).

19   In the opinion of Gobineau (1915: 27–28), 'we are driven to admit that for a very large number of human beings it has been, and always will be, impossible to take even the first step towards civilization; if, again, we consider that these peoples are scattered over the whole face of the earth ... we must conclude that a part of mankind, is in its own nature stricken with a paralysis, which makes it for ever unable to take even the first step towards civilization, since it cannot overcome the natural repugnance, felt by men and animals alike, to a crossing of blood.'

20   For Gobineau (1915: 125, original emphasis), 'the argument [is] that of the permanence of types', namely, that 'we have shown that the human races are each, as it were, shut up in their own individuality, and can only issue from it by a mixture of blood ... if the types are thus absolutely fixed, hereditary, and permanent, in spite of climate and lapse of time, mankind is no less completely and definitely split into separate parts ...'

21   Gobineau (1915: 138).

and 'hatred of violence'.[22] However, warns Gobineau, this is a state that lasts only as long as 'a race keeps its blood' pure, since 'as nations become greater, more powerful, and more civilized, their blood loses its purity, and their instincts are gradually altered.'[23]

The Good Things of This World

From the latter process stems the pessimism that Gobineau felt about the future of European civilization, the obstacle to further progress being, so he thought, the continuous nature of changes in its racial identity.[24] Listing the attributes that contribute to the formation of a civilization – among them literature, philosophy, metaphysics, and politics – he concludes that in Europe '[t]he capacity for infinite progress is ... not shown by the present state of our civilization'.[25] England, Holland, and Naples at that conjuncture (the mid-nineteenth century) were regarded by him as ethnically homogenous, retaining thereby their 'race instinct'. France, central Italy and Germany, however, where populations were ethnically heterogenous, a uniform idea of government was as a result less acceptable. In the latter contexts, therefore, society did not possess the same 'confidence in itself', and the stability on which civilization depends was lacking. As long as the dominant race remained dominant, insisted Gobineau, civilization exists and is guaranteed; once the race was no longer dominant, because of 'race-mixing', the civilization on which it is based declines.[26]

---

22 For these characteristics, see Gobineau (1915: 89–91). 'Civilization is not an event,' he explains (Gobineau, 1915: 77, original emphases), 'but an assemblage of events and ideas, a *state* in which human society subsists, an *environment* with which it has managed to surround itself, which is created by it, emanates from it, and in turn reacts on it.'

23 On this, see Gobineau (1915: 42, 90).

24 Gobineau (1915: 102–103).

25 Gobineau (1915: 161). A corollary of equating civilization with culture + scientific discovery + politics + philosophy is that where any or all of these characteristics were absent, civilization was deemed to be absent. This was expressed by Gobineau (1915: 86) thus: 'Show me a place where the introduction of printing has had results, similar to those in Europe, where our sciences are brought to perfection, where new applications are made of our discoveries, where our philosophies are the parents of other philosophies, of political systems, of literature and art, of books, statues, and pictures!'.

26 Hence the view (Gobineau, 1915: 104–105) that 'the active element distinguishing any civilization is identical with ... the dominant race. The civilization is modified and transformed according to the changes undergone by this race, and when the race itself has disappeared, carries on for some time the impulse originally received from it.'

When considering threats to race/culture/civilization, however, it is clear that Gobineau views these as emanating as much from home as abroad. Although the main target of his racist ideology remains the ethnically 'other' inhabitant of less developed societies, increasingly drawn into this same category are plebeian elements from his own society.[27] In a sense, this is unsurprising, given the cultural basis of his view about racial 'purity', whereby the aristocracy is deemed by him to be the main – if not the sole – repository of most characteristics and practices forming an 'authentic' national identity (politics, law, literature, music, painting). Within Europe itself, 'the lower strata of the French people have very little in common with the surface [as they] form an abyss over which civilization is suspended'. He continues: 'The peasants look on us almost in the light of enemies [and] understand nothing of our civilization, they share in it unwillingly, and think themselves justified in profiting, as far as they can, by its misfortunes'.[28] Similarly, those emigrating to North America are described negatively by Gobineau, who labels them 'a very mixed assortment of the most degenerate races of olden-day Europe ... the human flotsam of all ages.'[29] Both the French peasant and the European emigrant confirm what Gobineau derides as the egalitarian 'liberal dogma of human brotherhood'.[30]

Like the 'other' of less developed nations, therefore, peasants and workers located within 'civilized' nations belong to the category of those for whom

---

27   Gobineau (1915: 159) makes it clear that he objects to equality, not just between races and nations but also within them, or 'the right of all men to have their part in the good things of this world'. In short, he perceived a 'from below' threat from within the same context – by workers and peasants – as posing for those like him much the same kind of problem as 'race-mixing'.

28   Gobineau (1915: 97ff., 101–102).

29   His contempt for those who emigrate to the United States is hard to disguise. Hence for Gobineau (Biddiss, 1970: 160–61, 162) '[t]he American Union is in fact the one country in the world which from the beginning of the century and especially in recent years, has experienced a vast influx of heterogenous elements ... [t]hey are a very mixed assortment of the most degenerate races of olden-day Europe. They are the human flotsam of all ages ... an incoherent juxtaposition of the most decadent kinds of people ... The Americans, then, though claiming to be a young nation, are in fact made up of all the old peoples of Europe ... During the long, sad journey from Europe to the New World, the Atlantic air does not change them. They arrive the same people as when they left. A simple change in geographical location cannot regenerate races more than half exhausted.'

30   See Gobineau (1915: 38–39) who observes: 'The curious point is that the theory of equality, which is held by the majority of men and so has permeated our customs and institutions, has not been powerful enough to overthrow the evidence against it ... I do not think that the usual idea of a national character for each people has yet been reconciled with the belief, which is just as widely held, that all peoples are equal.'

civilization is unachievable. Together with the former, they contribute to the threat feared by Gobineau: peoples who cannot – for whatever reason – protect their own blood line, and thus their own 'racial purity'. Unsurprisingly, he viewed immigration simply in terms of 'blood-mixing', a process facilitating the descent as he saw it into degeneracy on the part of ethnically 'pure' – and thus superior – racial populations. This contention was illustrated with reference to the British case: although Gobineau commended the 'vigour' of the British, he argued that 'the ever-increasing commercial organization of society threw many [of its aristocratic classes] headlong into the plebeian masses, and Anglo-Saxon blood was gravely contaminated.'[31] Such an outcome was attributed by him to the 'birth of heavy industry [which] increased this tendency by attracting into the country workers from all non-Germanic races ...'.[32] Ultimately, therefore, blame in the discourse of Gobineau – not just for 'race-mixing' and its resultant 'degeneracy' but also and more broadly for progress, equality, and democracy – lies with capitalism, indicating that he, too, is an exponent of the anti-capitalist ideology emanating from the political right.[33]

Music, Speech, Passion

Writing and composing at the same conjuncture as Gobineau, Richard Wagner contributed substantially to racist theory structured by notions of innate and enduring cultural 'otherness'. Although holding similarly notorious views about race, Wagner – unlike Gobineau – was a vehement anti-semite.[34] Since for Wagner the marker of national identity was language, which in turn is connected by him to music, he maintained that while Jews do indeed speak the

---

31 For this view, see Gobineau (Biddiss, 1970: 145).

32 'The influx of immigrants from the continent continued and increased', observed Gobineau (Biddiss, 1970: 146), adding: 'Besides the recent inflow into England of part of the Irish, other ethnic influences have remorselessly gained ground, and instincts opposed to the Germanic mentality have continued indefinitely to abound ...'

33 Hence the argument by Gobineau (Biddiss, 1970: 147) that '[t]he aristocracy is being challenged; democracy, hitherto unknown, is making claims which were not conceived on Anglo-Saxon soil [but which have] been brought over from the continent', mimics precisely the defence of slavery by planters in the antebellum American South, on which see Chapter 2 (this volume).

34 Unlike Wagner, Gobineau (1915: 121–22) admired Jews both as a civilization and as a race, because they 'have settled in lands with very different climates from that of Palestine, and have given up their ancient mode of life', in spite of which they have retained their cultural identity.

tongue of the nation they inhabit, they do so only 'as an alien'.[35] As for them the vernacular is a learned and not a mother language, he further asserts, Jews cannot express themselves adequately ('idiomatically, independently, and conformably to [their] nature'). He maintains this is so because language 'is not the work of scattered units [= diasporic peoples], but of historical community; only he who has unconsciously grown up within the bond of this community takes also any share in its creation'.

The crux of his anti-semitic argument concerns the relation between nation, language, and music. Its logic is for Wagner straightforward: as Jews are not – and in his opinion can never be – part of a nation, they are unable properly to acquire its speech, language, and thus also its music. This is because for Wagner talk, and song, is the expression not just of feeling but also of *national* feeling. Hence the view that the 'true poet, no matter what branch of art, still gains his stimulus from nothing but a faithful, loving contemplation of instinctive life.'[36] In the opinion of Wagner, therefore, all art has – and can only have – a national origin, one that stems from an 'instinctive' passion or 'feeling' that can only be realized by those belonging to a historical community and speaking its language. In short, music – like speech, language, and all forms of culture – springs from a process of 'being in the nation'. Equating Jews with modernity, Wagner holds them responsible for the erosion of tradition and culture that forms the basis of national identity.[37]

Lacking both a nation, and hence the capacity to talk/sing as do those who are part of a nation, Jews are seen by Wagner as consequently unable to express themselves through music/language of a nation that culturally is not theirs.[38] Not the least problematic aspect of the anti-semitic perception

---

35 In the words of Wagner (Goldman & Springchorn, 1977: 51, 55, 56), 'The Jew speaks the language of the nation in whose midst he dwells from generation to generation, but he speaks it always as an alien ... [he] has never had an art of his own', since what is missing, what is not possible is 'going back to the folk source' of the nation. Consequently, for Wagner 'he merely listens to the barest surface of our art, but not to its life-bestowing inner organism ...'

36 Wagner (Goldman & Springchorn, 1977: 54).

37 On the basis of this claim, Wagner (Goldman & Springchorn, 1977: 52) proceeds to ask yet another question, one that invokes a familiar racist argument at the heart of anti-semitic discourse: lacking the ability to 'enunciate' music, due to an absence of the requisite national 'feeling'/passion, why are Jews prominent in the shaping of public taste about this particular art form? Wagner answers by calling upon the equally familiar racist trope (Belloc, 1922; Lewis, 1939): through usury, 'the cultured Jew appears in our society [where] our modern culture [is] accessible to no one but the well-to-do'.

38 According to Wagner (Goldman & Springchorn, 1977: 52, original emphases), 'if the aforesaid qualities of his dialect make the Jew almost incapable of giving artistic enunciation

by Wagner of 'otherness' is his view that, even when Jews successfully contributed to national culture their work nevertheless continued to be labelled
'Jewish'. Musicians who are Jewish point out, rightly, that when their gaze is
inwardly-focussed, they are accused of 'not belonging' to the national culture,
while when their gaze is outwardly-focussed, and engaged with the national
culture, they are nevertheless accused of infiltrating this with 'foreign'/'alien'
influences.[39] Either way, Jews are indicted as being innately 'other', and consequently inherently unable to 'belong' to a different national context.

Defined by Wagner as cosmopolitans without their own home, therefore,
Jews are perceived as doubly 'other': external both to the national context
from which culture derives, and thus also its creative impulse. Alienated not
just from people in this national context, but also from his own people, the
'cultured Jew' who utters 'mimicked speech' is accused by Wagner of producing also music that is culturally 'inauthentic'. Hence it is when this same but
'other' individual attempts to connect with 'the folk', that he is confronted by
'instinctive ill-will': the latter is the culturally determined explanation offered
by Wagner for the presence and reproduction of grassroots racism. Ironically,
and his anti-semitism notwithstanding, Wagner does not blame Jews for
this predicament: indeed, culpability for their exclusion is affixed by him to
'Christian civilization for having kept the Jew in violent severance from it'.[40]
His sole object, as he sees it, 'is to throw light on the aesthetic character of the
results', confirming thereby his intention to view race as an epiphenomenon
of culture.

---

to his feelings through *talk*, for such an enunciation through *song* his aptitude must needs
be infinitely smaller. Song is just talk aroused to highest passion: Music is the speech of
passion.'

39   This element of not-belonging invariably surfaces in the domain of popular culture.
During the immediate post-war era, marked by the rise of *film noir*, it featured in *The
Stranger* (1946), starring and directed by Orson Welles (on which see Higham, 1970: 100–
110). The narrative centres on a Nazi, Franz Kindler, who escaped justice at the Nuremburg
Trials, and was now hiding in small town America under the assumed name of Professor
Charles Rankin. On his trail is an agent for the War Crimes Commission, played by Edward
G. Robinson, who discovers the clue to the identity of the Nazi fugitive when it emerges in
the course of a discussion about the direction of post-war Germany, and how it could be
reformed politically. Kindler/Rankin states this is an impossible objective, since there is
no tradition of freedom in that country. When one of those present mentions Karl Marx
('Proletarians unite …'), Kindler/Rankin replies: 'But Marx wasn't a German, Marx was a
Jew'. It is this which alerts the Nazi hunter to the real identity of 'Professor Charles Rankin'
('Who but a Nazi would deny that Karl Marx was a German because he was a Jew?').

40   On this, see Wagner (Goldman & Springchorn, 1977: 51).

A Faint Uneasy Movement

Much of the same discourse as Gobineau is reproduced by D.H. Lawrence, but with one social difference. Whereas for the former the notion of 'blood purity' is located in the upper classes, to which Gobineau himself belonged, for Lawrence by contrast the same element – responsible for racial vitality/feeling – is found in 'those below'. Writing during the 1920s, Lawrence expressed disdain for American tourists who, because in his view they had 'no tradition ... no culture-history', were too easily overawed by what was seen in Italy.[41] The 'authentic' identity they should adopt instead, he argued, was indeed an ancient one, but not that based on European history and culture. It was, much rather, that based on the first nations within America itself, the inhabitants of which the settlers and colonizers had almost succeeded in wiping out.[42] Although this position is superficially progressive, it is nevertheless consistent with the broad argument that Lawrence makes throughout his writings: namely, the search for and innateness of an 'authentic' ethnic/national identity, one that is based on aesthetic criteria only and rooted in a blood-and-soil discourse.

For Lawrence, a sense of community – any community – derives ultimately from an innate and nativist instinctivism, an irrationalism that is almost animal, one that overrides any and all structural/organizational principles or social dynamics.[43] Amounting to a theory of biologistic determination, this

---

41   See Lawrence (1936: 87, 89, original emphasis) 'Americans in Italy ... are very humble and deprecating ... They prostrate themselves with admiration, they knock their foreheads in front of our elegant fetishes ... Italy consists of just one big arrangement of things to be admired. Every step you take, you get a church or a coliseum between your eyes and down you have to go, on your knees with admiration. Down go the Americans, till Italy fairly trembles with the shock of their dropping knees. It is a pity. It is a pity that American are always so wonderstruck by our – note the possessive adjective – cultural monuments ... Let the beauty of Venice be a sort of zenith to us, beyond which there is no seeing ... One begins to understand the barbarian rage against the great monuments of civilization. "Go beyond *that*, if you can." We say to the Americans, pointing to Venice among the waters. And the American humbly admits that it can't be done.'

42   'America, therefore, should leave off being *quite* so prostrate with admiration', counselled Lawrence (1936: 89, 90–91, original emphasis), adding: 'Let Americans turn to America, and to that very America which has been rejected and almost annihilated ... America must turn again to catch the spirit of her own dark, aboriginal continent ... America must take up life where the Red Indians, the Aztec, the Maya, the Incas left it off ... There lies the real continuity: not between the Europe and the new States, but between the murdered Red America and the seething White America ... To your tents, O America. Listen to your own, don't listen to Europe.'

43   Hence the view (Lawrence, 1968: 505): 'For blood is the substance of the soul, and of the deepest consciousness. It is by blood that we are ... [i]n the blood, knowing and being, or feeling, are one and undivided ...'

inborn sense – described by him variously as 'blood-sympathy', 'blood-contact', 'blood-passion', 'blood-desire', 'blood-sex', and 'blood-relationship' – is found in and then lost by the working class.[44] The latter initially subscribe to what for Lawrence was a positive attribute: a sense of community/kinship with landowner or squire, which in England was replaced in the view of Lawrence by a destructive sense of grievance ('class-hatred', 'class-consciousness').[45] As has been noted by those who knew him, such concepts and arguments not only informed much of what Lawrence wrote, but also amounted to a *weltan-schauung* that differed little from the ideology of Italian Fascism and German Nazism at that conjuncture.[46]

Of political significance, therefore, is that among the identities categorized by him as instinctively 'other' on grounds of 'blood-belonging' are gender and race.[47] Ironically, it was this latter identity as much as anything that lay behind the unease that Lawrence experienced when revisiting Germany in 1928, an unease that has been interpreted as his prescience as to the rise of Hitler.[48] Germany, noted Lawrence, was no longer part of European 'civilization' as 'the

---

44   For these concepts, see Lawrence (1968: 507, 508).

45   'The working-classes retain the old blood-warmth of oneness and togetherness some dec-
      ades longer', observed Lawrence (1968: 513, original emphasis), adding: 'Then they lose
      it too. And then class-consciousness becomes rampant, and class-hate. Class-hate and
      class-consciousness are only a sign that the old togetherness, the old blood-warmth has
      collapsed ... [t]hen we have these hostile groupings of men for the sake of opposition,
      strife ... This, again is the tragedy of social life today. In the old England, the curious blood-
      connection held the classes together. The squires might be arrogant, violent, bullying and
      unjust, yet in some ways they were *at one* with the people, part of the same blood-stream.'

46   Among those who knew Lawrence, perhaps the most damning critique is that by Bertrand
      Russell (1956: 104–108). Dismissing the 'dream-like quality of all his thinking', Russell
      altered his initially benign view of Lawrence, and came to regard him as 'a positive force
      for evil'. This was because 'he had developed the whole philosophy of Fascism before the
      politicians had thought of it'. Of particular concern was the 'mystical philosophy of blood',
      which Russell 'rejected ... vehemently, though [he] did not then know that it led straight
      to Auschwitz.'

47   Rejecting a rationalist approach to ethnic 'otherness', Lawrence (1930: 193–94) opts instead
      simply for one of feeling: 'The thought-adventure starts in the blood, not in the mind. If
      an Arab or a negro or even a Jew sits down next to me in the train, I cannot proceed so
      glibly with my knowing. It is not enough for me to glance at a black face and say: He is
      a negro. As he sits next to me, there is a faint uneasy movement in my blood. A strange
      vibration comes from him, which causes a slight disturbance in my own vibration.'

48   For this and what follows, see a letter written by Lawrence (1948: 150–54) It is described
      by the editor (Pritchett, 1948: v, 150) of the volume in which it is published not only as 'a
      famous example of historical prophecy', but also as indicating 'a remarkable sensitiveness
      to the trend of events in Germany at a time when Hitlerism, as we know it now, hardly
      existed'.

great leaning of the Germanic spirit is once more eastwards, towards Russia, towards Tartary'. This was regarded with concern: 'the positivity of Western Europe is broken. The positivity of our civilization is broken' since Germany was '[r]eturning again to the fascination of the destructive East, that produced Attila.' Dismay turned to fear ('Out of the very air comes a sense of danger, a queer, *bristling* feeling of uncanny danger'), as Lawrence sensed the approach of what he described as 'the ghost of the old Middle Ages of Germany ... the dangerous, lurking barbarians'[49]

What some mistook for a progressive misgiving on the part of Lawrence about the path German society was following, however, was nothing of the sort. It was precisely because of his views about the innateness and immutable nature of ethnic/national identity that he was able to recognize the process at work. 'It is a fate; nobody now can alter it. It is fate. The very blood changes ... the very constituency of blood has changed ... particularly in German veins'. Rather than being a warning against the rise of a far-right political mobilization, therefore, the observations by Lawrence of just such a development unfolding before him can be seen, much rather, as a perception on his part regarding the vindication of his own 'blood-belonging' views.

This is a discourse that Lawrence – like Gobineau and Wagner – applied both to himself and to everybody.[50] Thus he not only speaks of 'my old blood-affinity [with] the land' but also essentializes the Italian peasant as embodying an innate and thus 'authentic' closeness to nature ('his strong blood-presence') that Lawrence himself feels, and of which he approves.[51] Unlike workers, regarded as no longer possessing a community spirit based on 'blood-sympathy' with landlord and squire, peasants by contrast still embody this inborn sense. This is because the identity of a peasant is for Lawrence timeless, and its subject is depicted as unthinking, at one with the land, its proprietors, and the

---

49   'And it all looks as if the years were wheeling swiftly backwards, no more forwards,' he writes (Lawrence, 1948: 153): 'Like a spring that is broken and whirls swiftly back, so time seems to be whirling with mysterious swiftness to a sort of death. Whirling to the ghost of the old Middle Ages of Germany, then to the Roman days, then to the days of the silent forest and the dangerous, lurking barbarians.'

50   Asked whether he believed in equality, Lawrence (1968: 322–23) answered no, and although he considered himself superior to the peasant, 'it is only that I feel myself like the growing tip, or one of the growing tips of the tree, and him like a piece of the hard, fixed tissue of the branch or trunk. We're part of the same tree; and it's the same sap ... for his mindlessness, I would have chosen the peasant: and for his strong blood-presence'.

51   See Lawrence (1968: 321, 596), who refers to the presence of 'old-world peasants' having 'utterly blank minds', 'blindly going on with the little job in hand, the present moment, cut off from all past and future ...'

animals on it. Whilst peasants are not looked down upon, however, Lawrence nevertheless regards them as 'other', part of the same landscape in Italy yet different ('I want to live near them, because their life still flows').[52]

II

Moving on from an examination of the views held by those on the political right, who privilege race and endorse racism, it is necessary to consider how and why those on the left oppose racism together with its form of identity politics. Whereas Gobineau and Wagner see the presence of the 'other' as a cultural threat, both to the nation and to their race, Marxism by contrast sees the issue as involving a threat neither to the race, to the nation, nor to the culture. Instead, Marxists now and in the past interpret the question of the 'other' as one of political economy. Rather than the harbinger of liberalism and modernity, which is the way nineteenth century nationalists such as Gobineau and Wagner perceive the role of the 'other', therefore, Marxism regards the problem differently, and locates the whole question within an already established capitalism, and thus the capacity – or otherwise – of the accumulation process to reproduce itself systemically.

Accordingly, at issue is the extent to which the insertion by capital of the 'other' into a labour market that is increasingly global in scope is designed to undermine the consciousness and struggle of class. Early Marxists (Marx, Engels, Lenin) focused on the way racism was deployed by capitalists and their state as a weapon in the class struggle with labour, by appealing to ethnic/national/other identities within the working class in pursuit of divide-and-rule tactics. Later ones (Trotsky, Deutscher) shifted their focus somewhat, and looked at the social composition of those attacked in this manner, asking why this was. While Sartre gazes on anti-semitism from the outside, Trotsky and Deutscher address the same ideology as its actual or potential targets.[53] All are socialists, the latter rather more so than the former.

---

52   In Italy, therefore, Lawrence (1968: 595) describes how he lives 'in a certain silent contact with the peasants who work the land of this villa. I am not intimate with them, hardly speak to them save to say good day. And they are not working for me; I am not their *padrone*. Yet it is they, really, who form my *ambiente*, and it is from them that the human flow comes to me. I don't want to live with them in their cottages; that would be a sort of prison. But I want them to be there, about the place, their lives going along with mine, and in relation to mine ... I don't expect them to make any millennium here on earth, neither now nor in the future. But I want to live near them, because their life still flows.'

53   This predicament, faced by Trotsky as well as by Deutscher, is well described by the latter (Deutscher, 1968: 37) in the following manner: 'To Trotsky it came as a shock that Stalin used against him the anti-semitic innuendo. As a young man Trotsky had, in most

They Are Our Brothers

Throughout the early twentieth century Lenin condemned attempts by the Czarist autocracy to invoke non-class identities so as to turn workers of different ethnicities/nationalities against one another.[54] Countering such attempts to fuel dissention by means of the divide-and-rule tactic – both within and outside Russia – he emphasized that 'the duty of all class-conscious workers is to rise with all their might against those who are stirring up national hatred and diverting the attention of the working people from their real enemies'.[55] Particular criticism was aimed by him at Austrian Social Democracy for espousing cultural/national autonomy, pointing out that it licensed forms of 'otherness' (religious, educational), ideologies operating at the rural grassroots that would in turn not just reinforce chauvinistic tendencies in such contexts but also undermine thereby class solidarity.[56]

It was for this reason, above all, that Lenin clarified the Marxist position on ethnic/national forms of 'otherness' in the following unambiguous manner: 'Combat all national oppression? Yes, of course! Fight *for* any kind of

---

categorical terms, repudiated the demand for Jewish "cultural autonomy", which the *Bund*, the Jewish Socialist Party, raised in 1903. He did it in the name of solidarity of Jew and non-Jew in the socialist camp. Nearly a quarter of a century later, while he was engaged in an unequal struggle with Stalin and went to the party cells in Moscow to expound his views, he was met with vicious allusions to his Jewishness and even with plain anti-semitic insults. The allusions and insults came from members of the party which he had, together with Lenin, led in revolution and civil war. After another quarter of a century, and after Auschwitz and Majdanek and Belsen, once again, this time much more openly and menacingly, Stalin resorted to anti-semitic innuendo and insult.'

54   'Against the people's revolution, against the class struggle', argued Lenin (1962: 204–5) in 1905, the Czarist autocratic state 'must stir up national hatred, race hatred ... [t]his is precisely what the government is now doing when it sets the Tatars against the Armenians in Baku; when it seeks to provoke new pogroms against the Jews ... [o]f course, by fanning racial antagonism and tribal hatred, the government may for a time arrest the development of the class struggle ...'

55   See Lenin (1964a: 376–77), who condemned the fact that 'hostility is being stirred up against the Jews; the gutter press carries on Jew-baiting campaigns, as if Jewish workers do not suffer in exactly the same way as Russian workers from the oppression of capital and the police government ... [journalists] are straining every nerve to rouse the hatred of the people against China'. Differentiating the 'other' in terms of class, in much the same way as Deutscher later, Lenin (1965: 252) argued that '[a]mong the Jews there are working people, and they form the majority. They are our brothers, who, like us, are oppressed by capital; they are our comrades in the struggle for socialism. Among the Jews there are kulaks, exploiters and capitalists, just as there are among the Russians, and among peoples of all nations'. Similar views are expressed by him elsewhere (Lenin, 1964b: 470; 1968: 516–19, 520–21).

56   Lenin (1964b).

national development, *for* "national culture" in general? – Of course, not'.[57] In effect, he warned against turning what should for socialists be a struggle about class into a race war. Whereas the former promotes inclusivity across ethnicities, the latter by contrast fosters an exclusivity that often leads to antagonism between the same categories. Undermined thereby is solidarity based on class, the absence of which can only benefit capitalism. Although the dividing line between opposing racial/national oppression and promoting ethnic/national 'otherness' is imperceptible, nevertheless it exists: the political danger of not recognizing this break, and consequently moving from one to the other, is – as Lenin reminds us – something that cannot be ignored.

On the specific issue of anti-semitism, Trotsky outlines its pervasive nature in Czarist Russia, where such ideology found support among peasants, the urban petty bourgeoisie, the intelligentsia, and the 'more backward strata of the working class'.[58] The reason for this is ascribed by him to the fact that Jews inhabited urban areas, contexts in which the Russian government sought civil servants; since it recruited from the 'more cultured city population', those from the Jewish community found employment in the bureaucracy, 'particularly so in its lower and middle levels.' As to the cause of anti-semitism in Russia, this is linked by Trotsky to the antagonism felt by peasants and workers towards the bureaucracy, the tasks of which included enforcing the oppressive economic policy and legislative programme of the Czar. Consequently, opprobrium at the rural grassroots was directed at those deemed responsible for this and took the form of anti-semitism.[59]

Legislative ordinances enacted by the Bolsheviks that eliminated Czarist discrimination against ethnic minorities notwithstanding, it was Stalin who

---

57   Lenin (1964c: 35, original emphasis).

58   About this history, see Trotsky (1964: 207), who records many instances of anti-semitism and progroms during the Czarist era (Trotsky, 1934: 41, 157, 249; Trotsky, 1972: 132, 137). On the question of Bolshevik policy annulling Czarist legislation disadvantaging nationalities and ethnic minorities within Russia, Trotsky (1934: 892) observed: 'This formal equality gave most of all to the Jews, for the laws limiting their rights had reached the number of 650. Moreover, being city dwellers and the most scattered of all the nationalities, the Jews could make no claim either to state independence or even territorial autonomy. As to the project of a so-called "national-cultural autonomy" which should unite the Jews throughout the whole country around schools and other institutions, this reactionary utopia, borrowed by various Jewish groups from the Austrian theoretician, Otto Bauer, melted in those first days of freedom like wax under the sun's rays.'

59   'Even by a priori reasoning,' notes Trotsky (1964: 208), 'it is impossible not to conclude that the hatred for the bureaucracy would assume an anti-semitic colour, at least in those places where the Jewish functionaries compose a significant percentage of the population and are thrown into relief against the broad background of the peasant masses.'

encouraged anti-semitism by 'catering to the national feelings and prejudices of the backward layers of the population.'[60] Dismissed as unimportant both by Lenin and by Trotsky himself, the ethnicity of the latter was raised as an issue, and became politically significant, once Stalin was confronted by the Left Opposition.[61] Trotsky records that in public announcements by Stalinists he was increasingly referred to as 'Bronstein', since 'they wished to emphasize my Jewish origin', adding that '[t]he whole struggle against the Opposition is full of such episodes'.[62] In keeping with the approach of the majority of Marxists, therefore, Trotsky placed the rise, consolidation, and reproduction of anti-semitism within its historical context, determined neither by culture nor by psychology – as interpreted by those on the political right – but rather by politics and struggle of class.[63]

One's Own Free Will

Addressing the same question – what anti-Jewish racism is, and why it exists – Sartre moves away from the approach of Lenin and Trotsky. He essentialises anti-semitism, and thus dehistoricizes it, appearing to put it beyond the analytical scope of any explanation save a psychologistic one.[64] As interpreted by

---

60   About this, Trotsky (1964: 208–9, original emphasis) writes: 'The privileged [Stalinist] bureaucracy, fearful of its privileges ... represents at present [c.1937] *the most anti-socialist and most anti-democratic stratum of Soviet society* ... the leading cadre of the bureaucracy at the centre and in the provinces strives to divert the indignation of the working masses from itself to the Jews.'

61   On this, see Trotsky (1930: 292, 309–10), who comments: 'The question of my Jewish origin acquired importance only after I had become a subject for political baiting. Anti-Semitism raised its head with that of anti-Trotskyism. They both derived from the same source – the petty bourgeois reaction against October.'

62   See Trotsky (1964: 211, 212), who comments that 'the baiting of the Opposition back in 1926 often assumed a thoroughly obvious anti-Semitic character', noting further the stress put by Stalin on ethnic identity: '"Do not forget that the leaders of the Opposition are – Jews". That was the *meaning* of the statements of Stalin, published in all Soviet journals'.

63   The conclusion arrived at by Trotsky (1964: 213, original emphasis) about the spread of anti-semitic discourse in the Soviet Union is telling: 'Again: if such methods are practiced at the very top where the personal responsibility of Stalin is absolutely unquestionable, then it is not hard to imagine what transpires in the ranks, at the factories, and especially at the *kolkhozes*. And how can it be otherwise? The physical extermination of the older generation of Bolsheviks is, for every person who can think, an incontrovertible expression of Thermidorian reaction, and in its advanced stage at that.'

64   Despite conceding that 'there are certain historical bases to explain anti-semitism', Sartre (1948: 10) nevertheless proceeds to characterize this discourse as a pan-historical

Sartre, this form of racism has as its target a supra-historical identity devoid of context and conjuncture: hence the view that '[i]t is thus the *idea* one has of the Jew which seems to determine history, and not "historical evidence" which gives rise to the idea ... from whatever aspect we view the matter, the essential thing seems to be the *concept of Jew*'.[65] For Sartre, therefore, this kind of racism consists of an idea without a history, since in his view 'no external factor can instil anti-semitism'.[66]

Much like Wagner, for whom identity is defined simply as the product of instinct/passion/feeling, so anti-semitism is categorized by Sartre as 'a passion', which enables him to label it simply as an irrational urge: not just a demateri-alized ideology lacking a history, chosen at random and promoted assiduously by its adherent, but also a discourse uninformed by thought ('ruled by passion rather than by reason').[67] Sartre then dismisses this racism as 'a form of sick-ness', thereby pathologizing anti-semitism as a medical condition and not a political ideology capable of social analysis.[68] This sort of approach is unhelp-ful, not least when attempting to comprehend the origin, history, and political impact of racism, which is precisely what Marxism seeks to undertake.

It is when Sartre addresses the 'ordinariness' of the anti-semite that a miss-ing cause – competition fuelled by the accumulation process – is referenced, obliquely. No anti-semite, argues Sartre, asserts individual superiority over the Jews, not least because, unlike those in the latter category, the anti-semite is nothing more than an 'average man' and 'basically mediocre'.[69] That such

---

phenomenon without fixity to period or place, an ideology that seemingly reproduces itself regardless of anything else occurring at the time.

65   On this, see Sartre (1948: 12–13, original emphases).

66   'It becomes clear, therefore, that no external factor can instil anti-semitism in the anti-semite', he insists (Sartre, 1948: 13), since '[a]nti-semitism is something adopted of one's own free will and involving the whole of one's outlook, a philosophy of life brought to bear not only on Jews but on all men in general, on history and society; it is both an emo-tional state and a way of looking at the world.'

67   According to Sartre (1948: 14, original emphasis), 'it must be agreed that the anti-semite has chosen to let his life be dominated by his particular passion. A good many people, it is true, prefer to let their lives be ruled by passion rather than by reason'. See also Sartre (1948: 19–20).

68   For anti-semitism merely as a form of sickness, see Sartre (1948: 14), whose psychologistic depiction of anti-semitism mainly as the product of an irrational/diseased personality is to some extent true also of Horkheimer and Adorno (1973: 168ff.).

69   Hence the view (Sartre, 1948: 17–18): 'The anti-semite willingly admits that the Jew is intel-ligent and hard-working; he may even acknowledge his own inferiority in this respect ... The anti-semite cherishes no illusions about himself. He regards himself as an average man, and basically of the mediocre: one does not find instances of an anti-semite claim-ing individual superiority over the Jews'.

racism does not involve looking down on its victim, much rather the opposite, hints at the presence of another cause: it is the ability of the ethnic 'other' which is of concern, underlining thereby the role of competition – that is, economic rivalry – in fuelling the emergence and reproduction of anti-semitism.[70] Ironically, many of the examples provided by Sartre to illustrate anti-semitic discourse contain references by those holding such views to what is perceived by them as unfair competition for jobs.[71]

When the class origin of anti-semites is considered, however, Sartre depicts it as a specifically petty-bourgeois phenomenon, overlooking that racist ideology can also be deployed by plebeians experiencing acute labour market competition from workers of a different ethnicity or nationality.[72] For the petty bourgeois 'who possesses nothing', therefore, the self-image of the French anti-semite is that he possesses 'something worth stealing': France. This image of the French anti-semite as mediocre/average is then positioned by Sartre in a framework based on oppositions espoused by such racists: between on the one hand their national pride, espousal of rural tradition, and ownership of landed property, which together with their 'ordinariness' and anti-intellectualism, are contrasted by them with the urban-dwelling cosmopolitanism, the intellectual and commercial acuity they attribute to Jews.[73]

---

70   It seems that Sartre, for obvious reasons (he was writing at the end of the 1939–45 war), misses the way in which racism can change, and how this involves a different subject (petty bourgeois, plebeian) and cause (commercial rivalry, labour market competition). Though not absolute, this difference can take the following form:

Period	Discourse	Cause	Exponent	Target
Historical	Anti-Semitism	Commercial rivalry	Petty-bourgeois	Jews (already here)
Present	Racism	Labour market competition	Plebeians, workers	Immigrants (still to arrive)

71   Sartre (1948: 7–10).

72   About the class origin of those holding anti-semitic views, Sartre (1948: 20) comments that 'perhaps the majority, come from the lower middle class of the towns: Government clerks, office workers, petty business-men who possess nothing.'

73   'The true Frenchman, with his roots deep down in his own country, in his own small locality, sustained by a tradition of twenty centuries, benefiting from an ancestral wisdom and guided by tried and tested custom, does not need to be intelligent', observes Sartre (1948: 18–19): 'What merit he has is founded on the assimilation of those qualities with which things around him have been endowed by the labour of innumerable generations, and hence it is a merit arising from ownership ... The anti-semite fails totally to understand the principles underlying different forms of modern property, i.e. stocks

What is not mentioned by Sartre is that these same oppositions structure populism in general, and agrarian populism in particular.[74] Unusually for a Marxist, he misrecognizes the shared characteristics of racism and populism, a connection made by Marxists, then and since. Instead, Sartre argues that 'anti-semitism is a form of poor man's snobbery' constitutes evidence for a natural – as distinct from a manufactured – affinity that brings 'the duke and his coachman' together. The inference is that the construction of what Sartre terms 'an egalitarian community' is the result of plebeians voluntarily looking up to those at the top of the social hierarchy, rather than being persuaded as to overriding political usefulness to themselves of a shared national/ethnic identity. The latter is the populist aspect of political mobilization, a discourse that avoids mention of class differences separating those at the top and bottom of the social hierarchy who hold racist views in common, thereby recasting the difference of class as the sameness of ethnic/national identity. Not considered by Sartre is why this works when it does, and in whose interest it operates.

---

and shares, and so on. These are abstractions, mental entities which are connected with the abstract intelligence of the semite ... The anti-semite can conceive of only one type of acquisition – primitive land ownership – based on a truly magical relationship with possession ...'

74 According to Sartre (1948: 20), '[w]hen he [the anti-semite] contrasts himself with the Jew [it] is as the embodiment of feeling against intelligence, of the particular against the universal, of the past against the present, of the concrete against the abstract, of the possessor of landed estate against the possessor of transferable securities'. The oppositions informing the discourse that anti-semitism has in common with populism are presented in the following table:

Anti-semite	Jews
good	bad
feeling	intelligence
particular	universal
past	present
concrete	abstract
land	money/commerce
rural	urban
nation	cosmopolitan
tradition	modernity

To See with Distorted Vision

Where the cause and structure of anti-semitism are concerned, Deutscher followed in the footsteps of Marx, Lenin and Trotsky by the emphasis he placed on three things: the analytical primacy given to an historical materialist approach to the understanding of the origin and reproduction of anti-semitic discourse, advocacy of class solidarity between Jew and non-Jew, plus strong opposition to identity politics.[75] To this end he emphasized the historical, political and economic heterogeneity of Jewish populations in East and West, outlining the resulting social distinctions: in the East these remained important, but less so in the West, where assimilation was more pronounced.[76] Similarly, political emancipation occurred in the West, but not the East, where Jews were prevented by law from owning land or entering particular occupations.[77] Hence the rejection by Deutscher of the 'bonds of blood' argument underpinning claims as to the innateness of race, a position to which Gobineau, Wagner, and D.H. Lawrence all adhered.[78]

Like Trotsky and Lenin, Deutscher differentiated Jews in terms of their class position, and consequently also their politics and culture. For those on the

---

75   Speaking not just of Marx, Luxemburg, and Trotsky, but also of Heine, Spinoza, and Freud, Deutscher (1968: 36–37) noted: 'These "non-Jewish Jews" were essentially optimists; and their optimism reached heights which it is not easy to ascend in our times. They did not imagine that it would be possible for a "civilized" Europe in the twentieth century to sink to a depth of barbarity at which the mere words "solidarity of man" would sound as a perverse mockery to Jewish ears.'

76   'In Western Europe after the French revolution the Jews enjoyed formal equality in the eyes of the law', a development which, argued Deutscher (1968: 62), 'went hand in hand with ... growing assimilation ... In Eastern Europe the great masses of Jews ... lived in compact communities, separated from their non-Jewish environment [where] the way of life of the great mass of orthodox Jews had developed very little in the course of centuries.'

77   The political difference is outlined thus (Deutscher, 1968: 63): 'In Western Europe along with the assimilation went the emancipation of the Jews. Not so in Eastern Europe [where they were] not allowed to own land; certain occupations were closed to them, their position was little better than that of the Russian and Polish peasant serfs.'

78   This was an issue about which Deutscher felt strongly, as is evident from what he wrote in a 1966 essay (Deutscher, 1968: 51): 'To speak personally once again ... I have nothing in common with the Jews of, say, *Mea Shaarim* or with any kind of Israeli nationalists. I am attracted to the left-wing Marxists in Israel, but I feel just as close to like-minded people in France, Italy, Britain, and Japan, or to those masses of Americans whom I addressed in Washington and San Francisco at vast protest meetings against the war in Vietnam. Are we now going to accept the idea that it is racial ties or "bonds of blood" that make up the Jewish community? Would not that be another triumph for Hitler and his degenerate philosophy?'

political right, such as Gobineau and Wagner, opprobrium stemmed from the perception that Jewish culture was always and everywhere the same, regardless of context and time, a monolithic identity that spanned continents and epochs. Deutscher, by contrast, shows this to be untrue, since the Jewish population was not – and is not – homogenous.[79] In western Europe, therefore, it has been composed principally of those belonging to the middle class: merchants, businessmen, and bankers, not workers or artisans.[80] By contrast, in the East Jews were predominantly found among the poor – artisans, cobblers, tailors, and carpenters.[81] This distinction, however, is not made by the antisemite, for whom historically the Jewish population is homogenous, and consequently designated as such culpable for the all the ills of modernity and accumulation.[82]

---

79   'We all know how repellent are some of the Jewish milieus of the West', notes Deutscher (1968: 44–45), who continues, 'the milieus in which there is nothing but a few taboos and a lot of money. With us, in the [Eastern European] environment I knew, it was the reverse: no money, no taboos, but an abundance of hope, ideas, and ideals. We had a thorough contempt for the *Yahudim* of the West. Our comrades were made of different stuff.' He emphasizes the significance of this this distinction in the following manner (Deutscher, 1968: 52): 'To speak of the "Jewish community" as if it were an all-embracing entity ... is meaningless, and for a Marxist doubly so. The Marxist sees all societies primarily from the point of view of their class divisions. But the "Jewish community" contains not only antagonistic social classes; it has also been divided, so to speak, geographically.'

80   Hence the importance attached by Deutscher (1968: 61) to 'drawing a sharp contrast between the place of Jews in Western societies and their place in Eastern Europe and especially Russia ... [Thus] to look at the Jewish problem in Russia through the prism of Jewish life in Western Europe, is to see with distorted vision ... not for a single moment [must one] imagine that Jewish life and the Jewish community in Eastern Europe and in Russia resembled in any way the Jewish community in England, in France, or even in the United States.'

81   As recounted by Deutscher (1968: 61), '[t]hroughout the nineteenth century the Jews in the countries of Western Europe belonged mainly to the middle class. There were very few Jewish workers, not many Jewish artisans, some small shopkeepers. Most Jews were merchants, transacting their business on a large scale in many western capitals. Some of them were great bankers, and the House of Rothchild became almost a symbol of Jewish *haute bourgeoisie*. This predominantly bourgeois character of the Jewish community in Western Europe stood in marked contrast to the Jewish communities in Eastern Europe. True, in the East we also possessed our Jewish bourgeoisie, our merchants or shopkeepers. But the great majority of Jews were poor toilers, primitive artisans, cobblers, tailors, carpenters.'

82   On this point Deutscher (1968: 39) comments: 'It has been the misfortune of the Jews that, when the nations of Europe turned against capitalism, they did so only very superficially, at any rate in the first half of [the 20th] century. They attacked not the core of capitalism, not its productive relationship, not its organization of property and labour, but its externals and its largely archaic trappings which were so often Jewish. This is the crux of the Jewish tragedy.'

Presciently, already in 1966 Deutscher cautioned against going down the path followed by many nowadays, of seeing as progressive the reassertion of national/ethnic 'otherness'.[83] His concern then, lest economic crisis generated by the accumulation process would once again unleash the combined populism/racism that marked the 1920s and 1930s, has in effect been proved correct. At that conjuncture, however, he hoped – perhaps too optimistically – that any such development would face strong opposition from the intelligentsia in metropolitan capitalist nations. In his words: 'That is why I think that the role of the intellectuals – Jews and non-Jews alike – of those who are aware of the depth of the Jewish tragedy and the menace of its reoccurrence, is to remain eternal protesters ... to struggle for a society in which nationalism and racialism will at last lose their hold on the human mind.'[84] Although the future threat seen by Deutscher was specifically that of anti-semitism, his caveat at that conjuncture extended also to racism and nationalism in general.[85]

Half a century on, this fear about the dangers of opposing capitalism on the basis of nationalism/ethnicity rather than political economy – let alone socialism – is more relevant than ever, as indicated by the combination of neoliberalism and populism.[86] On the one hand, therefore, the emergence and consolidation of *laissez-faire* economic policies designed to maintain/enhance profitability by restructuring the capitalist labour process: downsizing/

---

83   Describing '[t]he *Yahudim* of the West, the bourgeoisie and plutocracy' as proponents of identity politics, Deutscher (1968: 46–47) continues: 'To someone of my background the fashionable longing of the Western Jew for a return to the sixteenth century, a return which is supposed to help him in recovering, or rediscovering, his Jewish cultural identity, seems unreal and Kafkaesque.'

84   Deutscher (1968: 58).

85   'I do not believe that anti-semitism is a spent force,' cautioned Deutscher (1968: 56–57, 58), adding: 'I fear that we may be living in a fools' paradise in our Western welfare state. The trustful feeling of freedom from anti-semitism may well be one more illusion, a particularly Jewish one, engendered by our "affluent society"...We may have the impression that anti-semitism is a spent force because in this our welfare state people are, on the whole, contented and satisfied and their social troubles are seemingly dispelled. Let this society suffer any severe shock, such as it is bound to suffer; let there be again millions of unemployed, and we will see the same lower middle class alliance with the *Lumpenproletariat* from whom Hitler recruited his following, running amok with anti-semitism. As long as nation-state imposes its supremacy and as long as the wealth of every nation is in the hands of one capitalist oligarchy, we shall have chauvinism, racialism, and its culmination, anti-semitism.'

86   As Deutscher (1968: 48) points out, 'European socialism as a rule accepted and encouraged the assimilation of Jews as part of a wider and progressive movement in consequence of which modern society was supposed to be shedding its particularist and nationalist traditions.'

outsourcing jobs, plus the search by employers for ever cheaper forms of casual/
temporary and low-paid labour-power drawn from the industrial reserve. On
the other, the reaction to the latter has taken an interconnected political and
ideological form: essentializing the race and nationality of the 'other' in the
postmodern discourse of the cultural turn, matched by an invocation on the
far right of similarly essentialized kinds of analogous 'selfhood'. Each not only
privileges such non-class identities as traditional – and thus desirable – forms
of empowerment, but also advocates political mobilization on the basis of
these sorts of ideology.

III

Warnings by Lenin, Deutscher, and others, of privileging non-class identities such as nationalism, and consequently disregarding the political and
ideological dangers inherent in continuing to view nationalism/ethnicity as
empowering discourses for mobilizing 'those below' against capitalism, have
largely remained unheeded. The connection between racism and the industrial reserve army, a link that historically Marxism has acknowledged and
addressed politically, is currently nowhere to be seen on the agenda of the
left. Instead, the issue surfaces in a different form, recast as one simply about
human rights and citizenship aspirations of the migrant. Rather than being a
question of political economy, involving the way the industrial reserve fuels
yet more labour market competition, how the mobilizing discourse of struggle
changes, shifting from class solidarity to ethnic/national identity and solidarity, and how such developments contribute to the project of capital, therefore,
the focus tends to be on the empowering nature of non-class identity as a way
of securing improvements within capitalism, and not its transcendence.

In ways that anticipate recent argument about withdrawal from EU membership so as to stem competition from the industrial reserve army, a century
and a half ago Marx advocated severing the link with Ireland precisely in order
to prevent migrants from competing with and undercutting English workers.
He insisted that working class emancipation in England depended ultimately
on Ireland following its own path of capitalist development, and to this end
international solidarity would take the form of support from English workers
for Irish equivalents in their struggle for economic and political independence,
as distinct from migrating to where this had already occurred.[87] In cases where
such an approach is not followed, and the issue is addressed instead by the left

---

87   See Marx (Marx and Engels, 1934: 289–90).

in non-class terms (human rights, citizenship), the result is that opposition to the industrial reserve is taken up by the political right, which uses it to gain working class support by recasting the issue in nationalist/racist terms.[88]

Avoiding the Question

The refusal by most of those on the left to address the issue of the industrial reserve army of labour, or to engage with it simply as a rights/humanitarian question, is difficult to miss. A case in point are contributions to what purports to be a Marxist approach to methodology, where the industrial reserve army is dismissed as 'functionalist' with nary a discussion.[89] Nothing more is heard about this concept, a vital theoretical and political weapon used by Marxists when opposing capitalism, with the exception of another contributor to the same volume who rather oddly links it merely to nutritional patterns.[90] As strange is the view of Novak, also a contributor, who ignores the industrial reserve, preferring to incorporate the migrant into what is termed 'refugee studies'.[91] The latter, it transpires, entails refocussing the issue of migration: away from political economy, with its emphasis on the need to control or regulate access to the labour market, since immigration 'cannot be reduced to capital's imperatives'; and towards a post-structuralist approach involving migrant 'political subjectivities [which] are irreducible to any synthetic representation.' In order to reveal 'the secret character of the refugee', therefore, Novak opts for commodity fetishism as the method for explaining

---

88   A case in in point was the way the rise of European fascism profited from the advocacy by
        Austrian Social Democracy of separatism on the basis of an ethnic/national 'other' iden-
        tity. As recounted by Whiteside (1975), towards the end of the nineteenth century Czech
        migration into the industrial districts of German Bohemia was used by employers to dis-
        place better-paid German workers. The result was that not only were hitherto socialist-
        leaning proletarian organizations and politics fragmented along ethnic/nationalist lines,
        but labour market competition between Czech migrants and German workers, together
        with the intense economic rivalry to which it gave rise, remained to a large degree unad-
        dressed and thus unresolved by leftist strategy.

89   See Bernstein (2021: 26, n 21), whose dismissive view about the industrial reserve is at odds
        with the declared intention of Mezzadri (2021: 10) in her introduction to the same book,
        where she announces that the 'insights from development studies can prove increasingly
        useful to investigate the socioeconomic changes taking place across the world economy.
        This is particularly evident with reference to the study of economic migration and the
        so-called refugee crisis'. This intention proved to be that, nothing more.

90   The single exception is Stevano (2021: 178–9).

91   For these views, see Novak (2021: 214–215).

such 'political subjectivities', a procedure, he accepts, is one at which 'many Marxists will despair', a conclusion that it is impossible to dispute.

Equally culpable in this regard are the views found in some leftist journals and magazines. Thus, for example, a 2014 article in *Socialist Worker*, based on a visit to a camp at Calais, presented its migrants as asylum-seekers.[92] Advocating an open-door approach, the question of migration was presented initially as a humanitarian one. In the course of the article, however, it emerged from what the migrants themselves said that reasons for wanting to go to the UK were 'to find a better life in Britain', because 'there is more chance of finding cash-in-hand work'. Accepting both that '[t]hese migrants tend to be young and want to work', and that '[b]osses will always try and use migrant workers to undercut wages', the argument for open-door access to the UK labour market concluded that '[t]he way to stop this is to defend wages for all', since '[w]here migrants are encouraged to join unions, wages can rise for all'. What this ignores are two issues in particular. First, that as long as business has access to the industrial reserve, there will be no pressure on them to improve pay and conditions. And second, unionizing migrant labour in a *laissez-faire* political environment is difficult; even if this can be achieved, as long as access to the industrial reserve is untrammelled, capital will retain the option of replacing such workers with 'green' labour.

Ignored thereby is the rich literature demonstrating the crucial role of the industrial reserve in restructuring the labour process, exerting thereby downward pressure on wages/conditions, and how workers in many different contexts and conjunctures have struggled to prevent attempts by employers to continue or enhance their access to the industrial reserve. Not the least important reason for its inclusion in any Marxist analysis of the way capitalism is reproduced is that a world-wide industrial reserve is currently the driver of resurgent populism.[93] Misrecognizing not only the connection between racism and the industrial reserve, but also how this features in the discourse of the political right, is far from common.

Thus earlier studies of working class racism in the UK, based on fieldwork conducted from the mid-1940s to around the mid-1970s, tended to depict it largely in psychological terms, categorizing support for the political right

---

92   See 'Scared, scarred and starved in Calais – the refugees locked out by Britain's borders', *Socialist Worker*, No. 2421, 16 September 2014.

93   All the contributors to this volume could benefit from a perusal of Marxist approaches – by, among others, Dobb (1955: 215–225), Sweezy (1946: 87–92, 149–50), and Glyn (2006) – to the way capitalism not merely benefits from but depends on a globally-enhanced industrial reserve.

simply as an effect of personality traits.[94] This despite containing glimpses of labour market competition, suggesting that even at that conjuncture racism was an ideology produced/reproduced by restructuring/displacing strategies pursued by capitalism, and not just innate.[95] It was an epistemology that pre-figured the later approach to the same issue by adherents of the 'new' populist postmodernism, some of whom extended the view by labelling racism as an innate characteristic of UK society.[96] Not the least problematic aspect of these approaches is the essentializing of racism, the inference being that, as it is ingrained, it is an ideology/discourse that cannot be altered, let alone eradicated.

Samuel Smiles Revisited

A different approach to the same issue is one that – because it too ignores the implications of labour market competition for workers in the receiving context – similarly regards migration in positive terms.[97] Mimicking what passes for leftism, but extending its logic in a consistent direction, the focus of this

---

94   See, for example, Robb (1954), Billig (1978), and Fielding (1981).

95   Robb (1954: 146) documents 'the complaint that the competition of foreign workers is so strong that it is always necessary for the worker to do what the employer wishes, whether he likes it or not, because the alternative is to be replaced immediately; as there are few jobs available, a quarrel with an employer means almost certain unemployment.' Such grassroots protests about labour market competition (Robb, 1954: 205) in the immediate post-war era notwithstanding, Robb (1954: 171–72) dismisses economic issues as having any explanatory value for an understanding of working class anti-semitism. Similarly, Fielding (1981: 93) records the following opinion at a later period: 'A "threat" posed by immigrants which strikes most directly at the working class heart is that immigrants provide a source of cheap labour. The Secretary of the [National Front wrote in 1975 that] "often immigrants do jobs at lower rates of pay, thereby undermining the position of workers. Coupled with this, many immigrants do an excessive amount of overtime, thus assisting unscrupulous employers ... endangering trade union rights and making a mockery of trade union struggle for a forty hour week"'. Having noted this, however, Fielding makes no further observation as to its role vis-à-vis the industrial reserve, and seemingly underplays the element of labour market competition, arguing (Fielding, 1981: 96) that for the National Front '[t]he essential negative attribute of immigrants is not their effect on ... jobs [but] that they are alien, strange, foreign.'

96   There are many examples of this currently, recognizable by the use of all-encompassing – and thus undifferentiated – terms like 'white privilege' and 'toxic whiteness'.

97   Of the UK Marquardt (2021: 146) opines that '[a]ny sane country should be at pains to attract young, dynamic people – not create a 'hostile environment' that pushes them away', a view heard nowadays not just from Goodfellow (2020) but also from employers and their political representatives.

kind of Panglossian approach is also migrant-centric. Advanced recently by Marquardt, it consists of the view that, because the global economy requires young workers, nations will always seek to attract them, enabling migrants themselves to choose the best offer.[98] His account is a litany of migrant achievement: a transition from rags, via an innumerable series of daunting personal setbacks overcome, to entrepreneurial acumen rewarded by riches, usually in the form of owning an innovative and prosperous business. Redolent of the 'self-help'/'self-improvement' ideology of Samuel Smiles, the migrant narratives of Marquardt depict how 'success has followed success', reinforcing his main argument: 'Improving one's social and economic conditions remains an important lever of migration'.[99]

When he attempts to explain why his rose-tinted vision about migration is not shared by 'those below' in metropolitan capitalist nations, Marquardt encounters difficulties. Addressing 'the pushback that immigration has received in recent years', he asks 'where is it coming from, and why?'. Rather than blaming those who – for whatever reason – contest open-door migration, he takes issue with 'the pro-migration stance of elites' on the grounds that such 'from above' support is detrimental to the cause of migrants.[100] This hostility by Marquardt towards elite support, however, is unconnected with the impact of migration on labour market competition, and stems instead from a desire on his part not to demean opposition to immigration so as then to engage with it and thus comprehend the cause.[101] The latter is attributed both to an

---

98   Hence the view (Marquardt, 2021: 221) about the 'economic benefits of leaving, and the entrepreneurial spirit it fosters. Economics can operate as a pull factor, with migrants, often young, drawn to dynamic economies ...' The Panglossian aspect is evident from an earlier comment by Marquardt (2021: 128) that '[u]nprecedented international mobility gave the young unprecedented leverage. By voting with their feet ... the young can turn the world into a beauty contest between cities, countries and regions vying to attract them'.

99   See Marquardt (2021: 144, 196). For the views not just about 'self-help', but also 'character', 'duty', and 'thrift' – all central to the self-validating image of the virtuous bourgeois in the Victorian era – see Smiles (1877, 1885, 1888, 1892). Confronting his critics, Smiles (1877: iv) in a later edition accepts that '[i]t has also been objected to the book that too much notice is taken in it of men who have succeeded in life by helping themselves, and too little of the multitude of men who have failed.'

100 Rightly dismissive of 'elitist liberal gatherings for very rich people' as nothing more than meetings of celebrities engaged in self-congratulation, thinking this sufficient 'to make the world a better place', Marquardt (2021: 213–14) then omits to interrogate this issue further; he veers off in another direction, as suggested by the second part of the following argument to the effect that 'there is something deeply problematic in the worldview and the pro-migration stance of elites and how that pro-migration stance can become such a liability for those who migrate'.

101 See Marquardt (2021: 208, 209–10).

unwarranted 'fear of the unknown' and to climate change, explanations which overlook that those who express concern about the economic impact of immigration know only too well what is involved, and that capitalism, not climate change is currently the most important determinant of mass emigration.[102]

Hence the inference that such 'fear' is unfounded/irrational is not correct; neither is climate change the sole or even most important cause of population movement.[103] Whilst it is indeed true that 'the pro-migration stance of elites' is problematic, Marquardt nevertheless misreads the reason for this. He fails to understand the material roots of the issues addressed, plus the connection between them: that elites are pro-immigration because, as capitalists, they benefit economically from an augmentation of the industrial reserve; and that plebeian opposition to immigration derives from the fact that, as actual or aspiring workers, they suffer economically from the same process. Underlined thereby is how little Marquardt understands the immigration debate, and why those working-class elements oppose attempts by employers to maintain or enhance access to the industrial reserve leading to an intensification of labour market competition. This is because he regards both capitalism (= entrepreneurialism) and competition (= economic dynamism) as positive.

Unsurprisingly, this also prevents Marquardt (and others) from recognizing the link between on the one hand accumulation, immigration, and the industrial reserve, and on the other the upsurge in racism and populism. Revealing interviews notwithstanding, the attempt by Payne to account for the decline of the Labour party in the Red Wall areas of the UK is bedevilled by its emphasis on what is presented as a rising incidence of prosperity. Consequently, the shift in political support from Labour to the Conservatives is attributed by him to the creation of new businesses and jobs; it is this increasing affluence that has contributed to the electoral backing for the Conservatives. In this reading, therefore, the driver of this changed allegiance is political optimism linked to economic wellbeing and gentrification, and not a populist appeal by the political right to the 'left behind'.[104] Not the least problematic aspect of this

---

102   Linking increases in immigration simply to climate change leads Marquardt (2021: 216–17, 220) to a somewhat curious solution, one that of course leaves capitalism intact ('Climate change activism is about moving around, it is about seeing more of the world, but doing so at a slower pace').

103   The case about 'fear of the unknown', linked by Marquardt (2021: 205) to the claim that 'anti-immigration rhetoric plays best in places where there are few or no immigrants', merely repeats an old canard that such concerns are unfounded or irrational, which in turn licenses the conclusion that people who express this fear are inherently racist.

104   Typical, perhaps is the description by Payne (2021: 78–79) of a former pit village where 'the basic amenities were still present: opticians, cafes, clothing and sportswear. Between this

rose-tinted interpretation is a methodological one. Like Marquardt, Payne focusses on economic 'success' stories, with the difference that the subject of his narrative is not the migrant but the local. Again, like Marquardt, those interviewed by Payne are drawn disproportionately from the ranks of the 'self-made' and the great-and-the-good (politicians, councillors, employers).

IV

After the Brexit vote, and as Covid-19 took hold, many immigrant workers in the UK returned to their eastern European countries, causing labour shortages across the host economy. What followed were three things, all interconnected. First, increased competition for workers resulted in a somewhat improved economic position of labour vis-à-vis capital.[105] Second, not just in the UK but across western capitalist nations, owners of the means of production were under pressure to increase wages and improve working conditions simply in order to attract or keep workers.[106] And third, there were as a result howls of outrage from employers and their organizations about the economically

---

and the new out-of-town shopping parks [the location] has everything you need.' On the question of gentrification, the same air of optimism prevails. Hence 'the streets of council houses morphed into semi-detached suburbia – triangular roofs, sloping driveways with space for two cars, well-kept lawns. Houses that were built for the aspirational middle-class lifestyle ...', maintains Payne (2021: 223). 'In every red wall seat I visited', he continues (Payne, 2021: 225–26), 'new housing estates have emerged outside the traditional town centres ... new detached houses were appearing in every spare corner', inhabited by persons such as the 'car-dependent middle manager'. These inhabitants of the norther red wall constituencies are portrayed thus: 'He used to vote Labour. But he'd bought his own house now [and] set up his own business ... the traditional Labour voter who switched to supporting Margaret Thatcher ... In 2019, the latest incarnation was Workington Man, representing the white middle-aged Brexit supporters residing in post-industrial towns.'

105 According to a first leader in the *Financial Times*, 'longer-term shifts are at play that could have profound effects – tilting the balance of negotiating power from capital towards labour', adding: 'The flow of migrant workers from central and eastern Europe to the wealthier west was already starting to reverse pre-Covid, as growing economies and salaries lured some home ... [l]onger term, without sizeable special visa schemes or a broad labour mobility agreement with the EU, filling the vacancies will mean having to offer better pay and conditions to UK workers.' See 'Britain's labour shortages boost workers' clout', *Financial Times* (London), 27 August 2021. See also: 'Wage growth stirs talk of "worker power" era', *Financial Times* (London), 3 September 2021.

106 See 'McDonalds lifts US wages as it struggles to attract staff', *Financial Times* (London), 14 May 2021; 'Worker shortages raise fears of higher wage costs in developed economies', *Financial Times* (London), 27 May 2021; 'Labour shortages hit Berlin's reopening', *Financial Times* (London), 29 May 2021; 'Bosses prepare bigger pay rises in effort to retain staff', *Financial Times* (London), 21 October 2021.

deleterious impact labour shortages and increased costs would mean for their businesses.[107] Invoking the necessity of having to make higher payments so as to attract or keep labour-power, this was used by capitalists and employer organizations as a reason why government should abandon immigration controls and reinstate the availability of migrant workers composing the industrial reserve.[108]

A Dearth of Workers

Protests coupled with the demand for continued access to foreign labour were heard across all economic sectors in the UK. This was particularly the case with regard to commercial transport, where a post-Brexit scarcity of lorry drivers had a multiplier effect on the distribution of goods. Historically, wages and work conditions of HGV drivers had undergone a decline, as employers competing for supermarket custom attempted to reduce costs. Below par wages and conditions were themselves a long-standing source of grievance: according to one driver, '[i]t's not a normal life for a human, it's like a prison – you do it like a zombie', while another confirmed that 'fair working conditions' was a desirable objective.[109] For their part, eastern European HGV drivers cited low wages and poor work conditions in the UK as reasons why they now sought better-paid employment available in Germany, compelling recruitment firms

---

107   Earlier instances of employer discourse expressing these concerns are examined by me elsewhere (Brass, 2017: Chapter 19).

108   Already there are signs that the UK government is facilitating continued access to the industrial reserve. See 'UK to ease immigration rules for care workers as shortage worsens', *The Guardian* (London), 24 December 2021. It must be emphasized that employer concerns about a contraction in the industrial reserve are not limited to the availability of immigrant labour. A similar attempt has been made by government to drive the jobless claiming universal credit into the labour market, both by broadening the kinds of employment sought and by shortening the amount of time spent looking for work. 'Amid an acute labour shortage, those able to work will be expected to search for jobs outside their former occupation from the fourth week of their claim, instead of three months. Those who do not comply will have their benefits cut.' See 'Unemployed will be told to broaden job searches', *Financial Times* (London), 27 January 2022.

109   See 'UK truck driver shortage signals a broken market', *Financial Times* (London), 24 August 2021; 'Shortage puts truck drivers on road to burnout', *Financial Times* (London), 31 August 2021; 'Driver troubles likely to worsen, says haulage boss', *Financial Times* (London), 21 September 2021; 'Lorry driver crisis "must be fixed in days or chaos at Christmas inevitable"', *The Guardian* (London), 25 September 2021; 'Johnson ready to ease visas for truck drivers', *Financial Times* (London), 25 September 2021; 'HGV visas deemed too little, too late', *Financial Times* (London), 27 September 2021.

in the UK to seek out replacements in non-EU Balkan nations (Serbia, North Macedonia).[110]

Much the same is true of food processing companies, where most of the labour employed is from eastern Europe, which leaves the sector 'exposed to post-Brexit immigration changes'.[111] As in the case of haulage companies, therefore, food processing employer organizations are lobbying government to extend visa schemes to low-skilled foreign workers, thereby enabling such companies to continue drawing on cheap labour resources available in the industrial reserve army.[112] Deprived of the usual source of foreign labour, '[t]his new regime was always going to be a shock to employers who had honed business models on the ready availability of low-skilled workers'.[113] The link between on the one hand labour shortages, improved bargaining power of workers, higher wages and better conditions, and on the other a contraction in the industrial reserve is hard to miss. Thus, an HGV driver observed that '[p]ay rates have gone up, and they [= employers] are fighting over a very small pool of drivers', whilst a trade union 'has negotiated a rise of 20 per cent in basic pay, with overtime rates rising from 150 per cent of basic to 200 per cent. That means overtime has gone up from about £20 to about £35 an hour'.[114]

---

110   See 'Eastern European truckers put brakes on return to work in the UK', *Financial Times* (London), 10 September 2021. According to the European Road Hauliers Association, 'European driver salaries were generally higher than in Britain; new EU rules had improved working conditions; and billions of euros had been offered to fund parking areas' adding that '[t]he UK doesn't have any of that ...' See 'European drivers "will not want to come to the UK"', *The Observer* (London), 26 September 2021. Another agency economist noted that 'the UK's offer [of temporary visas] could be unappealing in EU countries where demand for drivers had risen even faster, pushing up wages'. See 'Doubts cast on visa plan to ease driver shortages', *Financial Times* (London), 5 October 2021.

111   See 'Suppliers blame Brexit immigration rules for chicken shortages hitting KFC', *Financial Times* (London), 19 August 2021.

112   The British Poultry Council reported that '[w]e are facing a serious shortage of production operatives and processing staff that are classified as low-skilled workers ... but play an incredibly important role in keeping the food supply moving'. Government was requested to include such workers in the seasonal labour scheme applied to agriculture.

113   'Post-Brexit immigration curbs take toll', *Financial Times* (London), 1 October 2021. Much the same impact was being felt in other metropolitan capitalist economies. In the US, for example, a 'dearth of workers willing to drive trucks has become so severe ... that some fleet managers are petitioning to let more foreign operators into the country'. See 'US fleet managers beg to hire foreign truck drivers', *Financial Times* (London), 3 September 2021.

114   See 'McDonalds lifts US wages as it struggles to attract staff', *Financial Times* (London), 14 May 2021; 'Worker shortages raise fears of higher wage costs in developed economies', *Financial Times* (London), 27 May 2021; 'Labour shortages hit Berlin's reopening', *Financial Times* (London), 29 May 2021; 'Bosses prepare bigger pay rises in effort to retain staff', *Financial Times* (London), 21 October 2021.

Such developments are clearly of concern to capitalists. Observing that before Brexit '[m]any young people came here to work, study or both', and that '[t]hey provided a valuable and qualified addition to the labour market and were not taking advantage of this country in any way', one prominent employer concluded that '[t]he government ... must look at the requirements of the various industries experiencing shortages and allow people to enter ...'.[115] That wages have risen and conditions improved, if only marginally, suggests post-Brexit shrinkage in the industrial reserve leading in turn to labour shortages puts to rest the old canard that – in terms of jobs, working conditions, and wage levels – migration has (and can have) no impact whatsoever on the labour market.[116] Problematic aspects of this latter view are threefold. First, it ignores the presence and role of the industrial reserve. Second, as such it is indistinguishable from the position held by capitalist producers and their political organizations. And third, it leaves open the sole explanations of racism as being determined either by psychology (= racism-is-innate) or by imperial nostalgia (= harking back to the time of empire).

Steady Work, Job Security

Opposition to immigration, particularly that found among the European working class, is regarded by much post-colonial theory not just as racist but also as an effect of perceptions rooted in a colonial history which surface in the form of a still-extant imperial nostalgia.[117] Evidence for this points to views expressed by inhabitants of the so-called Red Wall areas in the North of England, where coal, steel and manufacturing employment used to be located. Recent studies of those who abandoned Labour in the 2019 election highlight a clear set

---

115   See Rocco Forte, 'Only a sensible immigration debate will solve our labour shortages', *Financial Times*, 4–5 December 2021.

116   That immigration has no impact on wages/conditions is a claim repeated endlessly by advocates of an open-door policy; most recently by Goodfellow (2020: 133ff., 281 n.13) who invokes Portes – a long-standing holder of the migrants-are-good-for-the-economy interpretation – in support of her view. For the epistemological affinity between the arguments of Portes and those emanating from libertarian economic theory, see Brass (2021: 248). Even the governor of the Bank of England agreed that '[t]he dispersion of pay growth has risen quite markedly ... [t]his could be a good thing, if it means above-average wage gains in sectors where low pay and poor conditions have led to a chronic over-reliance on imported labour.' See 'Business raises alarm over wage inflation amid labour shortages', *Financial Times* (London), 6 October 2021.

117   On this point, see Brass (2021), especially Chapters 3 and 7.

of interrelated causes that contributed to this shift in political allegiance.[118] Among its findings was that what concerned inhabitants of the Red Wall areas was the lack of high-paying jobs in the locality, together with the fact that most employment was anyway low paid.[119] The dearth of employment opportunities meant that people in such areas wanted to move south in search of work, but the high cost of housing there plus the intense competition for jobs made this kind of option prohibitive. These considerations fuelled not just opposition to immigration but also notions of an unfair North/South economic divide.

Hence the observation that '[t]here was another explanation for negative change in Red Waller's local area that I heard repeatedly: immigration'.[120] The latter process was thought by those interviewed to contribute to existing pressure on public services (hospitals, schools) that were already underfunded, the assumption being that once Conservatives had been voted into government, immigration would cease as a result of Brexit.[121] These deindustrialized locations not only voted heavily for Brexit, but also saw the loss of traditional electoral support for Labour which in 2019 switched to the Conservatives.[122] A feature of both these changes, some claim, is hostility to immigration on the part of a working class that is – and probably always has been – racist, an ideology that is itself rooted in a melancholic longing for an era when Britain possessed an Empire.

---

118   The studies in question are by Mattinson (2020) and Payne (2021).

119   This emerges from the study by Payne (2021: 163, 191, 210–11, 329), where nostalgia expressed in Red Wall constituencies was not for an imperial past but rather for the loss of relatively well-paid livelihoods ('steady work', 'job security') as a result of Thatcherite deregulation and deindustrialization, and their replacement with poorly paid, casual/part-time/temporary employment provided by theme parks and zero-hour contracts.

120   See Mattinson (2020: 74). Among those interviewed, she (Mattinson, 2020: 25) notes, 'regularly heard [were] complaints about workers from other countries taking jobs away from locals either by undercutting their wages or through employers' political correctness'. That such views have not changed is a point emphasized throughout her analysis (Mattinson, 2020: 75, 87, 115), along the lines of: 'Certainly, immigration remains a powerful issue in the Red Wall seats I visited'.

121   According to Mattinson (2020: 74–75), therefore, '[f]or workers, especially manual workers, the threat seemed very real. Immigration had risen to the top of the issues that voters were concerned about by the end of the last labour government.' By November 2019, however, 'it [had] slipped back down the ranking [because] many have assumed that "getting Brexit done" [would] also deal with the problem.'

122   In the words of a Labour politician interviewed by Payne (2021: 89), 'we could say until were blue in the face, "Look, it's not an open-door policy", but it was for the EU. You could go anywhere you wanted in the EU and live there with very few constraints, and that meant to the public, quite rightly, that's uncontrolled migration'.

However, even where attitudes formed by a working class towards migrant labour are indeed seen through a rear-view mirror, and thus constitutes looking backwards historically, evidence suggests this is not – as is usually claimed to be the case – to British imperial dominance. When invoked, therefore, the Golden Age seen by Red Wallers as desirable is not one of colonial or imperial rule, but rather the more modest period – a 'more positive past' – in which to be a member of the working class was a source of pride, when trade unions were politically efficacious, when employment was permanent, when jobs were well-paid, and when livelihoods were relatively secure (= 'a more positive future').[123] In short, a Britain not of the high Victorian 1890s but rather of the post-war era from around the 1950s to the end of the 1970s.[124]

Instead of being connected to historical images of cultural 'otherness' arising from British imperial nostagia, therefore, opposition to immigration was linked by Red Wallers to the broader economic issues of labour market competition and resource depletion/provision.[125] Much rather, Red Wallers emphasized that their concerns about immigration were unconnected with an innate disdain for the cultural 'other', one of those interviewed stating clearly that 'I worry about the amount of people coming into the country, but I don't want

---

123   'Being working class, it turned out, is not just about how you feel about yourself', notes Mattinson (2020: 86), 'it is also about how others see you ... many looked back to a more positive past, where the work that people like them did had dignity and commanded respect ... Back then, they believed, there was the promise of a more positive future, more opportunity and decent training with good apprenticeships: "when I left school, I was offered three apprenticeships with three different firms and I could take my pick. We all could."...As a worker back then you had clout. That meant better job security and pay. The trade unions were all powerful ...'

124   In the UK, this was an era when the Labour Party was frequently in government, but even when not, Conservative governments did not at this conjuncture depart substantially from the radical welfare programmes introduced by Labour in 1945.

125   That opposition to immigration took the form not of closing access from abroad but rather of regulation was accepted even by a Conservative politician, noting (Payne, 2021: 170–71) that '[t]here was an awful lot of the Brexit vote based on immigration' which, however, did not want 'migration to cease [only that] it needs more control'. The latter in turn was attributed by a UKIP politician (Payne, 2021: 300) to the fact that 'a lot of people were seeing their jobs threatened, lost their jobs or had to take reduced wages' as a result of increased migration from eastern Europe. 'These concerns were not xenophobic', he continued, 'Let's not blame these people [= immigrants]. If I was in Eastern Europe, you know, on five hundred quid [= pounds sterling] a month and I can get on a bus and come over to Britain and get fifteen hundred quid a month, I'd be on the first bus.' The significance of this utterance is twofold. Although capitalism is not mentioned, anti-immigration sentiment is nevertheless blamed on labour market competition linked to its reproduction, and does not entail racist images of the migrant him/herself.

to pick on them'.[126] Linking immigration to the issue of resource provision, in the sense that the former was seen as having implications for continued access to the latter, is clear also from the fact that the two major concerns raised by Labour supporters in Red Wall areas were open-door immigration and NHS underfunding.[127]

Conclusion

Although discourse concerning race is obviously central to any debate about capitalism, rather less so is how this link is reproduced, by whom, and why. At issue, therefore, are the different meanings attached to notions of ethnic 'otherness', and why these surface at some conjunctures but not at others. There is a tendency to approach this issue in an a-historical manner, and consequently to regard working class racism as innate, ever-present, and undetermined by events or circumstances outside its reproduction. Against this it is argued here that, without reference to context and conjuncture, it is impossible to understand crucial variations in and causes of racist ideology and its dynamics. For this reason it is argued here that an historical shift in the perception of the 'other' is crucial to the way in which the meaning not just of who but what this subject is has changed over time. Namely, from a perception of alterity as merely different, to different-and-inferior, and ultimately to an equal – and thus a serious competitor – in the global labour market.

A case in point is the way in the UK concepts of ethnic 'otherness' and selfhood fuelled opposition to immigration and EU membership. Where labour market competition in a particular national context is boosted by immigration, it is all too easy for employers to play existing workers off against incomers

---

126   Mattinson (2020: 137). According to a Labour politician (Payne, 2021: 166–67) from a Red Wall constituency, 'why we lost Labour voters to both the Tories, UKIP and the Brexit party comes back to the straw that broke the camel's back ... immigration ... [Labour] failed to understand people's concerns about Europe and about immigration'. She continued: 'You can suddenly find in a village, overnight, the workforce is 50 per cent from Eastern Europe. Now, it's not that people have got a thing against Polish people [but] those out of work in the Don Valley found themselves applying to employers who could find EU nationals willing to work for rates locals could not compete with.'

127   According to Mattinson (2020: 196–97), '[i]mmigration emerged as the second most voted for priority [in Labour focus groups] after investment in the NHS. The numbers revealed that some Urban Remainers must have voted for it [and several of them] told us that they had voted for "restricting immigration" despite being afraid to raise it in the group discussions. As one put it: "You see, even though no one dared to talk about [restricting] immigration, they've all voted for it. It can't be ignored."'

of another ethnicity or nationality, generating antagonism based on race. By turning first to migrants, and then to locals, capitalists are able to ensure that each component of the workforce is always in competition with the other. Presenting the issue as one of rivalry involving ethnic 'selfhood' against ethnic 'otherness', therefore, corporations are able to maintain or enhance profitability when engaged in competition with other enterprises for market share. This is what the defenders of unregulated immigration mean when they say that migrants are good for the economy; namely, that by keeping wages down and profits up, such workers enable accumulation to proceed apace. Not mentioned is the hidden meaning: an economic, political, and ideological subtext about how the reserve army is good only for capital and not for labour – either local or migrant, employed or unemployed.

What Gobineau objects to is the non-economic impact of immigration from continental Europe on English culture. This contrasts with Marxism, which opposes immigration not on cultural grounds – as does the political right – but rather on economic ones: namely, that it advantages capitalism and disadvantages the existing or aspiring workforce by increasing the level of labour market competition. Whereas Gobineau regards immigrants as lesser beings who decrease the 'purity' of the race, Marxism does not, agreeing that it is precisely their skills and work-ethic that makes them so attractive to employers. In effect, immigration prolongs the life of capitalism, and it is for *this* reason, and for this reason *alone*, that Marxism opposes such a process. Hence the opposition by Lenin, Trotsky, and Deutscher to the deployment by the left of non-class identity as the main weapon in the struggle against capitalism. Each of them insisted that, because these forms of 'otherness' were not themselves socio-economically homogeneous, it was necessary to differentiate such ethnic/national categories in terms of their different class elements.

In many ways, the views of Sartre about anti-semitism are, from the viewpoint of Marxist theory, the most problematic, in that the cause of racism is explained by him largely in instinctivist terms that are not so different from those of the political right. Moreover, unlike other Marxists, such as Trotsky and Deutscher, he makes little or no attempt to situate it within the context – and hence the outcome – of accumulation and the conflicts this generates. Describing the anti-semite in terms of someone who rejoices in his irrationalism, espouses tradition/custom, and regards his imperfect linguistic usages as empowering indications of long-term belonging, an organic development not shared by the 'other', Sartre does not contextualize these characteristics historically and economically: as part of the class struggle, waged 'from above' and 'from below', in the course of the accumulation process.

It could be argued that, where 'otherness' is concerned, postmodernism is the mirror image of Gobineau. Just as the latter essentialized nationalism/ethnicity, so the former re-essentialized the same non-class identities, over a century later. Whereas in the hierarchy of Gobineau the top position is that of the European while the lowest rung is allocated to non-European populations, the 'cultural turn' upends this same hierarchy, elevating hitherto subordinate forms of 'otherness' to the top and demoting its erstwhile dominant component to the bottom. In short, the privileging by the 'new' populist postmodern theory of identity politics is a present-day version of the same kind of discourse.

Accordingly, postmodernism has moved the concept of empowerment from class back once more to ethnicity/nationality, thereby making it difficult for socialists to pose questions about the industrial reserve army of labour without risking accusations of racism/xenophobia. Not the least problematic aspect of this transition is the accompanying claim that in the UK working class opposition to enhanced labour market competition of the migrant derives simply from the culture of the 'other', an innate/enduring antagonism rooted in imperial nostalgia. That such opposition can be linked much rather to economic causes, specifically rivalries for employment fostered by capital, is an issue considered in the following chapter, with regard to the antebellum plantation in the American South.

Anti-capitalisms (Lessons Unlearned by Postmodernists)

Every month brings forth its millionaire, and every day its thousands of new paupers.

A pro-slavery indictment of 1850s American capitalism by GEORGE FITZHUGH.[1]

• • •

Contending against capitalism ... the Narodniks throw all historical realism overboard and always compare the *reality* of capitalism with the *fiction* of the pre-capitalist order.

An 1898 indictment by LENIN of populist anti-capitalism in Russia.[2]

• •
•

Introduction: The Anti-capitalism of Pro-slavery Discourse

One of the more paradoxical issues currently facing the social sciences is how to account for the following contradiction.[3] Namely, the seemingly anomalous fact that in metropolitan capitalist nations, large numbers of the working class no longer support the left but instead vote into power not just conservative parties and politicians but also those led by rich men who palpably do not – and cannot – share the same political interests as themselves. The issue this raises is not so much that a conservative politician attempts to persuade workers that he – and only he – can best represent their interests (this he will try to do anyway) as to why this argument is so often successful: that is, believed by

---

1 Fitzhugh (1960b: 57).
2 Lenin (1963: 517, original emphasis).
3 Significantly, much of the 1850s proslavery discourse examined below based its arguments on the findings of the social sciences, maintaining that these were supportive of the case it made.

'those below'. What, in short, must be said by 'those above' to persuade 'those below' holding not just different but antagonistic class positions/interests that their comfort, welfare, and health – indeed, their livelihoods – are of equal concern to a conservative who (unlike them) is wealthy, frequently as a result of their own toil on his behalf.

One answer to this paradox is the capacity to mobilize politically and ideologically on the basis of non-class identities, such as nationalism and ethnicity, thereby shifting the economic struggle away from (for conservatism the potentially dangerous terrain of) class consciousness and struggle. Another, currently of increasing significance, is the fact that in metropolitan capitalist nations the print and/or electronic media are usually owned by the rich and powerful, which enables them to shape and/or control both the political agenda and how this is presented, in the process generating/reproducing what Marxism characterizes as false consciousness.[4] Less frequently addressed, however, is yet another reason: the invocation 'from above' of ideological opposition to capitalism itself, whereby in specific contexts antagonism is expressed by those with power and wealth towards the impact on 'those below' of the accumulation process.

This, it is argued here, is the anti-capitalism of the right, which is different from that of the left, and has to be distinguished from the latter in all respects (ideologically, politically, and economically). A failure to do so results in those on the left espousing identity politics, in the mistaken belief that because this, too, is a form of opposition to capitalism, such discourse must consequently be progressive. Where the anti-capitalism of the right is not differentiated from its leftist counterpart, therefore, socialists – and even some Marxists – who omit to make this distinction, mistakenly proceed to regard the anti-capitalism of the right as positive, and consequently a view that should be endorsed and supported politically.[5]

What the anti-capitalism of the right is, why it should be differentiated from that of the left, and the sharp lessons taught when this is not done, is best illustrated by reference to the way antebellum Southern pro-slavery discourse

4 Having castigated those socialists who continued to describe the ideological effect of capitalist monopoly exercised over the print and/or electronic media as generating 'false consciousness' among the working class, bourgeois commentators and politicians now apply much the same kind of conceptual apparatus ('post-truth', 'fake news') to the influence of populists.

5 The list of leftists, and some Marxists, who have subscribed to populism and/or postmodernism in the belief that the anti-capitalist stance of such views is progressive, and indeed no different from the same kind of critique made by Marxist political economy, is a long one. The reasons for their following this kind of theoretical trajectory have been discussed by me over the years, extending from Brass (2000) to Brass (2021).

opposed Northern capitalism in the period leading to the American Civil War. This negative appraisal of capitalism, which not only evinced sympathy for the plight of free labour composing its workforce, but also drew on arguments made by Socialists, has invited comparison with Marxist critiques of the accumulation process. From this apparent overlap stemmed a tendency among some on the left to view aspects of pro-slavery discourse – if not the discourse itself – in a more positive light, with particular reference to the claims made regarding not just the distinctiveness and empowerment conferred by traditional, rural, ethnic and national forms of selfhood, but also their historical longevity.

Much the same kind of epistemological approach currently informs the 'new' populist postmodernism, both opposed to development in many so-called Third World countries and supportive of analogous variants of identity politics – agrarianism, nationalism, ethnicity, tradition – deemed to empower an unheard rural 'from below' voice. Failure to differentiate the anti-capitalism of the right from its leftist equivalent, therefore, underlines the ease with which, now as in the past, it is possible to slide unknowingly into a conservative politics. It also highlights the crucial role of ideology in framing discourse; that is, a capacity to set – and then privilege – a political agenda, especially one which addresses in a populist fashion an issue linked to the formation, reproduction, or, indeed, dissolution, of 'from below' consciousness (and thus struggle) of class.[6]

The presentation which follows is divided into two sections, the first of which examines pro-slavery discourse in the antebellum South, with particular reference to its constituent elements (empowering nationalism, 'otherness,' tradition, and rurality). As an ideology it combined positive views about unfreedom (subsistence guarantee) with negative ones about capitalism (exploitation, labour market competition). The second considers the ideological affinities of pro-slavery discourse: superficially with socialism (and even Marxism), but more accurately with the 'new' populist postmodernism. The significance of the latter is linked in turn to current debates in the social sciences about how to interpret what is now a globally expanding industrial reserve army of labour.

---

6 This agenda-setting ideological role is effected through the process of inclusion or exclusion, not just of politics but also of options within a specific politics. In decades past, an article of faith on the left was that ownership/control of print and/or electronic media by a capitalist had a negligible political influence, since the object of acquiring such resources was for their possessor simply a matter of status enhancement, nothing more. Some of us knew better then, and rather more know better now.

I

The defence mounted by pro-slavery discourse in the antebellum South rested centrally on three interrelated arguments.[7] First, a challenge to the very definition of slavery itself, on the basis that unfree workers in the South were better off than free equivalents in the North. Second, the claim that those in the latter category, unlike slaves, were not only subject to labour market competition, diminished wages, and work intensification, but had to fend for themselves when capitalist crises resulted in unemployment. And third, approval for socialist antagonism towards free enterprise coupled with a warning that the latter system would eventually lead to a revolutionary overthrow by socialism of religion, family ties, private property, and the law. All these arguments were underwritten by the predominant image reproduced throughout pro-slavery discourse: that of the antebellum South as a benign form of non-capitalism, the 'other' of the Northern *laissez-faire* economy, in which master and slave co-existed harmoniously in what was claimed to be a pastoral variant of the agrarian myth.

For the Mutual Benefit of Both

Objecting to what it categorized as 'false and malicious representations' of antebellum society, and rejecting the terms 'slave'/'slavery' used by abolitionists as inapplicable to the South, pro-slavery discourse insisted that the relation was not as onerous as the concept implied.[8] Far from being a chattel or thing ('to be

---

7   Pro-slavery discourse refers here to the views expressed by George Fitzhugh (1960a, 1960b) and those contained in the volume *Cotton is King*. Edited by E.N. Elliott (1860), President of Planters' College, Mississippi, the latter text consisted of essays by David Christy, Albert Taylor Bledsoe, Thornton Stringfellow, Chancellor Harper, J.H. Hammond, Samuel A. Cartwright, the Reverend Charles Hodge, and Elliott himself. Of these, the contributions by Christy, Bledsoe, Harper, and Hammond focus on political economy, while those by Hodge and Stringfellow present the religious and Biblical argument for slavery. It is the former that constitute the main interest here. More broadly, and together with publications by Fitzhugh, the arguments in *Cotton is King* represent the most rigorous political economy case made by proslavery discourse during the antebellum era.

8   For this and what follows, see Elliott (1860: iii-xv). All the tropes deployed by antebellum pro-slavery discourse (slavery not that bad, no more than a form of equal exchange, black slaves are better-off than the free white labourer, all their subsistence needs are met) surface in a recent dystopian novel by Winters (2016) depicting an alternate vision of an America where the Civil War did not take place and slavery was never abolished. Controlled by means of a vast computer database containing every detail about each slave (= 'Persons Bound to Labor'), all modern-day plantation, factory, and mine labour throughout the

bought and sold, and treated worse than a brute'), therefore, in the South the relation was no different from that of a servant who, despite being obedient 'to the will of another', nevertheless possessed 'rights, privileges'. Although the word remains the same, its content has changed. Historically, slaves were at the mercy of their masters, since the person of a slave was owned, and as with any property could be used/abused by its proprietor. This, insisted Southern pro-slavery discourse, 'is not our labor system.'

The reality of Southern unfreedom was different, asserted pro-slavery discourse, arguing that 'slavery is the duty and obligation of the slave to labor for the mutual benefit of both master and servant,' an arrangement whereby the slave obtained in turn 'protection and a comfortable subsistence'. Accordingly, the slave is said to benefit from the provision by the master of a form of cradle-to-the-grave welfare, a 'subsistence guarantee' which its exponents maintained covered 'infancy, sickness, and old age', the whole cost of which was borne by the master.[9] This particular argument underwrote the pro-slavery claim that the 'subsistence guarantee' supplied by the master in the antebellum South ensured that unfree labour was better-off economically when compared to what the free worker received from employers and the market in the North.[10]

South continues to be both unfree and economically profitable. A familiar justification of slavery is repeated by a slave-owning businessman to an ex-slave who is black, now a bounty-hunter tracking runaways (Winters, 2016: 258, original emphasis): 'None of your cousins [= black slaves] got a thing to complain about down here, son ... This is not slavery of fifty or even ten years ago. People think about slavery, and they still think – *still* – about the whips and dogs and the spiky neck chains, all of that nasty business. But this is *now*. This is the twenty-first century ... Four thousand head in those buildings right there ... And you see that building in the center, with the turret-looking thing on top? From up there the guards can see into every single cell, and every single cell can see the guards, too. So everybody knows they're safe. Everybody's looking after each other.'

9   Hence the question asked – and answered – by pro-slavery discourse (Elliott, 1860: 569): 'But how is it that the existence of slavery, as with us, will retard the evils of civilization? Very obviously. It is the intense competition of civilized life that gives rise to the excessive cheapness of labor, and the excessive cheapness of labor is the cause of the evils in question. Slave labor can never be so cheap as what is called free labor. Political economists have established as the natural standard of wages in a fully peopled country, the value of the laborer's existence ... where competition is intense, men will labor for a bare subsistence, and less than a competent subsistence. The employer of free labor obtains their services during the time of their health and vigor, without the charge of rearing them from infancy, or supporting them in sickness or old age. This charge is imposed on the employer of slave labor, who, therefore, pays higher wages, and cuts off the principal source of misery – the wants and sufferings of infancy, sickness, and old age.'

10   For details of the 'subsistence guarantee' defence of slavery, see Fitzhugh (1960a: 82–83). The 'other' of this defence is that faced by the free worker: 'The men without property, in free society', noted Fitzhugh (1960b: 18), 'are theoretically in a worse condition than slaves.'

In the words of pro-slavery discourse, the reality of what it regarded as the 'subsistence guarantee' consists of the fact that '[c]apital exercises a more perfect compulsion over free labourers than human masters over slaves; for free labourers must at all times work or starve, and slaves are supported whether they work or not.'[11] When economic crisis ('commercial revulsion and distress') occurs, and a free worker has to fend for himself, therefore, the subsistence needs of the slave by contrast are guaranteed by the master.[12]

In this way slavery is recast as merely a form of equal exchange, one involving nothing more than a reciprocal transaction (subsistence/protection ↔ obedience/work) between its subject and the master.[13] Ideologically, it is an image consistent with and supportive of a crucial strand of pro-slavery discourse: namely, that the economic system of the antebellum South not only operated along pre-capitalist lines (= feudalism), but as such also corresponded to the aristocratic pastoral variant of the agrarian myth.[14] Overlapping with the foundation myth and populism, the agrarian myth projects two complementary but antithetical views: the urban, its inhabitants, and socio-economic system (capitalism, class) are portrayed negatively; the latter are all contrasted with idealized images (= 'natural', unchanging) of the countryside (unequal

---

11   See Fitzhugh (1960b: 32). Elsewhere it is argued, also by Fitzhugh (1960a; 63), that even '[t]he advocates of universal liberty concede that the labouring class enjoy more material comfort, are better fed, clothed and housed, as slaves than as freemen ...', a defence of slavery based on claims about a 'subsistence guarantee' reproduced *verbatim* one hundred years later in the revisionist case of Fogel and Engerman (1974).

12   Hence the pro-slavery (Elliott, 1860: 569–70) view: 'In periods of commercial revulsion and distress, the distress in countries of free labor falls principally on the labourers. In those of slave labor, it falls almost exclusively on the employer. In the former, when a business becomes unprofitable, the employer dismisses his labourers or lowers their wages. But with us, it is the very period at which we are least able to dismiss our labourers; and if we would not suffer a further loss, we can not reduce their wages.'

13   Reciprocity is central to pro-slavery discourse, in that it licenses the notion that the slave, too, benefits from work done for his owner. All profit from the relationship: by working for his master, the slave is said to repay 'the advances made for his support in childhood, for present subsistence ... for guardianship and protection,' as well as the costs 'for sickness, disability, and old age.' Presented thus, the slave is working to pay the master for a form of social insurance that nowadays is provided in metropolitan capitalism by the welfare state. The difficulty with this benign interpretation is that whereas in the latter instance provision is an entitlement, in the case of the slave it is not, and provided – if at all – at the discretion of the master. Substantial evidence from many different historical contexts suggests that manumission – turning an aged slave adrift by freeing him – occurred as soon as he ceased to be productive, so the claim by pro-slavery discourse about reciprocity does not hold.

14   For the characteristics of the agrarian myth, see Brass (2000, 2014).

but harmonious), its inhabitants (landlords, peasants), and its traditional values/institutions/identities. This dichotomy (rural = good, urban = bad) structures the differences highlighted by pro-slavery discourse: free market capitalism is depicted not just negatively but also as a specifically urban phenomenon (wealth centralized in cities), inferentially to be contrasted with the benign regime of slaveholders in the countryside.[15] An analogous dissimilarity extends to the portrayal by pro-slavery discourse of 'those below' in each location: between the 'degraded'/oppressed urban workers in the North, and the antebellum South where plantation slaves were provided with a 'subsistence guarantee'.[16]

Pro-slavery and/as (Conservative) Anti-capitalism

Just as the antebellum pro-slavery case rested principally on its negative portrayal of Northern capitalism, so the main plank of the latter argument was in turn the deleterious impact on free workers of labour market competition, the economic 'other' of the 'subsistence guarantee'. The case for the defence of slavery depended on a positive/negative combination forming a two-pronged polemical approach: not just on the attempt to demonstrate that it was a benign relational form, therefore, but also and simultaneously on undermining the defence/justification of capitalism and its *laissez-faire* philosophy.[17] Denouncing political economy as the philosophy of free society that promoted

---

15   The agrarian myth polarity (urban = bad, rural = good) is evident from the way Fitzhugh (1960b: 57) describes the consolidation of wealth in urban contexts: 'Liberty and political economy beget and encourage free trade, as well as between different localities and different nations as between individuals of the same towns, neighbourhoods or nations ... The effect of international free trade ... is to centralize wealth in a few large cities, such as New York, Paris, and London, and of social free trade to aggregate wealth in a few hands in those cities.'

16   'There never can be among slaves a class so degraded as is found about the wharves and suburbs of cities', notes Fitzhugh (1960a: 63, 64), who then contrasts the urban North with a picture of 'merrie England' ('The peasantry of England, in the days of Cressey, Agincourt and Shrewsbury, when feudalism prevailed, were generally brave, virtuous, and in the enjoyment of a high degree of physical comfort – at least, that differed very little from that of their lords and masters.'). It could be argued that the policy of sending free blacks to Africa was similarly informed by the plebeian variant of the agrarian myth, whereby Africa is portrayed as a region inhabited by 'natural' peasants.

17   Hence the importance attached by Fitzhugh (1960b: 52) to the view that slavery could not be defended until 'we succeed in refuting or invalidating the principles on which free society rests for support or defence.' As will be seen below, this second objective – attacking capitalism – was in a large part based on the criticisms made by socialists.

free market capitalism, pro-slavery discourse contended that by privileging 'social, individual, and national competition,' political economy 'naturalized' the process of competition as an inescapable feature of society, maintaining that 'all competition is but the effort to enslave others'.[18]

Equally clear is both the extent of the employer advantage that such labour market competition conferred, and also the emphasis place on this by pro-slavery discourse. Hence the focus of the latter on the fact that the only beneficiary of *laissez-faire* was the capitalist, to whom it gave the whip hand over the free worker adrift in a competitive labour market which guaranteed him nothing.[19] This is the crux of the pro-slavery indictment aimed at capitalism (= free society), which compares the relative absence of power to control by the strong in a state of nature (= pre-capitalist society), and how such power/control increases substantially once the strong own the earth ('They are masters without the obligations of masters, and the poor are slaves without the rights of slaves.').[20] It is a contrast between the absence of power wielded by the master over the slave in the antebellum South, and the absolute nature of power that the capitalist exercises over the free worker in the North.

In support of this aspect of its case, pro-slavery discourse indicated that opposition to emancipation was not confined to the South, but found also in the North, where free workers did not want 'to have the North filled up with

---

18   See Fitzhugh (1960b: 25, 27), who adds: 'Civilized society has never been found without that competition begotten by man's desire to throw most of the burdens of life on others, and to enjoy the fruits of their labours without exchanging equivalent labor of his own ...' The political economy to which he objects is that of Adam Smith, Say, and Ricardo (Fitzhugh, 1960b: 58–59).

19   Observing that conceptually the idea of a free society is underpinned theoretically by the social contract of John Locke, Fitzhugh (1960b: 13, 19) challenged this, arguing that 'the only true theory of capital and labor ... proves that the profits which capital extracts from labor makes free labourers slaves, without the rights, privileges, or advantages of domestic slaves, and capitalists their masters, with all the advantages, and none of the burdens and obligations of the ordinary [*sic*] owners of slaves ... Where a few own the soil, they have unlimited power over the balance of society ... Free society asserts the right of a few to the earth.'

20   'What is falsely called Free Society is a very recent invention,' comments Fitzhugh (1960b: 72–73), who continues: 'It proposes to make the weak ignorant, and poor, free, by turning them loose in a world owned exclusively by the few ... to get a living. In the fanciful state of nature, where property is unappropriated, the strong have no weapons but superior physical and mental power with which to oppress the weak. Their power of oppression is increased a thousand fold when they become the exclusive owners of the earth and all things thereon. They are masters without the obligations of masters, and the poor are slaves without the rights of slaves.'

free [blacks]'; that is, rivals in the labour market.[21] Couched in the language of race, the focus of this 'from below' objection was economic: competition for jobs, and a fear lest additions to the labour market would lead to a decline in the pay and conditions of those already in it.[22] That capitalism posed a threat to the livelihood of the free worker was further underlined by two additional warnings. The first, drawn from European history, demonstrated that once emancipated, serfs became free workers required to labour more intensively; workloads increased while their remuneration declined.[23] Merely to obtain subsistence, therefore, the outcome was that erstwhile serfs – now free, and vulnerable to employer demands – were faced with a much larger burden of work in exchange for lower returns. And second, as threatening to the employment interests of 'those below' were two further sources of labour market competition: externally, from European migrants arriving in America (which 'overstocks permanently the labour market on the Atlantic board'), and internally, from a burgeoning lumpenproletariat (consisting of the 'most wretched members of society', a 'very large nomadic class' that is composed of 'poor thieves, swindlers, and sturdy beggars') already there.[24]

---

21   See Elliott (1860: 25), where the following exchange is found: in Kansas, the 'free coloured man [was excluded] from the rights of citizenship. "Why is this," said the author to a leading German politician of Cincinnati: "Why have the free State men excluded the free coloured people from the proposed State?" "Oh," he replied, "we want it for our sons – for white men – and we want the [black man] out of our way: we neither want him there as a slave or freeman, as in either case his presence tends to degrade labor."'

22   On labour market competition in the North at this conjuncture, together with the kinds of conflict this engendered, see Fite (1968: Ch. VII), who outlines how capitalists fomented divisions within the Northern workforce, by replacing well-paid labourers with cheaper equivalents recruited from Europe.

23   Fitzhugh (1960b: 73).

24   On these points, see Fitzhugh (1960b: 11, 16, 78), who elsewhere (Fitzhugh, 1960a: 66, 69) notes that migrants arriving in the North, fleeing Europe, contribute to the very problem – labour market competition – they were trying to avoid in their home country, hinting at the presence of an industrial reserve army. Identifying 'competition for employment' as the principal reason for enhancing inequality between capital and labour, the pro-slavery discourse of *Cotton is King* (Elliott, 1860: 566–67, 568) argued that 'the tendency of population to become crowded, increasing the difficulty of obtaining subsistence. There will be some without any property except the capacity for labor. This they must sell to those who have the means to employ them, thereby swelling the amount of their capital, and increasing inequality. The process still goes on. The number of labourers increases until there is difficulty in obtaining employment. Then competition is established. The remuneration of the labourer becomes gradually less and less; a larger and larger portion of the product of his labor goes to swell the fortune of the capitalist; inequality becomes still greater and more invidious.' If one did not know otherwise, this critique of the way

Forging New Chains for Themselves

Pro-slavery discourse in the antebellum South demonstrates both how the anti-capitalism of the right deploys arguments favourable to the working class, and also how it is possible consequently to mistake this kind of critique as progressive, simply because its target is capitalism. Ostensibly as sympathetic to the political interests of workers is the pro-slavery endorsement of a similar critique emanating from socialists, fuelling yet further erroneous perceptions of such anti-capitalism as necessarily progressive, and thus deserving of political support. Among the views expressed by pro-slavery discourse that coincide with those of leftists, therefore, is on the one hand support for the labour theory of value, for the existence both of a class hierarchy and its concomitant form of struggle, and on the other hostility towards the unequal distribution of income, towards increasing wealth consolidation by the rich, towards the oppression of urban workers, and towards the impact on their livelihoods of labour market competition. It was an ideological combination designed to attract popular support in general, and that of labour in particular.

That a similarity existed between the pro-slavery anti-capitalist critique of Fitzhugh, involving both hostility to Northern producers combined with sympathy for the plight of their free workers, and a socialist anti-capitalist critique, has been noticed by his biographer, who maintained consequently that Fitzhugh was influenced by Marx.[25] Another and slightly different interpretation notes that 'Fitzhugh exploited and quoted extensively from many of the sources that Karl Marx used ten years later in the first volume of *Capital* to marshal evidence of the inhumanity of British industrial capitalism.'[26] It is argued here, however, that such an overlap extended well beyond the sources themselves, and included a number of concepts – among them class, class struggle, and a version of the labour theory of value, drawn perhaps not from Marx but from French Socialists – that are fundamental to leftist political theory.[27] If the language and concepts used by pro-slavery discourse appeared

---

        capitalism develops, together with the accompanying reference to who benefits and who
        suffers as a result, could easily have been written by Marx himself.

25   See Wish (1943), whose interpretation of the Fitzhugh/Marx connection is disputed
        by Genovese (1969: 182ff.). Earlier, however, Genovese (1968: 342–43) seemingly held a
        contrary opinion: 'It would be difficult for a Marxist not to agree with much of George
        Fitzhugh's criticism of bourgeois society.'

26   See the Introduction to Fitzhugh (1960b: xxv) by Vann Woodward.

27   Fitzhugh (1960b: 93, 98) not only mentions by name Proudhon, Owen, Louis Blanc, and
        Fourier, but also 'the German and French Socialists and Communists', so a knowledge of
        Marx cannot be excluded.

closer to those of socialism than is thought by recent opponents of this view, this was because the object of such discourse was not just to defend slavery but also to do so by disparaging capitalism.[28] However, criticism of the latter *tout court* was problematic, given the presence in the South itself of capitalist enterprises (see below).

Rather than being a challenge to the whole capitalist system that required its overthrow, as is the case with Marxism, such pro-slavery discourse had a less radical purpose: to disseminate a positive image of slavery by comparing it with its negative 'other' in the North; to persuade non-slaveholders that the antebellum South be permitted to retain its form of unfreedom; and to garner support among non-slaveholders for these objectives.[29] Very clearly, pro-slavery arguments were not designed to *promote* Marxist or Socialist political economy. As is also argued here, while there was agreement as to the negative aspects (oppression, exploitation) of capitalism, pro-slavery discourse and Socialist theory disagreed profoundly about the political solution to this problem. Misunderstanding or underestimating the latter distinction in terms of fact and cause lies at the root of conflating the anti-capitalism of the right and left, an error that in the case of one eminent Marxist scholar of antebellum historiography led him to find merit in the ideas of Southern conservatism, including exponents of pro-slavery discourse.[30]

---

28   Other pro-slavery positions (Fitzhugh, 1960a: 61; 1960b: 49, 77, 94) which fit with broadly leftist ones included a call for more State intervention to regulate capital and opposition to imperialism.

29   Attributing to pro-slavery discourse a desire to overthrow the entire capitalist system, Genovese (1969: 130–31) maintains 'I wish to claim two things for Fitzhugh: that he was the most consistent exponent of the slaveholders' worldview, ... and that he alone saw the necessary last step in the argument, which was that slavery could not survive without the utter destruction of capitalism as a world system.' While the former claim is not problematic, the latter is: it is now clear that, far from being incompatible with the accumulation process, capitalism thrives on unfree labour. For this reason, it is not possible to argue – as does Genovese – that pro-slavery discourse sought the destruction of capitalism.

30   This is precisely the epistemological trajectory followed by Eugene Genovese (1968, 1969, 1975, 1994; see also Genovese & Fox-Genovese, 1983), the Marxist in question, an effect of whose failure to distinguish between progressive and reactionary forms of anti-capitalism was both to look with favour on opposition by Southern conservatives to Northern *laissez-faire*, and – consequently – to endorse their wish to retain a place for traditional culture (myths, legends, religion, institutions). Half a century later, many academic exponents of the 'new' populist postmodernism (= the 'cultural turn') are following exactly the same epistemological trajectory.

All Capital Is Created by Labour

Dividing the class hierarchy into four strata, composed of (I) the rich, (II) the professions and skilled workers, (III) 'poor hardworking people', and (IV) 'thieves, swindlers, and beggars', pro-slavery discourse went on to describe those in categories I and II as 'masters without the obligations of a master', whilst those in III and IV were 'slaves, without the rights of slaves.'[31] The way in which the class structure was outlined by pro-slavery discourse, and how its distinct components stood in relation to one another, not only differed little from that of Marxist theory, but would have resonated with 'those below' who perceived both the hierarchy and its interrelationships as accurate reflections of the reality with which they were familiar.[32] As familiar to them, and similarly in keeping with Marxist theory, would have been the endorsement by pro-slavery discourse of a view akin to the labour theory of value, a position designed equally to appeal to non-slaveholding wage-earners and poor farmers who sold not the product of labour but labour-power itself.[33]

31　See Fitzhugh (1960b: 16–17), who delineates the class structure in the following manner: 'Throwing [black] slaves out of the account, and society is divided in Christendom into four classes: the rich, or independent respectable people, who live well and labour not at all, the professional and skilful respectable people, who do a little light work for enormous wages; the poor hardworking people, who support everybody, and starve themselves; and the poor thieves, swindlers, and sturdy beggars, who live ... without labour, on the labour of other people. The gentlemen [exploit], which being done on a large scale [requires] a great many victims ... whilst the rogues and beggars take so little from others that they fare little better than those who labor.'

32　The following table compares the way the class structure is perceived both by Marxism and by the pro-slavery discourse of George Fitzhugh:

Pro-slavery discourse		Marxism
I	the rich	capitalists
II	professions, skilled workers	middle classes, bourgeoisie, petty-bourgeoisie
III	poor hardworking people	working class
IV	thieves, swindlers, beggars	Lumpenproletariat

Source: Compiled from Fitzhugh (1960b: 16).

33　The dependence of capital accumulation on labour-power is set out by Fitzhugh (1960b: 19–20) thus: 'Give you a palace, ten thousand acres of land, sumptuous clothes, equipage, and every other luxury; and with your artificial wants you are poorer than Robinson Crusoe, or the lowest working man, if you have no slaves to capital, or domestic slaves. Your capital will not bring you an income of a cent, nor supply one of your wants, without labor. Labor is indispensable to give value to property, and if you owned every thing else, and did not own labor, you would be poor.'

Having constructed a model of the class hierarchy and its non-egalitarian attributes which socialists would recognize, pro-slavery discourse indicated the nature of the exchanges predicated on such a structure. The object of accumulation, therefore, was quite simply to benefit from the labour of others, a situation made possible because labour was the source of value ('for all capital is created by labor, and the smaller the allowance of the free labourer, the greater the gains of his employer', 'capital was but the accumulation of their labor, for common labor creates all capital').[34] In words that could have been written by Marx or Engels, pro-slavery discourse outlined how accumulation merely increases the work done by the poor whilst simultaneously cutting their wages: thus workers 'are continually forging new chains for themselves.'[35] A description, in short, that recognizes both that capitalism is based on a process of accumulation, and that the latter operates against the interests of the worker. Extending the analysis yet further in the same direction, pro-slavery discourse invokes the arguments of French socialists in order to categorize the capital/labour relation as one of surplus extraction amounting to exploitation, an 'abstraction, directly or indirectly, from the working classes of the fruits of their labor'.[36]

The sympathetic attitude of pro-slavery discourse towards socialism was not merely limited to its critique of capitalism, but also coupled with a warning about where socialism itself might lead. On the one hand, therefore, approval was expressed because political economy promoting capitalist development had been criticized effectively by 'the Socialists [who] have left it not a leg to stand on'.[37] However, on the other was a fear that, as economic crises generated by accumulation became more acute, the rejection of capitalism would make way not for a return to the kind of pre-/non-capitalist society advocated by pro-slavery discourse, but rather for revolution and a transition to socialism.[38]

---

34 On these points, see Fitzhugh (1960b: 25, 27, 38).

35 According to Fitzhugh (1960b: 32), therefore, 'since labor alone creates and pays the profits of capital, increase and accumulation of capital but increase the labor of the poor, and lessen their remuneration. Thus the poor are continually forging new chains for themselves.'

36 For the use by pro-slavery discourse of terms such as exploitation, a form of surplus extraction, see Fitzhugh (1960b: 41–48).

37 Fitzhugh (1960b: 52).

38 Noting 'the alarming increase in socialism,' Fitzhugh (1960b: 10) pointed out that 'Western European Society [had] been engaged in continual revolution for twenty years,' which suggested that 'Free Society every where begets Isms, and that Isms soon beget bloody revolutions.' Ambivalence towards socialism on the part of pro-slavery discourse is expressed by Fitzhugh (1960b: 24) in his observation that Socialists 'show us that, by means of taxation and oppression which capital and skill exercise over labor, the rich, the professional, the trading and the skilful part of society have become the masters of the

The latter possibility was of concern because it threatened what pro-slavery discourse regarded as 'the most essential institutions': religion, family ties, private property, and the law.[39] Hence the support for the socialist critique was tempered by disapproval of its desire to build socialism on the ruins of capitalism.

In making the argument opposing economic competition engendered by accumulation, pro-slavery discourse appears to agree with Marxist theory. Even the language and concepts deployed by pro-slavery discourse against *laissez-faire* and labour market competition is in many respects no different from that used by Marxists.[40] Suggestive of this is the view that the object of labour market competition is 'to prevent that association of labour without which nothing great can be achieved,' together with an acknowledgement of class struggle ('[i]t is impossible to place labor and capital in harmonious or friendly relations').[41] That such views are progressive – let alone Marxist – is deceptive, however, since of particular concern to pro-slavery discourse was that class antagonism generated by capitalism would in turn build support for socialism, and thus lead inevitably to revolution.[42] The issue of 'from below' struggle – '[l]iberty places those classes [rich and poor] in positions of antagonism and war' – was invoked not so much as an indictment of capitalism *per se*, therefore, as an expression of disquiet about the 'from below' struggle it might produce, and what it prefigured systemically.[43]

---

labouring masses, whose condition, already intolerable, is daily becoming worse. They point out distinctly the character of the disease under which the patient is labouring, but see no way of curing the disease except by killing the patient.'

39 Fitzhugh (1960b: 6).

40 Strongly hinting at the presence of class structure, class struggle, and even false consciousness, Fitzhugh (1960a: 56–57) indicates that the market necessarily 'arrays capital against labor ... In all old countries labor is superabundant, employers less numerous than labourers; yet all the labourers must live by the wages they receive from capitalists. The capitalist cheapens their wages; they compete with and underbid each other, for employed they must be on any terms. This war of the rich with the poor and the poor with one another, is the morality which political economy inculcates ... This process of underbidding each other by the poor, which universal liberty necessarily brings about ... places all mankind in antagonistic positions, and puts all society at war ... Thus does free competition, the creature of free society, throw the whole burden of the social fabric on the poor, the weak and ignorant. They produce every thing and enjoy nothing.'

41 Fitzhugh (1960a: 57; 1960b: 31).

42 The poor themselves are all practical Socialists', maintained Fitzhugh (1960a: 68–69), adding: 'They unite in strikes, and trade unions ... [t]he professed object is to avoid ruinous underbidding with one another, but this competition can never cease whilst liberty lasts. Those who wish to be free must take liberty with this inseparable burden.'

43 Fitzhugh (1960a: 68).

To this end, pro-slavery exponents raised the spectre of the 1789, 1830, and 1848 revolutions in France so as to illustrate the warning to all those opposing them about the impact on the poor of a 'free society'.[44] Described as 'insurrections of labor against capital,' these nineteenth century revolutions were attributed to destitution and famine 'among the labouring classes': revolution was the outcome of consolidation at the top of capital and at the bottom of labour, in the process having deprived both monarchy and nobility of power.[45] The logic of the pro-slavery position was simple: unlike slave society, where labour is provided with a subsistence guarantee that covers all the needs of its subject and family, free society guarantees its worker nothing. For this reason, free labour has to organize politically to remedy this lack (strikes, trade unions, political parties), and in doing so brings into question the property relation of capitalism. It was, maintained pro-slavery discourse, a case of 'infection' that had spread to 'the lower classes' throughout Europe, creating revolutionary momentum. Moreover, abolitionism would not be content with emancipation, because slavery was so closely bound up with all the other institutions of society that these, too, would have to change.[46] The threat, cautioned pro-slavery discourse, was not just to Southern institutions and society, but also to private property and capital itself.

II

(Pro-slavery) Contradictions, (Postmodern) Similarities

It hardly seems necessary to have to point out that, when pro-slavery discourse moves from attacking capitalism for its treatment of free labour to defending slavery as a benign alternative, it encounters major difficulties.[47] According to

---

44   See Elliott (1860: viii-ix) and Fitzhugh (1960a: 66). In the words of Fitzhugh (1960b: 65), 'Mobs, secret associations ... social and communistic experiments are striking features and characteristics of our day, outside of slave society. They are all attempting to to supply the defects of regular governments, which have carried the [*laissez-faire*] practice so far ...'

45   See Fitzhugh (1960b: 119ff.).

46   On this point see Fitzhugh (1960a: 84): 'No one who reads a newspaper can but have observed that every abolitionist ... is trying to upset other institutions of society as well as slavery in the South. The same reasoning that makes him an abolitionist soon carries him further, for he finds in slavery in some form so interwoven with the whole framework of society, that he invariably ends by proposing to destroy the whole edifice and building another on entirely new principles.'

47   This attribution of a positive view of unfreedom to its subject is evident, for example, from the following claim made by Ulrich Bonnell Phillips (1929: 196): 'In the main the

pro-slavery discourse, therefore, 'the person of the slave is not property' but 'the right to his labour is property', and as such can be transferred by its owner to another – sold on, in other words.[48] What is not said, however, is that the owner of the labour-power in question is the master, not the slave himself. Furthermore, conceptualizing the slave/master relation as an exchange of value for value freely entered into by each party not only mistakenly depicts the transaction as voluntary (= chosen by master and slave alike), but also banishes its elements of exploitation and unfreedom. Contrary to what pro-slavery maintains is the case – that the black 'slaves of the South are the happiest, and in some sense, the freest people in the world,' because children, the aged and infirm do no work, females 'do little hard work' and are protected by 'kind' masters, and slaves generally enjoy lots of leisure time – such claims are demonstrably false.[49] If Northern capitalists did not 'care' for the free workers they employed, then neither did planters in the antebellum South, claims by the latter to the contrary notwithstanding. Slaves were not free, nor were they happy and well-cared for when ill or old; women had to work as hard as men in the fields, and were subject to sexual predation by overseers and/or owners.[50]

American Negroes ... were more or less contented slaves, with grievances from time to time but not ambition'.

48 This attempt by pro-slavery discourse to redefine slavery as the ownership not of a person but simply of his labour-power is clearly designed to 'normalize' unfreedom by shifting the concept in the direction of free wage labour. It fails, since the redefinition overlooks the fact that where slavery is concerned, the seller of labour-power is not the same as its subject. Hence the ownership by another of the person of the slave prevents the latter from transferring/alienating his labour-power in person: that is, choosing to sell – or not to sell – his only commodity according to the interests of the subject of the relation. When such a sale took place in the antebellum South, the subject of this transaction had little or no say in the matter, which is a very different undertaking from the kind of arrangement governing the purchase/sale of labour-power belonging to a free worker, as interpreted by political economy generally and Marxist theory in particular. The issue is centrally about who does – or does not – own the labour-power in question: whereas the sale of the labour-power belonging to the slave is done by someone other than the slave, the sale of labour-power by a free worker is done by the subject him/herself. Pro-slavery discourse ignores this distinction.

49 In his methodological critique of the cliometric historiographical case (Fogel and Engerman, 1974) about the operation of a subsistence guarantee on the antebellum plantation, Sutch (1975) demonstrated that claims regarding the enhanced levels of diet, medical care, clothing, and housing allegedly enjoyed by slaves were all empirically incorrect.

50 Tadman (1989) has shown the extent to which slave families were forcibly separated in order to be sold on individually in the course of a thriving and profitable interstate trade in slaves throughout the antebellum South.

Similarly problematic is the connection between the antebellum slave economy and capitalism. An influential argument deployed by one strand of abolitionism consisted of the retardation thesis: namely that, because the presence of the slave plantation was an obstacle to the development of capitalism in the South, its form of unfree labour should therefore be eradicated.[51] The contention was that economically the South ought to become more like the North, a position which reflected the interests of impoverished farmers and workers who, due to the lack of employment, were the real victims of slavery.[52] Contrary to claims made by pro-slavery discourse, therefore, labour market competition was not confined to the North: it also occurred – and had a similarly negative impact – on landless workers in the antebellum South.[53] Because the legislative process in the antebellum South was controlled by slaveholders, however, the interests of non-slaveholding whites in the economic development of capitalism were ignored.[54]

Some pro-slavery discourse perceived capitalism as the enemy, the antithesis of the slave system, while others – such as the contributions to *Cotton is*

---

51   See Helper (1860: 18, 21, 24, 25, 84). 'Of all the experiments that have been tried by people in America,' insisted Helper (1860: 81), 'slavery has proved the most fatal; and the sooner it is abolished the better it will be for us, for posterity, and for the world.'

52   Described by his biographer (Bailey, 1965) as a racist for advocating the deportation of black slaves to Liberia, Hinton Rowan Helper was indeed different from other abolitionists and supporters of emancipation, such as Frederick Douglass and Paul Robeson, who promoted unity between black and white labour. Like other abolitionists, however, he (Helper, 1860: 47, 86, 93) opposed the purchase/sale of any person, and condemned the impact of slavery on whites and blacks alike. Significantly, Helper expresses sympathy for the poor whites of the South in much the same way that Fitzhugh does for the free white labour in the North: workers in each context are perceived as a victims of an iniquitous economic system – slavery in the South, and capitalism in the North.

53   Among 'the most common reasons for the mobility of many landless whites,' was the search for work (Bolton, 1994: 8). They 'had to possess a wide range of marketable skills since the existence of slave labor meant that stable, long-term employment was quite hard to find ... landless whites were constantly driven to relocate to the next neighborhood or to a distant state to take advantage of essentially temporary employment opportunities.'

54   Since 'the despotic adversaries of human liberty are concocting schemes for the enslavement of all the labouring classes, irrespective of race or color,' maintained Helper (1860: 103), '[i]t is against slavery on the whole, and against slaveholders as a body, that we wage an exterminating war.' As Wish (1960: 34) observes, 'Republicans urging the election of Abraham Lincoln found the Helper appeal to the white farmer useful in the doubtful counties of the Old Northeast where the animosity for the planter was accompanied by no sympathy for [black people]. In those states where [black] migrants were not

King – saw plantation slavery as an important part of world capitalism, to the extent that it could no longer be eradicated. Not the least ironic aspect of pro-slavery discourse, therefore, was that, notwithstanding its critique of Northern capitalism and its claim that the antebellum South was non-capitalist, a major argument deployed against opponents was that slavery had become too much a part of the global economic system to permit abolition.[55] So integrated into world capitalism, and consequently so important for accumulation, was slavery that, although once upon a time abolition might have been possible, this was no longer the case. Supported by 'numberless pillars', slavery was now 'too powerful to overcome'.[56] Among those who regarded the slave economy of the Southern plantation system in the immediate pre-Civil War era as already capitalist was Marx himself.[57]

The apparent overlap between arguments supportive of slavery and socialist theory suggests neither that Marxism is reactionary, nor that it supports antebellum conservatism, but rather that pro-slavery discourse – in true populist fashion – sought to influence and secure backing from non-slaveholding plebeian elements in the South and North alike. Maintaining that the solution to labour market competition was a return to the pre-capitalist paternalism of the antebellum South, pro-slavery discourse was in fact the antithesis of Marxism, which posits a solution in terms of a progressive transcendence of capitalism. Whereas pro-slavery discourse advocates a return to a past that is familiar, Marxism by contrast backs a transition to a future yet to be realized.

---

welcome, it was difficult to use anti-slavery arguments based on humanitarian grounds, but the small farmer could understand the monopolistic power of the planter as it cast its shadow across the vast unused lands in the West.' In the immediate post-Civil War era, even abolitionist Republican politicians (Kelley, 1866) continued to invoke arguments from *Cotton is King* supportive of American workers, as did twentieth century apologists for slavery (Phillips, 1918, 1929, 1939).

55   See Elliott (1860: 55ff.). 'The coercion of slavery alone is adequate to form man to habits of labor,' argued Elliott (1860: 552) in making the case for the centrality of this production relation to the reproduction of the capitalist system: 'Without it, there can be no accumulation of property, no providence for the future, no tastes for comfort or elegance, which are the characteristics and essentials of civilization.' Endorsing the interpretation of Nieboer (1910), the same pro-slavery discourse (Elliott, 1860: 564) made the point that '[h]aving the command of abundance of land ... wealth accumulation depends on the "command of slaves."'

56   Elliott (1860: 63, 64).

57   See Marx (1986: 436).

Pro-slavery, Postmodernism, and Identity Politics

Ostensibly, there is little to connect 1850s pro-slavery discourse with 1980s postmodernism.[58] The latter rejects not only the Enlightenment project and metanarratives as inappropriate Eurocentric impositions on rural Third World countries, but also and therefore is hostile to concepts such as class formation/consciousness/struggle. Currently, postmodern theory still exercises considerable influence over debate in the social sciences, and especially on analyses of development issues undertaken in academic, journalistic, and NGO circles. This kind of approach extends from systemic categories used (Empire), via the kinds of identities said to be possessed by 'those below' (subaltern, multitude), to the very forms taken by mobilization itself (everyday-forms-of-resistance).[59] Displacing revolutionary action designed to take control of the state, quotidian agency at the rural grassroots represents for postmodernism the unheard voices of plebeian elements in Third World nations.

In terms of epistemology and argument, however, not only are there ideological similarities between antebellum pro-slavery discourse and recent postmodern theory but such parallels are hard to miss. To begin with, these

---

58 A case in point is the issue of labour market competition, on which a difference seemingly exists. Whereas proslavery discourse blamed Northern accumulation for the negative impact on free workers of labour market competition, the privileging of cultural 'otherness' by postmodern theory is supportive of migration to capitalist nations. However, the issue of labour market competition resonated in the South as well. Poor whites and free blacks, who sold their own labour-power, opposed slavery because, as a form of cheap/unfree labour, it ensured that the South remained a low-wage economy. This was because members of the antebellum ruling oligarchy were able to lease their slaves to urban enterprises, the wages earned thereby accruing not to the slave but rather to his owner. Attributing the lack of industrial development in the antebellum South to the fear by slaveholders lest manufacturing 'would aid in developing a class consciousness among white labour [that] would be hostile to slavery', Russel (1923: 53ff.) underestimates the presence of an additional cause. Namely, a desire 'to drive the slaves from the cities and from [skilled] employments, and restrict them to agriculture'. What free white labour feared, therefore, was economic rivalry resulting from the deployment by slaveholders of cheap slave labour into urban occupations. Although Russel depicts hostility by free whites to slavery as seemingly progressive, the issue concerned opposition to labour market competition operating within the South.

59 Grouped under the rubric of the 'new' populist postmodernism, therefore, are the following: the subaltern studies project of Ranajit Guha (1982–89); Empire and multitude as conceptualised by Michael Hardt and Antonio Negri (2000; 2005); and the everyday-forms-of-resistance associated with the work of James Scott (1985). Taken together, these approaches have in effect colonized the social sciences in general, and development studies in particular.

cases are made on behalf of contexts outside metropolitan capitalism, rural locations (the American South in the mid-nineteenth century, so-called Third World nations a century later) that are said to be fundamentally different economically and untainted by accumulation. At each context/conjuncture opposition to capitalism is expressed in the name of an alternative and better society, which together with its specific institutional forms (slave plantation, peasant smallholding, bonded labour), are – its exponents insist – not capitalist structures. Both pro-slavery discourse and postmodernism are antagonistic to modernity and development, and each privileges cultural 'otherness' as empowering for 'those below'; in the antebellum South, that of black slaves, while in rural Third World, that of the indigenous population.

Notwithstanding the different contexts and conjunctures involved, the logic of each case is the same: namely, that traditional and long-standing production relations (slavery, smallholding, debt bondage) are emblematic of a particular identity, cultural, regional or national.[60] Moreover, pro-slavery discourse and postmodernism claim to be progressive simply on the grounds that they are opposed to capitalism, in the course of which each draws attention to the exploitative and oppressive character of the accumulation process that erodes an innate historical identity, and how the subject championed (the slave, the peasant, the bonded labourer) fares better in a traditional socio-economic process outside (and against) the capitalist system. The latter is seen as an external phenomenon: as interpreted by postmodern theory, opposition to capitalism then derives from a hitherto undiscovered, but authentic, grassroots voice, that can be depicted as depoliticized, uninfluenced by Eurocentric metanarratives. What these similarities emphasize, therefore, is that opposition to the market, to *laissez-faire* policies, or to capitalism generally, is not of itself an indicator of a progressive, let alone leftist, politics.

Just as antebellum pro-slavery discourse indicted the capitalist North as representing an alien systemic form, in the process disregarding the presence in the South of the same accumulation process, so British colonialism is incriminated by postmodernism as the harbinger of capitalist penetration of the Indian countryside. Not only does this similarly overlook the existence there of accumulation, but it also enables postmodernism to argue that it was a foreign colonialism that was responsible for privileging free labour as the 'other' of bonded labour and/or slavery.[61] Rejecting a political economy approach

---

60   As a result of the crop-lien arrangement, many small farmers and tenants in the antebellum South were – like their counterparts in Third World nations today – bonded by debt.

61   For the application of postmodern theory to an analysis of the free/unfree dichotomy, see Prakash (1990a, 1990b). Not only does he dismiss Enlightenment discourse, therefore, but

founded on whether the rural workforce was free or unfree, postmodern theory emphasizes instead the 'cultural' formation of labour.[62] Decoupling production relations from their material base in this manner, it become possible
not merely to deny the efficacy of power-exercised-from-above (= class rule),
but actually to invert this. The inference that – had they wanted – agricultural
workers and bonded labourers could have challenged their subordination but
chose not to do so, which lends credence to the postmodern claim that debt
bondage was a non-coercive relation.

As in pro-slavery discourse, postmodern interpretations of debt bondage in
rural India attempt to redefine the relation: such workers indebted to landlords, it is claimed, are not unfree, but merely 'dependent farm labourers'.[63]
Quite how and in what way those in the latter category, who are unable personally to commodify their labour-power as long as debts owed to the landlord remain unpaid, differ from unfree workers, is never explained. Equally
problematic is the postmodern contention that the debt relationship was non-
existent because bonded labourers 'contested' their subordination, a view akin
to saying that slavery was negated by the mere fact that its subject disliked
unfreedom.[64] Again like antebellum pro-slavery discourse, bonded labour in
India is depicted by postmodernism as an essentially benign arrangement, a
form of landlord patronage that is described as 'the economy of gentleness'
based on the provision of subsistence guarantee, whereby both the unfree
worker and his the family were 'certainly never in want of food'.[65] A similarly
benign interpretation is extended by postmodernism to what is one of the

---

this is coupled with a declared intention to challenge the very meaning of bonded labour
in India ('to unsettle the calm presence that the term "bondage" occupies').

62   See Prakash (1992: 3, 11, 34, 35–36). Although the focus here is on the latter, other postmodern interpretations of unfree labour-power that recast it as a form of 'cultural otherness'
include Taussig (1984), Rodríguez García (2016), Tappe and Lindner (2016), and Müller
and Abel (2016). Because Prakash (1990a: 185; 1992; 1992: 6, 16) conceptualises unfreedom in Foucaultian terms, as a 'corporeal' relationship whereby power takes the form of
physical control by a landholder over the body and not the labour-power of the worker,
it is easy for the absence of actual violence to be interpreted as evidence of either the
benign nature of bondage (= the 'economy of gentleness') or even the non-existence of
unfreedom.

63   Prakash (1990b: 185).

64   For the contestation ≠ bonded labour claim, see Prakash (1990b: 179, 205).

65   Prakash (1990a: 185ff.) maintains 'that the [bonded labourers'] poverty fell well short of
starvation, and that their subsistence was aided by their larger harvest earnings, when
compared to the ordinary labourers.' Even when he accepts that the labour regime is
'harsh', it is nevertheless the case that 'the [landlords'] gentle acts of domination were
visible in matters concerning the reproduction of the [debt bonded] family.'

most acute political issues facing the left currently: the effect on working class formation/consciousness/struggle of a globally expanding industrial reserve army of labour.

Empowering Populism

Historically, the anti-capitalism of the right can take a number of forms: that of landlord hostility aimed at a developing industry which 'steals' its tenants, providing them with alternative and better-paid economic prospects in towns and cities; that of middle-class resentment generated by economic crisis that results in the loss of savings; or that of those employed in the bureaucracy when the neoliberal state cuts their number. Perhaps the most effective instance of rightwing anti-capitalism is the 'from above' political sympathy expressed for 'those below' facing displacement as a result of capitalists employing cheaper workers composed of migrants, in the process undercutting pay and conditions secured by locals over years of organization and struggle. It is the latter situation in particular which generates multi-class alliances – uniting workers and bourgeois parties/politicians sharing a common ethnic or national identity – that breeds populism.[66]

Accordingly, a corollary of not differentiating anti-capitalism is not just advocacy of a return to the past but also the dilution of class struggle. Failure to recognize politically distinct forms of anti-capitalism leads in turn to forming alliances with categories that are antagonistic only to certain kinds of capital, and as such regarded by Marxists as uninterested in or hostile to working class empowerment and socialism. Composed of a broad range of components

---

66   That a populist anti-capitalism of the right was necessary to counteract that of the left was best expressed by Julius Evola (1898–1974), a fellow-traveller of Italian fascism, whose reactionary views – denouncing modernity while advocating a return to ancient 'spiritual values' and hierarchy – have influence the Italian new right. In order to avoid criticisms from the left, therefore, Evola (2002: 114–115) argued for the adoption by those on the right of 'a general view of life and of the State that, being based on higher values and interests, definitely transcends the economic plane, and thus everything that can be defined in terms of economic classes'. He added that if 'things were set up in this way, by absolutely refusing to set foot in the field where the Left trains its aim on the "*faux* target", its polemics would be rendered totally ineffective.' The significance of his concluding words (Evola, 2002: 231, original emphasis) on this subject is unambiguous: 'In the contemporary era it is absolutely important that *the struggle against a degenerate and arrogant Capitalism be waged from above* ... rather than leaving to the Left alone the right of accusation and protest.'

outside the working class (including undifferentiated peasants, lumpenproletarians, and 'marginals'), political and ideological unity among these socioeconomically heterogeneous elements requires – and indeed rests on – the adoption/promotion of cultural and/or non-class identities. It is precisely this objective that licenses the populism + postmodernism combination. Major intellectuals who formulated, promoted, or embraced either populism or postmodernism include Laclau, Derrida, Foucault, Lyotard, and Baudrillard: a political characteristic shared by them all was, to a greater or less extent, hostility towards socialism, Marxism, and Marxist theory.[67]

Because it privileges cultural identity as empowering, therefore, postmodern theory is complicit with nationalism. In this way, postmodernism moves into an ideological space occupied historically by populism. To the postmodern argument emphasizing the cultural identity of the migrant-worker -as'other'-nationality, therefore, the far right counterposes an argument similarly emphasizing cultural identity, only this time of the non-migrant worker. In the absence of socialist ideas/practice, and as capitalism spreads across the globe, this form of nationalist discourse can be deployed effectively by populists who claim it is the only way to safeguard/retain workers' jobs and living standards. The political outcome is not difficult to discern: consciousness of class, together with its accompanying forms of struggle, quickly give way to ideology and mobilization based on national identity.

Any working class unity, solidarity, and struggle achieved hitherto rapidly fragments along ethnic/national lines, and along with it unravelling political and economic gains made by leftist parties/organizations. Labour market competition involving workers and migrants possessing different ethnic/

---

67   Thus, for example, Foucault (1996: 90–91) and colleagues have defended the inclusion
      of the lumpenproletariat (= undifferentiated worker) within anti-capitalist social movements because it is composed of 'marginals'. Lamenting that 'the lumpenproletariat, in
      Marxist theory, is a sort of residue [which the authorities] do their best to "stigmatize"',
      a colleague of Foucault states that 'we are discovering ... there is a possibility of bringing
      the real marginal into social and political action which would be that of all workers'. To
      this Foucault replies that 'there is a split between the proletariat on the one hand and
      extra-proletarian, non-proletarianized plebeian on the other ... We should not say: there
      is the proletariat and then there are these marginals. We should say: there is in the overall mass of plebeians a split between the proletariat and the non-proletarianized plebeian.' Another discussant then adds that 'the Marxist perspective must be broken with.'
      Significantly, much the same case on behalf of the lumpenproletariat has been made by
      leftists (van der Linden and Roth, 2014) who maintain implausibly that such a view is not
      only consistent with Marxism but also unconnected to the 'new' populist postmodernism.

national identities quickly breeds racism, an ideology that populism foments and reproduces so as to obtain grassroots support, thereby dividing the work-force.[68] Components of the latter are encouraged to see themselves – and organize – as members not of the working class but rather of a particular non-class identity/group. This in turn is legitimized by postmodern theory, which proclaims the not just the irreducibility and innateness of non-class identity, but also its culturally empowering nature. Not only does this kind of shift deflect from divisions of class, therefore, but mobilization/struggle based on non-class identities – religion, ethnicity, nationalism – generates support for non- or anti-progressive ideologies/movements.[69] The result is a populist defence of non-class forms of 'otherness', and of their empowerment, sim-ply because they are 'other', regardless of what is advocated ideologically and politically.

The kind of problem this generates is clear. To begin with, it ignores peri-odic warnings by Marxists – among them Lenin, Trotsky, Luxemburg, and Marx himself – that such an approach is not merely not leftist but risks endors-ing political/ideological movements that are backwards-looking, and thus opposed to concepts of progress and democracy, let alone socialism. Hence the current enthusiasm on the part of postmodernists – and some leftists – for more ideological 'inclusiveness', with the object of constructing a political alliance consisting of anyone opposed to *laissez-faire*, an all-encompassing form of anti-capitalism that embraces categories outside (and even opposed to) the working class. Under the conceptual umbrella of terms such as 'mul-titude,' 'difference,' and hegemony, therefore, postmodern theory advocates incorporating elements like the lumpenproletariat, undifferentiated peasants, religious movements, and even sections of the bourgeoisie, into a broad alli-ance against the *laissez-faire* policies/programmes of the neoliberal state. Such populist movements – constructed around nothing more than a shared dislike of neoliberalism – overlook the fact that, politically and ideologically, these categories are not just uninterested in socialism but actively opposed to it, as

---

68   Not the least problematic aspect in terms of a racist outcome is when history presented
      by postmodern exponents of 'otherness' appears to all those who inhabit the receiving
      nation as though they were either not part of it, or were doing so illegitimately at the
      expense of others wishing to join their number.

69   Numerous instances of working-class abandonment of leftist parties/policies/pro-
      grammes in favour of reactionary equivalents on offer from populists and/or conserva-
      tives include not just Austria in the late nineteenth century, and Germany in the early
      twentieth, but also the UK in the early twenty-first.

evidence by their presence historically in counter-revolutionary and/or reactionary movements.[70]

An additional factor contributing to the current impact on working class livelihoods of labour market competition is that it is a problem that becomes more acute as capitalism spreads across the globe. Accumulation thrives on this expanding industrial reserve army, composed of erstwhile peasants who, separated from their means of production, contribute to a globally-available workforce that – because of deskilling – can now be employed alongside machinery in the advanced capitalist labour process. Improved communications and infrastructure in effect reduce distance between nations, travel no longer being the obstacle to migration that it once was. In the past, what immigrants to Western Europe brought with them was the identity of class as defined by the receiving nation to which they came. Now, increasingly they bring not only a particular ethnic/national identity, but also that of a nation left behind. The latter, it could be argued, is due in part to three interrelated processes. First, the role of NGOs, which nowadays act as a legal conduit for migrant rights, which although presented mainly in terms of asylum, inadvertently justify thereby the access to the host nation of what Marxism regards as an expanding industrial reserve army.[71] Second, the broad tendency to ignore political economy, especially that taking the form of Marxist analysis, when explaining how and why capitalism is reproduced systemically. And third, the role of academia generally, and in particular the adherents of the 'new' populist postmodernism, in legitimizing a discourse – currently hegemonic – privileging identity politics.

Conclusion

Traced here are the epistemological and political links between pro-slavery discourse in the antebellum South and theory espoused currently by the 'new' populist postmodernism. Since each is critical of accumulation and supportive

---

70 Agrarian movements exhibiting characteristics belonging to the anti-capitalism of the right extend from the Vendée in 1790s France, the Cristeros and Sinarquistas in Mexico during the 1920s and 1930s, to the new farmers' movements in India from the 1980s onwards.

71 For the most part, NGO discourse categorizes all migration as a process composed largely or wholly of refugees fleeing a nation for political reasons. On the centrality of the industrial reserve army of labour to Marxist theory, and in particular how its presence/expansion generates economic crisis within the capitalist system, see Sweezy (1946: 87–92, 149–50) and Glyn (2006).

of 'those below', both correspond to the anticapitalism of the right. Like pro-slavery discourse, postmodernism expresses hostility towards capitalism, and attempts to redefine unfreedom merely as a contextually-specific variant of traditional culture, one that empowers its subject. Consequently, postmodernism shares with proslavery discourse an idealized perception of pre-/non-capitalist systemic forms: the plantation in the case of the antebellum South, petty commodity production in the case of the Third World village. This expression of concern for 'those below', together with hostility towards their capitalist oppressors, is – it is argued – a populist combination. The latter in turn is at the root of the ideological power exercised by the anti-capitalism of the right over some on the left.

Denying that capitalism (= free society) was – or could ever be – based on a social contract between producers and workers, pro-slavery discourse attacked labour market competition as benefitting only the employer. Seemingly no different from leftist critiques of accumulation, this discourse expressed sympathy for free workers, supporting the labour theory of value whilst opposing the attempts by Northern capitalists to undercut wages/conditions. Without the subsistence guarantee that the discourse claimed was available to slaves in the antebellum South, free workers in the North – so the argument went – would organize to overthrow the accumulation process and usher in socialism. Coupled with this warning about the perils inherent in *laissez-faire*, the pro-slavery indictment of capitalism was designed to appeal to non-slaveholders (poor farmers, tenants, landless workers). Accordingly, the focus of this anti-capitalist variant was on how market competition favoured by Northern producers disadvantaged the free labourer who had to work harder for less pay, the avoidance of which was designed to generate 'from below' support for slavery which, by keeping black labour tied to the plantation, ensured they remained outside the labour market.

In certain respects, therefore, the critique by pro-slavery discourse of *laissez-faire* economics was as sharp as anything written by Marxism. Unlike the latter, however, the solution proposed was a return to what was presented as a benevolent pre-capitalist system, of which slavery in the antebellum South was the relational norm. Equally problematic were claims that accumulation and labour market competition were confined to the Northern economy. Much the same kind of logic – a return to a benign system claimed to be pre- or non-capitalist – informs the 'new' populist postmodernism. Such claims were and are obviously problematic, not least the attempt by pro-slavery discourse to deny that slavery constituted a form of property, or the insistence by the 'new' populist postmodernism that debt bondage did not correspond to unfreedom. In each instance, therefore, what was overlooked was that such labour-power was bought/sold/controlled not by its subject (the slave, the bonded labourer) but rather by the master or the landowner.

Recognition of these differences between pro-slavery discourse and post-modernism on the one hand, and Marxism on the other, has been rendered difficult by misunderstanding as to what the latter stands for politically. Over the past decades, and coinciding with the intellectual rise of postmodernism and neoliberalism, there has been a declining interest in Marxist theory. An inevitable consequence of this intellectual/academic unfashionability has been a corresponding inability to differentiate Marxist political economy, concepts, and theory, from non- or anti-Marxist equivalents. As predictable in terms of outcome has been what followed the epistemological lacuna that opened up during this period. Because they endorsed what is the anti-capitalism of the political right, with its privileging of non-class identities (nationality, ethnicity, religion), many who saw themselves as being on the left politically ended up not just supporting the reactionary theory/politics of the right, but also opposing leftist arguments challenging such positions. Not the least important of the many issues affected by this problem has been a failure to understand – let alone address – the significance of a globally burgeoning industrial reserve army and its deleterious impact on the working class in metropolitan capitalist nations.

In contrast to the anti-capitalism of the left, that of the right mobilizes on the basis of categories outside (and sometimes against) the working class. A shared dislike of neoliberalism underwrites the emergence and consolidation of the sort of identity politics endorsed by pro-slavery discourse and postmodernism: namely, nationalism, ethnicity, religion, and agrarianism. It was against these kinds of non-class ideologies that Marxism warned, indicating that they served to undermine the class interest of workers, and with it any prospects for a socialist transition. Under the banner of populism, the right has now moved to occupy the political space that is vacant, a colonization unwittingly abetted by those leftists (or 'leftists') who mistakenly saw this anti-capitalism – simply because it is opposed to capitalism – as a progressive development. The current significance of this shift is not difficult to discern. In an epoch marked by a global expansion of the industrial reserve army, and the populist reaction this has generated, involving as it does struggles not about class but about national, ethnic, and religious identity, this Marxist warning cannot be ignored.

Transitions (Real and Imagined)

The blinkered empiricist will of course deny that the facts can only become facts within the framework of a system – which will vary with the knowledge desired. He believes that every piece of data from economic life, every statistic, every raw event already constitutes an important fact. In doing so he forgets that however simple an enumeration of "facts" may be, however lacking in commentary, it already implies an "interpretation". Already at this stage the facts have been comprehended by a theory, a method; they have been wrenched from their living context and fitted into a theory.

> A still relevant warning issued a century ago by GEORG LUKÁCS.[1]

• • •

Whenever a Marxist attempted to write a history of capitalism it would come out as a wretched piece of work on the whole (laughs). Um, I won't mention names here.

> An observation by BANAJI about the shortcomings of Marxist historiography, made in the course of an interview during December 2020, a critique that might well apply closer to home than imagined.[2]

•   •
  •

Introduction: Simple Transitions?

Of the many forms a revision might take, three kinds in particular apply to the approach scrutinized in this chapter. Changes gathered under the term revision encompass the following epistemological shifts: that involving the object of study, or conceptually transforming the latter; that involving its politics, in effect a move away from Marxism; and that involving the approach itself,

---

1   Lukács (1971: 5).
2   "'Where is the working class? It's all over the world today": Jairus Banaji in conversation with Sheetal Chhabria and Andrew Liu – Part I', *Borderlines*, December 2020.

subject to unremitting change. Considered here, therefore, is the case made by Jairus Banaji, in articles and books from the 1970s to the present, about multiple historical transitions, from late antiquity to feudalism and from the latter to capitalism.

His is a curious yet familiar approach, since among the claims Banaji makes is that it presents an entirely new version of Marxism, replacing virtually every single preceding interpretation – including that by Marx – of these same transitions. Hence feudalism seems not to come from a process of economic decline: as in the case of late antiquity, therefore, what Banaji objects to are attempts by Marxists to explain the demise of particular modes by reference to 'catastrophist theory'. For this reason, the problematic claims he makes, not just about systemic transition but also about production relations and Marxist theory itself, cannot but prompt additional questions regarding his interpretation of the link between ancient society, feudalism and capitalism.[3]

The focus here is on the feudal mode of production, its vanishing from the original case made by Banaji, and the strange manner in which it subsequently reappears in his analysis. It is noticeable that, following initial critiques pointing out how his model of late antiquity left no space for a transition to feudalism, Banaji seemingly refashioned his approach so as to incorporate this missing systemic mode, yet one which at the same time retained both his argument and its core epistemological components ('disguised' wage labour, a 'new' aristocracy investing in agriculture, economic growth, etc.). Inevitably, the resulting framework is procrustean, a confused jumble of contradictory elements, an attempted resolution of which requires that he insert a space between late antiquity and feudalism.[4] Into this space are poured all the characteristics of his model, and from this same space are expelled all the concepts and claims belonging to Marxist theory which interprets the transition linking the fall of the Roman empire to feudalism as a continuous historical process.[5]

---

3 Problematic aspects of the way Banaji interprets ancient society have been outlined elsewhere (Brass, 2005; Brass, 2012; and Brass, 2021: Chapters 5 and 6).

4 Apart from the confusion arising from inconsistencies in the characterization of production relations, the attempt to construct a coherent pattern of systemic transition is beset by contradiction. Objecting to what is termed a 'linear history' projecting a 'simple transition from slavery to serfdom', Banaji (2010: 199–200, 205) suddenly appears to realize it is an approach that he himself is following. A similar objection to 'the half-baked conception of late antiquity as the precursor of feudalism' does not prevent Banaji (2010: 182, 215, 227) from arguing subsequently both that 'the West was defined by a tradition of tied labour inherited from the late Roman world' and that 'the *coloni* clearly were tied labourers inherited from the late empire'.

5 This approach does not prevent Banaji from believing that his alone is the only true Marxist paradigm about historical transition. Among the shortcomings Marxist historians such as de

Such difficulties are themselves rooted in the fact that what purports to be a Marxist analysis of the mode of production in ancient and modern economies is, much rather, a non-Marxist history of global trade and exchange. The central argument, outlined in his most recent books, is that a pan-historical form of capitalism stretches from ancient society to the present, in effect negating Marxist theory about the dynamics leading to a transition from one mode of production to another. In the case of feudalism, therefore, the emblematic form privileged by him turns out to be not natural economy but rather 'a commodity-producing enterprise', well-integrated into the market. Familiarity stems from two things. First, recent arguments made by Banaji are not in fact new, resting on earlier analyses (Brown on late antiquity, Hilferding on finance capital, Rodinson on Islamic capitalism). And second, the case he makes appears to be the latest in what is now a long series of attempts to debunk Marxism, and with it any prospect for a socialist transition.

Among the reasons invoked currently as to why Marxism is off the political agenda is that its historical subject – the working class – is either absent, too fragmented, or lacks interest in socialist objectives; that opposition to capitalism these days is best conducted by non-class categories and identities; that capitalism is not yet sufficiently developed to make a transition feasible; that it is not the right kind of capitalism; and that the contradictions generated by neoliberalism can be solved by returning to a 'caring'/'kinder' form of accumulation.[6] Most of these revisionist approaches have in common an initial endorsement of Marxism, quickly followed by its rejection on empirical or political grounds, a combination that can itself be traced to faulty methods and/or theory. This is also a route which Banaji himself seems to have travelled.

Ste Croix, Haldon, and Wickham are accused of by him (Banaji, 2010: 184, 199–200, 237) are variously 'a lack of a more sophisticated Marxist theory of the feudal mode', adhering to 'a simple transition from slavery to serfdom ... the famous metanarrative of vulgar Marxism', and being guilty of endorsing an interpretation of production relations 'less schematically than either Wickham or an earlier generation of Marxists have tended to do'. In the light of his own theoretical and methodological departures from Marxism, such criticisms applied by Banaji to other Marxists are problematic indeed.

6   These are positions held by exponents of, respectively, global labour history, the 'new' populist postmodernism, the semi-feudal thesis, 'financialization', and appeals to the patronage of a 'benign' capitalist state. Of late, others have shamefacedly returned to the Marxist fold, attempting unsuccessfully to persuade that they had never been away, on which see Brass (2017). In keeping with this, yet others have now espoused Marxism, having earlier mistakenly claimed that it misunderstood the acceptability to capital of labour-power that is unfree, but persist with claiming that the latter relational form can – and will – be eradicated by capital itself.

This chapter is divided into three sections, the first of which considers the different ways in which Banaji and others define antiquity, feudalism, and capitalism. The concepts deployed in this endeavour, the historical spaces into which they are inserted, together with their impact on the process of systemic transition, are looked at in the second part. Critically examined in the third are the supposedly Marxist theory and methods used in this process.

I

From the same stable as the term 'formalism', the word 'crystallized' applied by Banaji to what is presented by him as a concrete relational or systemic version pops up so often that it takes on a reified existence. Having at last got past the many references to 'crystallized' forms, what emerges is a reference apparently to something arbitrarily defined as the *non plus ultra* systemic configuration, a relation, condition or structure that – when reached – represents for Banaji the essential aspect of the phenomenon in question. Not the least curious aspect of this attempt to privilege a specific variant of a larger form as its distinctive trait is the absence of any reason as to why this variant and no other should be regarded as constitutive of a 'perfect' configuration, especially given the reluctance on his part to accept any of the remaining characteristics (land tenure, economic regime, production relations) said to be intrinsic to – and thus define – the model under consideration. This difficulty applies to each of the systemic categories in his approach: antiquity, feudalism, and capitalism.

The Parting to Come?

Along with non-Marxist historians of ancient society (including Tenney Frank, Rostovtzeff, Oertel, and A.H.M. Jones), leftists extending from Marx and Engels themselves to Kautsky, Luxemburg, Walbank, and de Ste Croix have all subscribed to a negative interpretation of the Roman Empire: not only did it decline, but its decay was due mainly to economic causes. Over the past half century, however, this negative view – the decline thesis – has been supplanted by academically entrenched revisionism, whereby the historiography of the Roman Empire has been transformed from a narrative about systemic decline to one about flourishing economic development. Many of those who oppose the decline thesis now espouse the concept 'late antiquity', a period which it is claimed was one of economic growth and general prosperity. This celebratory and positive interpretation – originally formulated by Peter Brown – has been accompanied not just by the erasure of leftist 'negativity' but also by

arguments for the presence in late antiquity of capitalism itself.[7] That Jairus
Banaji, a Marxist who during the 1960s/1970s participated in mode of production debate, is an adherent not of the decline thesis but rather of late antiquity,
seems to be an anomaly.

Seen from the broad perspective of Marxist theory, the difficulties with the
late antiquity framework which Banaji endorses are that it promotes what
amounts to a positive and a-historical image of capitalism, one that – because it
is crisis-free and seemingly benign – appears systemically eternal. It is a framework purged of all the processes which according to Marxist theory generate
systemic transition, among them crisis, struggle, and the non-development
of the productive forces. No fundamental economic transformation means in
turn no transition, and thus also no distinguishing characteristics separating
one mode of production from another. History – as depicted by this kind of
approach – becomes merely a narrative about an ever-present dynamic that
is progress. To back his contention about the presence in late antiquity of
an economic system akin to capitalism, it is necessary for Banaji to have to
identify the forms of the exchanges which his merchants, 'business classes',
'businessmen', and 'moderately affluent middle classes' themselves undertake.
This he does in two ways: on the one hand by stressing the multiple and positive aspects fuelling what he claims is unabated economic dynamism, and on
the other by downplaying (or denying) any negative economic processes and
effects. Much like Brown, therefore, Banaji denies the existence in late antiquity both of impoverishment and of overtaxation, forms of oppression and/or
appropriation central to so-called 'catastrophist models' informing the decline
thesis.[8]

Feudalism, what and when it was, is theoretically central to the debate
about the mode of production, particularly as this concerns the link between
pre-capitalist social forms and the transition to capitalism.[9] A crucial aspect
of this discussion concerns the economic structure, the production relations,
and the manner of their reproduction on the seigneurial system, as it existed in
Western Europe between the fifth and the fifteenth century.[10] As important is

---

7   Brown (1971, 1978).
8   For these views, see Banaji (2018: 7, 54, 86).
9   On this, see among others Hindess and Hirst (1975) and Hilton (1976). Insisting that
     'Wickham's characterization of the feudal mode is unrepentantly structuralist', Banaji
     (2010: 212) compares this approach to that of Hindess and Hirst, who equate feudalism
     with the expansion of tenancy.
10   The extent to which the European model of feudalism is applicable elsewhere, as Wickham
     argues, is also discussed by Archetti and Aass (1978), Wolpe (1980), and Goodman and
     Redclift (1981).

the question – much disputed – of two historical transitions: that from antiquity to feudalism, and from the latter to capitalism. Among other things, the European model of feudalism was closely linked to conquest, whereby a new ruler consolidated power by apportioning (or reapportioning) property to a landlord class. Not only was it loyal to him, but – in return for these property rights – feudal landowners henceforth agreed to provide the ruler with military assistance (men at arms drawn from among their own tenants).

Economically, feudalism is said to be characterized by the absence of a substantial market, either for labour or for other agricultural commodities.[11] In European contexts feudalism has been regarded as a social formation consisting mainly – but not only – of self-contained agrarian units: the demesne (or the manor) operated by a lord, and smallholdings leased by him to his peasant tenants. The latter paid rent to the dominant proprietor of their leased holdings in the form of labour-service, cash or kind. A crucial and defining aspect of such feudal relations, it has been argued, was serfdom.[12] Because rent was extracted by means of the extra-economic coercion exercised by the landlord over the tenant, production relations were as a result unfree. About these characteristics – the economic logic of feudalism, how its production relations should be defined, when/why a transition occurred, and from what to what – there is little agreement generally, and in particular by Wickham and Banaji, whose rival interpretations are compared here.

Arguing that, where feudalism is concerned, it is peasants, not workers that constitute the dominant relational form, Wickham cautions against drawing the opposite conclusion: that the existence of wage-labour in a feudal context amounts to evidence for the presence there of capitalism.[13] His view is that, as a mode of production spanning a period from pre-500 to post-1500, feudalism persisted because surplus extraction was based on the relation between lord and peasant, the latter providing the former with rent and taxes. Despite this, peasant economy survived, due mainly to the fact that smallholders – unlike

---

11   Slicher van Bath (1963).

12   On this, see Kosminsky (1956) and Dobb (1967).

13   See Wickham (2021: 5). Answering the question as to 'what feudalism is', he (Wickham, 2021: 9, 11) argues that 'in its economic sense as a mode of production, derived ... from Marx ... a socio-economic system based on the exploitative relations of production between peasants, that is to say subsistence cultivators, and lords. At its core are peasant family units, who work the land,' adding: 'Pure cash cropping, where peasants produce only for sale, and have to buy food in, was almost unknown under feudalism, and indeed was rare until the twentieth century under capitalism.'

lords – were central to the economic system.[14] Against the 'metanarrative of failure', which sees the non-development of capitalism as an opportunity lost, Wickham asks instead why should such a transition occur, on the basis of which a case is made for the longevity of the feudal mode of production.[15] The power of lords to extract rent and taxes from peasants, and the resulting pattern of consumption/underconsumption imposed on smallholders, had implications for the urban economy. When peasant consumption declined, therefore, production contracted, since in these circumstances it depended on the much smaller market of lords and their entourages.

It is to this this model of feudalism that Banaji objects. 'My own analysis highlights other features,' he proclaims, among which are 'huge monetary expansion and a tax-system less dominated by payments in kind than Marx believed or Wickham supposes', together with 'a widespread use of free labour coupled with more rigorous forms of subordination'.[16] Although his own model is presented by Banaji as an absolute departure from preceding ones, many of the issues he raises were already being discussed in the 1950s. By that point, historians had not only begun to question the equation of feudalism with natural economy, but also accepted that commercial activity and trade were more important than thought hitherto.[17] Despite the presence of some wage labour, however, it was 'not enough to change the old system': crucial elements of the feudal system endured, not least in production being geared to aristocratic consumption. As argued by Hilton – one of the historians of whom Banaji is critical – increases in production, trade, and population over the 13th and 14th centuries notwithstanding, 'the main features of the old social and political framework remained, not to disappear until the 17th and 18th centuries'.[18] Until the latter conjunctures, power was exercised by aristocracies and feudal monarchies, not industrialist or merchants; there had to be a bourgeois revolution before a full capitalist expansion was possible.[19]

---

14   Wickham (2021: 35, 37). As indicated by his insistence from the outset that 'coercive rent-taking is the feudal mode of production; it represents the exploitative relationship between tenant and landlord', Wickham (1985: 170) has remained consistent all along in his ideas, a point that can be seen as positive, in that he hasn't simply gone along with the latest fad – as so many have done, and still do – on the grounds that a whole 'new' interpretation is necessary (and fashionable).

15   Wickham (2021: 11).

16   Banaji (2010: 211).

17   For this see Hilton (1985: 268–69); the latter appears in a volume where his 1952 Past & Present article is reproduced.

18   Hilton (1985: 273–74).

19   In a direct challenge to the kind of case made now by Banaji, Hilton (1985: 274–75) noted then that 'the history of trade alone will not tell us how and when the characteristic

However, according to Banaji wherever the 'autonomous peasant enterprise' is found, there too is found capitalism, a teleology that can be shifted back in time, not just to feudalism but also to ancient society. On the one hand, not only were those designated by Banaji as a 'middle aristocracy' engaged in accumulation, but 'all sectors ... saw a substantial investment of private capital based on the individual pursuit of profit'.[20] Lest there be any doubt about this, Roman society is described as a context where 'the countryside clearly absorbed a great deal of investment'. On the other, numerous accompanying references seek to establish the widespread availability of hired workers, wage-labourers who received cash payments, day labourers and agricultural workers recruited on a casual basis, together with the view that 'the peasantry employed on such estates was largely proletarianized workforce'.[21] As to the descriptions contained in the legal (and other) texts cited by Banaji, his view is unambiguous: 'The crucial point is that such notions [in the sources] operated with respect to free labour'.[22] This point is emphasized in the conclusion of his 2001 book: 'Thus late antiquity throws up a social formation combining aristocratic dominance with free labour on a model that conforms to none of the historical stereotypes distinguishing the classical from the medieval and modern worlds.'[23] In other words, the combination of investment + trade + money + 'disguised wage-labour' = capitalism, no less in ancient society than in the feudal system.[24]

Trading Places

Turning to the issue of capitalism itself, what Banaji understands by this term is – as with so many of the concepts he deploys – theoretically problematic, and his efforts to rectify this are consequently replete with contradiction.

---

relations of feudalism gave place to those of capitalism ... [t]he growth of capitalist production cannot be measured simply by estimating the level of commodity production.'

20   Banaji (2001: 219).

21   These descriptions of the workforce are found throughout the account by Banaji (2001) of the rural economy in the eastern Mediterranean over the period 300–700 A.D. On estate peasants as a 'proletarianized workforce', see Banaji (2001: 181).

22   Banaji (2001: 209).

23   Banaji (2001: 217).

24   Money is at the root of what Banaji argues is a mode of production. Epistemologically, this approach leads in turn to a familiar relay-in-statement: money signals the historical ubiquity not only of economic growth and wage-labour (albeit everywhere 'disguised') but also of capitalism itself.

Although he begins by insisting that in all cases ancient economy must be differentiated from modern capitalism, any distinctiveness – never strong – soon recedes into the background. Disavowing the notion of ancient society as capitalist, he nevertheless opts instead for the presence there of 'individual capitalists', on the grounds that their existence was 'well attested throughout antiquity'.[25] For this reason, he settles for the opaque construction that around the start of the Principate an 'unproductive capitalism' amounted to 'a characterization of the economic activities of particular capitalists or groups of capitalists and not of the economy as a whole.' At this point, however, Banaji adopts a more sweeping and all-embracing definition, asserting that 'there was surely no period of Republican, imperial or late antique history when *capitalists* were not active in major sectors of the economy or when indeed some of these, or parts of them, were not organized on capitalist lines.'[26] Additional observations made by him suggest his view is that the Roman economy of late antiquity was indeed capitalist.[27]

When trying to account for the presence or absence of capitalist development in European or non-European contexts, Banaji also encounters fundamental theoretical difficulties, nowhere more so than with the role of the state. Although the latter is central to his entire case, Banaji seems unsure as to precisely why, how, and where. Agreeing that 'there is nothing inevitable about capitalism [because] its emergence depends, crucially, not just on markets but on the state', he qualifies this 'or at least a particular kind of state', one that 'sets out to encourage and bolster commercial expansion'.[28] However, precisely what was 'particular' about this kind of state, and why it was so in some contexts and conjunctures but not in others, is not explained. Problems generated by this lacuna keep on surfacing throughout the narrative. Emphasizing the contribution to profitability of circulating capital velocity, Banaji manages to overlook the important role of the state in providing infrastructure.[29] Having indicated that the state was itself central to the existence/success of commercial capitalism, Banaji then maintains it was a political apparatus the dominance of which rested neither on imperialism nor colonialism – state-dominant economic

---

25   Banaji (2018: 48–49).
26   Banaji (2018: 49, original emphasis).
27   See Banaji (2018: 2, 51), who elsewhere (Éwanjée-Épée, Boggio & Monferrand, 2015: 5) states clearly that what is to be found in late antiquity is indeed capitalism.
28   Banaji (2020: 120).
29   See Banaji (2020: 113–14). This, perhaps, might even qualify for the elusively 'particular' aspect of the state.

forms regarded by Marxism as the historical *sine qua non* of capitalist penetration/expansion.[30]

Moreover, for some reason, the process of trade and commerce is depicted as the efficiency/success largely of non-European agency, endeavour, and/or organization. On the one hand, therefore, there are positive references to 'indigenous Asian capitals' and Greek Levantine dominance.[31] On the other, there are a number of rather less positive references: Portuguese 'royal capitalism' is described as being 'cloaked in religious zeal and a great deal of both ignorance and bigotry'; the cosmopolitanism of mid-nineteenth century British trade expansion is questioned on the grounds that it was carried out by those of non-European identity based in England; and 'nobody in London had any knowledge whatever of conditions in India', while British trade efficiency was anyway down to merchants belonging to the Greek diaspora.[32] Quite why it is necessary to depict economic rivalries – which certainly existed – in precisely this non-economic manner remains something of an oddity, especially in an approach that claims an affinity with some variety of Marxism.

That some form of capitalism was historically present in the Islamic world was an issue addressed during the mid-1960s by Rodinson, much of whose approach – what sort of capitalism, the role of the state, the work of Ibn Khaldun – is reproduced by Banaji.[33] To the same question posed earlier by Rodinson – why did a modern capitalist economy not emerge in the Islamic world – Banaji answers that 'the non-development of capitalism was less about a failure to emerge than about the failure to acquire a more collective, corporate form that could express and contribute to the solidarity of a class.'[34] The irony structuring this view is hard to miss. Having spent many of the preceding chapters in his most recent book outlining how what passed for European commercial acuity was much rather down to the fact that trade was conducted efficiently on the basis of locally pre-existing social/cultural/economic networks by a whole range of non-European 'others' – including Middle Eastern merchants – Banaji now declares that what these same dynamic elements lacked was a 'collective'/'corporate' identity. A more egregious contradiction is hard to imagine.

The influence on Banaji of Hilferding is inescapable, the debt owed by the former to the latter being evident from how closely the argument made now

---

30   Banaji (2020: 121).
31   Banaji (2020: 63, 78ff.).
32   For these views, see Banaji (2020: 41, 73, 99–100, 121).
33   See Rodinson (1974) and also Banaji (2020: 125ff.).
34   Banaji (2020: 132).

follows that made by the Austro-Marxist in his 1910 book.[35] Although the latter analysis is mentioned by Banaji only twice, much of the case Hilferding
outlined a century ago, about how the economic system was developing – the
increasing centralization of capital, the formation of cartels, the role of banks,
finance, credit, money, joint-stock companies, and the state – prefigures that
of Banaji.[36] For this reason, the same critique made by Sweezy of Hilferding's
finance capital argument – how it not only breaks with Marxism but also (and
more importantly) precludes a socialist transition – applies with equal force to
the present case advanced by Banaji.[37] One way or another, capitalism is not –
or is no longer – what we thought it was, the inference being that its political
overthrow is either postponed *sine die* or else undesirable, and anyway now
impossible. Of course, all such prognoses cannot be but music to the ears of
capitalists themselves.

II

Epistemologically, the case made by Banaji about what happened between
late antiquity and feudalism, and thus also a transition not just from one to
the other but also ultimately to capitalism, rests in turn on two interrelated
issues: the concepts deployed, and whether or not these define and justify the
specificity of the historical space he wants to create.[38] His framework about the
antiquity/feudalism transition depends, therefore, on the validity of the production relations grouped under the term 'servile labour': the latter is inserted
by him after 'pure slavery', and before the 'peasantry proper', underwriting the

---

35   Hilferding (1981).
36   For these references to Hilferding, see Banaji (2020: 70, 85).
37   'Hilferding's error is a serious one in at least two respects', writes Sweezy (1946: 268–
      69): 'For one thing the preconception of financial dominance precludes an understand-
      ing of the most important recent changes in the character of the accumulation process,
      particularly the growth of internal corporate financing. And for another thing, it leads
      to profound illusions about the nature and difficulty of the task involved in achieving a
      socialist society. Already in 1910 Hilferding expressed the view that "the seizure of six big
      Berlin banks would mean the seizure of the most important spheres of big industry." Even
      at the time this was far from the truth ... But today the entire banking system could be
      "seized" in the United States, for example, without causing more than a temporary ripple
      in the ranks of big capital.'
38   The existence of this space requires that Banaji (2010: 234) dismiss the views of those –
      such as Wickham and Hilton – who argue for a slavery-to-serfdom transition. Accordingly,
      both 'eliminate the historical distinction between a middle ages dominated by a diver-
      sified servile labour-force exploited by estates which are not strictly bilateral [divided
      between landlord demesne and tenant holdings] and one characterized by manorial
      estates, labour-services and a renewed assault on the peasantry.'

distinctiveness of the period he claims existed from the end of late antiquity, one that preceded but led to the 'feudal reaction' of the eleventh and thirteenth centuries.[39]

Into this space Banaji decants a number of ideal types that are problematic in terms of Marxist theory: a 'mass of servile labour' that – contradictorily – was simultaneously free and unfree; a Chayanovian model of a 'pure' peasant economy; and an interpretation of slavery as being the *only* form of unfree production relation (= 'pure slaves'). Despite the fact that none of them are Marxist categories or interpretations, his case depends on each of these ideal types being a theoretically valid description of the phenomena to which they are applied. Whether each of these concepts – 'pure slavery' as the only form of unfree labour, 'pure peasantry', and 'servile labour' – together with the interpretation of transition they support, requires interrogation.

Feudalism, but Not Yet …

Trying to avoid making the link between tenancy/colonate and feudalism, Banaji sets up a distinction between 'peasant tenures' and 'allotments', the latter depicted almost as a form of 'hobby farming'.[40] The 'not-peasantness' of the latter is reinforced by the additional claim that allotments were 'an integral part of the estate system', as if 'peasant tenures' – or tenancies, when land was not owned by the smallholder but leased from a landlord – were in some economic sense wholly separated from the estate. In a bid to emphasize yet further this contention about 'not-peasantness', Banaji argues that the occupants of these allotments were 'a class of workers', composed of slaves and the free who were 'endowed with service-holdings rather than self-sufficient farms'. The term 'service-holdings' gives the game away, revealing as it does that its subject was indeed a tenant, the issue of self-sufficiency or otherwise notwithstanding.

---

39   Thus the kind of transition envisaged by Banaji (2010: 236–37) takes the form of 're-assembling what would later and only gradually become a peasantry proper [in the process throwing] up a vast array of intermediate categories between pure slaves and pure peasants, and it is this mass of servile labour that formed the backbone of élite-agriculture down to the feudal reaction of the eleventh to the thirteenth centuries and the imposition of serfdom.'

40   Hence the view (Banaji, 2010: 229) that 'the Merovingian *mansi* were not primarily peasant tenures but allotments … unlike the peasant-tenures … these allotments were still an integral part of the Merovingian *Gutwirtschaft* and their occupants a class of workers, both slaves and freedpeople, endowed with service-holdings rather than self-sufficient farms.'

In order to sustain the historical space inserted between late antiquity and feudalism, therefore, it is necessary for Banaji to adopt an ideal type of 'self-sufficient small peasantry': a definition that was unconnected either with tenants or with feudal serfs, enabling the assertion that estate labour was composed of landless workers residing there, and not peasants who were tenants. Not the least difficulty with such an interpretation is that it is based on the late-nineteenth century concept of the Russian peasant family farm associated with the neopopulist theory of Chayanov, for whom the form taken by peasant economy was based on the demographic cycle (= the producer/consumer balance within the peasant family).[41] Unlike Marxist theory, which maintains that what happens in and to peasant economy is governed by an external dynamic – the economic system as a whole – that of Chayanov treats the peasant family farm as an hermetic unit, the reproduction of which is determined simply by an endogenous logic.[42] Having erected an ideal type – Chayanovian peasant economy – Banaji is then able to make three claims: that it did not exist in the period covered; that consequently neither did feudalism; and that the non-existence of an estate tenantry paying rent meant what existed was actually a 'worker' in receipt of a 'hidden wage', a form of 'disguised wage labour'.

However, this interpretation is faced with several difficulties. To begin with, the peasant economy argument of Banaji ignores the role of kinship, and the division of labour linking tenant and landlord: hence it would be the wife, brothers, sisters, sons, and daughters of the tenant who would discharge labour-service obligations on the demsne, while the male household head cultivated the holding. Accordingly, the absolute opposition between 'peasant tenure' and 'allotment' does not hold; this is because Banaji perceives the kinlessness division of labour as a zero-sum arrangement, whereby a single allotment-holder has to work full-time for the landlord, and therefore seemingly cannot obtain subsistence from production on his own behalf. Not only is this ironic, given his endorsement of a Chayanovian model of a peasant *family*

---

41   For more on Chayanov, see Chapter 8 this volume. Not the least of the many ironies is that reifying a Chayanovian ideal type of peasant economy admits within his framework the same concept of 'natural economy' to which Banaji (2001: 3) strongly objected earlier.

42   Some of the many criticisms made by Marxists of the way Chayanov (1966) interpreted peasant economy are outlined by Kerblay (1966a: lxix-lxxiv), Not only did Chayanov ignore the role of productive forces, together with their differential distribution among peasants, and conflate middle peasants and kulaks, but in his model value was not objectively determined, as it is for Marxism, but rather an subjective assessment (made by the individual members of the peasant family farm) as it was – and is – for neoclassical economists.

farm, but it also suggests that allotment is seen as nothing more than 'hobby farming'.

As important are the issues of payment levels, how these changed (or not) over time, to whom payments were made, and the units of labour-power such disbursements covered. Of particular significance is whether the payment received was for a single unit of labour-power in instances where labour-services were undertaken by a variety of kinsfolk, which – being so – can hardly be categorized as a wage, 'hidden' or 'disguised'. Where this is the case, then work done is not for a wage, as Banaji maintains, since payment does not cover the quantity of labour-power provided by tenant kin. Consequently, such work cannot be regarded as being remunerated for the sale of this commodity, but rather as labour-rent due for the lease of land.

Free but Tied?

No concept generates quite as much difficulty for the arguments Banaji seeks to make – both about antiquity, feudalism, capitalism, and the transitions to and from each of these systemic forms – as does the distinction between free and unfree labour-power. As in the case of peasant-not-tenant, a view sustained only by insisting unfeasibly on a 'pure' kind of peasant economy that excludes all non-owning cultivators (tenant, sharecropper), so Banaji perceives only slavery as being unfree labour, similarly excluding all other kinds of work arrangement (debt bondage, attached labour), designated by him as 'free'.[43] The kinds of problem resulting from this interpretation are impossible to miss. Hence the notion of slavery as the only form of unfree labour (= 'pure slaves') generates yet more confusion, resulting in curious terms such as 'free but tied *coloni*'.[44] Seemingly oblivious to the history of the debate about this

---

43   The claim by Banaji (2010: 9) that 'no historians of late antiquity have ever invoked slavery as the fundamental reason for the fall of the western empire' is quite simply wrong. Among the historians who have made precisely this claim is Walbank (1946), who attributed the decline to how the cheapness of slaves prevented the occurrence of a labour-displacing technological breakthrough that would have enhanced the level of the productive forces. A consequence of cheap/unfree labour-power being available was a wider process of impoverishment, underconsumption, and retardation, leading in turn to economic crisis, ruralisation, and decentralisation that in turn paved the way for the eventual transition to feudalism.

44   See Banaji (2010: 234, 238), who elaborates: '*Coloni* were a category of permanent farm-labour which the government sought to tie to estates in the general interests of fiscal efficiency. They were free persons in the legal sense that they were not slaves, but restricted

odd free-but-not-free relational form, and his own part in it, Banaji maintains that 'on the heated issue of the *colonatus* a minor orthodoxy has emerged in late antique studies which consciously seeks to downplay the element of coercion that characterized the subordination of these workers.'[45] Not only was the latter view one he espoused previously, but it is also the way neoclassical economic theory – not Marxism – interprets such work arrangements.

In a 2003 article he dismissed the case made for unfree labour as a production relation, revealingly labelled by him 'so-called' (= non-existent), maintaining that as coercion is ubiquitous, and applies to all forms of working arrangement, there is – and can be – no difference between free and unfree labour.[46] This, he argued further, was the view of Marxist theory. Regardless of whether or not they were paid, Banaji at this stage opposed the conceptualization of bonded labour as an unfree production relation, insisting that all such relational forms are 'disguised wage-labour', to which he then appended the term 'free'.[47] His argument was directed at another Marxist approach: the latter took the form of theory about deproletarianization, which argues that in the course of class struggle capital restructures its workforce by replacing free labour with unfree equivalents, a process of workforce decomposition/recomposition.[48] Where such workers, who earlier have personally commodified

---

in their movements and subject increasingly to social downgrading and control of their employers ...'

45   In an accompanying footnote, Banaji (2010: 234, n. 83) complains that in a contribution to *The Cambridge Economic History of the Greco-Roman World* published in 2007, Andrea Giardini 'reproaches me with failing to see that the late-Roman *coloni* were unfree'. Interestingly, this is exactly the same criticism of Banaji as that made by me in 2003, both Giardini and I being of the view that Banaji did indeed regard the *coloni* as 'free labour', and that consequently he was one of those who downplayed 'the element of coercion that characterized the subordination of the workers.'

46   Banaji (2003).

47   The theoretical problem with the concept 'disguised' wage labour, deployed by Banaji in debates about the mode of production and late antiquity, is clear. Because it reifies the wage, this term confuses the fact of payment made to a worker (= wage labour) with labour-power that is free. The two aspects are, of course, distinct: one has to do with the kind of production relation linking a worker to his/her employer, while the other concerns the form taken by the remuneration for labour expended. Epistemologically, the problem generated by conflating payment of a wage with labour-power that is free is obvious. Throughout history many different kinds of worker who were relationally unfree nevertheless received payment whilst in the employ of another. That they were paid did not of itself signal the presence of labour-power that was free, as many examples of payments made to workers who were also chattel slaves, indentured labourers, debt peons and attached or bonded, all attest.

48   Brass (1999).

their own labour-power cease to be able to do so, what has occurred, this Marxist approach contends, is a relational transformation that corresponds to deproletarianization.

Responding to Banaji, a defence of the deproletarianization approach published elsewhere but in the same year, not only rebutted the case made by him, but also challenged his theoretical affinity with Marxism, pointing out that his assumptions and concepts were much rather based on bourgeois economics.[49] Central to this defence was the view that Banaji conceptualized free labour in the same way as neoclassical economic historiography, not the way Marxism does.[50] Utilizing marginalist theory about freedom of contract, he equated a free production relation with the capacity of a labourer simply to enter an employment arrangement: that such a worker is then unable to withdraw from the relation is for Banaji of no consequence. Marxism, however, interprets wage labour that is free, and thus constitutive of its subject being a proletarian, somewhat differently: as the ability not just to enter a work relation but also to leave it. What is important for Marxism in defining a work arrangement, therefore, is the reproduction of the *whole* relation (entry into + exit from). Accordingly, in cases where a worker enters a contract voluntarily, but is subsequently unable to exit from it, the production relation is not – and cannot be regarded as being – free in the sense understood by Marxist theory.

Contradicting the position held in his 2001 book, where he denied that bonded labour was unfree, claiming it meant only that its subject was tied to land, therefore, Banaji now accepts that 'in practice everyone understood that tying workers to the soil meant attaching them to their employer.'[51] The reason for imposing such restrictions has also been amended, since he admits that labour-tying stemmed from the fear by landowners who 'stood to lose a younger labour-force if they could not ... stop such individuals from pursuing

---

49   For this response, defending the deproletarianization approach, see Brass (2003a).

50   Maintaining in effect that there is no such thing as unfree labour, Banaji equates the latter with nineteenth-century liberal ideas about freedom as consent. All historical working arrangements are conceptualized simply as 'disguised' wage-labour that is free, a theoretically problematic claim first made during the Indian mode of production debate. Such a view ignores the fact that unfree workers get paid and also appear in the labour market, but not as sellers of their own commodity. By abolishing the free/unfree labour distinction, and adopting instead the view that all rural workers are 'disguised' hired labourers who are contractually 'free', Banaji aligns himself with neoclassical economic historiography (Robert Steinfeld, Robert Fogel, Stanley Engerman). This is why his claims to be a Marxist, and more broadly about what is and what is not Marxist theory, should be treated with caution.

51   For the original claim, see Banaji (2001: 210–11); for the contrasting view held now, see Banaji (2010: 197–98).

their freedom' by seeking better-paid jobs elsewhere.[52] In an effort to rescue his case based on the production relation between the slave of antiquity and the serf of feudalism being that of a 'worker', Banaji opts for another definition, that of 'half free' labour, 'an intermediate status' between free and slave.[53] However, much like its free-but-not-free counterpart, this 'half-free' characterization is not merely not part of Marxist theory but also fails epistemologically to replace the usual production relations informing political economy (serfdom, bonded labour, tenancy, sharecropping or the *colonatus*).

Workers, or Tenants?

Problems conceptualizing a peasant economy that is 'pure' are replicated in the case of what Banaji terms 'servile labour'. The latter is a vague, catch-all term, amounting in effect to nothing more than people-who-work, an amorphous category that soon runs into trouble when he tries to present its subjects as 'more proletarian than peasant-like'.[54] This opens the door to concepts like 'disguised wage-labour', and with it the claim that – just as in the case of antiquity – feudalism is really a form of capitalism. Accordingly, it is when he attempts to characterize 'the rural labour-force in the post-Roman West' that the differences between Banaji and Wickham emerge. Whereas Banaji regards 'slaves and freedpeople provided with plots of land as *workers*', Wickham sees them as peasants.[55] That it is the latter designation (of Wickham) which is correct, and not the former one (advocated by Banaji), is evident from the

---

52   Seemingly in line with criticism (Brass, 2003a) of his original position, Banaji (2010: 196) now agrees that 'landowners stood to lose a younger labour-force if they could not ... stop such individuals from pursuing their freedom, that is, migrating from estates that would otherwise hold them down as tied labourers.'

53   See Banaji (2010: 196, 227).

54   This claim surfaces and is emphasized constantly (Banaji, 2010: 200, 206, 207, 216, 229, 230–31, 234, 235, original emphases). 'A substantial part of the rural labour-force of the sixth to eighth or even ninth, centuries', one is informed, 'comprised groups who ... were *more proletarian than peasant-like*'. Subsequently, '[t]he main point ... is that the typical Merovingian estate exploited a *landless* workforce.' Again, such labourers 'were a a class of farm-workers'; 'bound together by their common condition of landlessness and servility ... the best characterization we have of the rural labour-force in the centuries between the fall of the Western empire and the imposition of serfdom [is] as farm workers and a class distinct from the peasantry'. Yet again, *coloni* existed 'into the sixth century but were increasingly absorbed into a less and less differentiated labour-force that I have characterized as "servile"'. And so on and so forth.

55   Banaji (2010: 189, original emphasis).

characteristics attributed by Banaji himself to those he terms 'workers'. Hence the claim that estates had 'a resident labour-force' – that is, composed of 'groupings of workers within the estate' – is itself qualified by a footnote on the same page indicating that they 'were given land as wages': in short, they were *tenants*.[56] Similarly, around the year 600 the rural labour-force in the eastern provinces of the Roman empire 'is best described as a landless peasantry that survived on short-term leases or by labour-tenancy on the large estates'.[57]

Sensing, finally, that his interpretation of the transition to feudalism was in trouble, and that those he criticized may be right after all, Banaji nevertheless tries to prevent his analysis from unravelling.[58] To this end he insists on the necessity of eschewing 'abstraction' when defining production relations, a criticism aimed both at Wickham and at other Marxists; not the least ironical view about this defence, however, is his own deployment of reified concepts such as 'pure' slavery and a 'pure' peasantry.[59] In an endeavour to rescue his argument, Banaji indicates a willingness to compromise, and accept the hybrid designation 'worker-tenants' rather than tenants, a 'solution' that resolves nothing.[60] What he still appears to misunderstand is that tenants/*coloni* get access to land on condition that they provide its owner with work, an arrangement that commits the lessee to deliver a stipulated quantity of days of labour-service per month. So work is anyway part of a tenancy agreement on the rural estate, an

---

56   On this, see Banaji (2010: 207, n.128). This uncertainty about the characterization of production relations is reflected also in the fact that at some points the view of Bloch about the labour regime on the estate system is endorsed, but criticized at others (Banaji, 2010: 193, 198, 226, 239).

57   Banaji (2010: 215).

58   A growing feeling of desperation, as the specificity of his characterization dissolves, is difficult to ignore. 'Now, viewed teleologically, in terms of some inexorable evolution towards the manor and its eventual triumph,' he observes (Banaji, 2010: 238), 'the allotment-holders of the post-Roman/early-medieval countryside may seem like a transitional type, a sort of station between two terminals, one called Antiquity, the other Feudalism; or, if you prefer, between Slavery and Serfdom.' This concession is followed immediately by reasserting the aptness of his own view: 'But this, I suggest, is absolutely the wrong way of approaching the issue.'

59   In a case of the pot calling the kettle back, Banaji (2010: 237) asserts '[t]hat a more substantial or autonomous peasantry existed or was emerging is incontrovertible (the feudal reaction would be incomprehensible without it), but to understand its emergence we have to describe the context of the relations of production within which it developed with less abstraction and certainly less schematically than either Wickham or an earlier generation of Marxists have tended to do.'

60   'If we choose to call them tenants', concedes Banaji (2010: 238, original emphasis), 'then *worker-tenants* is a better description of these groups than the tenants that Wickham seems to have in mind.'

intrinsic aspect of production relations involving tenants, not some indication
of proletarian status or hired wage-labour.

According to Banaji, two distinct forms of labour organization were deployed
on the estate system during the era of feudalism proper: that deployed either
by the landlord demesne or by 'an autonomous small peasant producer'.[61] It
is a method of framing the distinction that paves the way for discarding feudalism and replacing it with capitalism. The logic of his argument depends
on recasting the tenant – whose access to land is conditional on the payment
of rent, and consequently is not and cannot be regarded as an independent
proprietor – simply as 'an autonomous small peasant producer, an enterprise
of small peasant production'. Reproduced within the non-demesne sector of
the feudal estate, therefore, is nothing other than the Chayanovian model of
peasant economy. Having conceptually substituted this kind of 'autonomous'
smallholding enterprise for that of the economically-dependent tenant, Banaji
then recasts peasant economy yet further, arguing that – under feudalism
proper – even when the simple commodity enterprise not only undertakes
cultivation on its own land but also gets to sell the product of this endeavour, it
is 'a quasi-enterprise with the specific social function of wage-labour'.[62]

What the smallholding rural producer receives as a result of this sale,
Banaji insists, is actually 'a concealed wage', since 'behind the superficial
"surface" sale of products, peasants under this form of domination sell their
labour-power'. By this legerdemain a rural proprietor who cultivates his/her
own land and sells the output thereof – to all intents and purposes selling the
product of labour and not labour-power itself – is transformed by Banaji into
a 'disguised wage-labourer'.[63] In a sense this is an epistemologically necessary

---

61   Banaji (1976: 302–3).
62   See Banaji (1977: 34), according to whom a petty commodity producer does not actually
      have to sell his/her own labour-power in order to be categorized as being in receipt of a
      'hidden wage', and thus a 'disguised wage-labourer'. The wage element is simply imputed
      to the economic activity in question, whatever it might be. This goes against the distinc-
      tion made by Marxist theory, which distinguishes between a peasant selling the product
      of labour from one selling labour-power itself. This difference, central to the process of
      peasant differentiation on which Marxism bases its case about class formation, class con-
      sciousness, and class struggle, underwrites in turn the dynamic entailing a transition from
      feudalism to capitalism, and from the latter to socialism. It is anyway hard to see how a
      CEO of a multinational corporation, who not only receives payment for what s/he does,
      but also insists that – as in the case of his employees – it is no more than just remunera-
      tion for his/her labour, could on the criterion invoked by Banaji, not also be categorized
      as a 'disguised wage-labourer'. Indeed, currently this is the self-image of many highly paid
      capitalists who own/control global business empires.
63   Those who remain unpersuaded by the 'disguised wage labour' argument of Banaji
      include Wickham, an historian whose pathbreaking research into and understanding of

recategorization, in that it prefigures – and indeed clears the way for – the corollary. From this preceding relay-in-statement, therefore, it is but a short step to his next claim: that the production relation encountered in the feudal estate, one that Banaji recasts and essentializes as 'disguised wage-labour', itself signals the presence of the sort of capitalism now claimed by him to be a pan-historical form.

III

Tracking back through what Banaji has written over the decades is an experience akin to trying to describe the colour of a chameleon which refuses to remain in a single hue for more than a couple of seconds. Hence the difficulty confronting anyone examining the case made by Banaji about anything is the frequency with which he changes his mind. What he takes Marxism to be is subject to constant alteration, so much so that it is almost impossible to state categorically that a view to which Banaji subscribes on a particular day will be the same one he holds on the day following. Over the years he has endorsed – and then dropped – a number of modes: semi-feudalism, the 'colonial' mode, the peasant mode, and the tributary mode.[64] To these he now adds yet more: the Late Antique economy is labelled by him as a case, variously, of 'proto-industrialization', 'proto-modernity', 'quasi-capitalism', or 'commercial capitalism'. Unfree labour, dismissed out of hand by Banaji in 2003 as 'so-called' (= nonexistent), re-emerges in analyses published during 2007/2008, now no longer 'so-called' but an epistemologically acceptable form of production relation.[65]

---

feudalism is intellectually and methodologically somewhat more rigorous than that of Banaji. Wickham (2021: 12, note 13) is surely right when he observes that 'I resist Banaji's [claim] that some peasant tenures were so circumscribed by lords, and so difficult to live off, that they really constituted a 'wage in land', and can thus be assimilated to wage-labour; as far as I can see, most of these examples [referenced in the article by Wickham] were still subsistence, peasant, cultivation.'

64   For details, see Brass (2003a, 2012). During the mode of production debate, Banaji originally commended the semi-feudal thesis as the analytical way forward. It was only when another contributor to that debate pointed out the errors of his analysis that he changed his mind, and came out against the view he had originally advocated. Banaji did exactly the same over the colonial mode of production, which he initially advocated, only changing his mind – again – when the mistaken theory he was so enthusiastic about was criticized by others subsequently. None of the modes Banaji claims exists is found in Marx; neither is Banaji's own interpretation of modes of production, based as it is largely on monetary expansion.

65   Compare Banaji (2003) with Banaji (2010: Chapter 7), between which appeared the response by Brass (2003a).

Modes and Beams

Significantly, not least in the light of the view he now holds, Banaji earlier derided historians who maintained that capitalism existed in ancient Rome.[66] Terms such as 'bourgeoisie' and 'entrepreneurs' applied to 'groups of capitalists' who were engaged in economic activity such as investing in land and labour were dismissed by him initially as unjustifiable 'clichés in Roman historiography'.[67] Four decades on, however, these very same 'clichés in Roman historiography' are ones to which Banaji himself currently subscribes: as will be seen below, his view now is that capitalists were ever-present throughout ancient Rome, the economy of which was 'organized on capitalist lines'. Much the same is true of the way the role of merchant capital has metamorphosed. Originally, therefore, when addressing the components of feudalism, Banaji expressed agreement with Marx that merchant capital extracts surplus labour from small peasants, the mode of production being 'not yet determined by capital, but rather found on hand by it'.[68] On this, too, it seems that he has changed his mind, since now merchant capital has become for him a pan-historical form determining both economic activity and social organization of the labour process in every known mode of production.

---

66 Castigating Marxists such as Hilton, Dobb, and Sweezy, plus other historians, for what he regards as too abstract a definition of feudalism, Banaji (1976: 300) proceeds to identify what he deems to be a parallel and similarly mistaken interpretation: 'For a long time the history of classical antiquity worked with a similar illusion: what impressed the historians of the Roman world was the formal existence of capital, the fact that groups of capitalists were well-attested for the late Republic and early Empire, that they "invested" heavily in various speculative forms of activity, from the supply of slave-labour to the buying and selling of land or the "farming" of provinces. "Bourgeoisie", "entrepreneurs", "slave-holding capitalism" became clichés in Roman historiography.'

67 After this date, scorn for those who place capitalism in ancient Rome is not heard of again. It is absent both from an article dealing with much the same issue published the following year (Banaji, 1977), and also from the version of the latter reproduced subsequently in book form (Banaji, 2010: Chapter 2).

68 See Banaji (1976: 301) who elaborates: 'A given mode of production *in its crystallized or adequate form* posits not simply its typical enterprise, but this enterprise functioning to a process of labour which corresponds immanently to its inherent motion. Only in these conditions is it possible to speak of the productive agent as *master* of the labour process' (original emphasis). What he defends here is nothing less than Marx's theory about how 'perfection' in the case of accumulation ('its crystallized or adequate form') is reached only when industrial capital has taken charge (= 'master') of the labour process. This is a view he has discarded in favour of an essentialist model of merchant capital.

This problem of a constantly shifting viewpoint is itself compounded by additional and interrelated difficulties. To begin with, his failure to ask what his sources mean by terms they use, the assumption being that all concepts follow a uniform meaning, in accord with the way Banaji himself interprets them. Rather than considering in detail what is contained in the records located in the archives, Banaji all too often relies on what is said to be the case by those who have done this. Missed thereby are the assumptions guiding analyses which have looked at the primary data, assumptions which cannot but inform what the records are said to contain, and the arguments supported or negated as a result.[69] As significant is his hostility towards any prefiguring analyses by Marxists, not least those by Marx himself. Instead Banaji invokes non- or anti-Marxist sources – regarded by him as positive – in support of what he claims is a Marxist approach to the issues being considered.[70]

Most difficult in methodological terms is the way he resorts to comparison when upholding or rejecting a case being made: this involves skipping from one place or conjuncture to another and completely different one, thereby conflating what are distinct histories, contexts (locations, regions, countries), and periods.[71] In a sense, this is a necessary procedure, since by constantly rejecting interpretations for their supposed 'abstraction' or 'formalism' Banaji is driven into a corner of his own making: championing empiricism. Not the least ironical result is that, in the absence of evidence for the case he seeks to make Banaji resorts to comparison across time and space. Hence the parallel drawn by him with the Latin American *hacienda* because the Roman estate 'exploited a landless workforce comparable [to] the *gañanes* in Mexico'.[72] Describing the latter as a 'landless workforce' is incorrect, however, since *gañanes* were

---

69 This does not prevent Banaji (2010: 185, 189, 201) from describing texts he agrees with in positive terms ('seminal', 'convincing') and those he disagrees with in negative terms ('reiterated').

70 The list of non- or anti-Marxist theorists regarded by Banaji as having made positive contributions to the matter in hand is very long, and extends from neo-classical economists and cliometric historiography to Cold Warriors (Alexander Chayanov, Witold Kula, Arnold Bauer, Robert Fogel, Stanley Engerman, Richard Pipes, Karl Wittfogel).

71 Criticizing the view of Pirenne who 'saw the survival of the large estate as the decisive link between the post-Roman world and the middle ages proper', Banaji (2010: 205) maintains that a better model for that time is that of landed properties let to 'entrepreneur[s] engaged in short-term financial speculation who assumed the management of the estate for the period of the lease'. In a note at the bottom of the same page, however, one is informed that the model in question refers to 'early twentieth-century Apulia'!

72 See Banaji (2010: 226), who makes the same comparison subsequently (Banaji, 2018: 153–54).

tenants to whom the proprietors of large estates in Mexico leased land: in short, *gañanes* were not as Banaji supposes a 'landless workforce'.[73]

As problematic is the confusing manner in which chronology features in the historical process Banaji attempts to trace. At one point, therefore, he states that 'the watershed that divides Roman from late Roman history' occurred in the fourth century; later, however, the concept of a watershed – an historical conjuncture at which a fundamental break occurs – is shifted forward, to the seventh century.[74] Compounded by uncertainty as to the nature of production relations, what are presented as specific forms – 'pure' slavery, 'servile tenantry', 'tied labour', 'pure' peasantry, serfdom – appear, disappear, and then reappear across an era stretching from the fourth to the eleventh century. Again, the irony is unmissable: Banaji objects to a periodization whereby a single production relation (tenancy) lasts for a thousand years, but himself has no qualms about claiming that a single relational form ('disguised wage-labour') has existed for two thousand years.[75]

How Do We Know?

It is only when the evidence Banaji claims exists is scrutinized that real difficulties emerge. Time after time, therefore, reference is made to proof furnished by archaeological data without asking what such evidence (not presented) can tell us.[76] Assertions concerning the occurrence of an 'archaeological revolution' remain unaccompanied by explanations as to what precisely it actually demonstrates.[77] Maybe because of this one encounters an occasionally tentative observation ('My own feeling is ...'), together with equally sporadic admissions concerning the lack of evidence/data/information corroborating the argument, claim, or case that Banaji is making.[78] Ironically, he questions

---

73   On this point, see Góngora (1975: 152–53) and Duncan, Rutledge, and Harding (1977: 37). What this underlines is the danger of making a comparison with what for Banaji is an unfamiliar agrarian context.

74   See Banaji (2010: 185, 244).

75   This objection by Banaji (2010: 231) is aimed at Wickham.

76   See Banaji (2018: 8–9), who announces early on that he does not intend to discuss his sources (Banaji, 2018: xvii). For similar references to this sort of evidence, along the lines of 'the archaeology has now made a decisive difference to the way economic histories should be written', see Banaji (2018: 11, 18).

77   Banaji (2018: 62–63).

78   These kinds of admission are encountered intermittently. Thus he (Banaji, 2018: xv, 58, 68–9, 78 original emphasis) accepts the absence/paucity of data/sources for his concept 'private economy' (contracts, accounts, correspondence), plus other similar references

the case made by the decline thesis on the grounds of 'how do we know?', forgetting perhaps that this very question has been raised about the claims he himself makes.

Because of a tendency to base his account on particular sources, many of the claims made by Banaji consequently rest on an equally narrow range of opinion, the epistemology, politics, and methodology of which never surface, let alone are interrogated. Not only does the narrative skip from one geographical context to another, and from one historical conjuncture to another, but the focus throughout is mainly on the advantages/disadvantages of trade rivalry and business practices.[79] Surprisingly for an analysis deemed to be Marxist, in his most recent book not much is said about production and next to nothing about relations of production. Scattered throughout the narrative are passing references to unexplored or hastily consulted sources, along the lines of '[t]he following pages summarize some of the historical work ...', 'as the following rapid survey of examples shows', '[o]f particular note, not highlighted here', '[n]one of this has been mapped here', and 'descriptions of this sort could be multiplied almost indefinitely if one consulted a wider range of sources than I have, but they seem quite enough to me to suggest ...'.[80]

This problem is itself compounded by two interrelated points. Hence the lack of references to 'commercial capitalism' is ascribed by Banaji to 'Marxist reticence' on the part of English-language historiography, the inference being that for some reason Marxists have ignored the concept.[81] There is, however, an alternative explanation: since 'the historians listed [included] only a handful [who] were consciously working in a Marxist tradition', this dearth may be due to the absence from their analyses of what is a Marxist concept. Linked to this is the acceptance by Banaji that his own 'forms of capitalism' were not ones found in Marx, because the latter 'had never properly discussed [them]'. In short, they too may not actually be Marxist. Underlined thereby are the

---

along the lines of 'we have no way of quantifying the role of direct grants of land', '[o]ne reason there is so little explicit evidence of this side of their economic activities ...', and '[t]he dispersion of merchant colonies throughout the Mediterranean *may* imply a transformation of commerce ... [t]he famous financier ... was bound to have had late antique counterparts, but we know almost nothing about them'.

79 So much so that at times support for the argument – for example, Banaji (2020: 96) – resembles evidence drawn from a compendium of business histories. It comes as no surprise that a similarity exists between the approach of Banaji and that of Maher (2021): the latter, described as 'written from a practical business perspective', also finds numerous parallels between present-day capitalism and the economy of ancient Rome.

80 Banaji (2020: 89–98, 108, 119, 131).

81 Banaji (2020: 8).

difficulties raised by a failure to address the methodological and theoretical aspects of work and/or texts cited approvingly.[82] Dismissing what he categorizes as 'Western Marxism', all that remains is no longer recognizable as politically leftist, let alone Marxist.[83]

The second point concerns difficulties linked to the general invisibility in his latest book of production relations.[84] A failure to differentiate weaving in terms of class leads Banaji to connect the merchant as bearer of commercial capital directly to the weaver as producer, with the result that the latter appears tied to the former in an unmediated way.[85] However, there are two

---

82   Not the least important consideration is what do those using the term 'commercial capitalism' understand by this, and is there a theoretical consistency across all its usages (one suspects not)? In most instances the term appears to be nothing more than shorthand for trade, which certainly occurred in pre-capitalist systems; however, this is not the same as saying trade = capitalism, which is how Banaji interprets it.

83   Claiming that 'Marx's Capital remains incomplete', creating thereby an epistemological space into which then to place his own views, Banaji (1979: 40) seemingly rejects the theoretical legitimacy of Marxist analyses simply on the grounds that that they are 'Western'. Hence the assertion by him that '[w]hat is remarkable here is not that Marx should have left the book incomplete but that close to four generations of Marxists should have done so ... one of the most striking manifestations of the underlying crisis in the movement as a whole is the contemporary state of Western Marxism – the ecstatic leap from the uppermost floors of an imposing skyscraper of immobilised dogma to the granite pavements of confused eclecticism.'

84   On the question of the acceptability to capital of production relations that are unfree, Banaji appears to have changed his mind. A decade ago, Banaji (2010) declared abolished the free/unfree distinction as applied to production relations like debt bondage, indenture, and sharecropping, on the grounds that all rural workers – in late antiquity no less than modern capitalism – are simply hired labourers who are contractually free. Since the latter relation was present throughout ancient society, he concluded that capitalism itself must be an eternal systemic form. Now, however, it seems that even when it is reproduced by capital, Banaji (2020: 109) no longer regards unfree labour as 'so-called' (= non-existent).

85   Banaji (2020: 60–61, 88–89). Because he misunderstands the division of labour, Banaji assumes that the only link of consequence is that between the small putting-out unit or 'cottage industry' and the merchant, the latter exercising organizational power over the former. However, the capacity to organize production – when this is not done by a master-weaver himself (see below) – is a task that the local merchant or middle-man (= broker) discharges on behalf of a much larger and more powerful industrial capitalist enterprise. This is particularly important where the chain of command extends from the metropolis to a distant colony, and those on the ground possess 'local knowledge'. To regard the latter as evidence for autonomous control exercised by a local contractor or merchant – as does Banaji (2020: 102, 104, 105–6) – is not correct. What is perceived by him simply as putting-out by merchant capital is in the era of globalization a process of restructuring, outsourcing, and relocation – on which see Brass (1999, 2011) – undertaken by manufacturing industry in order to cut labour costs and thus restore, maintain, or increase profitability.

categories of weaver: the master-weaver owning the means of production, and the weavers who – as bonded labour – work for him. In such instances, the subject who controls/organizes/operates the means of production is not the merchant, who merely advances the cash to set the labour process in motion and collects the product at the other end, but the master-weaver.[86] Moreover, and as Chayanov indicated with regard to peasant farmers (see below), some better-off producers (like master-weavers) are on occasion able to free themselves from control exercised by a merchant – especially when backed by the state, a weaving cooperative, or industrial capital – and as a result generate sufficient funds to set their own labour process in motion.

Since the Beginning of the World

Initially depicting Marx as an adherent of the revisionist interpretation, Banaji claims that as Marx, too, saw merchant capital as dominant – even as industrial capitalism developed – he can be said to share the same view. Accepting that Marx insisted on an 'unbreachable separation' between merchant and industrial capital, Banaji nevertheless asserts both that 'there are clear indications [Marx] would *not* have reacted with horror to the idea that merchant capitalists might "dominate production directly"', and that consequently Marx 'allowed for a more active role for commercial capital'.[87] Nevertheless, almost immediately Banaji accepts that Marx did not posit 'a distinct form of accumulation that one could identify as *merchant* capitalism specifically'.[88] Unsurprisingly, therefore, the effort to conscript Marx for his own cause is overturned, as Banaji subsequently reinstates his original critique.[89] Reversing even this, and generating yet more confusion, the latter part of his most recent book appears to concede what it started out by denying: that industrial capital does indeed end up by subordinating its commercial equivalent.[90]

Despite the attempt by Banaji to recruit Marx himself to his own view about the subordination of industrial capital to merchant capital, evidence suggests

---

86 On the division of labour between weaver and a master-weaver who is still an artisan, see Marx (1976: 1029–30; 1981; 1981: 451ff.).

87 Banaji (2020: 8–9, 10, original emphasis).

88 Banaji (2020: 11, original emphasis).

89 See Banaji (2020: 85, original emphasis), where he states that 'Marx's own recurring characterization of commercial capital as inexorably subordinate to industry and to industrial capital obscures the fact that historically a wide range of industries worked *for* merchant's capital'.

90 Banaji (2020: 121–22).

otherwise. In volume II of *Capital*, for example, Marx describes both commercial capital as the 'primary form of which is always money, since the merchant as such does not produce any "product" or "commodity"', and money capital as 'the object of manipulation of a special kind of capitalist, in the circulation process of industrial capital'.[91] In the third volume Marx refers to Kiessellbach, who holds a view similar to that of Banaji, as 'still living in a mental world where commercial capital is the general form of capital', and consequently as 'not [having] the slightest suspicion of the modern meaning of capital, as little as Herr Mommsen when he speaks of "capital" and the rule of capital in his *Römische Geschichte*'.[92] The strength of feeling Marx had about this issue is also evident from his commendation of Richard Jones, who 'by no means shares the illusion that capital has been in existence since the beginning of the world.'[93]

Nowhere is this break with Marxist theory more evident than in the way the process of subsumption is interpreted. To begin with, Banaji links subsumption – an act of complete economic subordination – simply to commercial capital, and not to capital *per se*, as Marx himself argued. Speaking of mid-nineteenth century India, Banaji maintains that '[p]easant family labour was the productive base of most of the produce trades, and its *subsumption into commercial capital* through the channels of circulation described here involved the appropriation of vast amounts of unpaid family labour.'[94] However, this is not the way Marx used the term. Consequently, the large amount of unpaid labour extracted accrues not to commercial capital (as Banaji claims) but rather to capital *per se* (as Marx shows).

Furthermore, Banaji fails to differentiate the concept internally, between its two distinct – and historically significant – components. Accordingly, subsumption to capital is defined by Marx as either formal or real.[95] Formal refers to capital using the labour process 'as it finds it', with absolute surplus-value extracted by the usurer who, although providing materials/tools/money, does not intervene in the production process. This variant, as Marx pointed out, is encountered in pre-capitalist systems. By contrast, real subsumption occurs when there are changes in the division of labour, machinery and technical

---

91   Marx (1978: 497).
92   Marx (1981: 444–45, n.46). This criticism of Mommsen is significant, in that – like Banaji himself – he equates the commercial variant with capital *per se*, as a result of which Mommsen ends up locating capitalism in ancient Rome, again much like Banaji.
93   Marx (1972: 399).
94   Banaji (2020: 110, original emphasis).
95   Marx (1976: 1019–38).

inputs are deployed, and relative surplus-value is extracted. Capital has now 'taken over control of production', and 'the merchant turns into an industrial capitalist,' *not* the other way round, as Banaji maintains is the case. For real subsumption to be in place, therefore, 'the capitalist must be the owner or proprietor of the means of production.' It is this variant that is confined to – and, indeed, signals the presence of – industrial capitalism.

Banaji also tries to enlist the Russian Marxist historian Pokrovsky to his cause, insisting that he, too, was an ardent exponent of the 'commercial capitalism' approach, suppressed by 1930s Stalinism. However, it is clear from the source Banaji cites in support of this claim that Pokrovsky did not in fact hold the view attributed to him.[96] Having tried, unsuccessfully, to co-opt both Marx and Pokrovsky, Banaji then attempts to do the same with the Russian neopopulist Chayanov, claiming the latter represents not just a 'major breakthrough of theory' but also and somewhat contradictorily 'an innovation in Marxist theory'.[97] According to Banaji, therefore, Chayanov showed that merchant capital effected a vertical concentration of the peasant family farm, in the process subordinating it economically to commercial firms ('Vertical concentration was how commercial capitals established a degree of control over rural households and their labour powers'). Not only does this ignore the antinomy between class differentiation of the peasantry that informs Marxism and the homogeneous smallholder of populism, but it also overlooks the fact that Chayanov qualified his view, indicating how the better-off agrarian unit 'frees itself from any influence of trading capital'.[98]

Conclusion

Running through the analyses by Banaji is a single thread: ranging across a variety of different modes (antiquity, feudalism), each relational form he

---

96   'About the exact character of "commercial capitalism"', notes Barber (1981: 59), 'Pokrovsky was more than a little vague ... P.I.Kushner in May 1929 correctly observed that Pokrovsky "nowhere calls commercial capitalism a specific formation" ... It was certainly not part of his case that the central features of classical capitalism – large-scale industry, proletariat, bourgeoisie – were also typical of commercial capitalism'.

97   See Banaji (10–12, 99) and Chayanov (1966).

98   See Chayanov (1966: 263–64, emphasis added), who notes both that funding was provided by states or industrial capitalists, and that 'control of trade, elevator, irrigation, credit, and processing undertakings that concentrate and guide agricultural production in part or in whole belongs, *not to the holders of capital*, but to organized small commodity producers who have contributed their own capital to these undertakings ...'

encounters, whatever it might be (slavery, bonded labour, *coloni*, tenant, small-holder, 'peasant tenures') is recast by him as nothing more than 'disguised wage-labour'. This is turn paves the way for two additional claims: first, that what has existed throughout history is capitalism; and second, that the ubiquitous variant incorporating all modes corresponds simply to merchant capital. Although Banaji always begins by disclaiming a connection between modern and ancient capitalism, he quickly eradicates any such difference, and maintains that what exists in late antiquity is indeed capitalism. In a sense this ought not to surprise, since he claims to have found the presence in ancient society of all the characteristics and processes associated with capitalism. Hence the coupling at that conjuncture of wage-labour (designated by him wrongly as 'free'), 'new' sorts of producer (landowners who invested in means of production), and gold (wrongly seen as used to pay workers).

Rather than defining feudalism in terms of a single rent-taking form, Banaji maintains that every mode actually contains a plurality of relational forms, wrongly interpreted by him as evidence for the fact that 'peasant tenures' of every kind were no more than a 'wages in land'. Resident on the estates was a workforce he defined as both landless and a form of 'servile labour': because the latter was akin to 'disguised wage-labour', the production relation was not that of a tenant but much rather of a 'worker'. For this reason, insists Banaji, the kind of labour-power a landlord employed on the estate must be conceptualised as being that of a proletariat. This attempt to cast the 'worker' as an intermediate relational form, one that licensed a break separating the slave of antiquity from the serf of feudalism, constitutive of an historical space that is reducible to neither, is faced with a number of problems.

Not the least difficulty with Banaji's approach, is that what he presents as a hired labourer who is free turns out to be an unfree worker or peasant bonded by debt, a result of having to work off cash loans borrowed from employers. In other words, not the proletarian that is linked by Marxist theory to capitalist accumulation. However, it is necessary for Banaji to claim that such labour was not unfree, since – along with money and merchant capitalists – a free worker is crucial to his broader claim that capitalism was ever-present from late antiquity onwards. When he talks about a plurality of relational forms, therefore, this is misleading. It does not mean that, where feudalism is concerned, alongside labour-rent or payment-in-kind there are found other production relations like chattel slavery, bonded labour, or sharecropping. Much rather, all the latter are said by him to correspond to a single form: hired labour that is free ('disguised wage labour'), and consequently that what exists on the ground is a capitalist workforce.

The voluntary entry into a production relation, but the involuntary retention within it, means that the resulting work arrangement cannot be regarded as free. Overlooked thereby is the fact that labour-power bonded by debt is not a free production relation, and thus cannot be defined as belonging to a proletariat as understood by Marxism. Neither is it the case that the subjects of these production relations were landless, since the estates leased them holdings in exchange for which they provided landlords with labour-service. In short, they were tenants, and thus part of the colonate, forming an unbroken link between antiquity and feudalism, or the element of relational and historical continuity that Banaji is at such pains to deny.

All too often, the argument made by Banaji – now as earlier – is simply that wherever there is trade, there too is capitalism. In one crucial respect, however, the case he makes currently appears to have changed. Initially, therefore, the presence of capitalism was linked epistemologically to the characterization of 'those below', an approach based on the redefinition of peasants as workers. Conceptualizing smallholders as 'disguised wage-labour' enabled him to present them both as a workforce licensing capitalism, and consequently as evidence for the eternal presence historically of the accumulation process. Of late, this particular strand of the case seems to receive less emphasis, perhaps because of criticisms pointing out theoretical flaws in the characterization of the workforce, a result of his following a non-Marxist interpretation of production relations.

Now Banaji has adopted a different path in order to reach the same end: an analogous and similarly non-Marxist characterization, but this time of 'those above', whereby all capital is redefined as 'commercial capital', which – as before – permits him to argue that capitalism is historically ever-present. Unavoidable, therefore, is a somewhat baleful conclusion: for around four decades, he has tried repeatedly not so much to rewrite as to supplant Marxism, described by him as an 'immobilized dogma'. In the process all its core theoretical components have been discarded, and replaced either with reinterpretations as to what Marx really meant or (more usually) with versions of his own. On the basis of the case made in his latest books, the only remaining mystery is why Banaji is still perceived by some as a Marxist.

CHAPTER 4

Trajectories (To and from Unfreedom)

Debt, n. An ingenious substitute for the chain and whip of the slavedriver.

Freedman, n. A person whose manacles have sunk so deeply into the flesh that they are no longer visible.

> Definitions, no doubt humorous, by AMBROSE BIERCE as to the unrecognized but continuing efficacy of unfree labour.[1]

∴

Introduction: Quo Vadis, Domine?

What makes labour-power unfree, and whether or not such production relations are compatible with economic growth, are political issues that have a long historical lineage, particularly where the focus of debate has been on the development of capitalism. It is precisely in the course of the latter process – the struggle between capital and labour – that the free/unfree distinction becomes significant, not least for Marxist analysis of what nowadays is categorized as 'globalization'.[2] Although never dormant as an issue, unfree labour re-emerged to occupy centre stage in the debate about rural development during the years following the end of the 1939–45 war, when a political concern of Keynesian theory was not just economic reconstruction (mainly in Europe and Asia) but also planning (in the Third World).

---

1 Bierce (1967: 58, 103).

2 In epistemological terms, Adam Smith argued that labour-power was a source of value, while Hegel indicated that labour-power was owned by its subject. These positions found their synthesis in the analysis of Marx, who combined them to show how, since labour-power is both the property of its subject and also the source of value, under capitalism it can and does become a commodity that is sold to commercial employers by workers. Marx then outlined the way in which, as a result of this transaction, surplus-value was extracted by capital from the owner of the commodity labour-power, an appropriation which in turn corresponded to the economic dynamic that fuelled the accumulation process.

A crucial aspect of the ensuing discussion concerned the extent to which different relational forms constituted obstacles to capitalist development, and why. Central to these deliberations was the link between capitalist development and modern forms of unfree labour (peonage, debt bondage, indenture, chattel slavery). From the 1960s to the mid-1980s, neoclassical economists generally, and a specific form of Marxist theory (the semi-feudal thesis) asserted that, as unfreedom and economic development were – and are – incompatible, accumulation in Third World contexts would be accompanied by the spread of free labour. From the 1980s onwards, however, this claim was disputed by an alternative Marxist interpretation (the deproletarianisation approach).

About the importance of this debate, both in terms of political economy generally, and more specifically development studies, there can be no doubt. Where unfreedom has been reintroduced into a labour process that is capitalist, political economy teaches that such a development corresponds historically to a regression. This is because so much – politically, ideologically and economically – hangs on whether or not worker emancipation has been achieved. During the post-war era, therefore, the connection between forms of labour-power that were unfree and capitalist accumulation was a central aspect of two academic disputes. The latter involved rival explanations as to the nature of the labour regime not just on the plantation system in the American South but also structuring the mode of production in India.[3]

Originally confined largely to discussions about Third World countries, the capitalism/unfreedom debate has shifted, and now includes developments in the labour regime of metropolitan capitalist nations. Looking at the way unfree labour as a concept has been constructed and then reinterpreted over time, it is clear that in terms both of its desirability (working arrangements good for the worker) and of its systemic efficacy (working arrangements good for business), each of these views not only conflict but also invoke the same primacy of national economic needs and objectives (good for the country at large). Equally clear is the fact that, as the debate unfolded, a whole swathe of academic commentators, especially in the field of development studies, has been wrong-footed as a result of endorsing unexamined assumptions structuring

---

3 Contrasting views about the slave labour regime on the antebellum plantation in the American South – opposed by abolitionists on the grounds that unfreedom was coercive/exploitative but defended by pro-slavery discourse as a benign form of 'subsistence guarantee' that meant slaves were better-off than free workers – underline the polarized nature of the debate. Equally divergent views about unfree labour were on show during the mode of production debate in India, on which see Rudra *et al.* (1978).

the discussion. First in the 1960s, and then again in the 1980s, the upshot was over-optimistic prognoses about the trajectory or meaning of unfree production relations.

This wrong-footing occurred for two reasons. First, a consequence of mislabelling unfree labour as pre-capitalist ('feudal', or 'semi-feudal') residuals, and then insisting on the necessity of their demise together with the inevitability of their replacement by free equivalents. And second, equally incorrectly misrecognizing such labour-power as nothing more than benign/voluntary forms of 'traditional' culture. It is argued here that both these interpretations of unfree labour-power, either negatively, as a form of worker disempowerment that is destined to vanish as capitalism spreads, or positively, as a 'from below' form of empowerment, are wrong.

Since theoretical inconsistences resulting from unannounced changes of mind affect not just the trajectories and chronology of the capitalism/ unfreedom debate but also have political consequences, it is further argued such instances are not – and cannot be dismissed as being – of little or no significance. For this reason, the focus here is on the contributions and disagreements, over specific conjunctures after WWII. In part, this conspectus is a necessary corrective to a recent and problematic attempt at reviewing Marxist contributions to the debate, an intervention that succeeded only in misleading because of a failure adequately to comprehend past and present discussion vis-à-vis Marxism and unfree labour.[4]

To this end, the first of three sections in this chapter traces the capitalism/ unfreedom debate across three conjunctures: 1950–1980, 1980–2000, and 2000 to the present. In each of these periods, contributions to the discussion are examined in terms of epistemological consistency and influences, together with their respective theoretical and political implications. The next two sections consider the adequacy (or otherwise) of the way in which the whole debate has been reviewed, plus issues raised by the connection between methods and theory in case studies from India and the UK.

---

4 The review in question is by Rioux, LeBaron, and Verovšek (2020), the shortcomings of which are considered below. When compared with late-comers to a debate, one of the very few advantages enjoyed by those who participated from the outset is a more sustained engagement with the minutiae, and consequently a relatively enhanced capacity to track all the details across the whole trajectory. An important aspect of this advantage is the avoidance of the main problem facing late-comers: namely, the inevitable shedding of minutiae (= loss of detail) that occurs in the course of a drawn-out debate.

I

1950 to 1980

Throughout the period up to and following the 1960s 'development decade', contributions to the capitalism/unfreedom discussion linked to modernisation theory, the semi-feudal thesis, and the mode of production debate, all followed colonialism in seeing unfree labour as obstacle to economic development in newly independent Third World nations. This was the orthodoxy that dominated the conjuncture: those who maintained that, because unfree production relations were incompatible with accumulation, included not just bourgeois modernisation theory but also some Marxists writing about development in Third World countries. Eradicating unfree labour was for modernization theory part of a larger package of reforms aimed at ending pre-capitalist tenure in the agrarian sector.[5] This, it was argued, would permit economic growth, and contribute thereby to a capitalist transition in the underdeveloped nations of the Third World. For modernization theory, the desired objective was, amongst other things, to enable the formation of a labour market composed of free workers, providing local employers both with a workforce to produce commodities and simultaneously a domestic market to consume manufactures.

Like bourgeois modernization theory, Marxist adherents of the semi-feudal thesis also maintained that eliminating unfree production relations was necessary in order to generate economic growth. The object, again one shared with modernization theory, was that abolition would lead in turn to the next stage, as exponents of the semi-feudal thesis saw it: a transition to what for them was a still-absent capitalism. For this variant of Marxism, therefore, accumulation was incompatible with the presence of unfree production relations, a view upheld at this conjuncture by many of those engaged in the study of development both in India (among them Terence Byres, Jan Breman, Pradhan Prasad,

---

5   That unfree labour was regarded by modernization theory as an obstacle to capitalist development in Third World nations is clear from the observation by Weiner (1966: 306–307) that 'discipline and control of workers usually lay in some other not strictly economic institution, usually of a quasi-political nature, such as an aristocrat and the workers on his own lands', and consequently 'recruitment rarely depended on the attraction of workers in the open market [since] the right to withdraw from plantation employment was sharply circumscribed [by] indebtedness and "company stores"'. Modernization theorists included not just Myron Wiener but also Walt Rostow (1960), whose stages framework – passing from traditional society, through take-off and maturity, to high mass consumption – was an idealised justification of capitalist development as benign evolutionary process, designed explicitly as a political alternative to the revolutionary class struggle of Marxism.

Amit Bhaduri, Utsa Patnaik, and Jairus Banaji) and in Latin America (Ernesto Laclau, Eric Hobsbawm).[6]

During the 1970s, two additional and important contributions to the capitalism/unfreedom debate emerged from non-Marxist sources (neo-classical economics, world systems theory). Although each of them recognized the existence of a positive connection between capitalism and labour that was not free, both nevertheless stopped short of claiming that accumulation in the advanced capitalist economies of developed countries depended substantially on the employment there of workers who were unfree. For its part, cliometric historiography accepted that plantations in the antebellum south were capitalist, and thus economically efficient, but was as a result compelled to recast slavery as non-coercive.[7] This enabled cliometricians to argue that as a slave was essentially a choice-making subject, voluntarily opting to remain on the plantation, the workforce in the latter context was akin to free wage-labour. Consistent with a neo-classical economic approach, therefore, the plantation could be declared a capitalist enterprise.

The second major intervention in the capitalism/unfreedom debate at this conjuncture was that of world systems theory, a dualistic approach which maintained that although unfree labour continued to exist, it was a coercive relational form confined to the underdeveloped periphery.[8] In the advanced capitalist nations at the core of the global economy, however, those employed consisted of free workers. According to the dualism of world systems theory, because coercion applies to those engaged in peasant smallholding agriculture, unfree labour remains external to capitalism proper of the kind found in metropolitan capitalist countries. For cliometric historiography, therefore, the presence of capitalism was accepted, but this required in turn that unfreedom be denied. By contrast, in the case of world systems theory, it was unfreedom

---

6   The case made by these adherents of the semi-feudal thesis is examined critically elsewhere (Brass, 1999, 2011, 2018).

7   Where the labour regime on the antebellum cotton plantation is concerned, this argument is associated principally with the revisionist approach of Fogel and Engerman (1974).

8   Wallerstein (1979) is the main exponent of this world systems theory dualism (unfreedom on periphery, freedom at core). Broadly speaking, the case made was part of the wider 1970s debates about the new international division of labour, and its implications for capitalist development in metropolitan contexts. The shift of manufacturing, away from the latter and towards Asia (Japan, Korea, India and China) was possible because of two developments. First, the Green Revolution drove peasants off the land, and made them available to capital as workers. And second, technological/transport improvements such as containerization erased distance as an obstacle to marketing. This process, it was argued by Wallerstein and others, had profound implications both for metropolitan capitalist nations, newly industrializing nations, and for an understanding of the way capitalism itself would develop.

that was accepted, but only on global periphery. That unfree production relations, although epistemologically drawing ever closer to the accumulation process, might actually be central to the reproduction of the economy within the metropolitan capitalist heartland itself (= capitalism proper) was at this point an argument yet to be made.[9]

1980 to 2000

From the 1980s onwards, the global spread and integrated nature of capitalism undermined claims by the semi-feudal thesis that accumulation was incompatible with unfree production relations. In methodological terms, semi-feudalism thrived during the 1960s, when social scientists were engaged in trying to explain why economic development had seemingly bypassed rural areas in the Third World. This generated the notion of non-capitalism (at village level) in the midst of capitalism (the city), a form of dualism common then (particularly for those discussing the mode of production) but untenable now.[10] Recognition of this fact during the 1980s saw yet another paradigm shift

---

9   Adding to the catalogue of inaccuracies characterizing the capitalism/unfreedom debate, Watts (Little & Watts, 2022: 200, n. 3) claims not only that contract farming as a form of unfree labour 'is worth further exploration' – as if this remained an unexplored issue – but also labels the work of Miles (1987 – miscited by Watts as 1991) as 'canonical'. Unlike others, Miles accepts the existence of a connection between capitalism and unfree labour; however, like many others (Miles, 1987: 179–80, 196ff.) characterizes the latter relation as a pre-capitalist socio-economic form encountered in the periphery, and thus not part of the capitalist mode of production found at the core. In short, his view is essentially the same as that of world systems theory formulated by Wallerstein. This difference is set out in Brass (1999: 152–3, 170 n. 30). Misrecognizing this distinction is the sort of error Watts has made before, when misattributing the critique of 'new' populist postmodernism to Kitching, who actually made no mention of postmodernism, post-colonialism, post-development, etc. Details about this earlier mistake by Watts are contained in the second Index compiled by *The Journal of Peasant Studies* (Volume 32, Number 1, January 2005, pages 172–73, note 34).

10   What exponents of the semi-feudal thesis refuse to confront is the impact of outsourcing/ restructuring on the production relations available to capital. They still think a group of permanent workers enjoying trade union rights and employed for a good wage under one roof in a big factory is the next step, whereas the reality nowadays is very different. Subcontracting of production by large off-shore corporations to many smallscale sweat-shops (frequently located in the countryside, out of sight of government regulation, the workforce consisting mostly or entirely of women) where coercion and bonded labour relations are rife. Coming across the latter, exponents of semi-feudal thesis declare them to be evidence for the absence of a 'fully functioning' capitalism, rather than what such units actually are: evidence precisely for the existence/operation of a 'fully functioning' – or a mature – capitalist system.

in the debate about labour regimes. From that conjuncture onwards, therefore, the hitherto orthodox view that capitalist development required the eradication of unfree production relations was challenged by the Marxist deproletarianization framework.[11]

The latter showed, much rather, the opposite to be the case: in many instances, producers were restructuring the labour process by replacing free workers with unfree equivalents. In a global economy where producers have to become increasingly cost-conscious so as to remain competitive, therefore, enterprises reproduce, introduce, or reintroduce unfree relations in preference to labour-power that is free, a process of workforce decomposition/recomposition. As such, deproletarianization is part of the way class struggle is waged 'from above'. Along with downsizing/outsourcing, this is a method whereby nowadays capital restructures its labour process, cutting costs so as to maintain/enhance profitability.

An expanding industrial reserve army makes this kind of restructuring not just possible but also necessary, enabling multinational corporations, rich peasants, and commercial farmers to compete with rival enterprises. Whereas in the past the colonial state in India attempted to eliminate debt bondage and similar unfree working arrangements there, because they were thought to be obstacles to economic development, currently the neoliberal state (lip-service apart) is content to see them continue – and even flourish – as they contribute to profitability.

The 1990s also saw the entry into the debate of postmodern theory, which – following in the footsteps of pro-slavery discourse in the antebellum south – recast unfree production relations as part of traditional culture.[12] Just as antebellum pro-slavery discourse indicted the capitalist North as representing an alien systemic form, in the process disregarding the presence in the South of the same accumulation process, so British colonialism is incriminated by postmodernism as the harbinger of capitalist penetration of the Indian countryside. Not only does this similarly overlook the existence there of accumulation, but it also enables postmodernism to argue that it was a foreign colonialism that was responsible for privileging free labour as the 'other' of bonded labour and/or slavery. Rejecting a political economy approach founded on whether the rural workforce was free or unfree, postmodern theory emphasizes instead

---

11   On deproletarianization and its centrality to an understanding of the role of unfree production relations in the class struggle between capital and labour, see Brass (1999, 2011).

12   For the application of postmodern theory to an analysis of the free/unfree dichotomy, see Prakash (1990a, 1990b).

the 'cultural' formation of labour.[13] Again like antebellum pro-slavery discourse, bonded labour in India is depicted by postmodernism as an essentially benign arrangement, a form of landlord patronage that is described as 'the economy of gentleness' based on the provision of subsistence guarantee, whereby both the unfree worker and his family were 'certainly never in want of food'.[14]

If unfree labour is neither an 'economy of gentleness' nor a pre-capitalist remnant, but in many cases a coercive relation of choice where capital is concerned, used as much by a national bourgeoisie as by a foreign one, then it is difficult to see how entering alliances with the employing/owning class within the nation to further the cause of capitalist development there is still on the political agenda of workers' organizations. This suggests that it is socialism, not a progressive form of capitalism, which should be the objective of any 'from below' political mobilization and programme. Furthermore, the use of these kinds of unfree production relation tends to hinder and/or undermine the formation of class consciousness among labour, particularly when they involve the recruitment of migrants (who are unfree and thus cheaper to employ) in order to displace unionized and politically militant workers (who are free and thus more costly to employ). Since employers benefit from unfreedom, and consequently the state permits its continuance, abolition of such oppressive/ exploitative forms will be achieved only by a working class organized in pursuit of socialism.

Linked to world systems theory, of which it was an epistemological outgrowth, the 1990s additionally marked the emergence of a discourse privileging commodity chains or global value chains.[15] This approach, like that of world systems, was based on a core/periphery dualism informed by geography. Commodity chains discourse attempted to dissociate what it conceptualized as problematic elements located at specific points in the accumulation process, which – so exponents argued – could then be 'fixed' to the benefit of all concerned (capital and labour alike). By shifting the focus away from the economic system as a whole, so the argument went, and instead placing it on the operation of those stages (= links in the chain) where problems were deemed to occur, the latter would be remedied in order that the economic system could

13   See Prakash (1992: 3, 11, 34, 35–36).
14   Prakash (1990a: 185ff.).
15   Exponents of the commodity chain approach include Gereffi, Humphrey and Sturgeon (2005) and Gereffi (2018).

then proceed as before. Exponents of this approach have attempted to re-interpret the presence of labour-power that is unfree, by arguing that – when encountered in the accumulation process – such production relations are simply 'anomalies'; when bought to the attention of employers, these 'glitches' will rapidly be eliminated.[16]

Made in defiance of what history teaches about the centrality to accumulation of labour-power that is unfree, such naïve claims by commodity chain exponents posit a benign capitalism, operated by owners entirely unaware of the kind of production relations in the labour process they control.[17] Much like those who maintain that the problem of unfree labour can 'solved' from within the existing capitalist system, by appealing to the state to enforce its legislation outlawing bonded labour, thereby returning to a 'kinder'/'caring' form of accumulation, so the commodity chain framework also locates solutions to unfree labour inside capitalism. It is an approach that diverts the critical gaze away from the system as a whole and onto parts of it that exponents claim can be 'remedied', thereby making good the entire system, and thus ensuring its continued reproduction.[18] It comes as no surprise that – in the name of 'governance structure' and 'business systems' – such a piecemeal reformist approach is endorsed by defenders of capitalism, among them the World Bank and the United States Agency for International Development.

---

16   For the application to labour relations of a commodity chain approach, see among others Barrientos (2019) and Komlosy and Musić (2021).

17   Lest anyone imagines that commodity chain approach to unfree labour is in any way compatible with Marxist theory, a recent account by Pegler (2015) of production relations in rural Brazil disposes of such a view: his analysis fails to mention the presence there of unfree labour, completely out of keeping with most other reports from such areas in rural Brazil (Esterci, 1987; Martins, 1997). Much rather, one is presented by Pegler (2015: 947) with an idealized image of debt relations, described in the following positive manner: 'Traders are seen to play an important role, not as "exploiters" (i.e. via debt servitude) but because they are there when needed ...' Announcing that his object is 'to develop responsible [sic] chain diagnostics', Pegler (2015: 1062) dismisses an earlier Marxist analysis of these same relations on the grounds that it 'presents a familiar story of internal class relations, enclosures [that] remain encapsulated [sic] in very traditional Marxist historiography reminiscent of Maurice Dobb half a century ago'.

18   Rather than viewing the issue in terms of class, the commodity chain approach is a way that claims can be made about the insertion of particular non-class categories into employment, on the grounds that these subjects are underrepresented or undervalued as workers, and their inclusion would contribute to economic growth. Not only is such positivity acceptable to capital, but can be used by the latter to justify further restructuring of its labour process.

2000 to the Present

Since the class struggle argument based on deproletarianisation amounted to a rather more negative appraisal of the way a capitalist labour regime was developing, it caught off-guard those overoptimistic prognoses which earlier had proclaimed the necessity to the accumulation process of labour-power that was free. Having been demonized by many in the sphere of development studies, the view that capitalism was compatible with unfree labour quickly – and in several cases unaccountably – metamorphosed from a heterodox theory to a new form of orthodoxy. This in turn generated the proliferation of claims to have 'discovered' the compatibility between unfree labour and capitalism, some of which were then mistakenly endorsed in subsequent reviews of the debate. One outcome, therefore, was that some contributors who had merely taken up what earlier analyses had already established, or indeed had never said anything about this issue, were suddenly and unaccountably lionized as a result.

Accordingly, some exponents of the semi-feudal thesis dismissed the deproletarianisation argument on the grounds that it was a departure from theories about development – especially Marxism – premised on the view that accumulation necessarily and always required a workforce composed of free labour-power.[19] Other exponents of the same thesis, by contrast, having attacked the deproletarianisation approach, then adopted it, either deploying

---

19   Among them were Byres, Prasad, Patnaik and Banaji. A case in point was Breman (1985: 311), whose view at this conjuncture was that it 'is no longer the case' that permanent farm servants are bonded, 'even when ... indebtedness is a persistent feature of the labour relationship', and although casual workers receive loans and maidservants live in the house of their employers, 'their situation does not constitute an unfree working relationship either'. His view then was categorical and unambiguous: 'To my mind', he asserted, 'it is unsound to deduce from this [the existence of debt] that unfree labour continues in either the same form *or a new one* ... [t]he binding which accompanies this cannot ... be equated with unfree labour' (emphasis added). Similarly, 'I shall regard as unfree only that form of debt-labour which is rooted in non-economic coercion ... *this relationship has nothing to do with the essence of present-day control over agricultural labour*' (emphasis added). What was happening, by contrast, was 'the transition from a traditional agrarian economy to *a free labour market* in the countryside [and] the acceleration of a capitalist mode of production in agriculture' (Breman, 1985: 443–4, emphasis added). Taking issue with the deproletarianisation approach, Breman was adamant: dismissing the argument that what was happening amounted to 'replacing free workers with unfree equivalents or by converting the former into the latter', his view was that 'such reasoning implies that a process of capitalist transformation is in progress in the Indian countryside in which free labour is disappearing to make place for a regime of unfreedom,' concluding unequivocally: 'In fact the trend is the reverse.'

the framework under a different label or arguing implausibly that it was an interpretation to which they had subscribed to all along. Understandably, such claims, involving as they did unacknowledged changes of mind, triggered confusion and chronological inconsistencies in later attempts to construct a theoretical lineage for the whole capitalism/unfreedom debate.

Perhaps the most curious of all these trajectories has been the sudden, unacknowledged, and complete reversal of opinion by Jan Breman, whose many interventions in the capitalism/unfreedom debate have been based on fieldwork in Gujarat, Western India from the 1960s to 2013.[20] Over this period, his views have changed dramatically: from his original pre-1990s claim, strongly made, that unfreedom is unconnected with debt and anyway declines as capitalism develops, to a post-1990 contention, also strongly made, that capitalists do in fact prefer bonded labour which is invariably the result of debt. Yet he persists – even now – in denying that such a *volte face* ever occurred.[21] However, that an about-turn has indeed taken place can be illustrated with reference to any one of the many pre-1990 statements by Breman to this effect, and contrasting it with what is said in everything he has published since.[22]

---

20   These interventions extend from Breman (1974) to Breman (2019). Not the least curious aspect is that, notwithstanding substantial evidence of this *volte face*, neither Breman nor the majority of others contributing to the capitalism/unfreedom debate address this issue (e.g., de Neve, 2005), let alone consider its implications for any reviews or accounts of the different paths taken by contributors/contributions to the discussion. In a fundamental sense this is a departure from most other debates in the social sciences, where issues such as who said what and why, and how views were – or were not – transformed in the course of exchanges, are a standard (crucial, even) aspect of any intellectual dispute.

21   The list in his latest book (Breman, 2019: 34) of what he has written about 'neo-bondage' excludes any reference to a pre-1990 text, which appears finally to confirm the point that the concept emerged only after the case about the compatibility between unfree labour-power and capitalist development had already been made elsewhere.

22   That around the 1990s Breman changed his mind, without saying this is what he had done, is evident from the switch to the claim that a 'new' form of bonded labour – the hitherto unmentioned 'neo-bondage' – was indeed present in the capitalist agriculture of Western India, notwithstanding the fact that this contradicted all earlier pronouncements by him on the subject. The extent to which this is so can be gauged from comparing different accounts of the same fieldwork. In his initial analysis of sugarcane production in Bardoli, therefore, Breman (1978) characterized labour contractors as benign, debt bondage as a feudal/pre-capitalist relation, migrants as being 'free in their choice of where to go', and capitalism as necessitating 'a class of free and unattached wage-earners.' In later books, however, his account (Breman, 2013: 336ff.; 2019: 196) of the same capitalist labour regime at that same conjuncture has altered substantially, and is now presented as an example not of 'free and unattached wage-earners' but rather of 'neo-bondage'. The full extent of this *volte face* – currently still unacknowledged and unexplained – is evident from his present view (Breman, 2019: 38) that 'neo-bondage is a form of labour attachment that

The extent of this U-turn is clear from his latest book, where one encounters right at the start a forthright declaration that 'bondage and capitalism are not mutually exclusive', a construction repeated verbatim at intervals throughout; the conclusion ends similarly, with the observation that he has 'substantiated the contention that capitalism and bondage are not mutually incompatible'.[23]

Not the least problematic aspect of such unacknowledged U-turns is the way a Marxist agenda is replaced with a non-Marxist one. More recent contributors to this debate maintain – wrongly – that capitalism and its state can and will indeed eliminate unfree labour, thereby returning in part to the earlier claim that accumulation on a world scale can do without such oppressive/exploitative relational forms.[24] As problematic, therefore, is the absence of any mention about sudden and unexplained changes of mind, treated as unimportant, despite the fact that in particular instances such transformations entail an attempt to attach a non-Marxist political agenda to what was originally a Marxist one, an issue that is hardly of negligible importance.[25] Equally

---

is thoroughly capitalist in nature, widely prevalent in both the rural and urban economy, found in agriculture, industry and construction, as well as in other sectors, and in practice immobilizes migrant or local workers. The attachment varies in intensity, length, selectivity and shape but indebtedness is crucial to it.'

23 See, for example, Breman (2019: 34, 183, 237, 264). Part of the difficulty is the presence of many undefined concepts and odd linguistic constructs scattered throughout the analysis (Breman, 2019: 79, 148, 210, 212), among which are 'the past mode of production', 'reified mode of production', 'accumulation-dispossession syndrome', 'mercantile-financialized type of capitalism', 'mercantile-cum-financial capitalism', and the term 'elope' when in all probability what is meant is 'abscond'. Such oddities are themselves compounded by other misunderstandings. Thus, for example, Breman (2019: 263) cites the large volume edited by Brass and van der Linden (1997) as evidence for the claim that unfree labour is no longer of any significance. What that volume argued was exactly the reverse: not only that the incidence of unfreedom had been underestimated, was on the increase, but also that such forms of labour-power and capitalism were and are compatible.

24 Substantial and continuing evidence periodically confounds the oft-heard claim that, because capitalism is able to 'self-regulate', it will always and everywhere seek out and eliminate those (residual) production relations that are unfree. That the presence of the latter will not be 'solved' by capitalism, however, is underlined by the regularity with which 'scandals' – involving sweatshop conditions, low payment, and coercion – surface, are quickly said by employers to have been addressed, and then vanish from the headlines, only to resurface subsequently as 'scandals', often featuring the same enterprise. A case in point is the way the pandemic uncovered the fact of underpaid/overworked sewing machinists employed in 'fast fashion' clothing sweatshops, when the rising incidence of Covid-19 in one particular city (Leicester) was traced to the fact that such machinists were required to come in to work, regardless of whether or not they displayed pandemic symptoms.

25 Among the many who currently maintain – implausibly – that capitalism and/or its state can and will eradicate unfree labour are Breman (on which see Brass, 2018: Chapter 5),

problematic is the corollary: the longer a socialist transition is postponed, by not putting this objective on a leftist political agenda, together with that of migration – free and unfree – and the industrial reserve army, the more workers will in periods of crisis move towards reactionary populist solutions which seemingly offer to protect their jobs, culture, and livelihoods.[26]

By shifting the emphasis from the economic role performed for capital by an expanding industrial reserve army of migrant labour to the attainment by the latter subject of citizenship in the receiving nation, this kind of reformism envisages only piecemeal changes to unfree labour and downgrades the importance of class struggle.[27] Significantly, therefore, it is in reviews of the capitalism/unfreedom debate that difficulties inherent in a return either to pre-capitalist social order or to nicer/kinder form of accumulation surface.

Fudge (2019) and Kenway (2021). Such optimism ascribes to neoliberalism (or its state) a moral duty to look after the welfare of its workforce, a sentiment expressed by appeals to an 'uncaring' state that ought to know better. This idealised notion overlooks the nonexistent moral code where neoliberalism is concerned, a point made by Milton Friedman, the high priest of *laissez-faire* economic theory. In a 1970 *New York Times* article he observed bluntly that 'the social responsibility of business is to increase its profits', adding that 'discussions of the "social responsibilities of business" are notable for their analytical looseness and lack of rigor'.

26   None these days makes a distinction between the supplementing and displacing function of migrant labour, and thus miss its implications for political economy. Seeking legislative interventions designed to achieve what is termed an 'appropriate balancing' between migrant and local worker, ends up regarding the State as benign, almost above the fray. This despite the fact that currently the State is not merely a capitalist but a neoliberal institution, the agency of which is to formulate/implement legislation favouring the accumulation process. For those holding this view, the assumption is that, even in such a *laissez-faire* environment, it is still possible to protect the rights of migrants and locals, whereas employers attempt to enhance competitiveness/profitability by playing one off against the other. Under a neoliberal capitalist labour regime, therefore, the State will not seek to disadvantage producers striving for economic growth by protecting the rights of their migrant and local workers, much rather the opposite: any rights labour has managed to gain over the years will be stripped away. Hence the fatuity of a search for 'appropriate balancing,' an objective that amounts to no more than legislative tampering within a rampant market system.

27   Shorn of a role in the transition to socialism, such relational forms are henceforth to be situated somewhere along a continuum of capitalist occupations, their place determined by nothing more than subjective perceptions of how 'nice'/'nasty'/'very nasty' unfreedom is thought to be. Mapping the distinction between free and unfree labour onto the citizen/migrant binary also overlooks the fact that workers who are already citizens can become and remain unfree, no less than those deemed foreign.

II

Theory, Methods, Problems

In what purports to be a review of Marxist contributions to the capitalism/
unfreedom debate, a new account by Rioux, LeBaron, and Verovšek displays
a striking misunderstanding of this discussion and its political implications.[28]
To begin with, their claim that during the 1970s Banaji made the connection
between capitalism and unfree labour is incorrect: what he argued at that
point was that unfree labour was acceptable to feudalism, not to capitalism.[29]
The capitalism/unfreedom claim was made by him only much later. In keeping
with this Rioux, LeBaron, and Verovšek privilege recent interpretations – in
particular those by a co-author of the piece in question – and misrepresent,
downplay, or ignore earlier and more radical contributions to the debate.[30]

Not only are a number of participants wrongly identified as Marxists, therefore, but Rioux, LeBaron, and Verovšek also fail to point out that what they
term 'a more faithful Marxist tradition' is nothing other than the class struggle
argument based conceptually on theory about deproletarianisation.[31] Missing

---

28   See Rioux, LeBaron, and Versovšek (2020). The kinds of problem generated by more
      recent contributions to the debate can be illustrated by reference to arguments made by
      Kenway (2021). In her account, slavery itself dissolves conceptually, and becomes no more
      a point on a 'continuum' extending from 'nasty' to 'nice' work conditions. Eschewing the
      definition of employment as free or unfree according to the capacity of its subject to exit
      from the work relation, slavery is instead characterized as 'severe and varied forms of
      exploitation'. As understood by political economy, chattel slavery along with other vari-
      ants of unfree labour, has in effect ceased to exist as a socio-economic construct. Instead,
      and like other recent contributions to the debate, Kenway (2021: 114–15) proposes that
      such relations be positioned at the 'sharp end of a continuum of working conditions with
      no clear dividing line between what is being called modern slavery and what isn't'. Since
      this criterion applied to modern slavery is one that might be applied also to historical
      variants, which could equally be said to be no more than a point on a 'nice'/'nasty' con-
      tinuum, chattel slavery as a *sui generis* relational form vanishes. Ironically, Kenway (2021:
      116–118) then concedes that the specificity of positions located along the 'continuum' are
      'not easy to separate', and that 'the lines between what "is" and "isn't" the right kind of
      exploitation to be termed "modern slavery" are hugely blurred as a result'. In effect, she
      undermines her own case.
29   For details, see Chapter 3 (this volume). Where claims made by Banaji are concerned, it
      is always necessary to invoke a caveat. Having asserted earlier that bonded labour was
      not unfree, since all it meant was that a subject was attached to the place where s/he was
      born, Banaji now accepts that bondage can involve attachment not just to the soil but also
      to an employer. As the latter is the definition of unfree labour, it contradicts his previous
      claim about this issue.
30   Absent are key texts by Lichtenstein (1996) and Moulier Boutang (1998, 2018).
31   Jairus Banaji is one of those described by Rioux, LeBaron, and Versovšek as a Marxist
      who formulated theory about the acceptability to capitalists of unfree labour. As outlined

from the review is any reference to the crucial detail that some who have now joined 'a more faithful Marxist tradition' – rather late in the day – had earlier dismissed the very views they currently endorse. Frequent references to the publications of late adopters misleadingly conveys the impression that they have always and consistently supported this view.

Moreover, the review also overlooks the additional fact that their claim about the longstanding neglect of unfree relations was an inaccurate accusation levelled by them at Marxist approaches.[32] Not only do these late adopters receive a relatively privileged consideration in terms of weight given to their publications and arguments, therefore, but they all feature in the conclusion as representing the way forward in the capitalism/unfreedom debate. The Marxist who originally made the case about deproletarianization ('a more faithful Marxist tradition'), however, does not, despite having formulated many of the arguments subsequently taken up by the late adopters. Much the same kind of error pervades others contributing to the same capitalism/unfreedom debate, who either omit to mention deproletarianisation, or – like Rioux, LeBaron, and Verovšek – mistakenly insist that all those deemed to be the ones to carry forward the debate are the same ones who previously denied its central premiss – the class struggle argument on which 'a more faithful Marxist tradition' is based.[33]

Much the same difficulty faces another recent attempt to establish 'what Marxism is', this time with reference to methodology, in contributions to a book edited by Mezzadri.[34] Hence an unfamiliarity with Marxist theory is

---

in Chapter 3 above, Banaji is neither a Marxist nor does he subscribe to the concept of labour-power employed by capitalists as unfree; much rather the opposite, since his view has been that all production relations consist of 'disguised' hired workers that are free. In short, he denies that such a relational form as capitalist unfree labour exists (on which see Brass, 2011: Chapter 4). However, a caveat is in order: again, as is outlined in Chapter 3 above (and elsewhere), his views on unfree labour – as on much else – are subject to endless change and constant reinvention.

32   The accusation was made by Barrientos, Kothari, and Phillips (2013) in a symposium – to which LeBaron also contributed – about the unfree labour debate. The reply, pointing out its many errors, was made by Brass (2014a).

33   Arguing that 'the time was ripe for new conceptualisations', Shah and Harriss-White (2011) endorse both the 'neo-bondage' concept of Breman and the semi-feudal approach to agrarian transition of Byres as solutions to the analytical problems facing those who study Indian development, notwithstanding extensive critiques of their contributions to the capitalism/unfreedom debate. Much the same is true of a more recent intervention in this debate by Natarajan, Brickell, and Parsons (2021), an approach that draws specifically on the Marxian concept of unfree labour ('Insights from this study thus show the need to understand modern slavery as unfree labour ... embedded in and reproduced by wider processes of capital accumulation') yet fails even to mention the concept deproletarianisation.

34   The volume in question is edited by Mezzadri (2021).

nowhere so evident as the discussion of labour-power that is unfree, a production relation that features centrally in the volume.[35] That even its editor misunderstands the meaning of unfree labour-power bodes ill for the ensuing discussion, the difficulty being the confusion displayed by the editor herself over the concept 'deproletarianisation'.[36] This is a common mistake, one that associates the term proletarianization simply with separation from means of production (land, tools), forgetting thereby that freedom as envisaged by Marx also required that the labour-power of a worker not be owned/controlled by an employer or landlord. Whereas proletarianization involves the untrammelled ability of the worker personally to sell his/her own labour-power, the only property this subject possesses, deproletarianisation entails the sale of this commodity by someone other than its owner.[37]

In the case of LeBaron, who not only co-authors the review about the Marxist free/unfree debate but also contributes to the volume on Marxist methodology, there is a discernible pattern of error. Along with Barrientos, Kothari, and Phillips, she was one of those who attacked Marxism for having overlooked the extent to which unfree labour-power is compatible with accumulation. This mistake was pointed out in a reply showing much rather the longevity of Marxist theory making precisely the connection deemed to be absent: namely, that in the course of class struggle capitalists do indeed resort to labour-power that is unfree.[38] LeBaron then asserted that Marxism had also failed to pay attention to the role of the state in the reproduction of unfree labour. This inaccuracy, too, was corrected by a reply listing the many

---

35   It is the main issue addressed in contributions by Mezzadri (2021: Chapters 1, 5 and 15), by Lombardozzi (2021: Chapter 11), and by LeBaron (2021: 208–212). Mezzadri (2021: 10) is quite simply wrong to claim that unfree labour is one of the 'less explored themes in political economy'.

36   See Mezzadri (2021: 72).

37   Although this double meaning of unfreedom is recognized by Lombardozzi (2021: 147ff.), she adopts instead the non-Marxist view that 'between freedom and unfreedom lie a set of degrees', adding that '[i]n this perspective the dichotomy of what is free and unfree is dissolved in a continuum'. The difficulty with this is simply stated. Unfreedom dissolves conceptually and becomes no more a point on a 'continuum' extending from 'nasty' to 'nice' work conditions. Eschewing the Marxist definition of employment as free or unfree according to the capacity of its subject to exit from the production relation, unfreedom is instead characterized merely as a severe form of exploitation. As understood by political economy, chattel slavery along with other variants of unfree labour, have in effect ceased to exist as socio-economic constructs. This difficulty surfaces in a recent contribution to the debate about unfreedom by Kenway (see below), who – like Lombardozzi – proposes that unfree labour be positioned on a continuum of working conditions, erasing the distinction between such relational forms and free equivalents.

38   For this reply, see Brass (2017: Chapter 17).

analyses making precisely this point, including virtually all Marxist accounts of the South African apartheid regime, and most dealing with unfree labour in India, Latin America and the United States.[39]

To these misinterpretations are added yet others. Hence the claim by LeBaron that, because they are race and gender blind, 'Marxist understandings of unfreedom are not currently optimized to grasp these dynamics' not just of prison labour but also of categories such as child and female workers.[40] Again, this is quite simply wrong: the best account of prison labour in the United States, one not mentioned by LeBaron, is by Alex Lichtenstein, who happens to be a Marxist.[41] That age- and gender-specific labour is unfree and crucial to accumulation is recognized not just by Marx but also by most Marxists.[42] The attempt by LeBaron to distinguish between unfree labour deployed by private enterprise and that utilized by the state overlooks the fact that in Germany during the early 1940s and South Africa under the apartheid regime the labour of concentration camp inmates or prison convicts – by definition unfree – was in each instance leased by the state to large corporations or commercial farmers.

A notable exception to this kind of criticism is an earlier and much better review of the same debate, by McCusker, O'Keefe, O'Keefe, and O'Brian, whose discussion of labour regimes in general, and deproletarianisation in particular, is more informed – and thus more accurate – than the analyses provided either by Rioux, LeBaron, and Verovšek, or in the volume edited by Mezzadri.[43] Accepting that 'geography as a discipline has tended to sidestep issues of class in development and agrarian studies in favor of cultural and identity politics', therefore, McCusker, O'Keefe, O'Keefe, and O'Brian intend to 'pay attention to rural class formation'. Central to their argument is that deproletarianisation 'has the potential to explain a great deal about rural livelihoods', not least

---

39   See Brass (2018: 141–43). The confusion on the part of LeBaron as to what constitutes a Marxist analysis of unfree labour is outlined elsewhere (Brass, 2022).

40   LeBaron (2021: 210).

41   See Lichtenstein (1996). References to the unfree nature of convict/prison labour can also be found in Brass (1999: 161, 162, 164, 177; 2011, 162, 164, 177; 2011: 12, 178, 182–3, 198, 277).

42   The same claim, that a particular category of worker has not been addressed by – and is consequently missing from – Marxist analyses of unfree labour, is also made elsewhere by her (LeBaron & Gore, 2020: 1097), announcing an intention to 'underscore the role of unequal family relations' since 'this remains largely new terrain'. Once again, it is a claim that is incorrect: the presence within the kinship domain of female labour-power that is unfree has long been known about, not least as a result of 1970s fieldwork conducted in rural Peru (Brass, 1986). For more evidence that age- and gender-specific categories of worker have been, and are, central to Marxist analyses, together with the fact that such forms of labour-power are unfree, see Brass (1997: 38ff.).

43   See McCusker, O'Keefe, O'Keefe, and O'Brian (2013).

because the concept has been tested by 'very detailed responses [made] to almost all authors who have critically engaged with [this] work'.[44] For this reason, McCusker, O'Keefe, O'Keefe, and O'Brian conclude that it is an approach that 'deserves closer examination from a geographic perspective'.

In their conclusion to the review of the Marxist contributions to the debate, Rioux, LeBaron, and Verovšek emphasize the need to move beyond 'theoretical and formal questions at the expense of studying the real world', which conveys the impression that those who initiated the discussion about the acceptability to capitalism of unfree labour-power did so without 'studying the real world'. This is a familiar trope invariably aimed at Marxists, and is quite simply incorrect when applied to deproletarianisation. The latter theory was – and is – based on fieldwork conducted in Peru and India, so the inference that this Marxist class struggle argument is not grounded in what happens in 'the real world' is palpably untrue.[45] When defending deproletarianisation, moreover, lots of the criticism made of other interpretations concerns not points of theory but rather aspects of 'the real world' that have been overlooked, misinterpreted, or just ignored. This is an issue which highlights the vexed connection between methods and theory informing not just reviews but also contributions to any discussion about the capitalism/unfreedom link.[46]

III

As the following examples indicate, methodologically there are three forms of misrecognizing the capitalism/unfreedom link: avoidance, denial, and redefinition, each of which involves turning unfree labour-power either into

---

44   This point by McCusker, O'Keefe, O'Keefe, and O'Brian underlines the contrast with Rioux, LeBaron, and Versovšek, who note criticisms made of the deproletarianisation approach without, however, mentioning those made by the latter of other interpretations.

45   That the class struggle argument based on deproletarianisation emerged as a result of fieldwork conducted in Latin America and India is evident from Brass (1999: Part I – Case Studies), a monograph about the capitalism/unfreedom link that Rioux, LeBaron, and Versovšek failed to consult.

46   Difficulties raised by unresolved issues linking theory and methods are evident also in the contradiction at the root of the approach by Carstensen (2021: 2, 14). Having announced that she has no intention of addressing the capitalism/freedom debate ('This article makes a conceptual contribution regarding the relationship between racism, migration and unfree labour. I do not aim to develop a comprehensive theory on racism and unfree labour [since] I am not interested in reconstructing the structural function of race in capitalism') she then proceeds to dismiss any element of determination ('I highlight the need to examine policies against unfree labour in terms of whether and how they exacerbate inequality, sexism and racism, since these are neither an effect nor a cause but a central element of a capitalist economy') without having examined its presence (or, indeed, absence).

or about something else. Covering different chronologies (the eighteenth century to the present) and contexts (India, the UK), these case studies illustrate how the presence of a connection between such production relations and the accumulation process is either not addressed, overlooked, or dismissed as nonexistent. The deleterious political consequence in each instance is clear: reinforcing nationalist ideology; putting on the agenda a transition to capitalism, not socialism; and advocating not opposition to but an expansion of the industrial reserve army.

India: 18th Century Onwards

The first concerns the decoupling by Satya of unfreedom and the accumulation process, rather than its continuation but with a changed economic content. At issue, therefore, is the point at which a particular relational form – the *baluta* – can be said to have ended, and why. Described as 'share of the produce', the *baluta* system which operated throughout Deccan villages in Central India over the eighteenth and nineteenth centuries was an unfree relational form akin to *jajmani*.[47] A master/servant relation whereby lower caste workers (*asami*) provided those belonging to the upper caste (*balutedar*) with unpaid labour-power, the *baluta* arrangement applied historically to village servants whose freedom to work for others was constricted. As presented by Satya, this issue is depicted as one of India versus Britain, an undifferentiated dichotomy that informs much nationalist discourse.[48]

Central to the debate is the question of when the *baluta* system disintegrated, and why. On this Satya is doubly adamant, maintaining not only that it continued until the end of the nineteenth century, insisting 'that by 1895 the *balutedari* system was a thing of the past', but also equating this with the onset

---

47   On this history, see Satya (1997b; 2004).

48   Elsewhere Satya (1997a) adopts a similarly nationalist approach, contrasting pre-colonial Banjara society with a uniformly malign colonial state. On the one hand, therefore, there are romanticized images of pre-colonial society, along the lines of the Banjaras, whose 'songs represented their truthfulness and bravery', travelled on 'long winding country roads jingling to the bells of swaying and swinging Banjara bullock carts', the latter 'slowly disappear beyond the horizon leaving behind a large cloud of dust gently drifting in the sunset', a context which 'in pre-colonial times exhibited the vibrancy of buyers and sellers travelling great distances', etc. On the other, the colonial state is depicted as a paranoid institution that was 'suspicious', and displayed an unwarranted level of fear about the 'other'.

of and as a result of British colonialism.[49] Other sources, however, contradict this, reporting its continued existence in different villages of the Deccan into the early twentieth century (1917 and 1928–29).[50] It is simply not possible to dismiss this as does Satya, by saying that what happens in the historical period after the one he is writing about is of no consequence to his analysis. This is rather like declaring an animal extinct in one century, only to see it coming out of the forest in the next.[51]

---

49   Hence the view (Satya, 1997b: 50): 'The local aristocracy was so thoroughly eliminated that by 1895 the *balutedari* system was a thing of the past.' Of additional significance is that the *baluta* was destroyed as much by from below political activity as by from above legislative fiat. Hence what village servants wanted was the ending of labour-rent, and – as Ambedkar argued in 1928 – its conversion into cash-rent. They were quite happy with one aspect of the *baluta* – access to land – but unhappy with the rental form demanded of them by the caste *balutedars*. In a context where capitalist development was taking place, cash payment was in real terms less costly to erstwhile village servants than continuing to work for their masters at a given level of intensity for a specified number of days annually. At this conjuncture, therefore, not only was the *baluta* relation still in being, but this was a result of 'from below' pressure that it continue in a different form. Ambedkar's words on that occasion are instructive: 'Whenever ... any Mahar community in any particular village desires to make progress in any particular direction and that direction is not liked by the ryot, the one immediate step that the ryot takes is to stop the baluta and to proclaim a social boycott ... [S]uch a system which enslaves the whole population, which smothers the spirit of progress, which blocks the way for furtherance, is a system which, I think, no right-minded person ... will sustain or justify ... My honourable friend the Revenue Member will take it from me that the whole of the Mahar population – I say that without fear of challenge – is absolutely tired of the system and is desirous of getting rid of it as soon as possible.'

50   Hence Mann and Kanitkar (1921: 122) note the following: 'The institution of *balutas* or the payment of village servants by an annual charge against the crops which are grown is [in 1917] one of the characteristic features of a Deccan village. The actual payment consists of a fixed amount of grain and fodder on the crops cultivated for grain and fodder ... there were 31 families receiving *baluta* for services rendered'. In a similar vein Jagalpure and Kale (1938: 226–28) observe that in the rural Deccan *balutedars* 'are [in 1928–29] hereditary village servants useful to the community of cultivators [as agricultural labourers]'. Significantly, in his preface to the resurvey carried out in 1952 by Diskalkar [1960] of that same Deccan village, Mann [1967: 140] notes: 'One point which has interested me much is the apparently complete breakdown of the *Baluta* system which has for centuries been a feature of village life.' He goes on to outline the economic changes that occurred since his own investigation was conducted there in 1917: the intensification of agriculture and the provision of milk for the urban population, as a result of its proximity to Poona. So the *baluta* system did break down, but in the twentieth century not the nineteenth, and as much a result of domestic capitalist development as foreign colonialism.

51   Satya admits that his 'data and research doesn't go into the twentieth century', which raises a rather obvious methodological problem. If one has not actually looked for evidence of its continuation in the twentieth century, how is it possible to be sure that no such evidence exists?

Part of the difficulty is that, because no attempt is made by Satya to consider the *jajmani* system, it is correspondingly difficult to understand that – like *jajmani* – some aspects of the *baluta* relation continued beyond the nineteenth century.[52] As many of those who have conducted research in India attest, *jajmani* which some have pronounced a pre-capitalist/feudal relation has in some instances continued to flourish in what is palpably a capitalist agriculture. Since the *baluta* system survived into the era of British colonialism, it is necessary to address its connection with capitalism. Like the *jajmani* relation, therefore, being absorbed into the capitalist system did not prevent it from retaining the outward appearance of a pre-capitalist relation. What happened in such instances was a decline in the *ideology* of reciprocity (= equal exchange) historically accompanying the *baluta*, and not the latter itself. The obligation to work as unfree labour – a central aspect of this relation – would in such circumstances have continued as before.

India: 1960s Onwards

The second example, like the first, concerns a refusal to address changes in a labour regime long regarded as being of a specific systemic form. During the Indian mode of production debate, Purnea district in the northeastern state of Bihar was invoked by one contributor to the debate as an exemplar of semi-feudal agriculture.[53] No tractors, no commercial agriculture, few markets, just a vast array of small peasants, engaged in subsistence cultivation and subordinated to traditional landlords by the debt bondage mechanism. Fieldwork conducted there in 1990 indicated things had changed.[54] Not only were there tractors and a thriving commercial agriculture, but landlords were now investing in tubewells, fertilizer and obtaining bank loans for agricultural improvements. However, smallholding agriculture remained, in that poor peasants not only retained access to land but were also bonded to commercial employers (= landlords).

---

52   Beidelman (1959: 6–7) equates *baluta* with the *jajmani* system, while Fukazawa (1982: 252) makes the distinction that 'the *balutedārs* were not employed by individual peasant families (as under the "*jajmāni* system") but by the village as a territorial whole.' The way Satya characterizes the *baluta* system, however, does suggest that in one important respect it was similar to the *jajmani* relation: namely, that it was informed by the ideology (*not* the economic reality) of reciprocity, or the view of an exchange between dominant and subordinate elements that both parties considered equal.

53   The contributor in question was Prasad (1974, 1989).

54   For details, see Brass (1999: 124–126).

The differences that had emerged in Purnea during the intervening period were crucial. Poor peasants migrated, and the bonded labourers who remained behind to work for commercial employers were composed of females from peasant households. They paid off debts incurred for migration, and were subject to coercion that prevented them from working elsewhere as long as money was owed to an employer, a commercial farmer. The role of money-lending had altered: instead of being a way in which unproductive landlords extracted rent from tenants, it was now a form of productive investment the object of which was to purchase labour-power through cash advances, thereby keeping wages low in an economic context where labour costs would otherwise rise.

When informed what had been seen in Purnea, the contributor to the capitalism/unfreedom debate who had conducted earlier research there responded unambiguously: 'This cannot be, places like Purnea don't change like that, they are still semi-feudal'. No amount of argument, data or photographic evidence (tractors, large work gangs in the fields, bursting grain-stores ready for market, etc.) to the contrary would convince him otherwise. And so it remained. The point in telling this story is that it illustrates where on occasion the problem lies: not in the fieldwork context itself, which changes, but in the reluctance of cherished and long-held interpretations to recognize this fact.

UK: 2015 Onwards

The third example substantially relocates the same issue in terms of context: originally confined to discussions about Third World countries, the capitalism/unfreedom debate has shifted, and now includes developments in the labour regime of metropolitan capitalist nations. Such is the background to a recent book by Kenway, the latest addition to this already well-investigated topic. Like other recent contributions to the discussion, therefore, she is faced with one difficulty: each succeeding newcomer to the debate tends to discard earlier detail and complexity. Issues, problems and solutions long known about are liable consequently to be presented as new discoveries, a problem she is unable entirely to avoid.

In support of the contention that the new abolitionism favours the establishment, Kenway outlines how in 2015 the UK conservative administration proposed to curb immigration in the name of anti-slavery, attempting thereby to regain those of its electoral base lost to UKIP.[55] However, she omits to

---

55   Kenway (2021: 28, 30).

mention the two things that happened next. First, the backlash from many business organizations and thinktanks (The Institute of Economic Affairs, the Confederation of British Industry, the Institute of Directors, the British Chamber of Commerce) all of which complained of the adverse economic impact that would result from no longer having access to cheap migrant labour. And second, the hasty backtracking by government which assured them post-Brexit exemptions would in fact allow continued recruitment/employment of migrant workers.[56] Rather than being just a Tory device, therefore, this episode underlines the contradictory aspects of capitalism: a disjuncture between a political objective (anti-immigration to attract working class voters) and an economic one (pro-immigration to ensure capitalist profitability).

The teleological structure of her argument is clear. Conceptually, modern slavery generates a new abolitionism supportive of conservative politics, in that it permits the latter to target immigration in an apparently humanitarian manner, along the lines of concern for migrants exploited by traffickers. Because in her view migrants are not forced to come, but want to come, they should be accepted by the host nation on that basis. Once migration is made legal and safe, Kenway then maintains, traffickers will go out of business. Accordingly, since 'exploitation is a product of bad immigration policy', the state must be prevailed upon politically to legalize a 'safe migration pathway'. Accordingly, her argument concerns not so much slavery as how a discourse about modern slavery affects the perception of migrants and immigration.[57] As the narrative proceeds, therefore, the focus of Kenway undergoes a two-fold shift: from slavery to migration, and from coercion to exploitation. In the course of this mutation, slavery itself dissolves conceptually, and becomes no more a point on a 'continuum' extending from 'nasty' to 'nice' work conditions. Eschewing the definition of employment as free or unfree according to the

---

56 On this see Chapter 1 (this volume).

57 A further contradiction arises in the course of the analytical shift from slavery to immigration. Having rightly condemned the way corporations resort to outsourcing and subcontracting in order to access cheap sources of labour (Kenway, 2021: 126, 130), she also seems to endorse the open door policy (Kenway, 2021: 45, 56, 65–66) advocated by business interests, on the grounds that, just as employers want migrant labour, so migrants want to work for them. Although she is rightly critical of the rush by celebrities, the wealthy, and corporations to declare themselves against slavery, more problematic is her labelling (Kenway, 2021: 1, 20, 34, 36, 47–48, 61, 113) of all those subscribing to the 'new abolitionism' as unwitting allies of conservative politicians wishing to pursue anti-immigration policies. Overlooked thereby is the leftist case and its reasons for combatting unfree labour (see Brass, 2014).

capacity of its subject to exit from the work relation, slavery is instead characterized as 'severe and varied forms of exploitation'.[58] As understood by political economy, chattel slavery along with other variants of unfree labour, have in effect ceased to exist as socio-economic constructs.

In place of slavery as a relational form Kenway – like other recent contributions to the debate – proposes that such labour-power be positioned at the 'sharp end of a continuum of working conditions with no clear dividing line between what is being called modern slavery and what isn't'.[59] Since this criterion applied to modern slavery is one that might be applied also to historical variants, which could equally be said to be no more than a point on a 'nice'/ 'nasty' continuum, chattel slavery as a *sui generis* relational form unsurprisingly vanishes. Ironically, she then concedes that the specificity of positions located on the 'continuum' are 'not easy to separate', and that 'the lines between what "is" and "isn't" the right kind of exploitation to be termed "modern slavery" are hugely blurred as a result'.[60] In effect, she undermines her own case.[61] As ironical is the fact that eliminating the relational distinctiveness in this manner, by maintaining that unfree labour is in the end no different from that which is free, replicates the claim made not just by Banaji (see Chapter 3, this volume), but also by 1860s pro-slavery discourse in the antebellum South, and by cliometric historiography during the 1970s.[62] The latter insisted that unfreedom was a 'normal' work arrangement, no worse – and in many instances much better – than free equivalents.

---

58   Kenway (2021: 114).

59   Kenway (2021: 114–15).

60   Kenway (2021: 116–118).

61   Part of the difficulty stems from her use of a restricted concept of ownership: of the person, and not of the labour-power belonging to the person (as political economy defines unfreedom). Since her view is that ownership of the person by another – the historical variant known as chattel slavery – is no longer the case, modern slavery as a concept therefore cannot be valid. However, the ownership of the labour-power belonging to the person by another – as in the case of bonded labour (a work arrangement to which she refers) – indicates that such forms of unfreedom not only exist but are reproduced by capital in preference to free equivalents. Because 'modern slavery' subsumes these unfree relations, it cannot be dismissed in the manner Kenway wishes. In short, her problem derives from her use of the term 'slavery' rather than 'unfreedom': the latter concept was the one deployed much earlier, in the debate about institutional obstacles to economic development, a discussion not considered by her.

62   On 1860s pro-slavery discourse in the antebellum South, see Chapter 2 (this volume).

Conclusion

The capitalism/unfreedom issue has been a key part of the post-war debate about development, not just in Third World countries but now also – and increasingly – in metropolitan nations with a long history of accumulation that is well established. Outlined here, therefore, have been the many theoretical and political shifts in interpreting capitalism/unfreedom that occurred throughout this period. During the immediate post-war era, each of the dominant paradigms – modernisation theory, the semi-feudal thesis, and cliometric historiography – addressing the issue of economic growth decoupled accumulation and unfree labour. The latter was seen as an obstacle to economic development, and consequently as a relational form to be abolished.

It could be argued that the politics of the semi-feudal approach were merely another way of postponing/abandoning socialism. This it did by maintaining – incorrectly – that as long as 'semi-feudal' relations were found anywhere in the countryside, on the agenda was a transition to capitalism (not socialism) and alliances with (not struggle against) a 'progressive' national bourgeoisie in order to establish a benign capitalist democracy. However, recent writings about class struggle and unfree labour show that not just Marx and Engels but also Lenin, Trotsky and others all subscribed to the view that such relations were central to the way owners of the means of production organized and protected their accumulation process, and thus not part of any pre-capitalist system that such producers sought to discard. As such, they become a problem of capitalism *per se*, not an indicator that a benign form of the latter is still on the political agenda.

Accordingly, a paradigm shift took place from the 1980s onwards, when a Marxist interpretation argued that, because employment of unfree workers enhanced profitability, such labour-power was actually compatible with accumulation. Restructuring the labour process through decomposition/recomposition of its workforce, deproletarianisation – the Marxist class struggle argument – conceptually repositioned unfreedom within capitalism *per se*, not as an outlier found only in the periphery but present also in the metropolitan contexts of the core. Departing from the prevailing 'whips and chains' concept – whereby the presence/absence of unfreedom was associated simply with visual images of physical oppression – deproletarianisation also restored the sale/purchase of labour-power to definitions of work arrangements that were not free. Similar emphasis was given to unfreedom as characterized by the reproduction of the *whole* relation (entry into + *exit from*) rather than the manner simply of its inception (entry into).

Whereas for modernisation theory, the semi-feudal thesis, and neoclassical economics, the object of political struggle was to bring about a capitalism deemed to be absent, for deproletarianisation by contrast the struggle was about class, against capitalism, and to bring about socialism. Among other things, therefore, deproletarianisation has brought a more radical Marxist theory to bear on the discussion. However, subsequent contributions to the debate which adopted much of its approach, resurfacing under different labels, nevertheless discarded the link to a socialist transition, opting instead for amelioration within the existing capitalist system. The latter, in effect, remains intact, underlining thereby the political break with the more radical Marxist class struggle approach.

PART 2

On Travel

∵

[Boat from the Barbarigo map of Venice]

FIGURE 2   Ship (de' Barbari)

Travellers, or Tourists? (Journeys Outside Europe)

WACO KID: 'Where are you headed, cowboy?'
BART: 'Nowhere special'.
WACO KID: 'Nowhere special ... I've always wanted to go there'.
BART: 'Come on'.

> An exchange between the Waco Kid (played by Gene Wilder) and Sheriff
> Bart (played by Cleavon Little) at the end of the film *Blazing Saddles* (1974),
> directed by MEL BROOKS, hinting at the familiar trope of travel writing;
> that the search for pristine locations to visit is at an end.[1]

Introduction: An Instinctive Simplicity, a Thoughtless Idealism

Those who write about travel, whether or not formally designated travel
writers, tend to adopt one of two methodological approaches: either exploring the self in relation to the context visited, or else compose a record of
travel that is less inward-oriented, the focus being outward – more on the
context itself. That the distinction is not absolute is clear from the case
of Graham Greene. Lacking maps as a guide to where he was going, he set
off on his 1935 journey across the Liberian interior unprepared in terms of
knowing where he would/could go and how this would/could be achieved,
a process described by him as 'letting myself drift with Africa'.[2] Taking 'into
new country [,] an instinctive simplicity, a thoughtless idealism', Greene
was adamant that he did not want to be mistaken for a tourist; he was a
traveller, and the arduousness of the journey was for him proof of this

---

1 See Brooks (2021: 222–23).
2 See Greene (1936: 46, 75). His plans for the itinerary 'came to nothing', Greene (1936: 51)
   admits to the 'vagueness of my ideas when I landed at Freetown [in Sierra Leone]. I had
   never been out of Europe before; I was a complete amateur at travel in Africa. I intended to
   walk across the Republic [of Liberia], but I had no idea of what route to follow or the conditions we would meet.' Later he observes (Greene, 1936: 70): 'It is difficult to understand what
   control [there is] over the border; natives pass freely to and fro; indeed with a little care it
   would be possible to travel all down West Africa without showing papers from the moment
   of landing. There is something very attractive in this great patch of "freedom to travel"...one
   felt the happy sense of being free.'

identity.[3] This seeming amateurishness is offset by a detailed account, both of politics and of the exploitative role of external corporations in Liberia; his description of a nation in debt to foreign capital is far better than that of many current travel writers, who tend either not to address the role of capitalism in the country visited, or do so only in a politically superficial manner.[4]

In many ways, the trajectory followed by travel writing mimics that of its academic rivals (social sciences, development studies). At issue, therefore, is the form taken by opposition on the part of travel writers to the impact on societies they visit of the accumulation process. Described variously as 'Westernization', 'Europeanization', or simply modernity, such antagonism quickly translates into advocacy not of a progressive 'going beyond', let alone a socialist outcome, but rather of the preservation/conservation – or, where absent, a return to – of an earlier 'pristine/primitive' selfhood. A defence of the latter, in travel writing and the social sciences alike, entailing as it does resistance against any kind of economic development, slides imperceptibly into the conservative politics of the agrarian myth and the 'new' populist postmodernism. Because the focus of these two interrelated discourses is on the erosion of traditional beliefs/ practices brought about by economic development, they – much like travel writing itself – tend to privilege (and support) the cultural identity of the 'other'.

This chapter is divided into two sections. Section I examines a recent analysis of the tourist phenomenon by D'Eramo, an all-encompassing approach which is methodologically problematic. Its model, concepts, and claims serve as the background to the travel writing considered in the second part of the chapter. Section II is a comparison of travel accounts at two distinct conjunctures: early twentieth century narratives by, among others, Lévi-Strauss, Peter Keenagh, Graham Greene, and Paul Bowles; and those by Paul Theroux and Norman Lewis later in the same century. Most of these 'travellers tales' refer to journeys outside Europe; addressed in the subsequent two chapters will be a variety of accounts involving travel within Europe.

I

Beginning with the issue of tourism and how to analyse it, here – unlike in the case of those who, as will be seen below, write about travel – one encounters a problem of methods. Statements about what motivates the plebeian mass tourist have to be treated with some caution, since methodologically what the

---

3   See Greene (1936: 116–17, 179), for whom the 'junk of civilization' encountered in one particular village where 'tourist bait' was available reminded him that he was not far from the tourist trail, something to be avoided at all costs.

4   See Greene (1936: 285ff.).

plebeian mass tourist thinks about what s/he does is not easy to access. Travel writers whose accounts purport to address this issue ignore two things: first, that despite being 'a personal way of seeing the world as it is', those who write about travel for a living are for a number of reasons – funding, book contract, trip duration, etc. – not themselves 'ordinary' tourists.[5] And second, apart from the brief information (weather, places visited, people met) contained on the back of postcards sent from trips abroad, 'ordinary' tourists generally leave no extensive written record as to precisely why they go where they go, and what they visit and look at when they get there. Needless to say, it is unfeasible to regard as substitutes for such accounts the complaints about inadequate service provision found on customer review websites in tourist destinations.

The kind of difficulties to which this methodological lacuna gives rise is evident in the most recent attempt to examine and account for the nature and effect of mass tourism. A consequence of improved transport and communications, tourism is said by D'Eramo to be a nineteenth century invention, one which flourished during the twentieth, categorized accordingly as 'the tourist age'.[6] Definitions of tourist motivation considered both by him and by other writers (Enzenburger, Adorno, Horkheimer, Barthes) include a desire simply to escape from the present, alternatively a yearning to escape from capitalist alienation, and a wish to construct 'otherness' on the basis of what is seen.[7] Labelling tourism itself as a form of 'ambulatory determinism' (= the need to travel), D'Eramo opts finally for an oblique concept of 'having the world at our fingertips', a vague and unhelpful term which seems to refer to the speed of travel, being able to go from A to Z in the shortest time possible, regarded perhaps as itself being an exhilarating or sufficiently fulfilling experience.[8]

Hello, I Must Be Going

The analysis of tourism by D'Eramo is a rambling account of an important subject, one which manages to omit that which should be included and to include that which should be omitted. Along the way digressions multiply, spurious connections are made, and arguments disappear down a cul-de-sac. In the course of this meandering, travel is depicted as an all-encompassing phenomenon outside of which exists nothing, not unlike a history of breathing. As presented by D'Eramo, the moment a person gets out of bed in the morning, s/he

---

5   See Theroux (2018: 260).
6   For this claim, see D'Eramo (2021: 9, 19, 24, 28).
7   D'Eramo (2021: 38, 40).
8   D'Eramo (2021: 197).

is already a tourist. In his approach, therefore, travel seemingly corresponds to a form of perpetual movement, 'a two-way flow' that entails 'both coming and going', akin to the process expressed by a song in a Marx Brothers film.[9]

According to D'Eramo, we now live in what he terms 'the age of tourism', as the number of international travellers has jumped from 25 million in 1950 to 1.4 billion in 2018.[10] Linked to this is the growth in airports, railway stations, and hotels, with the result that in his opinion 'tourism is the most important industry of the century'. Its economic significance can be gauged from the fact that, as he notes rightly, '[t]he pandemic has proved the centrality of tourism through tourism's omission.' Although it 'is an essential component and aspect of globalization', tourism is nevertheless a phenomenon 'omnipresent, familiar, yet seldom truly explored in depth'. Asking '[w]hy hadn't tourism's importance fully registered before', D'Eramo answers his own question in a manner that will come back to haunt him: 'Because tourists themselves are hard to take seriously.'[11] Consequently, he maintains that 'new ideas' or 'original contributions' to the study of travellers and travel are lacking.[12]

---

9   'There is an extraordinary symmetry to the way that the city, at the same time it empties of its inhabitants who head to the seaside, fills up with urban tourists,' a process described (D'Eramo, 2021: 77) as amounting to a 'two-way flow – both coming and going – [that is] particularly marked in the so-called "tourist cities"'. The Marx Brothers film in question is *Animal Crackers* (1930), directed by Victor Heerman, in which Groucho as Captain Spaulding the explorer, just returned from a trip to Africa, sings 'Hello – I must be going, I cannot stay, I came to say, I must be going, I'm glad I came, but just the same, I must be going …'

10   D'Eramo (2021: 2, 19). In 2018 tourism accounted for 10.4% of global GDP, involving 319 million jobs or 10% of global employment (D'Eramo, 2021: 3).

11   When he first presented this argument to an audience in Italy during 2017, D'Eramo points out that no one took seriously its central premiss – that tourism is economically important. Why the claim that tourists 'are hard to take seriously' comes back to haunt him is outlined below.

12   Notwithstanding the claim about the absence of 'new ideas' and 'original contributions', the case made by D'Eramo is not as new as he thinks, its logic having been known about for some time. Much the same case, even using the same language, was made recently; by MacClancy (2002), who observes that 'tourism and leisure are now the largest industries in the world'; and by Hamilton-Paterson (2006), who notes that tourism 'is an industry determined to embrace you' and 'the swiftness with which mass travel is ironing out variety the world over'. This kind of argument – combining the demise of travel, the rise and deleterious impact of mass tourism, and the alignment of the latter with economic development – has been a staple of travel writing over the years, and is one made with particular force about the city of Venice (Morand, 2002; Debray, 2002; Martin, 2007). As noted by an earlier text (Elsner and Rubiés, 1999: 232), 'travel as a significant travel experience is no longer possible [due to the fact that] the world has become homogenous because of mass tourism'. Those who have made a similar point extend from Lévi-Strauss (1961), via Smith (1978) and Runciman (1991), to Holland (2018).

Forms taken by tourism proliferate exponentially, and extend from the sea-side holiday to include tourists going to festivals or on business, as well as travelling for sports, religious, sex, nudism, or medical reasons.[13] En route tourism is also conflated with pilgrimage and anthropological fieldwork.[14] This already long list is joined by school trips ('compulsory tourism') and one-way trips to die ('death tourism').[15] Labelling the latter as recent developments indicative of what is termed 'the age of tourism', sources not mentioned by D'Eramo indicate that many of the same kinds of reasons informed travel occurring in ancient society.[16] Moreover, nineteenth century tourist 'attractions' – such as visits to the sewers, the morgue, and to see executions – said to be no longer on the itinerary because they are now unacceptable, overlooks the fact that currently the bullfight in Spain is a spectacle kept going largely by tourism.[17]

Some of the explanations are puzzling, subject to contradiction, or else unconnected with the issue in question. Thus, for example, one is told both that 'the selfie expresses an irrepressible need to confirm one's existence', and that paintings of Venice by Canaletto and Guardi are simply equivalents of the 'modern tourist brochures' the object of which is enticing visitors to the city.[18] The comparison with tourist brochures is anyway somewhat curious, since those contemplating or undertaking the Grand Tour did not have to be invited. A more plausible reason for the painting and the selfie alike is that each image confirms to its respective audience *at home* that a visit has been made by the traveller/tourist concerned.[19] Accepting that 'the hitchhiker cannot compete at the level of luxury', the inference being that there are limits placed on where

---

13   See D'Eramo (2021: 51ff., 67). Compiling notes for this review, I observed early on that its author might have added to this list things like mountaineering, an invasion by a foreign army (veni, vidi, vici), or even time-travel, with a chapter on science-fiction. In fact, subsequently a whole chapter is indeed devoted to Martians and flying saucers (D'Eramo, 2021: Chapter 13).

14   D'Eramo (2021: 56, 195).

15   D'Eramo (2021: 58–59, 65). Missing from the list is political exile, an involuntary form of travel experienced by, among others, Trotsky (1930: Chapter XLV, the title of which is 'The Planet without a Visa'), Victor Serge (1963), Walter Benjamin, and Marx himself.

16   See Casson (1994) who records tourists in ancient society going on holiday to the seaside, undertaking travel for sports and health reasons, collecting mementoes of places visited, and making pilgrimages to the Holy Land during the early Christian era.

17   For these nineteenth century tourist 'attractions', see D'Eramo (2021: 24–25).

18   D'Eramo (2021: 43, 82–83).

19   Much later in the same text, D'Eramo (2021: 216) seems to accept this more prosaic explanation, observing that 'once they have returned home, tourists want to experience again the flavours they tasted on holiday just as they want to bring back memories of their trip by looking at photos and videos they shot.'

one can go and what one can do there, D'Eramo then subscribes to the opposite view, stating that '[i]t has become possible for each person – independent
of class or income – to be literally "a man of the world"'.[20] Digressions include
disquisitions on urban zoning, the art market, estrangement, and science
fiction.[21]

Tourists Who Are Not Tourists

Among the least persuasive arguments made by D'Eramo are three in particular: where present-day travel is concerned, that no difference exists between
oligarch and proletarian; that urban locations are an effect simply of tourism;
and recasting the latter as an industry by eradicating the modern/postmod-
ern difference. Less than convincing, therefore, is the claim that nowadays oligarchs are too busy working 'to experience the comforts of the "traveller" and
must succumb to the proletarian destiny of becoming a "tourist"'.[22] That the
yatch of a Russian oligarch can remain moored on the Riva degli Sciavoni in
Venice for months at a time, fenced off from access by the public, suggests otherwise, as does the fact that oligarchs travel by private jet, thereby prolonging
the duration of their stay in a place visited.

Equally debatable is the generalization that because '[h]uman civilizations
have traditionally had a sceptical relationship toward saltwater', evidence for
which is that cities are 'set back from the sea', the seaside holiday and its form
of tourism are consequently an anomaly.[23] From the premise 'that the coastal
agglomerations are all very new, all tied to the tourist industry', D'Eramo
extrapolates that '[a]side from the present day, no other human civilization
has witnessed the mass practice of seawater immersion [= seaside holiday]'.
Contrary to the explanation that urban coastal locations are due simply to
recent tourism, historically cities have indeed been placed near the sea, but
for economic reasons – maritime trade – that are unconnected either with an
aversion towards saltwater or with seaside vacations.[24]

As questionable is the claim that it was 'the demand for tourism [which]
triggered the collapse of a great empire [the USSR]'.[25] It transpires that

---

20   D'Eramo (2021: 158, 200).
21   See D'Eramo (2021: 139ff., 152, 164, 173–76, 178ff.).
22   D'Eramo (2021: 18).
23   D'Eramo (2021: 67–68).
24   Thus the location of Venice was determined by trading requirements long before the Lido
      became a fashionable holiday resort.
25   D'Eramo (2021: 5–6).

D'Eramo is referring to the way East Germans crossed into the West at the fall of the Berlin Wall in 1989, when tourist visas were issued to facilitate the process. What those with visas desired was not simply to 'visit' the capitalist West, but rather – if possible – to live and work there, to become 'Western'. Hence the episode to which D'Eramo refers was not about tourism at all. Subsequently, however, he returns to this issue, not only reiterating his initial claim but also extending the argument to include yet another phenomenon under the tourist rubric.[26] Inevitably, perhaps, migrants are categorized as tourists, despite the fact that the former visit to stay and work, whereas the latter visit only for a short while, to gaze and return home shortly thereafter. Accordingly, this conflation – migrant = tourist – ignores the different logics informing each process: the tourist is escaping from work, while the migrant is searching for it.[27] Unlike tourism, therefore, migration and the attempt to prevent it are both issues connected with the functioning (or otherwise) of the labour market.

Citing as evidence the case of Las Vegas, he rejects the view that tourism is no more than a 'postmodern frill', a 'superstructural rather than foundational' substitute for deindustrialization.[28] Much rather, he regards tourism as the epitome 'of the modern, of industrialized capitalist civilization, even in an apparently post-industrial and postmodern sector'.[29] This is because in his opinion no difference separates modernity (progress, industry, production, manufacturing) from postmodernity (consumption, pastiche, culture, the immaterial), since behind the glitz/excess there is an industrial economy

---

26 Subsequently D'Eramo (2021: 190–91) reiterates his claim, 'Very intentionally, I started this inquiry into tourism with the collapse of the Berlin Wall, an event hastened by an unstoppable avalanche of tourist visa applications ... in the unwritten constitution of the modern, totalitarianism and dictatorship are summed up in prohibitions against travel.'

27 Again, the problematic nature of this conflation is something D'Eramo almost recognizes ('These are tourists who are not tourists'), an apparent concession that does not prevent him from positing the migrant-as-tourist argument in the first place. 'A spectre is circling, avoided by all the discourses on tourism', he notes (D'Eramo, 2021: 237) about the migrant, adding: 'This is relevant not only because, in the first instance, the migrant and the tourist are the two complementary, symmetrical faces of modern travel ... it is also relevant because a good part of modern migration takes place under the guise of tourism – tourists who exceed their tourist visa, working in the country they are ostensibly visiting ... These are tourists who are not tourists.'

28 What D'Eramo (2021: 81, 132) opposes is the argument that because tourism is a substitute for deindustrialization, a city like Las Vegas – the 'intentionally tourist city par excellence' – appears to embody all the non-economic/immaterial aspects that postmodernism attributes to tourism.

29 D'Eramo (2021: 153). How can tourism be categorized as emblematic of modernity, when an important aspect of it involves, fundamentally, gazing on the past?

(casinos, hotels, workers).[30] Conflating the postmodern with modernity in this fashion, so as then to argue that tourism is not a service but an industry, cannot escape the basic contradiction D'Eramo faces. However much one tries to avoid the issue, Las Vegas produces no manufactured commodities (automobiles, rolling stock, white goods), and the ancillary economic activity (dormitory buildings, places to eat) that surround an electronic assembly factory or a car making plant does not of itself constitute the industrial status of such enterprises.[31] That Las Vegas is essentially a service-sector economy, not a manufacturing one, underlines its difference from what political economy has always defined as industry/modernity.

Although D'Eramo indicts the promotion by UNESCO of the world heritage site for complicity with tourist expansion, he omits to probe fully the intellectual context and its contribution to the politics of national identity, the cultural turn (= postmodernism), and populism.[32] When, finally, he gets round to the concept of 'the happy savage', this is linked not to the discourse of the agrarian myth (peasant = Nature = nation) but rather to issues such as nudity (= 'modern naturism') and the significance of 'brown skin'.[33] Building on this, D'Eramo records that at the end of the 1970s there emerged in the West an overlapping and mutually supportive ideological matrix, composed of identity + ethnicity + heritage, which was promptly appropriated by conservatives and the far right.[34] Nevertheless, he overlooks the epistemological connection between on the one hand the commodification of heritage, the rise of the far right, the consolidation of identity politics, and on the other what precisely

---

30 'What we see with Las Vegas', insists D'Eramo (2021: 133–34), 'is that its system of signs [= replicants that glory in their inauthenticity] has an efficiency and rationality that is in all respects industrial. Behind the appearance of glitz and excess lies a real economy of means. This contradiction is resolvable only if we understand the modern and postmodern not as contrasting but as tendencies that overlap or perhaps intertwine. The postmodern considers the modern as the grand narrative of progress, of industrialization and scientific rationality ... But in Las Vegas, tourism means precisely this ... when tourism (postmodern) becomes and industry (modern).'

31 D'Eramo (2021: 139) recognizes the difficulty in trying to label tourism as an industry, observing: 'No matter how often we tell ourselves that tourism is an industry, we never quite manage to picture it as such. In our minds, industry remains inextricably linked to hangars full of machinery, smokestacks and sulphuric fumes – and not to sandal-wearing shirtless hordes in their short trousers ... the tourist city still seems postmodern.'

32 For the promotion by UNESCO of 'authentic' heritage, inviting a melancholic gaze on ancient ruins, see D'Eramo (2021: 116–17).

33 D'Eramo (2021: 70–71).

34 D'Eramo (2021: 101–102).

brings them together with postmodern theory. In one sense this is unsurprising, not least because of his attempt to decouple tourism and postmodernism.

There is, however, another cause: the neglect by D'Eramo of the academic role in privileging 'otherness', directly, and indirectly contributing thereby to the conceptual recuperation of 'the noble savage'. The latter in turn played an important part in two interrelated processes: it fuelled the nationalist ideology, empowering conservatism and the far right; and it drove the replacement of Marxist interpretations of Third World development by the 'new' populist postmodernism. Opposed to the application to the rural 'other' of what it termed Eurocentric foundational discourse, 'new' populist postmodern theory licensed the intellectual search for and consolidation of an eternal (= 'authentic') subject at the rural grassroots. The national/ethnic characteristics (= identity) and struggle (= resistance/agency) of these subjects, it was then said, constituted an ever-present cultural 'heritage' in Latin America and Asia, underwriting the dominant academic paradigms of the era (subaltern studies, multitudes, everyday-forms-of-resistance). Why this aspect is missed by D'Eramo is, in part, due to his positive view of populism: notwithstanding their reactionary politics, his argument is that populist movements are progressive.[35]

The Ruin(s) of Time, the Time of Ruin(s)

Instead of re-essentializing the self and other of tourism, as does the agrarian myth of the 'new' populist postmodernism, a more fruitful approach requires de-essentializing these same two categories: the class position held by both the subject and object of the tourist gaze. Although the disdain felt by the 'traveller' for the 'tourist' coincides with aristocratic/bourgeois perceptions of the plebeian is noted by D'Eramo, unmentioned are crucial aspects of the way in which the class position of s/he who travels affects what is seen, by whom, and why.[36] Thus the element of scorn operates not just between classes, but also within the ranks of the same class.[37] During the Grand Tour, therefore,

---

35   See D'Eramo (2013).

36   See D'Eramo (2021: 11–12), who misses the fact that the camera enables a plebeian visitor to 'capture' that which has been hitherto a marker of cultural exclusivity, previously the object of gaze by the upper-class traveller alone. In effect, the camera enables the mass tourist to trespass on – indeed, to acquire – a form of cultural property which used in the past to 'belong' to members of the aristocracy and the bourgeoisie.

37   This element of not-keeping-up-appearances emerges clearly from the account by Szerb (2014: 53ff.), who records having to eat in cheap restaurants alongside workers during

aristocratic hostility was projected internally, against travellers occupying an analogous social position who departed from (or were ignorant of) the cultural norms governing this *rite de passage*. Whilst on a visit to Italy in 1765, for example, Boswell – to his obvious chagrin – was frequently chided by the tutor of an aristocrat travelling in the same group with his own lack of knowledge.[38] That Boswell should have been so concerned about this accusation is unsurprising: such cultural deficiency, it was inferred, posed questions about his right to move in such circles.

Class distinctions also extend to the different sources of information about travel instructions, destinations, and cultural discernment. This distinction was embodied in the contrast between manuals used by the aristocracy for the Grand Tour (recommending what should be seen), and guides used by everyone else on a tourist visit (containing advice about locations, travel arrangements, and cost). In the words of D'Eramo, '[b]etween the manuals and the guides we see the difference between the aristocracy, who were the intended readership of the first, and the bourgeoisie, that of the second'.[39] However, this distinctiveness is not as clear-cut as depicted. To begin with, information about 'how' to look was provided to aristocratic travellers not so much by manuals as by an accompanying guide/tutor, a knowledgeable 'bear-leader' present throughout the whole journey. And second, modern guides also include detailed information about what to look at and why (= how to look). Furthermore, present-day tourists – especially when in large groups – are often accompanied by a

---

a visit to Italy in 1936, repeating an earlier incident 'when I was a child and we used to travel abroad there would be times when my father, in an uncharacteristic fit of penny-pinching, and knowing none of his acquaintance would be likely to see him, would take us to the sort of lower-class restaurant, like the one I was sitting in now, that he would normally never set foot in. Even then, as a child, I was filled with shame.' He goes on to criticize himself for reacting like this, observing (Szerb, 2014: 59, 61): 'So there you have it: I'm no better than anyone else. And yet I loathe nothing in the world more than the sense of bourgeois superiority ... of course I too believe that my social rank is a matter of finding the right hotel room, eating in the right restaurant and having a suitable seat on the train. But I know perfectly well ... that my essential commonness [is because] I feel the force of the rules [about class]'.

38 On this episode, see Brady and Pottle (1955).

39 According to D'Eramo (2021: 16, original emphasis), '[t]he difference between the "manuals" for the Grand Tour and the modern "guides" gives us a clear idea of the image the authors had of their readers. The first was aimed at directing the prospective traveller's gaze toward certain objects and events, as the particular destinations were taken for granted; they explained *how* and not *where* to travel and look. In the case of the more modern guide, however, the reader is told where to go, how to get there and at what cost ...'

cicerone, a local guide with specialist knowledge about places to see, and why, in a particular locality.

It is only well into the narrative that the relationship between tourism and the ideology of class difference is addressed.[40] Visitors who gaze on a ruin are divided by D'Eramo between those who know what it is, its history and significance, and those who do not: between the aristocratic or bourgeois traveller, in other words, and the plebeian tourist.[41] Having said that the mass tourist – the plebeian – stares at ruins in ignorance of their meaning, D'Eramo contradicts this when observing that 'tourists dedicate the precious little spare time they have during the working year to the exhausting activity of sightseeing. What is surprising is not that they want to have fun, *but that they do so by trying to learn at the same time*.'[42] This, he then comments, 'has always been the real ambiguity of the tourist'. So, after all, the plebeian gaze is not necessarily that of someone who is ignorant.

That class determines who travels, where, when, and how, is an issue that cannot be avoided by any examination of the dynamics structuring tourism. There is a clear link between 'from below' class struggle, the formation of the welfare state, the provision of paid holidays, and the capacity of workers to enjoy travel.[43] It is when the analysis moves from the fact of travel to its rationale and effects – giving rise to questions such as 'what motivates the tourist?', and 'what does the tourist attraction consist of?' – that the story become more complicated.[44] It could be argued that, in one particular respect, those positioned at opposite ends of the social hierarchy, who travel in distinctive ways, at different conjunctures, to dissimilar locations, nevertheless do so for the same reason: not the formation but rather the confirmation of their class and/or national identity.

---

40   '[T]he reader will have noticed', comments D'Eramo (2021: 121–22), 'an element of class [since a] ruin is not any old ruined building, but rather must be the ruin of a palace, a mansion, a grandiose construction ...' He continues: '[T]he pleasure of a ruin is accessible only to those with cultural capital. It presupposes that the viewer knows what the ruin is the remainder of ...' That is, it 'distinguishes those with a consciousness [of history] from those in blissful ignorance ... who wander throughout the landscape without really noticing it.'

41   This difference (on which see Brass, 2014: Chapter 8) corresponds also to one between an 'initiate' (who understands the context) and an 'uninitiate' (who does not).

42   See D'Eramo (2021: 126, emphasis added).

43   As D'Eramo (2021: 18) notes, '[o]nly when everyone could enjoy paid holidays did travelling become a possibility for the masses'.

44   For these questions, see D'Eramo (2021: 35, 36)..

Is Your Journey Really Necessary?

Travel literature generally, and historically that connected with the Grand Tour, reveals the extent to which class struggle – at home and abroad – contributed to the formation of national identity.[45] Accounts by those belonging to the landowning class of journeys made throughout Europe confirm the shift from a cosmopolitan ideology shared with other members of the same class abroad to a nationalist one, held in common with subordinate class elements at home. In this the role discharged by the Grand Tour was crucial. Before the 1789 French revolution, the rural poor encountered during the Grand Tour were perceived as benign; after 1789 they were seen as a potential/actual menace, threatening to become the 'mob in the streets'. The latter, which caused such fear in the nineteenth century, has in the course of the twentieth been transformed into the plebeian mass tourist, currently seen by many travel writers as every bit as threatening as was the former.

It was this process as much as anything that occasioned the double transformation: a shift away from an internationally acquired ruling class culture, formed as a result of the Grand Tour, and towards an internally-forged identity that could – it might be claimed – be shared with plebeian elements. The formulation of a nationalist ideology, rather than the internationalism of those who rule, and its subsequent fusion with populism, can be traced to travel accounts by Herder (nationalism) and Herzen (nationalism as populism). In each instance European voyages opened up a comparative dimension, among other things enabling them both not just to observe the 'other' in the latter's own location but also – and perhaps more importantly – to surmise as to the cause and desirability of any differences (or similarities) encountered.

Characterizing tourism as 'a self-destructive practice', which succeeds only in converting 'the exotic other visited' into a copy of home, D'Eramo maintains somewhat pessimistically that '[i]n the end, there is no escape'.[46] Modern-day tourism is dismissed as being no more than a process of 'de-authentication', licensing for the most part 'the all-too-familiar litany of commodification ... standardization, homogenization, and falsification' that 'kills the city'.[47] That

---

45   What follows draws on three chapters in Brass (2014: Part 3), dealing with the connection
        between tourism and class formation, class struggle, nationalism and populism.
46   D'Eramo (2021: 74).
47   D'Eramo (2021: 115, 153, 167). 'Already today', he laments (D'Eramo, 2021: 154–55), 'Venice is
        a dead city: as one sees walking from canal to canal on a November night without finding
        a single window lit up.' This does not accord with my own experience of visiting the city,
        when at night-time there was not a window that was not 'lit up'.

D'Eramo himself subscribes to this disdain is evident from an account based on his own experience, which merits quoting at length. 'Not long ago', he writes, 'I went back to San Gimignano for the first time in thirty years. There was not a single genuine butcher, greengrocer or baker within its walls ... none of San Gimignano's inhabitants were to be found in the old city – they all lived outside its walls, in modern apartment blocks close to shopping centres.'[48]

This revealing cry of despair at the sight of so many tourists engaged in trampling across the globe suggests that D'Eramo is complicit with the anti-modern trope voiced by almost all those who have written and write still about travel and tourism. Namely, that the plebeian mass tourist cannot but defile the places visited, either by his/her presence alone, or by the necessity of having to provide him/her either with home comforts or with 'inauthentic' things at which to gaze. It projects, inferentially, a familiar and conservative sub-text: that, as high culture is not for the masses, they should be dissuaded from visiting places where it is located.[49] In this respect, D'Eramo comes close to reproducing the view of Marinetti and others (Robert Graves, Evelyn Waugh, Paddy Leigh Fermor) who object to mass tourism *per se*, either because it 'de-authenticates' by improving/modernizing, or because it prevents this from happening.[50]

'We Italians', laments D'Eramo, 'understand very well [that] residents of a tourist city live forever in the tourist gaze,' adding that '[i]t is like having your house full of unwanted guests.'[51] Subsequently he appears to retract this negative assessment, since '[t]aking pot shots at tourists seems like the world's most popular sport. Fire and brimstone abound (even in this book).'[52] Rather late in the day, therefore, D'Eramo admits he is guilty of regarding tourism simply as a blight, a kind of plague ('hell is other people'), which is how mass tourism has

---

48   D'Eramo (2021: 85–86).

49   That such views continue to circulate among the British ruling class is evident from comments made by Oliver Letwin, a wealthy old Etonian and Conservative Cabinet Minister, who in April 2011 opposed a new airport development on the grounds that 'we don't want more [working class] people from Sheffield flying away on cheap holidays.'

50   In fact, D'Eramo (2021: 108) confesses to 'some sympathy for Marinetti's intolerance'.

51   D'Eramo (2021: 89–90). From 1924 onwards, Benjamin spent much time travelling as an 'ordinary' tourist, including trips to Spain and Italy. After visiting Naples, for example, he (Benjamin, 1979: 167ff.; 2014: 145ff.) recounted his impressions of the city in both written and radio broadcast formats. Declaring his 'love of travel', Benjamin (2007: 171ff.) collected postcards – sent and received as part of what for him was an 'illustrated memory'. A brief reminiscence by him of a 1929 weeklong visit to San Gimignano prompts the following question: had he lived to revisit that town, would he, too, have been regarded as just another 'unwelcome guest'?

52   D'Eramo (2021: 157). Of the many anti-tourist diatribes circulating at present, a recent example is Meades (2021: 43, 190, 217–18, 815, 819, 825, 884–85).

traditionally been regarded by the upper-class traveller who resents the mass tourist – the plebeian from home – trespassing on what has been hitherto 'his' own property. In short, it is a well-known class attitude. A clue to the reason for this problem is found right at the end of the book. There D'Eramo confesses both to changes in the subject to be studied – from 'tourist city', via 'tourist civilization', to 'the age of tourism' – and to the late realization on his part that throughout the analysis he has been in lockstep with anti-tourist diatribes that have been issued periodically in the course of history.[53]

II

Any discussion (academic or otherwise) of travel outside Europe, who does it, what it means, how it has changed, and whether or not it ought to continue in its present form, sooner or later finds it necessary to address the observations made by the anthropologist Claude Lévi-Strauss about embarking on his initial fieldwork experience in Brazil during the mid-1930s.[54] Recounting how North American tribes allocate prestige to those who undergo and endure an ordeal that requires courage and resilience, he draws a parallel with a similar process in our own societies, where an arduous journey into a foreign land has been – and is – rewarded in a similar fashion.[55] His conclusion was that,

---

53   'As the reader ... will have realized', concedes D'Eramo (2021: 239, original emphasis), 'my plans changed even while I was working on this book. Indeed, my topic changed. I had undertaken to study the tourist *city*, as an urban aggregation unique to our time. Gradually, I came to understand that I was studying not the tourist city but rather tourist *civilization*. And, having got that far, I understood that what was taking shape was the *age* of tourism, which I would have to define ...' He continues: 'Even that does not suffice: for what changed was not just my topic, but my perspective and, lastly, the judgement I drew. Only while I was already on my way did I realize that I, too,...had allowed myself to become wrapped up in the cruel and childish game of making tourism the easy scapegoat for all the wrongdoings of the modern.'

54   See Lévi-Strauss (1961). Among those who refer to his observations about the nature of travel are Bowles (2006: xxii) and D'Eramo (2021: 241–2). Somewhat of a surprise, the recent biography of Lévi-Strauss by Godelier (2018) contains no analysis of the link between anthropology, fieldwork, and episodes of travel, despite the significance attached to the latter by Lévi-Strauss himself. The original French title of the book by Lévi-Strauss was *Tristes Tropiques*, a travel account he later recalled (Lévi-Strauss & Eribon, 1991: 58) it was not originally intended to publish as such ('It had never dawned on me to write about my travels ... I had to rethink my old adventures, reflect upon them, and draw some kind of conclusions').

55   'Once again', notes Lévi-Strauss (1961: 42), 'the parallel is very close: any young man who isolates himself for a few weeks or months ... and exposes himself to an extreme situation of any sort may count on being invested, on his return, with a kind of magic power ... [i]n our world the power comes out in newspaper articles, best-selling books, and lectures ...'

lacking any longer an indigenous society whose 'exotic' inhabitants and their traditional culture remained unknown to and unchanged by the world – an encounter with which represented the essential component of this rite of passage – a quest taking its subject (whether traveller or, indeed, anthropologist) into the terrain of a pristine 'other' had long ceased to possess validity.[56] For Lévi-Strauss, therefore, increasingly the element of difference has been erased by sameness, negating thereby any search for the presence of an authentic 'other'.[57]

Traveller's Tales

Despite attempts to conflate them, travel and anthropological fieldwork are distinct phenomena.[58] Like many travel writers, the tourist stays for a short time, without necessarily wishing to comprehend the totality of the social structure in the location visited. An anthropologist, by contrast, stays for a long – sometimes very long – time, endeavouring to become part of the social context studied, as befits the participant/observation methodology. Whereas the tourist – and to some extent also the travel writer – is always an outsider, an anthropologist is sometimes able to make the transition to that of an insider. On the basis of these and other differences, it is possible to situate those undertaking a journey at separate points on the same continuum. In terms of the kind of place visited, the duration of the visit itself, plus the intensity of social

---

In a conversation much later (Lévi-Strauss & Eribon, 1991: 22) his interviewer observed: 'It requires a great deal of courage and physical stamina to carry out this sort of expedition. In *Tristes Tropiques* you [Lévi-Strauss] write of riding over impossible terrain, crossing rivers, travelling by canoe.'

56   In the words of Lévi-Strauss (1961: 44, original emphasis), '[a]nd that is how I see myself: traveller, archaeologist of space, trying in vain to repiece together the idea of the exotic with the help of a particle here and a fragment of debris there. At this point Illusion begins to set its insidious traps. I should have liked to live in the age of *real* travel, when the spectacle on offer had not yet been blemished, contaminated, and confounded ...'

57   'There was a time when travel confronted the traveller with civilizations radically different from his own', laments Lévi-Strauss (1961: 90): 'It was their strangeness, above all, which impressed him. But these opportunities have been getting rarer and rarer for a very long time. Be it in India or in America, the traveller of our day finds things more familiar than he will admit.' This element of sameness is in marked contrast with the hopes experienced when starting out on his fieldwork in Brazil. 'I was in a state of intense intellectual excitement', explained Lévi-Strauss in an interview with Eribon (Lévi-Strauss and Eribon, 1991: 21), 'I felt I was reliving the adventures of the first sixteenth-century explorers. I was discovering the New World for myself'.

58   Just such a conflation informs the analysis of D'Eramo (2021: 195).

engagement with the locality and its inhabitants, therefore, it is possible to construct a spectrum from the anthropologist at one end, via the travel writer, to the tourist him/herself at the other.[59]

Perhaps because of these distinctions, and the perceived qualitative dissimilarity between their respective accounts, a discernible tension exists between those who, as anthropologists, conduct participant/observation fieldwork, and those labelled travel writers: the latter aspire to a scholarly respectability and academic influence enjoyed by the former.[60] Accordingly, a travel writer desires that his/her account be considered on a par with an ethnography; an anthropologist, by contrast, is glad this is not the case, and appears to resent the comparison when it is made.[61] Each tends to regard the approach of the other as epistemologically insufficient, because methodologically deficient. Whereas the travel writer deals with macro-level generalities, s/he often misses important processes operating at the grassroots: the opposite is true of the anthropologist, whose focus on the structural minutia existing at the grassroots frequently overlooks crucial economic and political determinants operating at the national or international level.

This difference between travel writing (more aware of the wider political context) and ethnographies (more aware of grassroots issues, greater detail about them) is acknowledged by Lévi-Strauss.[62] It is also a distinction

59   This spectrum is different from that attributed by Theroux (2018: 253) to Paul Bowles: 'He did not think of himself as a tourist: he was a traveller. The difference is partly one of time … whereas the tourist generally hurries back home at the end of a few weeks or months, the traveler … moves slowly, over periods of years, from one part of the earth to another.'

60   On the subject of influence, the self-effacing claim made by Lévi-Strauss is open to question: 'I even read recently,' he remarks (Lévi-Strauss & Eribon, 1991: 153), 'that the success of *Tristes Tropiques* was linked to the rise of the idea of the Third World. That is a misinterpretation. The societies I was defending or for which I was endeavouring to witness are even more threatened by the new setup than they were by colonization.'

61   That the travel writer craves the academic standing of the ethnography, and wishes his/her account to be considered on a par with that of the anthropologist, is evident from an observation by Theroux (2018: 263) when speaking of Somerset Maugham: 'His travelling off the beaten track makes this book [*The Gentlemen in the Parlour*] not just unusual but (to me the greatest attribute of the travel narrative) a valuable historical document.' The two most revealing phrases are 'off the beaten track' – that is, going to inaccessible places normally visited only by an anthropologist – and 'a valuable historical document', invoking thereby intellectual parity with the account written by an anthropologist of his/her fieldwork site.

62   'Shall I make a confession?', Lévi-Strauss asks his interviewer (Lévi-Strauss & Eribon, 1991: 159), before adding: 'After *Tristes Tropiques* there were times when I imagined that someone in the press was going to ask me to travel and write. If that had happened, perhaps I would have a clearer notion of contemporary problems [but] I wouldn't have

confirmed by a number of different travel writers. Witnessing tribal rituals in mid-1930s Honduras, for example, Peter Keenagh confessed that 'I have no right to put down the facts that we gathered as relevant pieces of tribal ethnography, because nine sentences of every ten are founded on guesswork'.[63] Emphasizing that 'I am not an anthropologist', Graham Greene exhibits an analogous form of deference at the same conjuncture when describing either the burial of a chief or the authority exercised over a village in Liberia by 'the Big Bush Devil', in each instance citing Diedrich Westermann as an authority.[64]

In a more defensive vein, Norman Lewis has the main character of a novel set in Laos during the immediate post-war era utter disparaging remarks about the relevance of anthropology to a proper understanding of the political context.[65] Anxiety on the part of the travel writer about not being on a par with the anthropologist is matched also by fear lest s/he be regarded as no more than an ordinary tourist. It is a concern about status diminution expressed by Theroux in the following manner: 'I was reminded of who I really was ... [i]n spite of my politics and my teaching in the bush school, I was little more than a tourist, taking advantage.'[66] Like those he disparages, however, in declaring that 'I love the African Bush, I hate African cities' Theroux confirms that he, too, subscribes to agrarian myth discourse.[67]

---

written the same books. Whether for better or for worse, I don't know. In any case, it would have been different.'

63 See Keenagh (1937: 174), who – somewhat disarmingly – accepts (Keenagh, 1937: XI) that 'neither the author nor [his companion] had the slightest scientific knowledge of any kind. For these reasons let no learned conclusions be drawn by the reader from the material of this book; and let him understand clearly from the start that the expedition was no more than an unjustified piece of elaborate and protracted inquisitiveness.'

64 See Greene (1936: 100–104, 106, 164), who displays a similarly respectful attitude towards anthropology when considering the power exercised by the village devil. 'Anthropologists, so far as I can gather', he notes (Greene, 1936: 107), 'have not made up their minds whether it is a real language the devil [in the village] speaks or whether the interpreter simply invents a meaning'.

65 The character in question (Lewis, 1953: 106), 'intent as usual on replacing instinct by misconceived intelligence, floundered hopelessly', because he had purchased 'an out-of-date book on Laos by a German professor and studied with great care the chapter on courtship among the Laotians', learning that 'it entailed an exchange of symbolic flowers at different phases of the moon ...' Overly reliant on this academic text, and consequently '[u]nder the influence of this study [he] bored [his Laotian girlfriend] for several days, until he renounced as hopeless the task of refining himself, and relapsed into the natural barbarity she so respected.'

66 Theroux (2018: 225).

67 See Theroux (2018: 227).

Objecting to 'traveller's tales' because such accounts essentialize the tribe or 'savage', Lévi-Strauss argues that perpetuated thereby is an image of an unchanging 'other' which he, together with other anthropologists, knows to be untrue.[68] This is indeed the case, as much travel writing has from the early twentieth century onwards included – and includes still – the objective of an encounter with a 'primitive other', either situated in the long-distant past or else currently hidden from sight in a far-off and inaccessible location. Hence the admission by Keenagh that in the course of an undeniably arduous journey upriver in Honduras during the mid-1930s, he was 'particularly anxious to find the tribes of this area, because they are almost pure Indian', adding that '[h]ere, if anywhere, was the untainted ancient stock'.[69] Much the same kind of 'pristine/primitive otherness' is evident in the way Lewis describes the indigenous inhabitants of Melanesia in the 1990s.[70] By contrast, the search by Paul Bowles for an authentic cultural identity that is American takes him in another direction, back to what he terms 'the childhood of our culture' embedded in European history.[71]

---

68   'I understand how it is that people delight in travel-books and ask only to be misled by them', explains Lévi-Strauss (1961: 39), displaying his scorn for the genre. He elaborates: 'Such books preserve the illusion of something that no longer exists, but yet must be assumed to exist if we are to escape from the appalling indictment that has been piling up against us through twenty thousand years of history ...'

69   See Keenagh (1937: 207). His surprise and disappointment on finding that he was not the first to have encountered the 'pristine other' once found was evident (Keenagh, 1937: 127–28): 'We had successfully made our way into the middle of a Zamba village without alarming the Indians, and as far as one could tell this was completely untouched ground. On the way to the hut we saw no single sign of civilization or white influence. The scales fell suddenly from our eyes. On the far wall, occupying a place of dignity and importance, was the red and green legend "Lucky Strike": and on one of the side walls this was matched by a more modest sign, "Coca-Cola"...I cannot remember ever having had a greater surprise than in that moment when we first went into the hut ... we knew that we were in the heart of the wildest Indian territory, yet there hung two glaring advertisements for the most modern American products.'

70   See Lewis (1998: 151ff.).

71   See Bowles (2010: 102–103): 'But I believe that what we Americans are searching for, and thus the most important thing we can bring back with us, is something more all-embracing. I should call it a childhood – a personal childhood that has some relationship to the childhood of our culture. The overwhelming majority of us are transplanted Europeans of one sort or another. Culturally speaking, the short time we have been in America is nothing compared to the infinitely longer time we have spent in Europe, and we seem to have forgotten this true past, lost contact with the psychic soil of tradition in which the roots of culture must be anchored.'

Ragpickers of History

Notwithstanding the accusation levelled by Lévi-Strauss against travel writing, that it essentializes the indigenous subject as an ahistorical and thus unchanging 'other', the same objection applies equally strongly to much anthropological discourse, including his own.[72] Ironically, therefore, he outlines his position on this issue as being one in which 'I defend the small populations who wish to remain faithful to their traditional way of life, away from the conflicts that are dividing the modern world'.[73] It is an approach that has informed most ethnographic research, extending from the early twentieth century to the present. Anthropologists conducting fieldwork in Latin America constructed the idea of an enduring and unchanging 'peasant society', the supposed passivity of which gave rise to concepts such as 'limited good', 'folk culture', the 'culture of poverty', Andean 'verticality', and latterly new social movements.[74] Those undertaking research in Asia have deployed similar frameworks, proclaiming the unchanging/unchangeable nature of a culturally innate 'peasantness' found there, a view embodied in currently fashionable paradigms like the subaltern, everyday-forms-of-resistance, and new farmers' movements, all of which subscribe to or are influenced by 'new' populist postmodern theory structuring agrarian myth discourse.[75]

This link is one that Lévi-Strauss not merely accepts but takes a pride in, pointing out that cultural relativism is 'one of the foundations of

---

72 Noting 'how thoroughly the notion of travel became corrupted by the notion of power', Lévi-Strauss (1961: 39, original emphasis) makes clear the reason for this: 'No longer can travel yield up its treasures intact ... commercial and military aircraft roar across the still "virgin" but no longer unspoilt forests of South America and Melanesia ... [t]ravel, in such circumstances, can only bring us face to face with our historical existence in its unhappiest aspects. The great civilization of the West has given birth to many marvels; but at what cost! ... What travel has now to show us is the filth, *our* filth, that we have thrown in the face of humanity.'

73 Lévi-Strauss and Eribon (1991: 153). Earlier in the same interview (Lévi-Strauss & Eribon, 1991: 56) he admits to being overwhelmed by his 'contact with the new world', an 'upheaval which still affects me, of a face-to-face encounter with a virgin and immense nature, while all that I had known before was nature of modest proportions.' Central to this reaction, therefore, was a classic illustration of Burke's sublime: the immensity of Nature and the 'natural', dwarfing what he had 'known before'. The later reference (Lévi-Strauss & Eribon, 1991: 93) equating 'virgin forest' with 'an unknown world' reinforces the anthropological trope regarding Nature as the abode of a 'pristine other' hidden from view.

74 On the contribution by anthropology to the construction and perpetuation of theory about grassroots rural identity in Latin America as 'other', see the volume edited by Brass (2003).

75 For details about these paradigms, see Brass (1995).

anthropological thought'.[76] A similar pride is taken in the fact that a book by him led to 'the rehabilitation of the primitive mind', which – when coupled with the recognition that anthropologists, including himself, 'flee from civilization' that is for them alienating – confirms why 'otherness' is seen by ethnographers and travel writers alike in a positive light.[77] Tracing the methodological debt that social history (= 'the new history') he notes that over the past three decades 'historians have understood the importance of minutiae in daily life that anthropology takes as its substance, details their forerunners tended to ignore.'[78] Ethnographers are described by him, memorably, as 'the ragpickers of history sifting through the garbage cans for our wealth', a practice that has been adopted by social history. It is precisely this connection, acknowledged so proudly by Lévi-Strauss, that led in turn to the methodological and theoretical validation – and eventual consolidation – of postmodern theory and the agrarian myth.

Difficulties facing such claims are not difficult to discern. Although the influence anthropology exercises on social history is undeniable, the assertion by Lévi-Strauss that consequently no difference can be said to exist between the source of fieldwork observations in anthropology and investigations by social history based on chronicles, memoirs, and literature, is problematic.[79] Whereas anthropologists in the field are able to question their informants about points of interest/relevance, this procedure is not open to social historians examining documents relating to episodes long past.[80] Take this specific approach – being face-to-face with the object(s) of study, a presence enabling live conversation to ensue (an exchange of views, of information, of ideas) – away, and the methodological advantage enjoyed historically by anthropology

76   On cultural relativism as the epistemological core of anthropology, see Lévi-Strauss and Eribon (1991: 147).

77   See Lévi-Strauss and Eribon (1991:110); the book in question is Lévi-Strauss (1966). As revealing is the following admission (Lévi-Strauss & Eribon, 1991: 67): 'For many anthropologists, perhaps, not just myself, the ethnological vocation is a flight from civilization, from a century in which one doesn't feel at home.'

78   For this and the following observations see Lévi-Strauss and Eribon (1991: 122).

79   On this issue, Lévi-Strauss states (Lévi-Strauss & Eribon, 1991: 122): 'Historians have discovered that this long-neglected refuse lying about in chronicles and memoirs as well as in literature is of the same nature as the observations made in the field by anthropologists, and that they could utilize it.'

80   This is a difficulty that seemingly escapes Lévi-Strauss. When asked about the future of anthropology, and whether or not it might be 'and endangered science' (Lévi-Strauss & Eribon, 1991: 146), he replies: 'It will change its character. If there is no longer an object to fieldwork, we will become philologists, historians of ideas, specialists in civilizations now accessible only through documents gathered by earlier observers.'

vanishes. In short, interrogating a person and a document are not the same, not least in the quality and quantity of information each practice is capable of yielding. In the case of a fieldwork interview, it is the fieldworker him/herself who sets the agenda of what is discussed, and why; in the case of a document, by contrast, the agenda has already been set, long ago and by someone other than the social historian.[81]

Equally problematic is the attempt by Lévi-Strauss to reconcile progress with what he accepts is the centrality to anthropology of cultural relativism. It is a difficulty rooted in his restricted use of the term 'difference', applied by him in a narrow sense to mean only culture.[82] Focussing on the latter, therefore, Lévi-Strauss declares – rightly – that cultural 'difference' cannot lead to a conclusion that one culture is better than another. In saying this, however, he ignores the element of economic distinctiveness that underpins culture, which permits two points to be made. First, that an advanced society, economically speaking, is indeed better than one that is not, especially in meeting the needs of its population (health, education, etc.). And second, this being so, that one can also speak of progress, insofar as this entails a transition from a less developed to a more developed systemic form, with all that such a transformation entails not just for the economy but also for politics and ideology.

Unevolved People

The travel writing of Paul Bowles and Graham Greene underlines the epistemological and political link between on the one hand idealized and undifferentiated concepts of 'pristine/primitive otherness' based on what is presented as an enduring traditional identity, and on the other agrarian myth discourse and that of the 'new' populist postmodernism. Both the latter are opposed to modernity, and its accompanying systemic developments (industry,

---

81   This is not to say that a fieldwork interview is devoid of problems; clearly, what is asked, and indeed what is answered, depend on the research agenda – and the politics – of the anthropologist concerned. However, the broad issue of the methodological distinction between anthropology and social history is unaffected by this particular question, internal to the fieldwork process itself.

82   'The notion of progress,' he argues (Lévi-Strauss and Eribon, 1991:147), 'implies the idea that certain cultures, in specific times or places, are superior to others because they have produced works that others have shown themselves incapable of producing. And cultural relativism ... states that there is no criterion that enables one to make an absolute judgment as to how one culture is superior to another ... [cultures] are not unequal (nothing makes it possible for us to decree them as such), but different.'

urbanization, class formation/struggle, socialism), and each perceives foundational categories which emerged from the Enlightenment as inappropriate to
an understanding of the rural 'other'. All the negative characteristics rejected
by modernity as backward-looking and conservative are much rather celebrated by agrarian myth discourse and the 'new' populist postmodernism, no
less than by travel writing, under the theoretical rubric of cultural 'difference'.[83]
Accordingly, traditional identities/practices structured by popular culture –
such as artisan craft, peasant economy, custom, religion, ethnicity, nationalism – are recast as benign politically, as functional economically, and positive
ideologically. Henceforth, insist exponents of agrarian myth discourse and the
'new' populist postmodernism, all such forms of 'otherness'/'difference' must
be regarded as empowering for the subjects concerned.

It is precisely this element of cultural 'difference' that informs what many
consider to be the two best pieces of fiction composed by Bowles: the novel
The Sheltering Sky (1949), and the short story 'A Distant Episode'.[84] Both depict
the unpleasant fate awaiting Western nationals (French, male; American,
female) who travel into the Sahel region, where each character encounters and
collides with what for them both is the cultural strangeness of the 'other'.[85]
Underlined thereby is the belief held by Bowles about the fundamental
incompatibility – the irreducibility, even – between a process of modernization (= 'Europeanization'/'Westernization') and the entrenched 'otherness' of

---

83   Hence the passing-of-a-'golden age' view about cultural disintegration in North Africa
     expressed by Bowles (Negri, 1990: 41): 'The collapse of a culture on the verge of breaking
     down is inevitable. When I arrived in Morocco in 1931 it was a very different world from
     today. Even the Sahara was different.' Unsurprisingly, changes accompanying independ-
     ence are perceived as negative (Bowles, 2010: 325): 'With the arrival of independence the
     local golden age was abruptly terminated. At the same time ... servants began to grumble
     about working for seven or eight dollars a month, and started asking for ten, or even fif-
     teen ...'

84   Assessing the literary reputation of Bowles, Edmund White notes that 'his love of tra-
     ditional culture made him one of the keenest observers of other civilizations America
     ever had. Unlike some of his countrymen he did not brashly set out to improve the rest
     of the world. For Bowles, Americanization was the problem not the solution.' See 'Paul
     Bowles: The Desert and the Solitude', *The New York Review of Books*, 14 June 2011.

85   In the *Sheltering Sky* the American female is taken captive by a desert caravan, and
     becomes mute and insane. Rather worse is the fate of 'the Professor' in the 1945 short
     story 'A Distant Episode' (Bowles, 1988: 39–49), a linguist undertaking research, in the
     course of which he has his tongue cut out and becomes the plaything of a desert caravan.
     The central feature of each narrative is the inability to communicate with the 'other', the
     resulting silence – violently enforced in both instances – emphasizing what for Bowles is
     the incommensurable nature of the meeting resulting from Western/modern incursions
     into a non-Western culture.

traditional culture, a view that informs not just his fiction but also the accounts he wrote about travel in North Africa, Asia, and Central America.[86]

Writing about what he saw in early 1950s India, Bowles expressed what might be termed a symptomatic combination of likes/dislikes. Hence his disapproval of the attempt there to become modern ('the twentieth century's gangrene'), a process he dismissed as an unwarranted/undesirable trend towards 'Europeanization' and 'Westernization'.[87] By contrast, Bowles is supportive of traditional culture in India as benign, innate and unchanging. In his view, modernity is for tourists only, not for those belonging to the local Indian population. What vexes him most is the hostility shown by 'politically minded intellectuals' to traditional religion; an antagonism, Bowles maintains, that in turn means they are as a consequence 'forced to hate the past'.[88] His conclusion at that conjuncture was a resort to Malthusianism, bemoaning the fact that scientific elimination of disease would eventually undermine those customary and reassuring 'beliefs and rituals' which he regarded as positive.[89]

---

86   In his introduction to the *Collected Stories* of Bowles (1988), Gore Vidal states 'the floor to this ramshackled civilization that we have built cannot bear much longer our weight. It was Bowles's genius to suggest the horrors which lie beneath that floor, as fragile, in its way, as the sky that shelters us from a devouring vastness.' This negative view about modern civilization generally (not just its capitalist variant) is in keeping with that of the author himself. Asked by an interviewer whether 'the Western value system' still works, Bowles (Negri, 1990: 41) replied: 'The so-called Western "values", what kind of values are they? I don't think, for instance, that the America of today is a country with values or "culture": it is a huge monstrous "non-culture", a "non-civilization". It's a long time since I've been to America, but I have many friends who tell me what's going on there. It's an apocalypse.'

87   For these views, see Bowles (2006: 47–48), who writes: 'In the past few years there have been visible quantitative changes in Indian life, all in the one direction of Europeanization. This is in the smaller towns; the cities of course have long since been Westernized ... There is at the same time a slow shutting-down of services which to the Western tourist make all the difference between pleasure and discomfort in travelling ...'

88   'The younger generation in India', he comments (Bowles 2006: 49), 'is intent on forgetting a good many things, including some that it might do better to remember. There would seem to be no good reason for getting rid of their country's most ancient heritage, the religion of Hinduism'. Lamenting the anti-religious challenge to perceptions of Gandhi as a god, Bowles continues: 'The young, politically minded intellectuals find this not at all to their liking [because] subconsciously they cannot accept their own inability to go on having religious beliefs. Then, belonging to the group without faith, they are thereby forced to hate the past, particularly the atavisms which are made apparent by the working of the human mind with its irrationality, its subjective involvement in exterior phenomena.'

89   See Bowles (2006: 52–53): 'I keep thinking about [a recent outbreak of plague in Southern India], and I wonder if the almost certain eventual victory over such diseases will prove to have been worth its price: the extinction of the beliefs and rituals which gave a satisfactory

This idealized perception of 'otherness' was itself reinforced during a visit to Madeira in 1960, where a friendly meeting with a peasant led Bowles to merge the persona of the smallholder with the countryside ('fitting to the general décor'), seeing both as part of Nature and in effect indistinguishable from it. For Bowles, the peasant was a 'natural' servant, and his physical appearance was described as being hand-made, an artisan product, to be contrasted as such with other faces seen by the same writer, referred to as mass produced.[90] In short, made by an industrial process, and thus – unlike the peasant – not natural. Although aware of his own tendency to romanticize what he terms 'unevolved people', subscribing much like other travel writers to the notion of the 'pristine/primitive' rural other, Bowles decides nevertheless that he is right to do so.[91]

Pristine Other, Untouched Land

Like anthropologists and others who write about travel, Graham Greene sub-scribes to agrarian myth discourse, insofar as he condemns the western 'self' whilst idealizing the indigenous rural 'other'. The 'authenticity' of the latter subject in the Liberian countryside during the mid-1930s is contrasted by him

---

    meaning to the period of consciousness that goes between birth and death.' He adds: 'I doubt it. Security is a false god; begin making sacrifices to it and you are lost.'

90   Elsewhere Bowles acknowledges his penchant for being waited on by the 'other'. In a let-ter to Gore Vidal, written in April 1950 while Bowles was in Ceylon, he noted that (Miller, 1994: 218) 'the way one is taken care of by the servants appeals to me ... there is no such thing as service in Europe or America after one has been attended to by Sinhalese. So the nightmare [a return to the West] is about to begin again, I suppose. One can't stay in Paradise forever.' In keeping with this, when on his own island off Sri Lanka, purchased from a rubber planter, Bowles (2010: 457) confesses to rather liking being addressed as 'Master' by his servants.

91   For these images of rural 'otherness', see Bowles (2010: 314–15): 'Soon a barefoot peasant appeared wearing the hand-made, archaic-looking costume fitting to the general décor, and I called down to him for a match. He looked up, smiled, and said: "I have none, but I'll go back and get you some." Then he turned and went back the way he had just come ... In ten or fifteen minutes he reappeared at the top of the hill, running. I went to meet him. Breathless and still smiling, he held out the box of matches he had just bought and, with a curious mixture of pride and reserve, presented it to me as if it were a valuable gift ... There was a definite difference between [his] face and the kind of faces I was used to seeing. It was as if this one had been made by hand, the others mass-produced. Even as this thought occurred to me I was aware of my own weakness for romanticizing about unevolved people. But this time I quickly decided I was right: here was the first Madeiran peasant I had spoken with ...'

with the destructive tendencies of the former, a specifically urban and coastal outgrowth of western 'civilization' deemed responsible for eroding the 'naturalness' of the 'primitive'/'native' population inhabiting the rural interior. Greene wanted to understand what was at the heart of the 'fascination' he experienced as he travelled through Liberia, observing that at other times and in other places it had been rationalized variously as imperialism, the search for gold, or conquest; all trying to get to grips with the 'feeling for an untouched land'.[92] Like anthropologists and travel writers, therefore, Greene expresses his sense of wonder at coming upon a pristine 'other' in an 'untouched land' by combining agrarian myth discourse with the Burkean sublime: a case, perhaps, of two forms of pristine 'otherness' encountered simultaneously.

Essentializing/idealizing the 'other' as possessing an eternally unchanging character – referred to variously as 'childlike', 'primitive', 'simple and uncorrupted' – Greene celebrates and simultaneously laments the demise of the 'noble savage' inhabiting villages in the Liberian interior.[93] The latter was where 'the timelessness, the irresponsibility, the freedom of Africa began to touch us at last'.[94] It was there, according to Greene, that he had 'the sense that one was nearer than one had ever been to the racial source, to satisfying the desire for an instinctive older gentler way of life'.[95] This closeness to nature, in both senses ('primitive others' = nature; the forest = nature), plus the desire thought natural (= 'for an instinctive older gentler way of life') underlines the extent to which Greene – like Bowles, Lévi-Strauss, and more recently exponents of the 'cultural turn' – subscribes to agrarian myth discourse.[96]

Consistent with agrarian myth discourse are the negative images – inhabitants of the urban and coastal region dominated by western 'civilization' – that

---

92   'It wasn't easy to analyse the fascination behind the dirt and disease' seen in the villages, he confesses (Greene, 1936: 162–3), 'but it was more than a personal fantasy ... Different continents have made their call to different ages, and people at every period have tried to rationalize in terms of imperialism, gold or conquest their feeling for an untouched land'. The sublime is expressed thus: 'Zigita itself is nearly two thousand feet up ... Onagizi ... rises another thousand feet, the home of evil spirits ... all round Zigita are hills and forests'. About the impact on him of the forest vastness, Greene (1936: 193) elaborates: 'it represented the huge difference between this nature and what I had previously known'.

93   For these terms, see Greene (138, 139, 141, 154, 182, 276–77). 'The "noble savage" no longer exists', he (Greene, 1936: 69) notes, adding regretfully that 'perhaps he never existed ...'

94   Greene (1936: 161–2).

95   Greene (1936: 193).

96   'I remember wandering round the village', comments Greene (1936: 234–35), 'and thinking that, after all, the whole journey was worth while: it did reawaken a kind of hope in human nature. If one could get back to this bareness, simplicity, instinctive friendliness, feeling rather than thought, and start again ...'

accompanies the positive one of the interior. For Greene, therefore, the coast is equated with a 'civilization' that is western and 'inauthentic', to be contrasted as such with the interior, inhabited by the 'primitive'/'native' who is the embodiment of 'authenticity'. In the Liberian interior, villagers 'had an air of chivalry, of an older civilization than in the tin shacks on the coast': compared to the latter, the interior was 'where there was a greater simplicity, an older more natural culture'.[97] Unlike the rural interior, the locus of desirable 'otherness', the urban population on coast was seen by Greene as no different from himself: 'It seemed to me that they, almost as much as oneself, had lost touch with the true primitive source.'[98] Significantly, the one village in the interior described by him as 'horrible', its residents 'so ugly, so diseased', was because they had in his opinion been corrupted by 'coastal civilization'.[99] In short, these were not the 'authentic' indigenous 'others' of whom Greene approved.

Not the least commendable trait of the impoverished 'native other' in the African interior was a passivity when compared with the poor in Europe.[100] This pro-rural-poor/anti-European-poor dichotomy is itself part of agrarian myth discourse, and corresponds to a trope frequently invoked by travel writers who, like Greene, flee 'civilization' in the West, only to see nothing but virtue and happiness in rural society elsewhere. Revealed thereby is a political subtext: the acceptability of the 'noble savage' image is due in part to its seeming docility, an apparent satisfaction with the little it has. This is regarded by those holding this view as positive, a sign of virtue, one that differentiates the 'primitive'/'native' subject from its more active – and consequently less well regarded – European counterparts; namely, workers who by means of 'shrill speech or sudden blows' have fought against their impoverished status.

This distinction between the pristine rural 'other' and those categorized as part of Western 'civilization' rests on the view that the former cannot become like the latter, no matter how hard an attempt is made to effect such a transition. Unlike Lévi-Strauss, who sought to reconcile progress with cultural relativism, Greene seemingly endorsed non-transcendent cultural separation, as evidenced by his mocking description of a 'fashionable wedding' involving

---

97   Greene (1936: 128, 302–3).

98   Greene (1936: 303).

99   About the village in question Greene (1936: 156) observes that: 'It was the only place until I got into Bassa country where coastal civilization has corrupted the natives, in which I found nothing to admire'.

100   'I never wearied of the villages in which I spent the night', he notes (Greene, 1936: 92–93): 'the sense of a small courageous community barely existing above the desert of trees … they never revealed the rasped nerves of the European poor in shrill speech or sudden blows.'

a bourgeois couple who are black attempting to imitate their white counter-parts.[101] Citing a fictional attempt at upward mobility portrayed by Ronald Firbank, Greene indicates that the episode he himself described fell well below that ('but alas! The smell of the fish laid fourteen deep in the roadway ...').[102] Whilst the racism of such a view, based as it is on the perception of ethnic 'otherness' as innate, is self-evident, that the celebration of a pristine 'other' identity at the centre of agrarian myth discourse might also be racist is less easy to see.

Conclusion

Any endeavour to compose a history of travel and tourism, indicating who undertakes this, when, and why, is faced with epistemological issues which, if these remain unaddressed or unresolved, quickly undermines the project. Just such a problem confronts the attempt by D'Eramo to construct a history of travel/tourism, not least at the level of how these phenomena are to be dif-ferentiated and defined. For this reason, his account is too inclusive: travel encompasses all forms of motion, outside of which there appears to be noth-ing. Among the more problematic claims are that tourism is itself an industry, not a service economy, and that in terms of time oligarchs face the same travel constraints as the mass tourist. Similarly overlooked is the role of agrarian myth discourse and academia in promoting the identity politics which under-write the way heritage, nostalgia, and tradition feature as tourist attractions. Ironically, he concludes that his approach is in the end no different from the anti-tourist position informing many narratives about travel.

Missing from his analysis is that what the aristocratic traveller on the Grand Tour and the plebeian mass tourist each sought in a different location visited was not just 'otherness' but also – and perhaps more importantly – a valida-tion of the 'sameness' informing their own sense of self. This the aristocrat did when travelling abroad, where s/he encountered a similar hierarchy, evidence for the presence there of a similar 'natural' order (landlord, peasant) as s/he saw it, or the 'sameness' of class as at home. The plebeian mass tourist also

---

101 Greene (1936: 37–38, 40–41).

102 'Sometimes it was almost Firbank', states Greene, to the degree that 'it recalled the Mouth family forcing their way into the highest social circles of the city of Cuna-Cuna'. The ref-erence by Greene is to a 1925 fictional account by Ronald Firbank (1951: 259–329) of the unsuccessful attempt at upward mobility by a black family in the rural Caribbean. Try as s/he might, Firbank infers, the non-white 'other' can never become like the white 'self'.

finds evidence abroad (English food, English pubs in Costa del Sol resorts) of his/her own 'sameness' at home. In effect, plebeian mass tourists reaffirm an already established selfhood which they take with them when visiting another country on holiday. Why this is so can be linked in turn to the history of class struggle, and the emergence – because politically it was in an important sense necessary – of populism.

That a crucial aspect of travel is its capacity either to endorse or to negate pre-existing notions of selfhood and alterity emerges from accounts in different forms of writing. Claims to the contrary notwithstanding, both anthropologists (Lévi-Strauss) and travel writers (Theroux, Lewis) and those who write about travel (Greene, Bowles) tend to essentialize and/or idealize the 'other' as culturally pristine and unchanging. Like D'Eramo, therefore, Lévi-Strauss complains that sameness erases difference, thereby de-authenticating both the object and experience of travel. Greene and Bowles each subscribed to agrarian myth discourse, opposing modernity and romanticizing 'otherness'. From the 1930s to the 1950s, therefore, those who travelled outside Europe rejected not just the label of tourist, an identity regarded as demeaning, but also progress and development – embodied in notions such as 'civilization', 'Westernization', and 'Europeanization' – as undesirable impositions on 'other' inhabitants of non-European contexts, anticipating thereby similar arguments made half a century later by the 'new' populist postmodernism.

In a sense the contradiction faced by Lévi-Strauss – wanting to reconcile progress with cultural relativism, but defining progress simply in terms of culture, and then declaring that culture is itself incommensurable – is unsurprising. Progress is not just about culture, which he regards as irreducible, ruling out comparative analysis, but also about economics and politics, which can be compared, but phenomena that Lévi-Strauss does not address. The wider concept of progress, its systemic operation, and the interrelationship of culture/politics/ideology, is what Marxism (and, indeed, political economy) teaches. As Lévi-Strauss himself makes clear, Marxism is not an approach that he regards as valid, either for comprehending 'otherness' or for an understanding of travel. Why this is not the case, especially where class together with components of agrarian myth discourse are relevant to interpreting accounts of travel within Europe, is an issue considered in the following chapters.

[Dog seen from the Vaporetto going round the Assassini]

FIGURE 3   Dog (Cannaregio)
© ANNA LUISA BRASS

Tourists, or Travellers? (European Journeys)

But it seems to have been always recognized that relating one's rambles viva voce is a somewhat chancy business; the wisest aunt telling the saddest tale is not always listened to; hence travellers have usually committed their trips to paper, knowing that the printed word breaks resistance down where the human voice does but strengthen it. Thus, it has always been the custom for returned travellers to write travel books, whether in the form of fictional narrative, or of true; and it is said that this form of literature is the greatest in bulk of any in the world.

An observation in an essay 'Telling travellers' tales', about travel writers, by one of their number.[1]

:.

Introduction: Songs of Travel

Generally speaking, accounts of travel outside Europe examined in the previous chapter are written during the pre-war era, whilst a number of those about travel inside Europe considered in this chapter appear in the post-war era. In terms of the place visited, therefore, the travel accounts focussing on locations outside Europe include Liberia, Brazil, Honduras, Melanesia, and the Sahel, all of which at the time were considered as 'exotic' and beyond the reach of the 'ordinary tourist'. By contrast, the accounts of travel within Europe examined here focus on Italy in general, and Sicily in particular, not least because of their importance as tourist destinations in the era of mass tourism.

This distinction notwithstanding, many of the tropes informing travel writing about contexts outside Europe apply also to the way similar accounts portray journeys within Europe.[2] Hence the reappearance in the latter context of

---

1 Macaulay (2021: 197).
2 Thus, for example, Green (1953: 148–49) regards the inhabitants of Sicily as in certain respects no different from those of the Middle East and Asia: 'I was aware of an almost exaggerated air of fecundity [in Palermo], a bursting tropical lushness in the air. I had found the same thing

agrarian myth discourse, but with at least one difference: whereas outside of Europe its indigenous subject was described by travel writers as the 'tribal', the 'primitive', or the 'native', inside Europe the same 'other' subject is now the peasant. All the remaining tropes resurface: idealization of the countryside, the rural community and its inhabitants; fear of being thought a tourist, wanting to be like an anthropologist; deploying avoidance mechanisms where tourism is concerned; and dislike of plus anxiety at the spread of urbanization and industrialization.

Accounts of travel exhibit a similar continuity in terms of different variants and combinations of the agrarian myth (pastoral/Darwinian, aristocratic/plebeian) across pre- and post-war eras and non-European and European contexts.[3] If the non-European travel accounts covered in the previous chapter – by Lévi-Strauss, Peter Keenagh, Graham Greene, Paul Bowles, Paul Theroux and Norman Lewis – all belong to the plebeian category, then so too do the ones about European travel by D.H. Lawrence, Peter Green, and John Mortimer in this chapter. By contrast, the travel writing of Guiseppe di Lampedusa about journeys within Europe, also examined below, corresponds to its aristocratic form. Most of the variants considered here constitute the pastoral version of the agrarian myth.[4] As important in terms of European travel are the two conjunctures involved: periods immediately following the two world wars.

The first corresponds to accounts of travel after the 1914–18 conflict, when it was thought that the aristocratic landowning class in European countries had lost its pre-war power and influence, an era marked also by outmigration to the US, a population loss in Italy that contributed in part to a resurgent Fascism. Accounts written after the 1939–45 war similarly reflect the different outcomes experienced by its participants. For the victors travel was seen in a number of distinct ways: as an escape from wartime austerity: as an opportunity to revisit places where they had served as soldiers; and in the case of beneficiaries of the American GI Bill, to embark on studies enabling travel

---

in India: unbelievable poverty of soil and habitat combined with a fierce productivity of the species that was reflected in every gesture, every word, every belief. I saw now the reasons for the Sicilian ethics; they did not differ so very much from those of Arab or Hindu.'

3   For the different combinations forming agrarian myth discourse, see Brass (2000). Both the plebeian or 'from below' variant, and the aristocratic or 'from above' version, exhibit a similar nostalgia and accompanying sense of loss for a vanishing rural landscape and its traditional values.

4   Although not accounts of travel, the narratives about rural Sicily by Giovanni Verga are the exception, being as they are the red-in-tooth-and-claw (or Darwinian) version of agrarian myth discourse. His stories are included here in order to indicate that descriptions of 'from below' society give a different picture from the one about a benign landlord power contained in *The Leopard*.

linked to anthropological fieldwork.[5] For those on the losing side, by contrast, the resulting destruction and poverty in their countries reinforced prefiguring tropes in travel writing. In the case of Italy, the combination of military defeat, urban destruction, and impoverishment, not only fuelled notions of the 'picturesque' and strengthened visitor perceptions about the economic and social backwardness of the country, but also fostered racist attitudes towards the inhabitants of the conquered nation.

Of the three sections in this chapter, the first examines the way accounts of travel within Europe are informed by agrarian myth discourse, and its a-historical characterization of rural inhabitants as 'other', while the focus of the second is how this same designation was subsequently transferred onto the mass tourist. The third section links problematic aspects of such travel narratives to other literary, filmic, and historiographical interpretations of the same contexts and/or episodes.

I

In his accounts of travel in Europe throughout the latter part of the 1920s, visiting France, England, Germany, and Switzerland, Lampedusa expressed what might be termed the symptomatic ideology of an aristocratic landowner. On the one hand, therefore, he voiced opposition to urbanization/industrialism, together with – as he saw it – their attendant squalor, poverty, filth, and decadence. On the other, approval was indicated for the countryside and pastoral landscape encountered in nations visited, together with their accompanying landowners, cultural framework and supportive institutional structure (dressing well, being a 'gentleman', and having good manners; ancient cathedrals and universities). This positive/negative combination was itself fused with agrarian myth discourse, in particular an anxiety concerning the historical decline in the position of his own class, and especially the power it once exercised.

A central component of this ideology takes the form of nostalgia, a perception of loss which, as expressed by Lampedusa, is twofold: internal, or for

---

5   On travel as a method of escaping post-war austerity in England, see Green (1953: 18). Among the beneficiaries of the GI Bill were the anthropologists Robert Murphy, Eric Wolf, and Clifford Geertz, all of whom subsequently undertook fieldwork; Wolf eventually returned to conduct research in an area where he had been posted as a US soldier (Cole & Wolf, 1974). The travel writing careers of Eric Newby (1971) and Norman Lewis (1978) were similarly rooted in accounts based on their experiences in wartime Italy, whilst travel undertaken by Leonard Cottrell (1960) tracing the route taken by Hannibal also has its origins in time spent in Italy as a war correspondent. It was during 1944 when convalescing in a Naples hospital (Cottrell, 1960: 14) 'listening to the far-off thudding of guns [that he] resolved that one day [he] would visit not only Lake Trasimene but the sites of other Hannibalic battlefields ...'

the power his own family once exercised; and external, or for that which the European aristocracy used to exercise historically. The internal variant emerges in the course of a journey in time undertaken by Lampedusa, tracing the route back to his early childhood travel from one property in Sicily to another part of the same island, where his ancestors owned more land and a large house, and where they were waited upon by retainers.[6] He recalls that, in addition to the four other houses once possessed by the family, the latter owned also a palace in Palermo; he reminisces about its vast size, furnishings, ancestral portraits, together with its ever-present servants.[7]

The external variant of nostalgia takes the form of regret at the decline of the power/influence once exercised by the aristocracy, and specifically a yearning for the position of the landlord class in pre-1914 Europe, described by Lampedusa as an 'easy-going' life before the break-up of Empires, the Bolshevik revolution, and war.[8] At the same time, when visiting Powis Castle in Wales, he declares himself 'overwhelmed' by its antiquity and treasures, noting with pleasure that 'Lord Powis is the biggest landowner in England'. However, this sense of affinity with those of the same class in a different country is tempered by the realization that, when compared to their English counterparts, landlords in Sicily are 'poor and we shall die poor.'[9] This prefigures the concern

---

6   It should be noted, however, that the decline in family fortune may not be as steep as
     depicted. In describing the valuable contents of the Palace in Palermo, he (Lampedusa,
     1962: 49) frequently notes that a given item (a book, a tapestry) is 'still in my possession'.
     That the invocation by Lampedusa of his familial straightened circumstances is, in part,
     special pleading, is further suggested by the following (Dummett, 2015: 192): 'In 1948
     Lampedusa bought an eighteenth-century property facing the seafront [in Palermo],
     where he lived until his death in 1957. It was here that he wrote his historical novel, *The
     Leopard*. The property ... has a magnificent view overlooking a terrace towards the sea
     [and] a number of elegant reception rooms, filled with sunlight ... decorated with furnish-
     ings from the belle époque. Much of the library came from the original family palace.'
7   See Lampedusa (1962: 41, 46), who describes the palace as 'spread over a vast expanse and
     contained about a hundred rooms, large and small. It gave the impression of an enclosed
     and self-sufficient entity, of a kind of Vatican as it were, that included state-rooms,
     living-rooms, quarters for thirty guests, servants' rooms, three great courtyards, stables
     and coach-houses, a private theatre and church, a large and very lovely garden, and a big
     orchard.' Of the theatre, he (Lampedusa, 1962: 62) notes in a mildly patronizing manner
     that 'the audience, partly of peasants, were attentive and warm in their applause.'
8   'The principal result of a journey to Switzerland,' writes Lampedusa (2010: 125–29) from
     Zurich in 1928, 'is that one travels in time more than in space. One lives in pre-war Europe,
     in the easy-going Europe of 1913 ... one is considered a nabob.'
9   Referring to his own landowning class in Sicily, Lampedusa (2010: 63–66) regrets that 'we
     are pale shadows of the true lords [English aristocracy]. We are poor and we shall die poor.'
     The latter is a sentiment later attributed to the Prince of Salina in *The Leopard*. Observing
     English aristocrats placing large bets on card games, he (Lampedusa, 2010: 23–26) feels

expressed by Lampedusa in *The Leopard*, regarding the political displacement of his own class during the mid-nineteenth century by members of the commercial bourgeoisie from Northern Italy.

City and Countryside

Lampedusa provides a brief description of his travels around Paris during 1927, observing at one point that 'the street plunges into mediocrity with a confectioner's and other low establishments', the disdain of the aristocrat for those in trade.[10] A year later, on another visit to the French capital, he records his delight at the fact he stays in 'one of the most aristocratic streets in this aristocratic *faubourg*.'[11] He continues: 'O gentle beauty of provincial Paris ... beauty ignored by so many people, who mistake the soiled cosmopolitan mask of Montmartre for the true aspect of this affable city.' Two years later, and now in Berlin, Lampedusa complains about the decadence of that city, an effect as he sees it of its being 'a metropolis'. His comment that '[n]othing is harder than this city' accurately conveys the presence of anti-urban sentiment, which combines with an invocation of the rural pastoral to form the aristocratic variant of the agrarian myth.[12]

Travelling across England in 1927, Lampedusa makes constant reference to four interrelated phenomena: the hideousness of large-scale industrial connurbations, the aesthetic character of the countryside, the antiquity of small towns, and the cultural role of institutions in producing the right kind of ruling class members. From York, he 'continues his pilgrimage through old England [which] takes him through the most ancient cities of this glorious island'.[13] Avoiding urban conurbations and 'industrial infernos', Lampedusa keeps instead to 'venerable cathedral cities [and] peaceful seats of learning'. Invoking the aristocratic pastoral version of the agrarian myth, he 'travelled through the amazing serenity of the English countryside: meadows with herds of cattle, lazy brimful rivers, gorgeous hills – a real pastoral scene ...' In

---

himself lacking because he cannot match them in this respect. A long, elegiac description, not a little envious, of London clubland around Pall Mall which he admires, merely serves to confirm the truism that Lampedusa (2010: 15–19) yearns for the lifestyle of the British aristocracy, in much the same way as Henry 'Chips' Channon (2021) – another outsider at that same conjuncture, looking in and wanting to be part of what he sees.

10   Lampedusa (2010: 75–76).
11   Lampedusa (2010: 121–24).
12   Lampedusa (2010: 151–57).
13   On this and what follows, written from York in 1927, see Lampedusa (2010: 27–33).

a similar vein, Chester is described as a place 'which is so ancient and graceful', and of Stratford-upon-Avon as 'the remarkable and truly divine gentleness of the countryside' where 'the immortal Shakespearean pastoral was born'.[14] He moves on subsequently to Oxford 'in which *everything* is beautiful': he 'was not surprised that from such surroundings, from Oxford and from Cambridge, *gentlemen* come forth.' When in London the next year, Lampedusa again expresses longing for the countryside: 'kilometre after kilometre of a city which will not bring itself to an end. Suddenly, after Kingston, open fields ...'[15]

The contrast between agrarian myth discourse and urban/industrial dystopic imagery is impossible to miss: it is a dichotomy evident in every step of the journey Lampedusa takes in England.[16] Avoiding what he terms 'industrial infernos', he describes how he passes through the 'venerable cathedral cities' and 'ancient university towns' of 'old England', in the process travelling through 'the amazing serenity of the English countryside', which he agrees is 'a real pastoral scene'. According to Lampedusa, the main purpose of the two ancient universities is to produce 'gentlemen' like himself, cultured and (where possible) titled. For him, being a gentleman is an aesthetic trait: knowing how to dress, how to speak, how to behave, and doing all this effortlessly.[17]

Consistent with agrarian myth discourse, at a later conjuncture Peter Green persists in labelling rural society in Italy as 'feudal', and the Greek landscape as 'timeless'.[18] These images are themselves reinforced by accompanying sentiments that stress the closeness of the population – or particular components of this – to the land ('The monastery was a pleasant place; its sunburnt monks lived close to the soil'; 'However modern and sophisticated Italy may show

---

14   For this and the following views, see Lampedusa (2010: 43–55, original emphases).

15   Lampedusa (2010: 105–114).

16   A similar dichotomy structures perceptions of home, where (Lampedusa, 2007: 68) on the one hand Prince Salina and a retainer, out hunting in the early morning, 'found themselves in the immemorial silence of pastoral Sicily'. On the other hand, about the location of the family home in the city of Palermo, Lampedusa (1962: 37) remarks: 'But if Via di Lampedusa was decent enough, for the whole length of our house at least, the streets into it were not;...crawling with poverty and squalor, and depressing to pass along ... there always remained a good stretch of filth and horrors to traverse.'

17   Touring Scotland and the North, Lampedusa (2010: 35–40) complains of his 'fragile finances', and commends the Director of the Wallace Collection in London as 'a gentleman graced with education, exquisite manners and extremely well-cut clothes.'

18   Thus Green (1953: 65) maintains that 'Italy is still, despite two world wars, an essentially agricultural country, and retains the peculiar feudal system that naturally belongs to an agricultural economy.' Elsewhere the same is said of Greece (Green, 1989: 136): 'We often forget that Greece was, and to a remarkable extent still remains, an agrarian peasant culture ... things have not changed all that much in the Greek countryside to this day.'

herself, one never gets far from the soil').[19] As important in bolstering agrarian myth discourse is the conflation by Green of poverty with acceptance, anticipating thereby concepts such as 'culture of poverty' and 'limited good' applied at that conjuncture by anthropologists to peasant society.[20] That he regarded rural community not just as an ageless way of life but also as positive is evident: 'I was conscious of being caught up and assimilated by something old and warm and elemental.'[21]

Observing, further, that the 'particular brand of stoicism which is the hallmark of a true peasant from Brittany to China', Green underlines the extent to which acquiescence/acceptance of what is old, traditional, 'natural' (= the soil) is for him a characteristic of a past consisting of a more 'authentic' form of rural livelihood.[22] In much the same way as pre-war travel writers, he invokes the sublime when describing mountains as 'the sudden fierce re-assertion of all the primeval power of nature'.[23] This idealized perception of the Italian countryside as harmonious is combined with the antagonism expressed by Green towards signs of modernity/industry/urbanization in a nation recovering from war.[24] His difficulty with modernity, coupled with a desire to escape into an idealized arcadia, highlights the presence of agrarian myth ideology and the degree to its discourse structures travel writing both outside and inside Europe and in pre- and post-war era alike.

Class, Race, Blood

It could be argued that Lampedusa displays all the stereotypical attitudes of the European landowning class at that period, ranging from nostalgia for a

---

19   On this see Green (1953: 87, 113).

20   'Nowhere else', writes Green (1953: 116, 117), 'could one find such a curious amalgam of modernity and antiquity, of luxury and poverty [and] the unquestioning acceptance of this phenomenon ... I was conscious of nothing but a dull unfeeling acquiescence, an almost paralysing air of resignation.'

21   Green (1953: 119).

22   For his view about the universal characteristics of 'the true peasant', see Green (1953: 126). The opinion that Green has about peasant acceptance contrasts with that found earlier in the stories of Verga; far from accepting their condition, peasants struggle against a fate which casts them invariably as subordinates whom those above exploit.

23   Green (1953: 32).

24   'The truth of the matter', confesses Green (1953: 147–48), 'was that we were tired of cities ... I at any rate was pining for open countryside ... and villages ... I was also somewhat tired of the chromium-plated speed and complexity of present-day Italy: I felt an urge for that peculiar solitariness which only the past surviving into the present can give.'

past era in which it exercised power, via anti-semitism and support for fascism, to a condescending attitude towards the peasantry. The latter are portrayed as accepting of their situation, and passive, living in villages 'all weltering in poverty and dog-days, and in an ignorance against which they never reacted with the very faintest of flickers.'[25] If anything, his view of the foreign plebeian was reactionary. Whilst passing through Lithuania, a letter written from Berlin during 1930 indicates that Lampedusa approves of anti-Jewish pogroms.[26] Significantly, his objection to Jews ('goatish stink, shrill oriental cries') is not just racist but also because they belong to 'the lower orders' – they are not wealthy. This is borne out by his subsequent observation, that 'I believe I shall see more appetizing ones in Livonia' – that is, Jews who are not poor.[27]

Such views, symptomatic not just of landlord ideology but also of the far right, hint at a potential sympathy for Fascism: indeed, when visiting Paris during 1925, Lampedusa expresses approval of 'the attack on Amendola [which] filled me with exquisite pleasure'.[28] At the same time, aware of the revolutionary history in the nation he was visiting, he professes himself safe because Mussolini is 'by my side'.[29] The positive view about Fascism as protecting the interests of landowners by keeping 'those below' – poor peasants and agricultural labourers – in their place was tempered by suspicion that, potentially, the

---

25   Lampedusa (1962: 64–65), whose benign self-image as landowner is reflected in the perception of the Prince of Salina 'loved ... the people, the sense of feudal ownership still surviving there ...'

26   He writes (Lampedusa, 2010: 145–49) that 'the station was packed with Jewish members of the lower orders ... the spectacle was grotesque to the highest degree ... men [with] sweat running down behind the pomaded ringlets; the goatish stink, the shrill oriental cries ... all this made many things clear to [Lampedusa], even including the periodical massacres carried out ... by the Russians.'

27   Echoes of this anti-semitism are found also in *The Leopard*, where Lampedusa (2007: 142) puts the following words in the mouth of Prince Salina, defending the power exercised historically by his family: 'Now even people here [in Sicily] are repeating what was written by Proudhon and some German Jew [= Marx] whose name I can't remember, that the bad state of things, here and elsewhere, is all down to feudalism; it's my fault, as it were. Maybe ... I don't believe that [the bourgeoisie] or the English squires or the French seigneurs governed Sicily any better than did the Salina.'

28   Lampedusa (2010: 5). Giovanni Amendola was a journalist and anti-fascist politician murdered by the Blackshirts in that same year. However, in the book (Lampedusa, 2010: 9) the endnote about this episode fails to draw out the political implications of Lampedusa's 'exquisite pleasure'.

29   Hence the view (Lampedusa, 2010: 8): 'Here [in France] I am in a potentially Bolshevist country. The [political] situation is very serious [but] I don't give a damn, because I know that even if a revolution breaks out, no one will touch a hair on my head or steal one penny from me, because by my side I have ... Mussolini!'.

same kind of antagonism could be directed at aristocratic landlords, or 'those above'. As will be seen below, this concern surfaces in *The Leopard*, where the Prince of Salina recognizes that a possible 'from below' threat is not abolition but replacement ('I understand now; you don't want to destroy us ... you just want to take our places ... all will be the same, just as it is now: except for an imperceptible change round of classes').[30]

For his part, Lawrence invokes his usual 'blood-belonging' criterion to describe what is presented as the 'primitive' character of Sicilians, according to him no different at the time he was writing from their 'classic Greek' ancestors.[31] This view is echoed by Peter Green, who in his account of a visit to Sicily in the immediate post-war era states that 'I knew I had been in contact with some inchoate but enormous primitive power, which the years had been unable to dispel'.[32] In keeping with this, he extols the Sicilian bandit Salvatore Giuliano as a Robin Hood character, beloved of the peasantry for attacking and robbing landowners, an idealization consonant with the depiction by Hobsbawm of social banditry.[33] Needless to say, this interpretation is one that has been challenged and shown to be wrong.[34] In a similar vein, Norman Lewis depicts

---

30 Lampedusa (2007: 25). The key point is made by the Jesuit priest, who – fearing the loss of church property, and its negative impact on the poor – warns Prince Salina (Lampedusa, 2007: 28): 'How will these desperate masses be placated? I'll tell you at once, Excellency. They will be flung first a portion, then another portion and eventually all the rest of your estates.'

31 'The Sicilians of today are supposed to be the nearest thing to the classic Greeks that is left to us; that is, they are the nearest descendants on earth', writes Lawrence (1936: 228, 230), adding: 'Perhaps the deepest nostalgia I have ever felt has been for Sicily ... Not for England or anywhere else – for Sicily, the beautiful, that which goes deepest into the blood.'

32 Green (1953: 207).

33 On this, see Green (1953: 154–58), who writes: 'I had hoped to meet Giuliano somehow while I was in Sicily, but it was not to be. He actually came into Castelvetrano the day after we left ... Then came the story of his death: and reading it a thousand miles away in England I felt something of the cold despair that must have swept over Sicily when the news was announced ... But all this was yet to come. While I talked, on this September day, with three peasants, Giuliano was still alive and roaming the western hills: and his presence sent a spark of hope and excitement through the length and breadth of Sicily, and who knows how much further?' For a similar idealization of Giuliano, see Hobsbawm (1969: 33), who maintains that 'bodies like the Sicilian Mafia ... might reach out to all who were outside and against the official structure of power [turning] banditry into a nucleus of effective political rebellion'.

34 See Blok (1972) for a critique of Hobsbawm, and especially his comments (Blok, 1988: 204–5) that 'bandits were used as instruments in the struggle against the peasant movement and the parties of the Left'; as reported by Lewis (1964: 150–53, 161–63), in 1947 the Giuliano band attacked a peaceful crowd of peasants after the political victory of the Popular Bloc,

the inhabitants of the Mafia heartlands in Sicily as beings not so dissimilar from their ancestors ('the descendants of an ancient non-European tribe').[35] Observing that 'the contemporary Florentine only differs in non-essentials from his fourteenth-century predecessor, whose tradition and manners he has inherited whole', Peter Green aligns himself with this pattern of cultural essentialism, a-historically depicting both the country visited – Italy – and its people as unchanging.[36]

II

Travel accounts examined in this chapter either depart from or reinforce what Walter Benjamin termed 'the inherited templates for viewing Italy'.[37] The latter draws one, rightly, back to the class position of the traveller or tourist, and how this structures what is sought and how this is seen. As outlined in the previous chapter, viewed thus the 'inherited template' may licence gazing on the 'otherness' of a history/tradition/ruin thought to embody a vanished past; alternatively, it may entail nothing more than a search for the aspects of home to be found in the location visited; or it might be a combination of these approaches. Again as outlined previously, and as noted also by Benjamin, whatever their differences visitors generally share the object of attempting not to be in the same

---

leaving eleven dead and 55 wounded. The political stance of Giuliano is evident from the fact that, according to Blok, '[t]he band left pamphlets in these places that appealed to Sicilian youths to join Giuliano in the struggle against Communism'.

35   'This was the earth as it had been in the depths of the past, before human interference', observes Lewis (2016: 98, 99, 101) about Sicily: 'It was also the former heartland of the Mafia [where] the villagers were the descendants of an ancient non-European tribe', a location which '[f]or many years ... had been the hiding place of bodies of the men of Corleone who had fallen foul of the Mafia'. For a similar account by the same writer, see Lewis (1998: 140ff.). In an earlier book about the same subject he (Lewis, 1964: 25, 27) not only described the Sicilian Mafia as belonging to 'the prehistory of humanity', akin to an African tribe in Mali, but also claimed it 'can be regarded as a form of primitive human society that has somehow survived in the modern Western world; its cruel laws are those of tribesmen...'.

36   Green (1953: 59). On economic changes and political conflict in post-war Italy, see among others, Regalia, Regini and Reyneri [1978: 101–158], Red Notes [1978], Autonomia [1980], Ginsborg [1990; 2003, 2004], and Lumley [1990]. Monographs chronicling agrarian transformation and political conflict in rural Italy include Paulson [1966], Lopreato [1967], White [1980] and Bull and Corner [1993].

37   See Benjamin (2016: 143), who in a review of a 1927 book about an Italian journey writes that, 'these jottings possess only a few rare passages of interest that is more than private', adding that the author of the book in question 'was on the point of freeing himself from the inherited templates for viewing Italy.'

place as others like themselves: the fellow traveller the 'avoidance of whom has always been the best and most difficult part of all techniques of journeying.'[38]

A discernible break exists between pre- and post-1960s accounts – both fiction and non-fiction – by British (and other) writers about European travel. During the 1950s, therefore, a subtext conveyed a sense of superiority on the part of those staying towards populations inhabiting the European countries visited, perceived as composing an external 'other'. Hence the negative expressions concerning aspects – food, odd locals, mosquitoes, non-existent plumbing, and nasty bugs – considered to be emblematic of the backwardness of the location.[39] From the 1960s onwards, however, both the sense of superiority and the focus itself shifts: visitor disdain is now transferred from locals – the external 'other' – for their alleged backwardness and onto the visiting plebeian who travels from home (= the internal 'other'). In keeping with this, the earlier and negative view of the location visited as 'backward' similarly metamorphoses into a positive one about culture.

Such changes are already prefigured in the early 1950s travel account of Peter Green. Passing through Northern Italy, therefore, he complains of turning a 'lovely resort into the worst kind of tourist area'.[40] Despite being in effect a tourist himself, Green feared being mistaken for one: 'Quite suddenly I felt completely alien, an interloper, with TURISMO written in large capitals all over me.'[41] The identity with which he declares an affinity is that of the anthropologist. This is because much like the latter even tourists gaze upon the 'other', claims Green, in the same way as participant/observation fieldwork methods dictate: taking part, yet classifying those external to the self.[42] The same kind

---

38   Of another travel account, also about Italy and written in the same year, Benjamin (2016: 144) remarks that '[n]ow for the first time we possess the ideal portrait of the "fellow traveller", avoidance of whom has always been the best and most difficult part of all techniques of journeying.'

39   In 1950s Positano, therefore, books fall apart, having been devoured by ants (Mortimer & Mortimer, 1957: 110–111), a metaphor perhaps for the destruction of intellect/reason by nature as seen by a visiting bourgeois from England.

40   Green (1953: 35).

41   See Green (1953: 42, 149), who also expresses the same concern subsequently ('I feel depressingly *turistico*').

42   According to Green (1953: 50–51), therefore, 'many people, including myself,...shy away very hard from the word "tourist"...It is a hard thing to realise that, with the best will in the world, the visitor to a country, whether he stays three days or three months, is going to carry away a completely idealised picture. In the first place, he is not, and cannot be, part of it himself. He doesn't depend on the country for his livelihood. This immediately puts a fence round him; his pocketful of money and lack of obligation suspend time – and judgment – for him. He unconsciously assumes the role of a detached observer, wandering (if

of shift is also evident in two accounts of travel to Italy – one fiction, the other non-fiction – written thirty years apart by John Mortimer.[43] Each involved longish stays, in different places, by a largish middle-class family from London. The earlier, and non-fictional, account was composed mainly of diary entries about a family holiday in Positano on the Amalfi Coast during the mid-1950s; the second, by contrast, took the form of a novel, but also recorded events occurring in the course of a stay by the same kind of bourgeois family in a villa located in Tuscany during the late 1980s.[44]

Away from Home

A novel about the experiences of an bourgeois family from England on holiday in Tuscany during the late 1980s, *Summer's Lease* involves principally a three-fold quest: for the disappearance of a vital resource (water), for a number of unexplained deaths among the ex-pat community (murder), and for the work of the fifteenth century artist Piero della Francesca (culture).[45] The fact that the novel about a foreign holiday in 'Chiantishire' – in a 'villa to let near small Tuscan town', Mondano-in-Chianti, Siena – is not only written by the same author of the *Rumpole* stories, but also – and like the latter – is a crime mystery, illustrates the way these two genres can overlap.[46] The result is a combination that places a quest to uncover a crime within a picturesque location, the latter

---

he is lucky) through an enchanted land; in his relations with local inhabitants an uneasy blend of newspaper reporter [and] anthropologist ...'

43　The first of these accounts was co-authored by John Mortimer (1923–2009) and his then wife, Penelope Mortimer (1918–1999). He was a prominent barrister and dramatist, she a journalist; both were well-known authors, he of *Rumpole of the Bailey* stories (1978–2007) and she of the semi-autobiographical book *The Pumpkin Eater* (1962).

44　Those staying in Positano during the mid-1950s consisted of a large family (2 adults and six juveniles) who live in 'semi-detached Victorian house in North London' (Mortimer & Mortimer, 1957: 11). Before going, the children (Mortimer & Mortimer, 1957: 29) display little knowledge about the destination ('Is Positano in London?', 'Is Italy in London?'). The fictional group holidaying near Siena during the late 1980s consists, similarly, of a large family (two adults, three daughters, plus a grandparent) – the Pargeters – from an equally fashionable and expensive part of London.

45　That the search for the works of Piero della Francesca leads to Urbino, and ultimately to the last of the deaths, emphasizes the interlocking nature of these quests. Among other quests which feature as sub-plots is the search by an aged grandfather for an old girlfriend.

46　'Chiantishire' is described (Mortimer, 1988: 66, 118, 123) as 'that old-established suburb of Wimbledon', a place where the lifestyle adopted by ex-pats enabled them to 'feel as though they had never moved out of Twickenham'.

in effect rivalling the former for the attention of the reader (or film audience). This is especially the case when such fiction is transformed into a television series – as did the production of *Summer's Lease* as a television drama on BBC2 in 1989 – enhancing thereby the visual aspects such as landscape. Images depicting the context in which the crime occurs are consequently transformed into more significant – not to say major – components of the narrative.[47]

What starts out as an investigation into a water racket in an area of Tuscany where this resource is scarce ends up uncovering murder, the former being a Hitchcockian McGuffin leading, ultimately, to the discovery of homicide. At first, therefore, the quest involves a search for 'vanishing water', a situation whereby the supply to holiday lets in this part of Italy ('Chiantishire') is turned off and reinstated only when the visiting family renting the villa pay for getting it back. A trick from which both ex-pats and locals profit, the water scam points initially to the deaths that occur. This is a false trail, however, since it transpires these murders are due not to economic causes (struggle over control of water profits) but rather to adultery (*crime passionnel*).

During the 1950s, negative views regarding Italian underdevelopment are placed by the Mortimers in the mouths of locals themselves, assessments from which the authors do not dissent.[48] About these views, they comment, somewhat condescendingly, that the local giving voice to them was 'like the

---

47   Although this genre combination generally entails a police investigation, it can – and in the case of *Summer's Lease* does – take the form of a search undertaken not by state authorities but rather by an unofficial individual (= amateur sleuth). The effectiveness of this genre combination (crime + picturesque context), amounting in some instances to a travelogue, is acknowledged to be the case in the following *policières* that have featured as successful television series:

Writer	Protagonist	Context
Donna Leon	Brunetti	Venice
Colin Dexter	Morse	Oxford
Andrea Camilleri	Montalbano	Sicily
Anthony Horowitz	Foyle	Hastings
Henning Mankell	Wallander	Sweden

48   'I have a good political understanding', observes one local (Mortimer & Mortimer, 1957: 100, 101–102), adding: 'It is arrested [= backward] here. Very arrested indeed. In Sicily they bring their pigs into their bedrooms. It is also arrested there.' Continuing in much the same vein, the local opines that 'In England the development is not arrested. In Naples there are a hundred thousand unemployed, ten people living in one room, and when you go to Sicily and see what I have seen in the bedrooms, that is very backward I assure you.'

intellectuals of every university from Swansea to Paris to Berlin: arrogant, misinformed, loquacious, comical and humane'.[49] Anticipating the way mass tourism would be perceived subsequently, the Mortimers lament the 'gigantic European movement [and] the steady infiltration [of Coca-Cola] into every corner of Europe'; that is, the combined modernisation/Americanisation that, to some extent, would form part of the wider process corresponding to the development decade of the 1960s.[50]

That opprobrium had shifted from Italian locals onto plebeians from home is evident from utterances by members of the bourgeois family holidaying in the villa during the 1980s.[51] One labels the plebeian tourist 'the English army of occupation in Chiantishire', and compares their impact to the sack of Rome by Charles V, adding that such tourists 'desecrate the holiest places with their flash-bulbs [and] do their best to make even our delightful local trattoria in Mondano sound like a Berni Inn in Basingstoke'.[52] Not only is the local trattoria – where upper-class tourists like themselves eat – referred to as 'our', but the family is also said to feel entirely at home in 'Chiantishire'.[53] In support of this self-perception as superior to other tourists from home, another family member asks 'Am I a gentleman?', to which he answers in the affirmative ('I suppose I have some of the right characteristics').[54]

---

49 Mortimer and Mortimer (1957: 103).

50 See Mortimer and Mortimer (1957: 115–16), who signal an awareness of the kinds of issue that mass tourism might eventually pose for upper-middle-class travellers like themselves, by observing (Mortimer and Mortimer, 1957: 150) that '[l]iking Capri may be an expression of bad taste ... On the other hand, not liking it would seem to be the most subtle form of snobbery'.

51 A local tells a member of the English family holidaying in the Tuscan villa that (Mortimer 1988: 88) 'I don't think you can ever understand Italians', indicating that for the former to continue to depict the latter as 'backward' is quite simply no longer acceptable.

52 See Mortimer (1988: 137–39, 196), for whom the 'otherness' of those belonging to the ranks of plebeians is defined as 'common', a description applied to anyone who installs in their home 'cocktail cabinets or tanks of tropical fish like a successful East Ender would flaunt at you'.

53 This is an element of class-specific belonging that Mortimer (1988: 140) makes clear: 'In the second week of their holiday', the Pargeter family 'felt that they had been living in [Tuscany] for ever. [England] seemed part of a distant world [they] could barely remember [while] life centred round the villa, the sunlit early mornings with their promise of great heat, fulfilled during long afternoons, and dinner on the terrace when the darkness fell.'

54 See Mortimer (1988: 124). The same family member continues: 'I have always owed money. I usually stand up when a lady enters a room ... and I have always been anxious to place my education and superior talents at the service of the Radical Left. My grievance against our present masters is that, quite frankly, I find most of them rather common ... I suppose you might call me a gent.'

III

Although the condescension displayed towards the 'other' in pre-war accounts of travel outside Europe to some degree changes with the onset of post-war mass tourism, and the element of disdain shifts to the plebeian self from home, familiar tropes nevertheless continue to surface in writing about journeys made within Europe itself. Chief among them is agrarian myth discourse, and the problems raised by the way in which its related components – landlord ideology, ethnicity, class, urbanization, development, and poverty – are reproduced in narratives about European travel across the pre- and post-war era are not difficult to discern. This is clear when travel accounts are themselves contextualized in terms of their accompanying cultural forms (novels, films, historiography).

Always Defeated?

Hence any assessment of views expressed by Lampedusa is necessarily based not only on accounts of his European travels during the late 1920s, but also on a memoir and short stories, together with the literary and filmic versions of the justly celebrated novel *The Leopard*.[55] The latter consists of a narrative about the decline of the Sicilian landowning class during the 1860s, the power and influence it exercised historically passing to an emerging capitalist class in northern Italy, composed of bourgeois liberals who pursued their own political and economic interests, embodied in the *Risorgimento*. Thematically central is the necessity, as the aristocratic protagonist (Don Fabrizio, Prince of Salina) sees it, of a marriage alliance between his nephew (Tancredi) and the daughter (Angelica) of a wealthy bourgeois (Don Calogero). As such, the novel reveals much of the ideological framework to which Lampedusa himself subscribed, complementing thereby the views he expressed in the course of his journeys throughout Europe.

---

55 Seen as a masterpiece in its own right, every bit as much as the novel on which it is based, the film *The Leopard* (1963) is directed by Luchino Visconti. In both film and book, the symbolism is explicit: as the embodiment of the aristocratic landowning class, Prince Salina is the leopard, whereas Don Calogero, who personifies the monied bourgeois, is the jackal. 'We were the Leopards and Lions', says the Prince (Lampedusa, 2007: 143), 'those who'll take our place will be little jackals, hyenas.' For Lampedusa (2010: 92ff.), therefore, the bourgeois is synonymous not just with a predator but also an omnivorous scavenger that lives off the carcasses of others: in short, it consumes an already dead landowning class.

A clear antinomy separates two images projected by Lampedusa in his writings: that of landowner contained in his account of travel, and that projected by him in his fiction. Hence *The Leopard* is self-serving landlord ideology advanced by its author to justify the class position he and his family occupied. Until the rise of the northern Italian bourgeoisie, so the argument goes, the Sicilian aristocrat – the main protagonist – is portrayed as the embodiment of *noblesse oblige*, a landowner who cared for his tenants and retainers. Following the alliance between the nobility and the bourgeoisie, however, market relations became dominant, and the Prince of Salina was advised by Don Calogero how to make yet more money from his land, by increasing the levels of rents/dues paid by peasants on the estates.[56] The Prince reluctantly went along with this, surplus extraction by him being 'feeble in application'. Nevertheless, the fortunes of his family continued to decline. What concerned the Prince most was the loss of reputation suffered by the Salina family as a result. These interrelated mishaps – a shift away from *noblesse oblige* and towards the market – are attributed by Lampedusa to the rise of the bourgeoisie, and unconnected with anything the benign Prince Salina might have done.

If the narrative of Lampedusa projects a 'from above' version of agrarian myth discourse, its aristocratic/pastoral combination, that of Giovanni Verga corresponds to a 'from below' variant that is both plebeian and Darwinian.[57] Although stories by Verga deal with the same period of Sicilian history as *The Leopard*, they project images of a rural society very different from the one portrayed by Lampedusa.[58] Whereas the latter depicts the landlord class as

---

56   Lampedusa (2007: 103) 'Don Calogero's advice, after listening to the Prince's report and setting it in order, was both opportune and immediately effective; but the eventual result of such advice, cruelly efficient in conception, and feeble in application by the kindly Don Fabrizio, was that as the years went by the Salina were to acquire a reputation as extortioners of their own dependents, a reputation quite unjustified in reality but which helped to destroy their prestige ... without in any way halting the collapse of the family fortunes.'

57   As in the case of others who write about rural Sicily, Verga subscribes to the view that its peasantry is instinctive/natural/spontaneous. According to Lawrence (Verga, 1928: 13), therefore, 'Verga's people are always people in the purest sense of the word. They are not intellectual ... He had a passion for the most naïve, the most unsophisticated manifestation of human nature.' Lawrence (Verga, 1928: 18–20, original emphasis) endorses this view, lamenting the defeat of rural 'spontaneity' by the 'greedy': 'It may be urged that Verga commits the Tolstoyan fallacy of repudiating the educated [= urban] world and exalting the peasant. But this is not the case ... Verga by no means exalts the peasants as a class ... [He] turned to peasants to find, *in individuals*, the vivid spontaneity of sensitive passionate life, non-moral and non-didactic. He found it always *defeated*.'

58   As well as portraying rural Sicily as seen through the lens of an aristocratic landowner in *The Leopard*, Visconti also used a story by Verga – *The House by the Medlar Tree* – as

benign, and inequality as seen by 'those below' as 'natural' and acceptable, Verga describes the same context as based on resentment and struggle.[59] His stories focus on the plight of sharecropping families who, unable to meet the rental payments owed to a landlord, go into debt as a result of which they lose access to land and housing, and their personal belongings are seized and sold.[60] Although 'those below', consisting of peasants and shepherds, struggle against this, they are presented as unable to resist the combined power of landlord, church, and state, in legal disputes over property rights, debt, and rent.[61]

For their part, members of the landowning class appearing in the narratives are far from benign: as seen by Verga, not only are they interested simply in maximizing the amount of surplus that can be extracted, but landlords also exhibit a characteristic that Lampedusa affixed not to the Sicilian nobility but rather to the emerging northern bourgeoisie.[62] For his part, Lawrence is dismissive of the concern Verga shows for the plebeian characters in the narratives about rural Sicily.[63] Objecting to such realism (*verismo*), he comments that in the stories of Verga '[t]here is too much, too much of the tragic fate of the poor ... a sort of wallowing in tragedy: the tragedy of the humble.' However, Lawrence accepts that the Sicily portrayed by Verga is 'essentially a true picture'.[64]

---

the basis for the 1948 film *La Terra Trema* (Visconti, 1970) about the travails faced by the inhabitants of a small fishing community in Sicily.

59   On being informed (Verga, 1929: 157) by a landlord that 'I've come round to make the collection [of rent]', a sharecropper replies: 'Lucky for you who reap without sowing ... I've got five children, and have to find bread for the lot of them.'

60   Verga (1929: 158–59) recounts how in cases where a sharecropping family cannot make a rental payment, therefore, the landowner confiscates personal belongings (livestock, cupboards, chests of drawers) and sells them.

61   Thus an indebted peasant is reduced to shouting at a moneylender (Verga, 1929: 40) 'What shall you want of me when I've got nothing left?'.

62   In what is a broad indictment of the landlord/peasant relation, Verga (1929: 155) remarks of the better-off rural inhabitants that 'you'll never get yourself out of their ugly books any more, nailed down by debt'.

63   Complaining that Italians are 'always borrowing somebody else's eyes to see with', because they 'have always borrowed their ideals of democracy from the northern nations', Lawrence (1936: 224–5) is critical of Verga for his 'emotional-democratic vision'.

64   See Lawrence (1936: 225), who not only translated the short stories of Verga but also championed his writings, arguing (Lawrence, 1936: 223) that 'after Manzoni, he is Italy's accepted greatest novelist.'

Land, Politics, Fascism

The relationship between Lampedusa and Fascism is similarly open to divergent interpretations. For his part, E.M. Forster claims that the short story by Lampedusa – *Blind Kittens* – about the new rich of 1900 who emerged from the ranks of the peasantry, includes a portrayal of one such who 'will become an eminent Fascist'.[65] This appears to be a reference to the main protagonist, Don Batassano Ibba, a 'near-baron' who came from peasant stock, and developed into a substantial and wealthy landowner as a result of his father's financial acumen – a money-lender who acquired property as a result of non-payment of debts. He 'took pleasure in contrasting the purity of the Ibbas with the corrupt background of the old nobility'.[66] In attributing this view to Ibba, Lampedusa is effecting a contrast between his kind of people – the old nobility who practised *noblesse oblige* – and the upstarts from the ranks of the peasantry, whose fortunes and power were built on commerce and usury.[67] It was they who, according to Lampedusa, were the supporters and beneficiaries of Fascism in the early part of the twentieth century.

This distinction, which fits in with his self-perception as a benign landlord, one who was opposed to Fascism and different from those who backed it politically, as represented by the fictional character of Ibba, is open to question. Although the translator of the book containing the story maintains that 'Don Giuseppe was always an anti-Fascist [because] he refused to hold public office during Fascism', this of itself is not evidence for his being labelled an opponent of Fascism.[68] Lampedusa may not have been an active Fascist, but he did not disprove of such politics either. As his letters about travel show, Lampedusa not only agreed with attacks by Blackshirts on anti-Fascists such as Amendola, and held anti-semitic views, but also indicated satisfaction with the guarantee

---

65   This view is expressed by Forster in his introduction to Lampedusa (1962: 7–8). For the story *Blind Kittens*, see Lampedusa (1962: 109–128).

66   Lampedusa (1962: 120). The contrast between a declining aristocracy of which he was a part and arriviste elements is underlined by Lampedusa (1962: 125–26) in his description of those such as himself witnessing 'the tragic jerking of a class which was watching the end of its own land-owning supremacy, that is of its own reason for existence and its own social continuity ...'

67   This disdain is reflected in the kind of criticism made by Lampedusa (2010: 7) of the bourgeoisie, condemned by him on aesthetic grounds, for its lack of taste culturally.

68   Whilst members of the aristocratic landowning class may indeed have regarded the plebeian component of Fascism with social disdain, they were most certainly not averse to the role of the latter in combatting organized labour and leftist political parties.

of safety that the reassuring presence of Mussolini provided for aristocrats like himself.

A politically analogous difference between film and literary versions of *The Leopard* occurs in the ball scene/episode.[69] In the novel, Colonel Pallavicino, an officer who fought Garibaldi at the battle of Aspromonte, is presented by Lampedusa in a more sympathetic light than in the Visconti film. As depicted in the book, the Colonel is a positive character: he is regarded by the Prince as 'one of us', as more knowing and understanding of the forces at work throughout Italy. Nor does he go off, as in the film, to supervise the execution of the Red Shirt prisoners who fought courageously alongside Garibaldi. In the film, by contrast, Visconti depicts the Colonel simply as a pompous braggart, eager to impress the aristocrats present by inflicting the death penalty on rebel soldiers; equally clear is that in the film version the Prince regards the prisoners with compassion, but views their captor with contempt. This divergence can be attributed to a desire on the part of Visconti, himself a member of the Italian nobility, to present the aristocracy in the best possible manner.

Peasants, Ancient and Modern

The clue to what Green writes about travel is also not difficult to discern: modern Italy and Greece are seen by him through the lens of a classicist.[70] In his view, the countryside now – Italy in the early 1950s, Greece in the 1980s – is as it has always been, and peasants are no different from what they were in antiquity. This is an idealisation, an a-historical one at odds with the changes recorded in the agrarian sector of Greece in the post-war era.[71] As significant is the way in which this is expressed in what he writes about travel; in terms of an anxiety about the loss of nature, 'naturalness', and closeness-to-the-soil. Writing about Italy in the immediate post-war era, therefore, it seems as if Green needed to reaffirm the Italy of his imagination: that the 'natural', eternal

---

69   In the novel Lampedusa (2007: 162ff.) indicates that the ball is an occasion when 'the few hundred people who made up "the world" never tired of meeting each other, always the same ones ...' Significantly, the Prince and aristocrats present judge the furniture and furnishings solely in terms of aesthetics, whereas Don Colgaro, the bourgeois, judges everything according to its value/cost.

70   Classical themes on which Green has written include historiography (Green, 1989, 1993), translations (Juvenal, 2004), and fiction, among which is a narrative about the life of Sulla (Green, 1957) which compares well with that by Graves (1960, 1961) about the Emperor Claudius.

71   On post-war changes to the agrarian sector of Greece, see Bika (2007).

Italy of classical antiquity was still there, despite the modernization and industrialization then taking place.[72]

In later writings, however, Green seemingly recognizes the fact of idealization to which he subscribes in his travel writing.[73] Criticizing what he terms 'Victorian Hellas', Green accepts that the industrial revolution shaped the way Victorians interpreted antiquity; however, the target of his disapproval is the negative impact of industrialization on the landscape is not merely consistent with agrarian myth discourse, but also suggests that this aspect of his views remains intact.[74] In keeping with this is his ambivalence towards the evidence of poverty, initially regarded as quaint and endearing as long as it was in its rustic setting, but seen by him as off-putting when encountered in urban contexts. Hence 'the cheerful poverty' of Naples in the end becomes for Green 'unbearable', 'a nagging sore on my conscience, a peculiarly nasty kind of embarrassment'.[75]

---

72   Observing that on the island of Lesbos 'nothing has really changed', for Green (1989: 60, 62) '[t]he Spirit of Sappho ... is, clearly, still alive and well, despite the encroachments of mass-communications and nuclear-based power politics. Long, against all odds, may it so continue.'

73   About this Green (1989: 36) remarks that '[m]odern Greeks, too, were included in this [Victorian] rose-tinted scene: happy Mediterranean peasants with less work and more food than would be their lot in the dank north ...' About the reason for this idealization Green (1989: 39) explains that 'the Victorian concept of antiquity was ... a stylised never-never-land done up in fancy dress ... it would be hard to find a Victorian essay in ancient literature, history, or philosophy that was not, at the same time, in some sense a work of propaganda.' Elsewhere he (Green, 1972: 11ff.) strongly opposes the idealization of the Golden Age of Greece, arguing that '[t]he myth of a Golden Age is endemic to humanity ... if man is not looking forward to the millennium he is looking back to some lost Eden'. Ironically, the latter is a view to which Green himself adheres in his travel writing.

74   Hence the argument (Green, 1989: 42) that '[t]he Industrial Revolution undermined (often in a most literal sense) the very foundations of English rural, and still predominantly aristocratic, landownership; by providing new avenues to greater wealth it opened up the closed circle of traditional political power; it destroyed old values as well as the landscape, and brought a dangerous air of of egalitarianism into society along with the poisonous smoke from its factory chimneys.'

75   Whilst in Florence, he (Green, 1953: 56–57) observes, 'I could not be unaware of the desperate poverty behind the prosperous façade; of the pinched faces and shrunken bellies of most of these children. When I came to Naples it became alarmingly apparent'. Green (1953: 104, 107) goes on to note: 'The poverty that one comes across in Florence, an unpleasant reminder of the social defects that one never thinks of abroad, is here [in Naples] unavoidable: it stares you grimly in the face on every street corner. I found the dirt delightful at first ... in the end it formed a nagging sore on my conscience, a peculiarly nasty kind of embarrassment.'

Like travel writing generally, this distinction – the acceptability of rural poverty, the unacceptability of its urban counterpart – indicates two things. First, that the criterion at work is an aesthetic one ('picturesque'), and not based on political economy; scarcity is perceived as 'natural' in the countryside but an eyesore in towns or cities. And second, it reproduces the dichotomy at the heart of agrarian myth discourse; the pro-rural/anti-urban antinomy. In the case of Green, and the impact on him of his Italian journey, the contrast between rural and urban society, and more generally the significance he attaches as a result to agrarian myth discourse, emerge most clearly from his concluding observations about travel-as-consciousness-formation.[76] Of the two conflicting approaches, one involves those who – like Green himself before his journey – are urban inhabitants ('city-dwellers'), bearers of an alienated existence he now wishes to discard (subjects 'detached from their background'); for these sort of people, humanity dominates nature, the 'natural'. The alternative, espoused when the journey ended, embraced a thematically-grouped set of concepts: pro-soil, pro-rural, and pro-'natural'; for these sort of people, by contrast, nature dominates humanity.

It was in the latter category that Green now found himself. When he left England at the start of his journey, he subscribed to the first view ('the limited horizon of the town-dweller divorced from the soil'), and as he travelled in Italy he shifted to the second (the 'natural forces in these Southern latitudes'). The tension between the two was resolved in the course of his journey; travel-as-consciousness-formation, and its corresponding transformation, occurred in Sicily, a place where nature/soil (= agrarian myth discourse) claimed not just its inhabitants but Green also. His conversion is made clear from the outset: 'This is the story of a journey', he declares, one that 'traces not only my progress through Italy and Sicily, but also the integral change in my own outlook

---

76   'Everyone has, sooner or later, to form for themselves an attitude to living', concludes Green (1953: 209–10), who then elaborates: 'Some people – mainly city-dwellers ... – can find their pattern in their fellow-men, isolated and detached from their background. Others, and today these form a minority, start from the physical bones of a country, the seasonal inscape, earth, rock and valley sculptured by time into a unique complex which shapes not only itself but those who live in it, till they take on the *ethos* of the soil which bred them ... When I left England, people – the ineffectual people I knew, the limited horizon of the town-dweller divorced from the soil – formed the fragmentary pattern of my existence. As I travelled on man receded into the enormous landscape of movement that enveloped me; was caught up and absorbed by natural forces that in these Southern latitudes still have free play ... In Sicily the final metamorphosis was achieved. The burning island, its soil ... had long ago claimed its inhabitants: and though I did not know it till long afterwards, silently and inevitably it claimed me also.'

on life that resulted from it: the awareness not only of the permanent imma-
nence of the past in the present, but also of the unifying force and significance
of a land itself lying behind those who live in it, and shaping them to its own
pattern ... what still remains for me the only true reality: the reality of the land,
which determine all history and every creed.'[77]

Conclusion

Like accounts of journeys outside Europe considered in the previous chapter,
similar narratives about European travel reveal continuities the former and
can be differentiated in a number of different ways. In terms of conjuncture,
therefore, accounts of travel considered here focus on contexts as they were
after each of the two main conflicts within Europe, that of 1914–18 and that of
1939–45. One effect of the latter war is that the initial condescension expressed
by the victors when visiting tourist destinations (Italy, Sicily) inhabited by
defeated populations is replaced with enthusiasm for these same attributes,
a transition whereby the underdeveloped and impoverished nature of place
and people is recast as evidence for a desirable – because authentic – cultural
alterity untainted by the intrusion of progress and development.

In the period immediately following the 1939–45 war, a subtext encountered
in accounts by British writers (Peter Green, Norman Lewis, John Mortimer)
conveyed a sense of superiority to populations inhabiting the countries visited, perceived as composing an external 'other'. This took the form of negative
views about the backwardness of the location, disapproval in the case of visits
to Italy and Sicily being expressed about aspects such as poverty, squalor, odd
locals, and unpalatable food. From the 1960s onwards, however, these opinions
gave way to positive ones, in the course of which the scorn projected in narratives of travel shifted accordingly, from the internal 'other' (Italians, Sicilians)
onto the external 'other', the mass tourist corresponding to the plebeian from
home. Hence the negative view of locals that inform what Mortimer wrote
about 1950s Italy and replaced in his 1980s account by positive ones, at which
point the subject perceived as undesirable is now the foreign tourist.

As significant, however, are the ideological continuities spanning these different conjunctures. Principal among these are components forming agrarian myth discourse: on the one hand idealization of the countryside, its rural
communities and inhabitants; on the other, hostility towards industrialization,

---

77   Green (1953: 9).

tourism and tourists, together with concern lest being taken for one of the latter. Both in the account of travel across Europe during the 1920s, as also in the fictional account of the 1860s Sicilian landowning class, Lampedusa deploys an ideological framework consistent with the aristocratic pastoral variant of agrarian myth discourse. Invoking aesthetic criteria, he condemns not only industrial conurbations (which he avoids visiting), but also Bolshevism. Similarly, his anti-semitism is class-specific, and extends to racist observations about working class Jews who are poor. By contrast, Lampedusa approves of the countryside throughout Europe, its ruling class owners, its traditional hierarchy and institutional supports.

Tropes about travel persist, not least in perceptions of rural poverty as unproblematic, almost as part of nature itself. Viewed in aesthetic terms, rural poverty in Italy was regarded by Green as picturesque, even after the 1939–45 conflict, while its urban counterpart elicited revulsion. For him there was little difference between post-war Italy and its socio-economic form/function in classical antiquity. In the case of Lampedusa, both travel narratives and fiction exhibit the same 'from above' worldview. Writing just after the end of the 1914–18 war, he regrets the demise of European aristocracy, a view embodied in both novel and film versions of *The Leopard*, expressing nostalgia for the historical era when it exercised power. The latter is depicted by him as noblesse oblige, a benign image contradicted in the 'from below' narrative by Verga, the focus of which is on the poverty and oppression of the sharecropper. Unsurprisingly, perhaps, Lampedusa also declares a sympathy for fascism and approves of its role in keeping the Italian left in check.

As will be seen in the chapter which follows, many of these same issues and themes surface in accounts of travel to and residence in Venice.

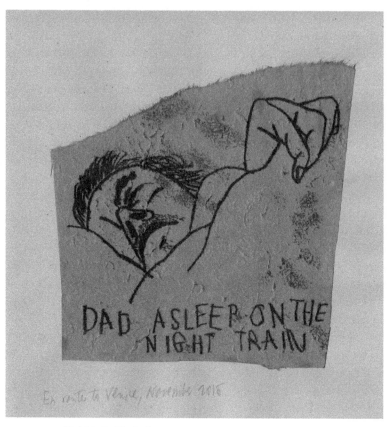

FIGURE 4   Night train (Venice)
© ANNA LUISA BRASS

Arrivals, Not Departures (On Never Leaving Venice)

It is easy to feel and to say something obvious about Venice.

> A truism acknowledged by JOHN ADDINGTON SYMONDS in the early
> 1880s, one noted in virtually all travel accounts featuring this city both
> before and since.[1]

• • •

Like *acqua alta* [high water], tourism came when it wanted, could
be stopped by nothing, and would gradually destroy the city.

> A trope encountered in almost all fiction and non-fiction writing about
> Venice, voiced here by Commissario GUIDO BRUNETTI, a Venetian
> detective in the 2021 novel by DONNA LEON.[2]

• •
•

Introduction: Venice, Tourism and the Agrarian Myth

Its urban character notwithstanding, how Venice is portrayed in travel accounts
is consistent with components of agrarian myth discourse, extending from its
small-scale nature, its traditional culture, and the absence of industrial development. Since the focus of most travel accounts has been and remains largely
on its culture, aesthetics, and image, however, the economic links between
the city and the surrounding countryside, and in particular the ownership by
Venetian noble families of large rural estates, remain hidden. For this reason,
where Venice is concerned the aristocratic pastoral version of the discourse
transects the urban/rural divide, in the process exhibiting typical agrarian

---

1 Symonds (1884: 169), who continues: 'The influence of this sea-city is unique, immediate, and
   unmistakable. But to express the sober truth of those impressions which remain when the
   first astonishment of the Venetian revelation has subsided, when the spirit of the place has
   been harmonised through familiarity with our habitual mood, is difficult.'.
2 Leon (2021; 206).

myth features.[3] Among the latter are support for traditional rural hierarchy; a belief in the existence of an harmonious rural idyll; nostalgia for the pre-modern coupled with a rejection of modernity; and opposition to the intrusion and effects of tourism.

Already in the late nineteenth century the presence in Venice of tourists was being seen by the upper-class visitor (such as John Addington Symonds) as a problem. Just as the Venetian aristocrat, in his/her capacity as proprietor of a large rural estate in the Veneto region, felt menaced by tenants, so the same individual in his/her capacity as a resident of Venice felt threatened by tourism. Nor were these sentiments confined to permanent inhabitants of the city. Visitors who at a later conjuncture became in effect residents, expressed conservative views no different from those espoused by Venetian landowning aristocrats. In part, this is because – mimicking the views of the latter – such visitors never really left the city, a spiritual affinity reflected in what they thought and wrote about Venice.

Thus, the Symonds – father and daughter – at an earlier conjuncture, together with L.P. Hartley at a later one, all of whom visited and stayed in the city, were supportive of rural hierarchy, its landowning class, and cultural tradition, but antagonistic towards modernity, its urban manifestations, and the working class, all in ways that uphold agrarian myth discourse. For those such as Robert Byron and Ethel Mannin, the same ideology was combined with disdain for the tourist. Similarly, for Rose Macaulay the destruction of Venice by water, and with it 'civilization', is a metaphor for the destruction of the city and its culture by tourism. This contrasts with travel writing examined in previous chapters, where 'civilization' is condemned as an undesirable imposition on the pristine culture of the indigenous 'other'.

Although the travel narratives examined here belong to two distinct conjunctures – before and after the 1939–45 war – they display similarities in terms of their likes/dislikes. Accordingly, this chapter is composed of three sections, the first of which considers the late nineteenth century accounts written by the Symonds, father and daughter, and the early twentieth century one by Byron. The remaining two sections deal with post-war accounts of visits to the city. Hence the focus of the second are two fictional accounts by Hartley, one set in Venice, the other in England, which display similar components of agrarian myth discourse, while the third looks at the way Venice features in narratives by Macaulay and Mannin.

---

3   It is important to note that agrarian myth discourse is not confined to what happens outside Venice, in the surrounding countryside, but operates also with regard to locations – Giardini Eden and Torcello – inside the city itself (Brass, 2014: Chapter 8).

I

Until his death in 1893, the poet and literary critic John Addington Symonds visited the city of Venice each year to stay with Horatio Brown. The focus here is on the description by Symonds of Venice in a chapter entitled 'A Venetian Medley' which, the overwrought prose notwithstanding, provides sufficient references enabling an assessment as to his views about not just local inhabitants but also fellow travellers visiting the city.[4] This is complemented by the travel account of his daughter, Margaret Symonds, based on visits over the 1888–1892 period to the Veneto region, including stays at the large domain in its countryside owned by Countess Pisani. Each account contains negative views about tourists and tourism, while that by Margaret Symonds records in some detail both the functioning of a rural estate and the extent to which its aristocratic owner subscribes to the landlord version of the agrarian myth.

The Ox Spoke

In the Ducal Palace, where the painting of Bacchus and Ariadne is described as 'Tintoretto's touch upon the pastoral', A.J. Symonds marvels at 'the slight effect' this art produced 'upon the ordinary public'. The latter correspond to German tourists who, it is inferred, gaze upon the painting with a lack of appreciation, tourists-as-philistines uncomprehending of the artistic treasure they see.[5] In the eyes of Symonds, therefore, the episode illustrates a double taint: not just tourists who are foreign, but also culturally uncouth (= uncivilized). Returning from a trip to the Lido, he sits down to a meal in a restaurant, surrounded by diners who are tourists of different nationalities, all of whom, according to Symonds, 'must be suffered gladly through well-neigh two long hours.'[6]

---

4   See Symonds (1884: 169–211), who states (Symonds, 1884: 170) that '[i]t is my present purpose to recapture some of the impressions made by Venice in more tranquil moods.'

5   'Sitting, as is my wont, one Sunday morning, opposite the Bacchus,' comments Symonds (1884: 183), 'four Germans with a cicerone sauntered by. the subject was explained to them. They waited an appreciable space of time. Then the youngest opened his lips and spake: "Bacchus war der Wein-Gott." And they all moved heavily away. *Bos locutus est.* "Bachus was the wine-god!" This, apparently, is what the picture tells ...'

6   Hence the view (Symonds, 1884: 206) that '[f]rom their separate stations ... the guests flit in to a gloomy gas-lit [restaurant]. They are of various speech and race ... here we must accept what fellowship the fates provide. An English spinster retailing paradoxes culled today from Ruskin's handbooks; an American citizen describing his jaunt in a gondóla from the railway station; a German shopkeeper descanting in one breath Baur's Bock and the beauties of the Marcusplatz;...all these in turn, or all together, must be suffered gladly

The disparaging terms used in his description – the alcoholic breath of the 'German shopkeeper', the pointless recitation of a guidebook by the 'English spinster' – leaves no doubt as to his condescension, and consequently his wish to avoid such company.

It is with apparent relief, therefore, that he remarks 'I have escaped from the hotels with their bustle of tourists and crowded tables-d'hôte.'[7] Leaving the context and negative aspects of this encounter with foreign tourists, therefore, A.J. Symonds retreats to an alternative *trattoria* where '[t]here is no noise, no bustle' and 'no *ahurissement* of tourists.'[8] The contrast is clear: instead of listening to tourists speaking loudly about things of which they have little or no knowledge, Symonds prefers the company of locals who discuss things quietly and knowledgeably. Despite avoiding the crowds of foreign visitors, and being interested mainly in how Venetians live and what they do, Symonds nevertheless differentiated those in the latter category.[9]

On a day trip to Chioggia, therefore, where '[t]he main canal is lined with substantial palaces, attesting to old wealth and comfort', he noted that 'from Chioggia, even more than from Venice, the tide of modern luxury and traffic has retreated. The place is left to fishing folk and builders of the fishing craft [a place where] we feel the spirit of the decadent Venetian nobility'.[10] However, whilst eating a meal there in the company of friends, their sojourn was interrupted in a 'somewhat unpleasant' manner by impoverished local inhabitants who 'crowded round to beg for scraps'.[11] This ought not to have been a matter for surprise, given that poverty has been a constant in the history of Chioggia.[12]

---

through well-neigh two long hours. Uncomforted in soul we rise from the expensive banquet; and how often rise from it unfed!'

7   Symonds (1884: 170).

8   Referring to both the cheapness and the 'excellence of the cuisine' in this trattoria, Symonds (1884: 208) invokes what for him is its principal advantage: 'There is no noise, no bustle ... no ahurissement of tourists. And when the dinner is done, we can sit awhile over our ... coffee, talking until the night invites us to stroll along the Zattere ...'

9   Symonds (1884: 170–71).

10   Symonds (1884: 175).

11   His alarm at being surrounded by begging locals (Symonds, 1884: 177) is evident from the portrayal of this episode: '[F]or the Chioggoti, in all stages of decrepitude and squalor, crowded round to beg for scraps – indescribable old women, enveloped in their own petticoats thrown over their heads; girls hooded with sombre black mantles; old men wrinkled beyond recognition by their nearest relatives; jabbering, half-naked boys; slow, slouching fishermen with clay pipes in their mouths and philosophical acceptance on their sober foreheads.'

12   On the poverty of those who live in Chioggia, an enduring condition throughout its history, see Godoy (1985).

Escaping from this encounter with indigent 'squalor', it is with relief that A.J. Symonds and his companions returned to Venice, described by him as 'a long enchanted chapter of romance'.

Many of the same kind of anti-tourist sentiments were echoed at that conjuncture by Margaret Symonds, his daughter. Hence the reproach that '[t]he vulgar desire of a tourist – the feverish wish to know about things and people', a vulgar desire of which she feels herself also to be guilty.[13] Her enthusiastic wish to explore her surroundings – 'what joy awaits the eager tourist!' – is tempered by a concern lest she be seen as too much of a tourist.[14] In a departure from most travel writing, therefore, she labels a wish fully to know and understand the context visited – 'the heart of that country unknown to any tourist' – as in some sense undesirable, an intrusion into that which must remain hidden from outsiders like her.[15] Adopting the same dual approach – criticism followed by self-incrimination – Symonds decries the tendency on the part of 'passing tourists' to lament the rundown condition of grand buildings once inhabited by the Venetian nobility, and to criticize the failure as the tourist sees it to maintain them in good repair.[16] This, she then explains, is because villas decayed after their aristocratic owners, crippled by high taxes, were unable to maintain them properly, and instead moved to the towns.

It Is Not Easy to Do One's Duty

Turning to the link between Venice and the deployment in that context of all the ideological components that combine to form agrarian myth discourse, its presence and history can be traced to the process of land acquisition by the

---

13   Critical of '[t]he vulgar desire of a tourist – the feverish wish to know about things and people', Symonds (1908: 164) nevertheless confesses that she, too, is prey to this: it 'had even tinged my joys with minutes of discontent. I was inwardly assured that [Padovana] was not an uncivilized and barbarous waste outside the limits of the Doge's Farm. I was aware that it had its society, its fashions, and its conversation [but] I still desired to turn its pages and to read them with my own inquiring eyes.'

14   At the foot of the Euganean hills, announces Symonds (1908: 94–95), 'what joy awaits the eager tourist! He will find there a whole set of little cities. Each has a tempestuous past written in its archives, and a small piazza, arcades streets, a church, a ruined castle'. The 'little cities' referred to are Monselice, Este, Battaglia, the villa of Cattaia, Praglia, Teolo, Valsan Zibio, and Arquia. All were located near to the Doge's Farm where she was staying.

15   Symonds (1908: 106).

16   'It is so easy for the passing tourist to criticize and to lament', she writes (Symonds, 1908: 175), adding that 'I myself confess to harbouring the domineering spirit of a crusader in search of holy tombs ...'

Venetian aristocracy throughout the Veneto region. An illustration of this is the Pisani family, merchants who from the fifteenth century onwards bought large rural properties in the Padovan-Venetian plain: powerful and wealthy, their ancestors provided the city with diplomats, Admirals, Cardinals, and in 1735 a Doge.[17] That the aristocratic variant of agrarian myth discourse as applied to rural Italy is confined neither to its landowning components nor to Italian nationals is evident from the account by Margaret Symonds of the labour regime and landowner ideology linked to capitalist agricultural production taking place on the Pisani estate towards the end of the nineteenth century.[18] That its aristocratic proprietor, Countess Pisani, was an exponent of this discourse is unsurprising; more surprising, perhaps, is that some components of the agrarian myth are endorsed also by Symonds herself.[19]

Despite owning 3000 acres of cultivated land 'with the accompaniment of Italian peasants, Italian bailiffs, and Italian government', and devoting her energies to the garden, the self-image of Countess Pisani was one of *noblesse oblige*.[20] This patriarchal identity is unsurprising, since as an aristocratic landowner she 'had inborn convictions about breeding and race, and the superiority of mind over matter'.[21] As 'a strong Catholic', moreover, the Countess 'brought a keen, if perhaps too conservative, judgement to bear upon the

---

17   Like other members of the Venetian nobility, the Pisanis invested money from trade in the purchase of land, in their case bought from senior army officers who had incurred debts. On their history, see Symonds (1908: Chapter 1).

18   As the daughter of a well-known poet and Italophile, it is unsurprising that Margaret Symonds tended to see the workings of the estate owned by Countess Pisani through rose tinted lens, an idealization exemplified in the view (Symonds, 1908: 262–63) that '[t]he young English ladies and their mother had a wonderful love for the native, which was evidently returned.'

19   After marrying into an ancient Venetian family in 1852, Countess Pisani managed its large estates in Northern Italy, where according to Symonds (1908: 13, 15, 16, 146), '[s]he took very little personal part in the management of the property. Her energies were therefore devoted to the house and garden …', adding that: 'When Count Almorò III died he left the whole of his property and the entire management of it to his wife. This lady knew nothing of farms or farming.' Symptomatically, what amounted to a commercial operation – the economic improvement of the estate so as to generate substantial profits – was displaced in ideological terms, and the focus shifted thereby onto maintaining the garden. In the winter the family members returned to Venice, and 'live awhile in their apartments in the Palazzo Barbaro'. Just as Lampedusa in *The Leopard* describes how Prince Salina travelled in almost a royal style to Palermo in Sicily during the mid-nineteenth century, accompanied by his entourage, so Symonds (1908: 36) indicates that Countess Pisani 'sometimes went to stay in her town house at Venice, taking with her all her country retinue. Then the beautiful rooms on the piano nobile of the Palazzo Barbaro were opened up.'

20   In the words of the aristocratic landowner (Symonds, 1908: 17–18), '"*Chi ha terra ha Guerra*" – It is a daily struggle and conflict … It is not easy to do one's duty'.

21   Symonds (1908: 29).

politics of nations'.[22] Tenants are regarded with condescension: 'They reason like children, and when you are kind to them they act like spoiled children.'[23] Noting that Countess Pisani 'never did much manual work [in the garden] herself, although she loved to imagine it', Symonds reports that '[a]fter her love for her oxen came her love for the garden'.[24] Although initially possessing only twenty oxen to plough an estate of 3000 acres – a shortfall of some 400 animals – the estate prospered economically, becoming 'one of the best managed in that part of the country', livestock numbers increasing to some 500 cattle.[25] When full, the granaries were said to contain 'hundreds of square feet of grain spread on their floors', near which 'are immense arcades where all the farm machines, sacks, seats, &etc., are housed and guarded by sheepdogs.'[26]

Not revealed is from whence came the capital investment necessary for this economic development: for her part, Symonds claims that improvements in farm production were not financed by higher rents.[27] However, episodes of labour conflict at that conjuncture suggest that all may not be as benign as claimed by the estate owner. Accordingly, it is difficult for Symonds to avoid

---

22   Symonds (1908: 38).

23   Although broadly sympathetic towards the downtrodden peasantry, Symonds (1908: 18) does not seem to distance herself from the view of Countess Pisani when infantilizing the estate tenants in this manner, merely observing that '[t]he Italian peasant in Central Italy is often refined and intelligent. In Padova [where the Pisani estate is located], he is of coarser and heavier mould, and his mind has been warped by centuries of apparently fruitless labour and an old tradition of serfdom. "How difficult it is to understand the peasants!" she [Countess Pisani] writes in one letter. "They reason like children, and when you are kind to them they act like spoiled children."'

24   See Symonds (1908: 24, 25), whose depiction of the rural hierarchy as viewed by Countess Pisani bring to mind the justly famous equivalent recounted by Silone (1960: 30–31) in his account of Fontamara and its landowner, Prince Torlonia:
    'God is at the head of everything. He commands in Heaven. Everybody knows that.
    Then comes Prince Torlonia, ruler of the earth.
    Then come his guards.
    Then come his guards' dogs.
    Then nothing.
    Then more nothing.
    Then still more nothing.
    Then come the peasants.
    That's all.'

25   There were two threshing machines on the estate, and each required a team of twelve oxen to pull it (Symonds, 1908: 218).

26   Symonds (1908: 87–88).

27   On this economic turnaround, see Symonds (1908: 146, 152–53), who denies that the source of capital was rental, commenting that Countess Pisani 'received small rents' from her tenants, and that '[i]t may be imagined [sic] that her income from the estate was small indeed ...'

the issue of harsh working, employment and living conditions of the tenants on the Pisani estate. Hints concerning this surface throughout the narrative about her visit there: hence the admission that '[t]he hours of work appeared to me to be very long' since '[t]he harvesters began at three [in the morning] and ended at seven [in the evening]', together with the fact that '[t]he women grow old before their time, and the men's hair turns early white'.[28] The subordination of the estate workforce is nowhere better illustrated than in an episode when villagers bow and uncover their heads as the carriage transporting Symonds to the Doge's Farm passes by.[29]

The presence of rural poverty is evident from two interrelated processes: the length and demanding nature of the working day during the grain harvest, and the importance to tenant families of post-harvest gleaning as a source of subsistence. During the harvest, the working day consists of 13 hours labour in the fields, a task undertaken by men.[30] This is followed by gleaning, when the females in tenant households gather the grains left on the ground after harvesting.[31] About this Symonds reports, somewhat naïvely, that gleaners were those who also composed 'an army of peasant girls who habitually weeded and watered the garden' on the Pisani estate, but that when gleaning occurs 'they get so excited in the fields that they even refuse to come to the garden'.[32] An alternative explanation for this absence suggests itself: unwillingness to work

---

28   Symonds (1908: 132, 134). On her return to the Doge's Farm after a day of sightseeing, Symonds (1908: 280) encounters tired workers, and observes, tellingly, that 'no one smiled'.

29   For this episode, see Symonds (1908: 73).

30   These arduous tasks required by estate agriculture are described by Symonds (1908: 202, 204, 221) thus: 'We drove into the property and found the men at work on the ... farm. They begin to work with the dawn – at three. It takes thirty men to cut a field, but the thirty will do twelve fields in a day ... At midday there is a pause [and at] three they begin again, and work till four, then on again till seven ... In the late evening the young men come from their work and carry the [full] sacks up to the granaries. This is the hardest labour of the year. The sacks are very heavy, weighing from 50 to 72 kilos each, and it requires both strength and agility to hoist them on the shoulders and run up the precipitous brick steps into the barns.'

31   'In the afternoon the women appear upon the scene', notes Symonds (1908: 205, 209), '[t]hese ladies have nothing to do with the reaping and stacking. Their main object is gleaning ... A woman can glean a franc's worth of corn in the day if she works hard enough ... When the corn is stacked ... the news is spread that in the field there will be gleaning at such and such an hour. If the property is large the crowd which gathers outside its gates will be proportionately big ..."

32   Symonds (1908: 28). It should be noted that the details acquired about gleaning and other agricultural tasks were the result, in the words of Symonds (1908: 212), of the fact that 'I indulged my harmless desires, such as joining the gleaners and conversing with them freely.'

on gardening is due not to the 'excitement' of gleaning but much rather to collecting grains missed by harvesting being an important source of income or sustenance.[33] Historically, gleaning is an indicator of rural impoverishment, in that it is perceived as a necessary supplement to wage or subsistence levels which are themselves inadequate.

Loaded Pistols, Ominous Chatter

In the light of these issues – hard work, inadequate subsistence – it is hardly surprising that tenants regarded Countess Pisani with hostility. She informs Symonds that 'we have had ourselves a fight, and eighteen men, armed with knives and spades and pitchforks, who assailed my party, dispersed them ... and took possession of the land'.[34] Observing that '[f]riends left me in the midst of what I call a strike', she then complains that '[t]he harvesters refused to go to work (not one man of last year came)'.[35] Having characterized her tenants as children, it is possible to comprehend how an aristocratic landowner might be taken aback by such displays of 'disobedience'. Outlining how for the Countess it was peasants who 'were the schoolroom', therefore, Symonds accepts that '[i]t is no easy matter to manage a schoolroom full of strong and overbearing young people', thereby indicating the extent to which their landlord equated tenants with unruly children (peasants = schoolchildren = infantilization) on those occasions when they questioned her authority or decisions.[36] It comes as no surprise, finally, to learn that Countess Pisani kept a loaded pistol above her bed, ready to use.[37]

---

33   The importance of gleaning to the economy of the estate workforce can be gauged from an episode recounted by Symonds (1908: 214–15), when fire broke out in a 'house ... let by [Countess] Pisani to a carter, who, against her advice, had admitted some families for the gleaning season. One of these was composed of three small children ... The mother, in her gleaner's madness [sic], had locked them into an upper room with all her gleanings and gone off herself to the fields.' That female workers found it necessary to put at risk the lives of their offspring by leaving them alone in a dwelling while absent gleaning – inappropriately termed 'madness', implying an unwarranted enthusiasm – confirms the economic centrality of such tasks. Significantly, exactly the same kind of phenomenon – a mother leaving her young children locked up in a house and unattended throughout the day while she was out at work – was encountered by me when undertaking research in rural Bihar during 1985.
34   Symonds (1908: 20).
35   Symonds (1908: 21).
36   Symonds (1908: 23).
37   Symonds (1908: 30).

Many of the same views expressed by John Addington Symonds and his daughter in their travel accounts are voiced also at a later conjuncture by Robert Byron. Staying in Venice on his way to Persia in 1933, he observed when visiting a Palladian villa that 'Europe could have bid me no fonder farewell than this triumphant affirmation of the European intellect', while his companion warned that 'It's a mistake to leave civilization'. In keeping with other accounts written about the city, Venice is equated with 'civilization'.[38] Like them, he also voiced objections about the presence there of English tourists, observing that '[a]fter inspecting two palaces ... we took sanctuary from culture in Harry's Bar. There was an ominous chatter, a quick-fire of greetings: the English are arriving'.[39]

A somewhat more benign view of tourists, tourism and crowds is that of a Hungarian writer, Antal Szerb, who spent time in Venice during his 1936 visit to Italy. In contrast to travel writers who view the prospect of increased mass tourism with horror, he lamented the impending closure of a right to travel, to which his own response was to treat every visit to a foreign country as if it were his last.[40] Furthermore, unlike many of those who write about Venice, Szerb was entranced as much by the aesthetically unprepossessing narrow alleyways (*calli*) leading off the canals as by the more obvious architectural splendours of the city.[41] Despite exhibiting many of the tropes circulating about travel – among them the visual impact on entering the city for the first

---

38   See Byron (1991: 20).

39   See Byron (1982: 19). Notwithstanding enthusiastic opinions and endorsements from other travel writers (for example, Paul Fussell and William Dalrymple), it is difficult to avoid the view that much of this supposedly classic account by Byron is little more than a laughing-at-foreigners narrative, since the text is peppered by frequent dialogues illustrating the difficulties, misunderstandings, and incomprehension the 'other' had with the English language when communicating with Byron and his travelling companions. These encomia can be found in the introduction by Fussel to Byron (1982: v–xii) and Dalrymple, 'The road to inspiration', *The Guardian* (London), 8 November 2003.

40   'My impressions of Italy', he observed (Szerb, 2014: 20), 'always feel like the last visions of a dying man.'

41   Emphasizing the delight taken in these most ordinary structures of the urban, Szerb (2014: 25) confesses that '[i]f I were compelled to speak with total candour, I would say that it is for these back alleys that I love Italy. For me, they represent what gardens were to the age of Goethe, and what "Nature" was to the Romantics. No snow-covered peak, no glacier, mountain lake or stream, no sea or parkland could move me like the back alleys of an old Italian city'. This surfaces in his novel, where the same view is expressed by the main character (Szerb, 2012: 9): 'Mihály first noticed the back-alleys when the motor-ferry turned off the Grand Canal for a short cut and they began appearing to right and left. But at the same time he paid them no attention, being caught up from the outset with the essential Veniceness of Venice ...'

time, a nostalgia induced by its decay/decline, coupled with suspicion towards progress – he nevertheless regards in a positive manner those travellers in the same space as himself.[42] Noting 'how cheerful, how proud and friendly' they are, Szerb comments that Italy – even under Fascism – 'has become a country of the self-satisfaction of the masses'.[43]

Lamenting the fact that an effect of the rail link to the mainland is that Venice was now more accessible to tourists than in the past, Byron made clear his regret at the access this conferred on those wishing to visit the city: 'Give me Venice as Ruskin first saw it – without a railway; or give me a speedboat and the international rich', adding that the 'human museum is horrible ...'.[44] Either by blocking the ease of entry into the city, or – once this was no longer possible – by escaping from the crowd once it had arrived, he underlines the importance for him of the element of exclusivity which upper-class travellers like himself had enjoyed, and was now in the process of being lost. Confirmed thereby is how, even three decades before the advent of mass tourism, the realization of the twin desires of those undertaking a journey – exploration and exclusivity – are thwarted: this in turn gives rise to resentment at finding similar kinds of selves present in the place visited, particularly encountering there the visitor from home and especially the plebeian tourist.[45] These anxieties became more pronounced in accounts of travel to Venice during the period after the 1939–45 war.

---

42   Describing Venice as 'this pampered city, crammed as it was with the world's fashionable riffraff', he (Szerb, 2014: 19, 21, 23, 24) nevertheless exulted that it had resisted 'the hammer blows of "progress"', remarking that: 'Here Western culture's Faustian rush to infinite expansion comes to a halt. Venice cannot "develop"'. For him it is a 'city that exists in the spontaneous sense of nostalgia experienced by everyone who feels, on arrival, that he must have been here before, though he has never previously set eyes on it.'

43   Szerb (2014: 73, 77).

44   For these sentiments, see Byron (1982: 20). In a letter written at the time he (Byron, 1991: 190) notes of the Palazzo Barbaro, where he was staying '[t]his palace is lovely ... I shall go to the Lido this morning [but] then I think it won't see me again ... life is very different here when one has a fast motor-launch always waiting at the door ... I regard myself as not really here at all, but simply staying in a large house somewhere with some friends I want to see. I have a large room with a marble floor overlooking the Grand Canal and so can stay in it and be alone if I want to ...'

45   That he subscribed to this exploration/exclusivity couple is evident from the following view (Byron, 1991: 30): 'You see most people go abroad and lead exactly the same Oxford lives in foreign capitals, drinking perhaps something new, but flitting from café to café etc. I don't want to do this: I want to go somewhere where there is not an Oxford life to be led, where a little energy is required and if such a thing is possible something new – different conditions of life.'

II

A writer from a petty-bourgeois background, who embodied all the posi-
tive/negative components of agrarian myth discourse, L.P. Hartley strongly
approved of the aristocracy, the rural, and tradition, whilst equally strongly
disapproving of the working class, the urban, and modernity. Whereas considered elsewhere was the way in which he deployed this approach in relation
to rural England at the start of the twentieth century, examined here is the
application of this same discourse to a fictional account of a holiday abroad, in
Venice during the period immediately following the 1939–45 war.

Real and Loveable?

It was when staying at a country house on a large rural estate in Norfolk during
the early twentieth century that Hartley encountered for the first time the two
main issues which informed his writing. On the one hand, 'the upper-class life
that was to so fascinate him, and would mean so much to him for the rest of
his life'; and on the other, the recognition that 'he was an outsider'.[46] Although
'never ashamed of his middle-class upbringing', Hartley nevertheless sought
'acceptance by the landed ... gentry [since] he had never had a natural place
among the titled people he loved to mix with [who regarded him] as an interloper'.[47] Both these issues structured his two principle works of fiction: the
Eustace and Hilda trilogy (which appeared over the 1944–47 period), and *The
Go-Between* (published in 1953).

The central theme in these books concerns an impoverished young man of
petty-bourgeois urban origin, who is 'taken up' by wealthier and aristocratic
landowning families for the duration of a short holiday in their company, either
in England or in Venice. Throughout this stay, he is patronized for not being
'quite like us', despite a continuous striving on his part for social acceptance.
This is the case in *The Go-Between*, the best-known of the novels, where the
young petty-bourgeois runs errands taking messages arranging secret assigna-
tions between the daughter of the landowning family and her lover, the tenant
farmer.[48] Like Hartley, the young petty-bourgeois occupies a liminal position,

---

46   For this and the following quotes, see his biography (Wright, 1996: 31).
47   'As an adult Hartley was happy to admit his middle class origins,' records his biographer
      (Wright 1996: 22), 'but seemed always to be making every effort to break free of them. He
      longed ... to rise up the social ladder ...'
48   For the discourse informing *The Go-Between*, and in particular the role of class, see Hartley
      (1953) and Brass (2014: 205ff.).

placed between two opposed class locations: on the one hand the aristocracy and merchant capitalist, and on the other the plebeian components (of whom the tenant farmer is emblematic). In the struggle between the latter elements, the character occupying this intermediary role ultimately sides with the aristocracy, again like Hartley.[49]

Contrary to the way *The Go-Between* is interpreted, whereby its celebrated reference to the past as a 'foreign country' is equated simply with childhood, here the term is seen much rather as symbolizing a similarly distant – but different – 'other' identity, one that for Hartley and his main protagonist was a desirable objective.[50] Namely, social acceptance into the ranks of the rural upper class, an unobtainable goal (= another place, or 'foreign country') to which he and his character both aspired but were in each case denied access. Hence the endorsing manner in which Hartley represented individuals in his fiction belonging to aristocratic and/or landowning families, a benign picture that drew praise from those sharing his idealised view of the English ruling classes.[51] Unsurprisingly, therefore, once he achieved success as an author 'those who made up his circle, a title, or reputation, or wealth, was almost a prerequisite'.[52]

Just as Hartley sought acceptance socially by 'those above' him socially (= aristocratic circles), so he was equally keen to distance himself from 'those below' (= plebeian elements), regarded by him with disdain. Attributing the presence of workers to what for him was an equally alien modernity, Hartley condemned them both.[53] Hence the antagonism he displayed towards the

---

49   This fictional characterization is consistent with that undertaken by its author. Thus, for example, in his reply to a hostile review by Leonard Woolf of Cynthia Asquith's 1915–18 diaries, Hartley (Wright, 1996: 241) came to her defence, challenging Woolf's claim that 'she and her generation of aristocrats (the very set with which Hartley had been intimately associated) had spent the war years in frivolous denial of the horrors that were taking place'.

50   Among those who regard 'foreign country' simply as a metaphor for childhood is Wright (1996: 219).

51   According to Wright (1996: 143), John Betjeman 'praised the fact that though Hartley's characters were from the privileged classes he had made them real and loveable'. In a similarly idealized vein, Bloomfield (1962: 8, 12, original emphasis) maintains that 'Hartley's aristocrats – the men – are on the whole *gentlemen* [who] have a regard for other people's feelings ... His soft spot for ease and elegance combined with the authority of tradition, as they sometimes are in the "well-born soul"...has by no means blurred his vision.' The same source (Bloomfield, 1962: 22) concludes in an analogous fashion: 'His function as a writer [is to be] the transmitter of a civilised ethos. If we want a more civilised world we had better know all we can about what it is like to be civilised'.

52   Wright (1996: 230).

53   Hence the 'sometimes desperate railing against the ills of modern life and the working class' by Hartley, who expressed particular dislike of the 'holidaying mass' (Wright, 1996: 212, 226). These mutually reinforcing pattern of antipathy takes the following

working class, a hostility evident in dealings with his own staff.[54] Although Hartley is described by his biographer as having 'affection' for his servants, it is clear that – as in so many instances – a positive attitude by an employer towards 'those below' was conditional on their knowing their place, and certainly not engaging in agency/organization aimed at those – like him – occupying positions at the apex of the class hierarchy.[55] Not only was he described by his tenants as 'a terrible snob', and being 'obsessed with the shortcomings of the working class', therefore, but there were instances when publishers also baulked at the 'snobbishness' contained in his books, thought to be 'dreadfully pronounced'.[56]

A Dream Long Lost

Thematically, the first part of the *Eustace and Hilda* trilogy, entitled 'The Shrimp and the Anemone', has structured the way in which the whole narrative is interpreted. Hence the view that, just as the shrimp is consumed by the anemone, so the trilogy concerns how the life of Eustace, the main character, is in effect dominated and absorbed by Hilda, his sister.[57] Although the process of devouring and being devoured is indeed central to the narrative, it is argued here that, important as the brother/sister relation is in this respect, as significant is another and different version of the same kind of predation. The latter takes a double form. First, it signifies the way the main character – the young petty-bourgeois – is absorbed visually/culturally by what he sees in Venice, a

---

form: modernity = working class = holidaying mass, or the arrival in places like Venice of the plebeian from home. That is to say, the era of mass tourism.

54   On this, see Wright (1996: 214, 217–18). On the subject of negative portrayals of working class characters in his fiction, Hartley observed in the 1960s that 'I often wish I *could* write a novel without moral preoccupations, but what I write about individuals is a reflection of what I feel about people in general ... For instance, I am almost obsessed by the way that the working-class, in England, only keep a promise if immediate financial gain results from doing so.'

55   About this issue his biographer (Wright, 1996: 223) notes: 'In fiction, Hartley could at least show the possibilities of joy that existed in the master-servant affection [*sic*], and could go on to show how the unfaithfulness of the servant was the one destructive element, the snake in the potential Eden.'

56   See Wright (1996: 142, 223, 226). An example of this was when he 'referred to the working class as the "w.c." [and went] on to describe them as "the Toilet"'.

57   As recounted by Wright (1996: 147), this 'focus on brother and sister' gives rise to 'the life-altering relationship that bestrides the novels' composing the trilogy. In the novel (Hartley, 1958: 612) they are described as not 'of a good family'.

place he is visiting for the first time. And second, it refers also, and crucially, to the way in which he is symbolically ingested ('swallowed up' and then 'spat out') by the aristocratic circles residing in the city, a social milieu to which he is attracted, but which continuously rejects him.[58]

The first and more subtle form of predation affecting Eustace is being 'devoured' by the city itself, and how this differentiates him from others in the sought after aristocratic social circle who have been in Venice much longer.[59] Unlike him, therefore, they are 'initiates' who possess not just an understanding but also a class-specific appreciation of its culture.[60] New arrivals joining the aristocratic social circle 'were not new to Venice, they were as much at home there as was Lady Nelly, and their knowledge ... was much more articulate. Names of churches that Eustace had only just begun to get sorted in his mind tripped off their tongues'.[61] As mortifying for the young petty-bourgeois

---

58 When invited to stay in Venice by Lady Nelly, around whom functions an aristocratic social circle in the city ('I've taken a house in Venice for July and August and September: it's very old, fifteenth century, so you'd feel quite at home ... she made things easy for him: it seemed to be her mission to make things easy for people'), Eustace appears to be deceived by its innocuousness (Hartley, 1958: 369–70). Later he recognizes his mistake, observing (Hartley, 1958: 499) that 'Lady Nelly belongs to the smart world ... and just because you want to seem to belong to it, which you never will, you have adopted some of their worst qualities'.

59 As a young first-time visitor to Venice (Hartley, 1958: 450ff.), 'his thoughts ... were still uneasily resisting the seduction of the undisciplined, unashamed opulence around him ... Everything Eustace saw clamoured for attention.' Like so much else to do with this character, it was a perception that reflected the experience of Hartley himself. Just before his death, Hartley – in a letter dated 17 November 1972 (Wright, 1996: 266–67) – finally came to terms with the fact that, after much time spent in the city, 'he would never see it again. Venice, a dream long lost, could still be remembered with affection ... In these final memories of the one place on earth where happiness offered itself to him, he seemed to have come to terms with the parting. He attached no blame to Venice now, defining it as "really a state of mind – not always a very happy one – Elizabeth Bowen once told me she leaned over a bridge and tears poured from her eyes, she knew not why! I think it is the sight of so much perfection, I think, to which one can add nothing, or take anything away. I used to have an acute nostalgia when I left it, but that wore off, and t last time I left I was glad to get away, with the heat pouring down like a great wet blanket. But I was much older then, and what I could get out of Venice I had had."'

60 The dawning of a realization on the part of the young petty-bourgeois that culturally he was different from aristocratic 'initiates' in Venice is recounted by Hartley (1958: 488) thus: 'Hitherto Eustace had been a systematic sight-seer, choosing his quarry beforehand and going straight to it. But privately he felt that this was touristy and crude.'

61 'Listening to them,' continues Hartley (1958: 574). 'Eustace realized how slight, how featureless, was the background of his Venice, a mirage in a desert of continental inexperience. Even the daughter [of an aristocrat] had been there before the war, the precocious child of a world-famous father ...'

was the fact that they were unimpressed by what he liked of what he saw, a divergence that emphasized the cultural distinctiveness of their respective class positions.[62] In short, he delighted in and approved of what aristocratic circles in Venice regarded as the 'wrong' kinds of things.

Much like his counterpart in *The Go-Between*, the main character (Eustace) in the final part of the *Hilda and Eustace* trilogy is an aspiring writer, a young man on holiday, staying with a family of a much higher social position, not in England but in Venice. On arriving in the latter context, he endeavours to become part of the aristocratic social scene in the city, but 'not everyone is fooled by his striving'. Those composing this aristocratic set quickly see through him, and his attempts to belong are endlessly frustrated.[63] The sole exception to this upper-class-based form of exclusion, some commentators maintain, is an older aristocratic female (Lady Nelly), who – unlike others of the same rank – accepts him, thereby treating the young petty-bourgeois character as a member of her social circle in Venice.[64] It is clear from what Hartley writes, however, that such an interpretation is incorrect: even she looks down on him.

The subordinate class position of Eustace, that of a retainer in an aristocratic household, is underlined incessantly, emphasizing that he is no more than a menial, taken up and discarded at will by those occupying a superior position in the social hierarchy. Challenged as to what he does in Venice, the young petty-bourgeois replies that he is working on his book, to which the questioner – a member of the social circle he wants to join – replies, crushingly, 'dancing attendance on her [Lady Nelly], I expect she makes you earn your keep.'[65] What 'dancing attendance' entails is clear: it amounts in essence to being constantly reminded by her of his position as a class 'outsider'. Reinforced thereby is his own self-image of not belonging, a process compounded by patronizing utterances and social humiliation.[66] Just like the young boy in *The Go-Between*

---

62   For these new arrivals in Venice (Hartley, 1958: 573), therefore, 'far longer was the list of sights they need not see – and these included many ... that were especially dear to Eustace. They did not care for Tiepolo ... until yesterday it had been his favourite picture in Venice.'

63   According to Wright (1996: 73) 'Venetian society seemed even more difficult to break into than its English counterpart ... It was, in its upper reaches, a snobbish society, at its core an Anglo-American colony of residents living in Venetian splendour.'

64   She is described by Bloomfield (1962: 13) as 'the really grand member of the family [and] too much of a real aristocrat to be snob', who, it is claimed by Wright (1996: 140), 'alone accepts [the young petty-bourgeois] for what he is, inviting him to be taken up in her Venetian life'.

65   Hartley (1958: 567).

66   Illustrated by Hartley (1958: 514) thus: 'Eustace glanced at Lady Nelly, who was obviously enjoying his embarrassment.' Whilst in Venice, the young petty-bourgeois comes

who is similarly patronized by a family higher up in the social hierarchy, and to whom a similar 'kindness' has been done, so Eustace is driven to imagining what her wealthy and/or aristocratic friends might be thinking.[67] Observing how English and Italian aristocratic members of the social circle interacted with each other, the young petty-bourgeois recognized – albeit reluctantly – the roots of his outsider status and consequent exclusion: not being of the same class as them, he could – and would – never 'fit in'.[68]

III

Described as 'an ardent Venice-lover', Rose Macaulay was taken there as a young girl in 1892.[69] Staying in the city more than sixty years later, it was still 'like living in some lovely poem.'[70] Like others who write about travel and place, she invokes only aesthetic criteria when enthusing about Venice, comparing it favourably with the 'ordinary ugly streets' of London.[71] Her outline for an unfinished novel, *Venice Besieged*, was sketched in note form during a stay in the city in 1957. Venice is depicted as a beleaguered city, the civilization of

---

across a sea-anemone, reminding him of the earlier time when he witnessed one devouring a shrimp. Remembrance of the episode is recalled in the third part of the trilogy (Hartley,1958: 543–44), further suggesting that the devouring/devoured metaphor applies not just to the brother/sister relationship but also to the petty-bourgeois/aristocrat one.

67   This element of social uncertainty takes the following form (Hartley, 1958: 500): they 'asked themselves "who is this strange young man that Nelly has got hold of?"', concluding: '"She is simply doing a kindness to a young man of genius, as she has often done before. Now we understand."' This self-doubt as to what her rich friends might think of him continues: 'he's just a young man she has picked up somewhere – Heaven knows who he is or what he does ... He's just a little imposter ...' The parallel with *The Go-Between* is exact.

68   Of this exchange between English female and Italian man occupying the same high position in the social hierarchy, the petty-bourgeois character observes ruefully (Hartley, 1958: 557) that the Italian participant 'was an aristocrat, he fitted in, and no doubt there were countless (if countless was the word) fine shades of understanding that she had with him that she could not have with Eustace.'

69   See Macaulay (1964: 24).

70   Macaulay (1964: 220–225, 285–86) stayed in Venice during May 1957, and again over August and September 1958.

71   Observing that 'Venice tends to get almost as sociable as London, after a few days in it. Of course it is a place everyone comes to, and one is liable to meet frends both visiting it and living in it'. Macaulay (1964: 225) continues: 'But what I like *much* the best is walking about it alone, seeing all the little streets & canals & bridges & squares & churches – every step brings one to some fresh beauty; it's like living in some lovely poem ... I shall miss it terribly when I'm back in London, and have to step out into ordinary ugly streets, & no glimpses of green canals and little bridges and campos ...'

which is threatened by barbarism. The city is overwhelmed by a catastrophe in the form of a deluge (= biblical flood), 'caused by a great tidal wave sweeping in from the Adriatic and submerging the lagoon islands and then Venice itself'.[72] She describes the process in some detail: the 'sea sweeps impetuously through Lido port [and] spreads through the channels in mudbanks, till they brim over and flood [the] whole lagoon.'[73] As the narrative continues, her account becomes apocalyptic: hence '[t]he tide flows on past Venice and Murano to [the] mainland [at which point] *Venice will disappear into sand and water*.'[74]

The irony of this narrative is difficult to miss: a decade after Macaulay wrote about a major flood in Venice, there was one, in 1966. An analogous fear of impending disaster, whereby Venice was not merely flooded but wholly submerged by the sea, was expressed also some seven decades earlier, by John Addington Symonds.[75] For the latter, as also for Macaulay, Venice flooded symbolizes the destruction of civilization; however, because she was a Catholic, in religious terms the flood also represents for her a cleansing process, a renewal akin to baptism. Additionally, therefore, it could be seen also as another form of purification, one in keeping with agrarian myth discourse. This corresponds to a sanitization, the washing away not of original sin but of tourists: that the latter are the object of such cleansing is suggested by her reference to the kinds of people who arrived in (= 'besieged') the city from the outlying island in the Lagoon, as '[w]ild primitive creatures there [who] swim to Venice, or come in

---

72   Macaulay (1964: 315) was clearly aware of the frailty of the sea defences protecting Venice, noting 'you hear the boom of the waves breaking on the Lido shore. If it gave way, [the] sea would roll in on [the] city, sweeping palaces and churches to destruction, as Tintoretto has pictured in Santa Maria dell' Orto.' The latter place, the Church of the Madonna dell' Orto, contained a painting by Tintoretto of The Last Judgment.

73   Macaulay (1964: 316–17).

74   See Macaulay (1964: 317, original emphasis), whose notes on the destruction of the city reads like the script for a disaster movie: 'Great tidal wave in [the] Adriatic submerges islands; their wreckage [is] swept into Venice – boats full of lunatics; wooden buildings, people, animals, trees, crops, flung onto Venice. Adriatic sweeps into the lagoon ... [the] campanile sticks up, and the domes and houses. All the debris of the islands flung into [the] Piazza. Piers, bridges, calles, campos, all submerged.'

75   'Lying awake in Venice, when the wind blows hard, one hears the sea thundering upon its sandy barrier', writes Symonds (1884: 199): 'On such a night it happened once to me to dream a dream of Venice overwhelmed by water. I saw the billows roll across the smooth lagoon ... The Ducal Palace crumbled, and San Marco's domes went down. The Campanile rocked and shivered like a reed. And all along the Grand Canal the palaces swayed helpless, tottering to their fall, while boats piled high with men and women strove to stem the tide, and save themselves from those impending ruins. It was a mad dream, born of the sea's roar ...' A similar fear about the sea defences being overwhelmed, and Venice flooded, was expressed by Mannin (1975: 27).

fishing boats'.[76] Those threatening the city were '[p]eople and animals besieging civilization', a process described further as being like an 'old house, partly ruined and discovered attics full of strange life'.[77] Negative terms such as 'wild primitive creatures' and 'strange life' are suggestive of an 'other' that causes anxiety, which in the case of Venice is the mass tourist.

Much the same kind of anxiety was expressed by Ethel Mannin who – like Rose Macaulay – was a novelist writing not just about travel but about Venice, a city she visited repeatedly and for the last time in 1973.[78] Again like Macaulay (and Margaret Symonds), her account of visiting the city exhibits the same two components of agrarian myth ideology: pro-rural and anti-urban discourse, embodied in positive depictions of the Italian countryside and its denizens coupled with negative ones of industrialization and mass tourism.[79] For two reasons, however, the negative views held by Mannin about industrialization and the presence in Venice of the mass tourist are unusual. First, as she was a socialist the expectation would be for a more sympathetic perception on her part concerning the desirability of industrialization. And second, she makes the important point that the presence of a crowd does not – cannot, and should not – lessen what the individual gaze is able to appreciate: in her words, '[n]othing can detract from it [= Venice], because it is *there*; beyond all telling in its beauty; and inviolate.'[80]

---

76   This reference by Macaulay to the city of Venice being besieged by 'wild primitive crea-
      tures' from the outlying islands corresponds to the Darwinian plebeian version of agrar-
      ian myth discourse, much like the fear expressed by Vidya Naipaul that in the Congo the
      rural inhabitant would emerge from what he called the 'the bush' and overwhelm 'civi-
      lization' – the economically developed, urban space in the nation (on which see Brass,
      2014: 309ff.).

77   Macaulay (1964: 315).

78   'When I was [in Venice] in 1964', comments Mannin (1975: 167, original emphasis), 'the
      tourists were thin on the ground; in the autumn of 1973 I often felt almost hysterical in the
      density of the throng milling [in the centre of the city]...by 1973 *everything* had become
      more "dense", tourism not least.'

79   It is clear from a meeting with a Venetian countess (Mannin, 1975: 27) that the aristocratic
      variant of agrarian myth discourse continued to circulate at that conjuncture. Hence the
      complaint by the Countess 'that the local crafts were dying out because young people pre-
      fer to work in modern factories on the mainland, and also to live there...'. This is a familiar
      kind of protest, associated historically with the objection by a landlord to the 'poaching'
      by industrial capitalists of the peasant workforce employed hitherto by the former.

80   Observing that 'Venice is unique; it is the world's most beautiful city [and] tourists from
      all over the world...cannot make the face of the basilica less than fabulous', Mannin
      (1975: 48, original emphasis) concludes that '[n]othing can detract from it, because it is
      there; beyond all telling in its beauty; and inviolate.'

This insight notwithstanding, in her 1973 travel account, not just of Venice but of Italy, Mannin deploys the familiar pro-rural/anti-industrial ideological combination that signals the presence of agrarian myth discourse.[81] Hence the aversion felt by Mannin for tourists is evident from their being part of the reason for locations she liked and those she avoided. Into the latter category, therefore, came the central area of Venice, described variously as 'dense with tourists' where 'camera-slung tourists milled and milled around', forming a 'density of camera-slung tourists', a location – 'the Tourist Belt' occupied by 'a mob of human beings [who] babble away' – from which to escape because 'I have a fear of crowds and wanted to get away'.[82] By contrast, a church in Venice is commended for being 'free of tourists', as is the Giudecca because this part of the city was a place in which 'there were no tourists'.[83]

Perhaps the most virulently pathological objection to the presence in Venice of the mass tourist is that of Andrei Navrozov, a paleo-conservative émigré from the Soviet Union who admits he is a 'bilious helpmate of the white counter-revolution'.[84] Just as 'totalitarianism' or communism is equated by him with plague, so too is mass tourism regarded as a pandemic, especially when this involves the unwelcome arrival of its subject in Venice over the summer months.[85] Conflating socialism and tourism, and then dismissing them both

81   Hence the following description (Mannin, 1975: 65): 'The road goes on and on through the wide beautiful valley, held in the golden evening light, with high wooded hills, fold upon fold of them [where] lie the farmhouses and churches, villages and scattered dwellings, with outcrops of vineyards, that constitute the natural scene, and it is impossible not to reflect on how traumatic an experience for the country people must have been the cutting of the gigantic motorway through the peaceful countryside, and not to wonder how much natural beauty and immemorial way of rural life was sacrificed to this vast feat of engineering.'

82   See Mannin (1975: 67, 68, 69, 121, 123, 166), who avoids a café 'for at all hours [it was] choc-a-bloc with tourists'. Ironically, Jan Morris (2001) who – like Mannin and others – also writes in a nostalgic mode about Venice and Trieste, upholding agrarian myth discourse and lamenting the intrusion of modernity and mass tourism into such places, nevertheless is herself critical of Wilfred Thesiger, another travel writer, for holding precisely the same kind of anti-modern views (Morris, 2021: 23–25).

83   For these views, see Mannin (1975: 113, 148).

84   On this self-description see Navrozov (2002: 146). About tourists coming to Venice he (Navrozov, 2002: 206) writes in a manner not so dissimilar from the overwrought prose of John Addington Symonds that: 'Summer in Venice means tourists. Do I hate them? No more, I assure you, than a patient striken with a mortal illness hates the individual viral agents…which are draining the nucleic-synthesizing energy of his body cells to replicate themselves.'

85   'The whole deadly drama of the epidemic that strikes Italy in the summertime Is the faceless uniformity of the tourist mass,' comments Navrozov (2002: 106–7), adding: 'Naturally here in Venice…the tourists wear the same-looking jeans, have the same-looking

in pathological terms, points to the common enemy of all those on the political right: the plebeian subject, either at work, in power, or at play somewhere
abroad, in a place regarded by the upper classes as historically their own cultural property. Symptomatically, therefore, the view of Navrozov about mass
tourism in the city borders on contempt, both for the tourist him/herself and
for the kinds of activities s/he does whilst there, projected negatively as 'the
greater Venice of unwashed tourist masses and the cheap cafes that presuma-
bly cater to them.'[86]

Conclusion

Ostensibly an unpromising context in which to encounter travel writing exhibiting components of the agrarian myth, narratives about journeys to and stays
in the city of Venice indicate this is not the case. Travel accounts examined
here contain many aspects of the discourse-for/discourse-against combination
informing this discourse: on the one hand supportive of rural hierarchy, traditional culture, and nostalgia for the pre-modern; and on the other antagonism
towards modernity, industrial development, and tourists/tourism. Broadly
speaking, negative views about tourists and tourism feed into agrarian myth
discourse in two specific ways: not just by eliciting and then foregrounding
national identity (of the resident self and visiting other) as part of the problem
to be addressed, but also by equating the mass tourist with a process of cultural
erosion.

Hence the disdain expressed by A.J. Symonds towards the end of the nineteenth century, is twofold. First, he disparaged tourists of whatever kind and
nationality, characterizing them as uncultured and/or ignorant. And second,
he felt revulsion when surrounded by aged and impoverished locals. For him,
therefore, the issue is the same as that invoked subsequently by others who
write about Venice: the unbridgeable gap between the self-as-initiate and the

---

knapsacks on their backs, and eat the same aeroplane food as they approach their destination'. Continuing in much the same vein, he (Navrozov, 2002: 107–8) asserts that: 'If one
believes as I do that the deadliest disease ever experienced by mankind is totalitarianism,
one can only assume that European tourism is yet another of the many ways in which the
citizens of Western democracies are preparing themselves, and being prepared, for this
imminent global plague.'

86 For this view, see Navrozov (2002: 126), compounded later in the same text (Navrozov,
2002: 150) by his observation that 'once every two years, in high summer, my beloved
Venice loses face and becomes a kind of cultural sewer. This is the season of the Biennale,
the witches' sabbath that brings all the world's scum to our canals...'

other-as-tourist. In her detailed account of a rural estate owned/operated by an aristocratic Venetian family, his daughter, Margaret Symonds, not only shares the anti-tourist disdain of her father – albeit extending the critique to include herself – but also enables one to detect the antinomy at the heart of the place visited. That is, between on the one hand the landlord pastoral version of agrarian myth discourse, as embodied in the benign self-image of *noblesse oblige* held by Countess Pisani, and on the other the inadequate subsistence provision combined with tough working conditions together with the antagonism towards her displayed by the estate workers on strike.

As important to an understanding of the way in which agrarian myth discourse is reproduced, therefore, is that which is not directly seen: the economic linkage between Venice and the surrounding countryside, whereby profits from seaborn trade are reinvested in the purchase of land, produce from which is then sold back into markets within the city. Revealed by travel writing is the contradiction at the heart of landlord ideology espoused by the owner of the Doge's Farm, which maintains that although rural society is unequal, it is nevertheless harmonious. By juxtaposing these antithetical elements, the narrative of Margaret Symonds indicates that struggle involving those regarded by the landowner as 'unruly children' counters and undermines this important component of the aristocratic variant of agrarian myth discourse.

Other visitors to the city, particularly those arriving during the post-war era – among them Macaulay and Mannin – similarly espouse agrarian myth discourse, not least hostility towards the presence of tourists. The Venetian travel narratives of each adheres to the familiar pro-rural, pro-tradition but anti-modern, anti-tourism combination. In a similar vein, Hartley – like Lampedusa – writes about the landowning class in an endorsing manner, but unlike him does not belong to the aristocracy: it is this form of exclusion, of being refused access to a hierarchical position to which he aspires, that fuels the social resentment displayed by his fictional characters. The latter seek acceptance by the landed aristocracy, in Venice as in England, and its refusal underlines their self-image of not belonging.

Although opposition to modernity and industrialization appear as a constant across the three chapters examining accounts of travel outside and inside Europe before and after the 1939–45 war, there is nevertheless a discernible transition in the structure of these narratives. Whereas travel accounts of journeys outside Europe defend the 'other' against the intrusion of 'civilization', the equivalent narratives about travel within Europe – especially those about Venice – protect 'civilization' against its overthrow by the 'other', albeit of a different identity. In the latter case, the 'other' consists of the mass tourist, the plebeian from home, as distinct from the former instance in which the 'other' is much rather the indigenous subject already at home. The manner in which the agrarian myth undergoes a transition, from discourse to become a political and economic project of neo-populism, and how also travel to Venice features in this, are issues examined in the chapter which follows.

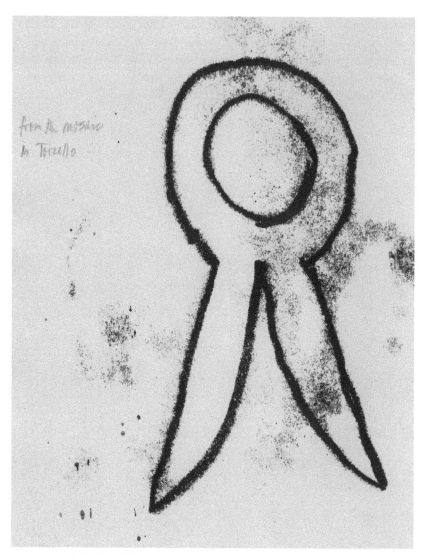

FIGURE 5   Lock (Torcello)
© ANNA LUISA BRASS

Other Worlds (Neo-populist Journeys)

> Populists ... combined in their ideology an anti-feudal bourgeois democratism with a petty-bourgeois conservative reaction against bourgeois progress.
>
> An observation by ANDRZEJ WALICKI that accurately captures the contradictory nature of Russian populism, opposed to the Czarist regime in the name of bourgeois democracy yet also to the pursuit by the latter of capitalist development.[1]

∵

Introduction: Worlds of Difference?

The current rise and global spread of populism has been accompanied by a corresponding endeavour in Western academia to relabel it politically, in positive terms as a sign of 'from below' ideological progress. Within the social sciences, and especially development studies, this has generated claims that specific variants of populism – agrarian, neo-populist – should now be regarded as potentially or actually leftist. In this process, the work of the Russian neo-populist Alexander Chayanov (1888–1939) has played a crucial role. Focussing largely on his publications about rural economy (the efficacy of the peasant family farm, the desirability of cooperatives) the drive towards the rehabilitation of a Chayanovian approach to peasant economy proceeds apace, markedly so in academic journals dealing with rural issues. Rather than seeing the neo-populism of Chayanov as the 'other' of Marxism, as an alternative to the latter that is itself non- or even anti-Marxist, these attempts at recuperation involve Procrustean efforts at assimilation. They extend from the view that neo-populism is different from but compatible with socialism, via the argument that no difference exists between neo-populism and Marxism, to an insistence that neo-populism itself is nothing more than a form of Marxism.

Against such views, it is argued that his politics, as revealed by an analysis of the discourse structuring the three Gothic fables examined below, tell a

---

1   Walicki (1969: 22).

different story. Whereas in his economic writings Chayanov sought principally
to make the case for peasant economy, in his non-economic publications the
focus shifted to a critique of socialism/Bolshevism. The latter was accordingly
foregrounded in his Gothic narratives, albeit taking the form of metaphor.
Considered here, therefore, is the link between the different intellectual genres to which Chayanov contributed: his economic work as an agronomist, his
political views as a neo-populist, and his literary output.[2] The focus is on the
latter, and in particular three stories by him categorized as belonging to Gothic
fiction, and as such apparently unconnected with the views he held either on
agriculture or on the politics of neo-populism. To demonstrate the existence
of this link where Chayanov is concerned, it is necessary to trace its presence
through a number of seemingly disparate histories/genres/concepts/processes
informing his views, among them Romanticism, neo-populism, travel, and the
agrarian myth.

A major protagonist in the stories of Chayanov is a sense of place, the
context in which events unfold providing an additional layer of symbolism,
thereby reinforcing the way characterization and narrative are depicted. This
is especially the case with regard to the manner in which the city of Venice features in his stories. Despite being widely acknowledged as a place emblematic
of urban civilization, Venice is nevertheless frequently depicted in popular culture as a location inhabited by ghosts, apparitions, and malign, other-worldly
forces.[3] The presence of the latter is in keeping with its identity as a place of
melancholy/mystery, the embodiment of tradition and yet simultaneously the
'other' of the rural. Like the agrarian myth, Romanticism and the Gothic literary genre, therefore, location is also centrally about the politics of nationalism,
socialism, populism, class, and the state.

The first of two sections in this chapter outlines the economic argument
made by Chayanov with regard to the dynamics of peasant agriculture,
together with the objections to this by Marxist theory. His three Gothic stories
are analysed in the second section, with particular reference to the political
symbolism informing each of them, and how this connects to the issues raised
in his economic writings.

---

2 As used here, the term 'other world' possesses a double meaning: that in addition to his
economic writings, Chayanov also writes fiction: in the latter, moreover, he enters the non-
material realm of the supernatural.

3 That Venice is frequently depicted in popular culture as doom-ridden – the locus of decline,
death, and the supernatural – is evident from, for example, the novel *The Haunted Hotel: A
Mystery of Modern Venice* (1879) by Wilkie Collins, films such as *Death in Venice* (1971) and
Don't Look Now (1973), directed respectively by Luchino Visconti and Nicolas Roeg, and the
supposed curse that blights ownership of the Palazzo Dario.

I

During the 1960s development decade, there was widespread concern among non-Marxist academics about the revolutionary threat posed by an economically backward agriculture in Third World nations, whereby a combination of population growth and food scarcity might fuel a challenge to the capitalist system itself. It was a fear that prompted much research into the modernization of peasant farming compatible with private ownership rights, an option that would not only increase output on existing smallholdings but also avoid substantial expropriation of landed property in rural areas. This political dilemma – undertaking an agrarian reform programme without at the same time jeopardizing either individual tenure or the accumulation process – gave rise to the renewed interest in metropolitan capitalist nations of the work of Chayanov.[4] As a neo-populist agronomist, he maintained that an homogenous peasantry composed of self-sufficient petty commodity producers constituted a pan-historical socio-economic category.

Chayanov: The Economic Case

Not only did this amount to a denial that capitalist penetration of agriculture in Russia entailed depeasantisation, but it was also the mirror image of the way Marxist theory interpreted the peasantry. Instead, Chayanov argued that peasant economy remained the same despite exogenous systemic transformations (feudalism, capitalism, socialism) to which it was impervious. This was because the economic reproduction of each individual peasant family farm was determined endogenously, by its demographic cycle.[5] According to

---

4   By the mid-1960s, as Kerblay (1966a: xxv) noted, Chayanov was forgotten in the USSR and largely unknown in West. As an early champion of his rehabilitation, Daniel Thorner (1966; 1980: 383ff.) argued for the relevance of Chayanovian theory about peasant economy to debate about difficulties confronting economic development in the rural Third World: 'Most of those who are today seeking to understand the economic behaviour of the peasantry seem to be unaware that they are traversing much the same ground trod from the 1860s onward by several generations of Russian economists. The problems that are today [1966] plaguing economists in countries like Brazil, Mexico, Turkey, Nigeria, India, and Indonesia bear striking similarities to those that were the order of the day in Russia from the emancipation of the serfs in 1861 down to the collectivization of agriculture at the end of the 1920s...'.

5   In Russia, Chayanov (1966: 67–68, original emphasis) noted, 'farms that sowed small areas gradually acquired a labour force as family age and size increased...[c]onversely, former large farms [shrink in relation to] small families created after division.' Consequently, 'the

Chayanov, therefore, landholding size, food output, and work intensity (= self-exploitation) by undifferentiated peasant households in the agrarian sector were all governed by a common set of factors.[6] These were the size of the peasant family itself, the ratio of working to non-working household members (= the labour/consumer balance), and the necessity of having to provide all the latter with their subsistence requirements (= drudgery of labour).[7]

Following in the footsteps of the *zemstvo* researchers who conducted rural investigation in Russia, he – like them – aimed to achieve economic growth not through the redistribution of land but rather by means of improved output on peasant farms: that is, 'to transform the entire *organization* of the peasant economy without waiting for political changes'.[8] Part of the reason for this was not wanting a confrontation with the Russian peasant, what was central to Chayanov's view about the agrarian problem was the peasant family labour farm. Private property, he maintained, was a reality, and had to accepted as such; it was dangerous to attack peasant ownership of land, since in his opinion 'no political power was able to force the peasant to change the nature of his farming'.[9] Because of this, argued Chayanov, the only viable option was to

---

demographic processes of growth and family distribution by size also determine to a considerable extent the distribution of farms by size of sown area...' He goes on to observe that 'when speaking of peasant farms...those in statistical circles have begun to use the expression *demographic differentiation*, thus avoiding the social significance formerly ascribed to this difference.'

6   On his concept 'self-exploitation', see Chayanov (1966: Chapter 2). As he (Chayanov, 1966: 6) explains, 'the degree of self-exploitation is determined by a peculiar equilibrium between family demand satisfaction and the drudgery of labour itself...[a]s soon as this equilibrium is reached, however, continuing to work becomes pointless.'

7   The link between the labour/consumer balance and the drudgery of labour is outlined by Chayanov (1966: 81)in the following manner: 'that the energy developed by a worker on a family farm is stimulated by the family consumer demands, and as they increase, the rate of self-exploitation is forced up...[i]n other words, we can state positively that the degree of self-exploitation of labour is established by some relationship between the measure of demand satisfaction and the measure of the burden of labour.'

8   See Kerblay (1966a: xxix). Such a project has its supporters today, who echo the optimistic sentiments of Chayanov himself. 'We are moving', states a current exponent of the Chayanovian model of the peasant family farm (van der Ploeg, 2017: 14), 'towards an agriculture made out of many richly-chequered, mutually-cooperating peasant farms that are strongly embedded in, and interwoven with, the regional economy through newly constructed nested markets'.

9   As pointed out by Kerblay (1966a: xxxviii, original emphasis), Chayanov regarded 'the predominance of the peasant farm based on family labour', as the unit around which to build progress in the countryside. 'Even if private property was not ideal,' he stated, 'it was a reality, dangerous to attack as long as the peasants' ideas remained unmodified...no political power was able to force the peasant to change the nature of his farming'. Accordingly, 'Chayanov felt that the solution to the agrarian problem lay essentially in the patient work

reorganize and improve peasant economy as it already existed. Agricultural productivity would be enhanced by accepting the presence of individual proprietorship and expanding output on such holdings.

This objective, which involved making available improved livestock, mechanization, fertilizers, and crops, was to be realized through a system of cooperatives.[10] The latter referred not to a single agrarian unit combining a number of producers but rather an external and separate institutional unit to which individual smallholders sold their crops and from which they received credit provided by the state. Since these kinds of marketing cooperatives would enable peasants to compete economically with larger agrarian units and merchants, it was a system that in the opinion of Chayanov was capable of raising output on petty commodity producing units whilst simultaneously ensuring the survival and prosperity of peasant agriculture. Such a view, needless to say, overlooked the influence that a peasantry already differentiated along class lines would have on the economic direction taken by an agrarian cooperative enterprise.

Based as it is on the peasant family farm and small-scale technology, Chayanovian theory presented the possibility of agricultural production without extensive alterations, both to ownership rights and to the prevailing agrarian structure. Insofar as it entailed neither rural property redistribution nor collectivization, his model was not merely compatible with capitalism but – perhaps more importantly – would also not lead to socialism. From the 1960s onwards, therefore, it was politics as much as anything else that made Chayanovian analysis so acceptable both to those formulating government policy and to those in Western academic institutions undertaking the study of Third World economic development.[11] Paradigms that currently dominate the

_____

of reorganizing the peasant economy. It was a question of finding the principles of organization which would increase *the productivity of agricultural labour*...'

10   Hence the view (Chayanov, 1991: 17) that '[p]easant cooperatives, as we know, constitute a part of the peasant economy which has been given a distinct identity in order to organize that economy on large-scale principles.' Accepting that 'cooperatives cannot be thought of in isolation from the social and economic foundations on which they are based [as a result of which they] organize those interests and aspects of the lives of groups or classes which already existed before cooperatives appeared', Chayanov (1991: 17–18) nevertheless persists in maintaining that such units 'in our opinion represent, in a highly perfected form, a variation of peasant economy which enables the small-scale commodity producer [to flourish] without sacrificing his individuality,' even to the extent of 'employing hired labour'. In other words, for him peasant essentialism overrides the palpable fact that cooperatives are transected by the kind of class relations which are redolent of capitalism.

11   Interest on the part of development theory in Chayanov's view of peasant economy can be gauged from the significance attached to his approach by, among others, Kerblay (1966a; 1966b; 1971), Sahlins (1972), Jasny (1972), Shanin (1971, 1972), Harrison (1975; 1977; 1979), Cox (1979), Durrenburger (1984), Shanin (1985; 1986), Ellis (1988), Danilov (1988),

study of rural development – such as the Subaltern Studies series, everyday-forms-of-resistance, 'multitudes' and 'global labour history' – are similarly informed by a Chayanovian framework, albeit not always knowingly so.[12]

Chayanov: The Economic Case Against

Conceptually, the dynamic informing the model of what Chayanov terms the peasant labour farm is an internal one: variables such as the size of holding, work intensity, cultivated area, and output, are all driven by the subsistence requirements of the family unit, beyond which there is no need for labour-power to expend additional energy. Once the labour/consumer balance is reached, therefore, and an equilibrium between needs satisfied and effort undertaken establishes itself, the limit set by the drudgery of labour on the part of its household members has been achieved. According to this effectively closed economic model, Chayanov treats the peasant farm as a socio-economically hermetic entity, largely unaffected by the wider system. The difficulty he faced was both economic and political, and stemmed from an obvious disparity between two contrasting models: the family labour farm as perceived by him was governed by an endogenous dynamic, whereas Marxism sought to account for the reproduction of the same agrarian unit exogenously, by what occurred in the economic system as a whole.[13]

Nove (1990), Shanin (1990), and van der Ploeg (2013). Discussions about the importance of a Chayanovian approach feature in two collections on rural development, edited by Wharton (1970) and by Mencher (1983). Of particular interest is the exchange about Chayanov, in the earlier volume, involving Georgescu-Roegen and Daniel Thorner.

12 On these paradigms, see respectively Guha (1982–89), Scott (1976; 1985), Hardt and Negri (2005), and van der Linden and Roth (2014). For the connection between all the latter and Chayanovian theory, see Brass (2000, 2014, 2017, 2018).

13 This is not to say that Chayanov (1966: 73) was unaware of this contrast, observing that 'we cannot deal with the conditions that determine the level of labour productivity, since they depend not so much on on-farm factors as on general economic factors affecting the farm's existence.' Listing the latter, he concedes that '[b]y their very nature, all these factors lie outside the field of our present investigation.' Nevertheless, he (Chayanov, 1966: 254, original emphasis) defends his view against that of Marxism by pointing out that 'Russian economists started to attach a somewhat different significance to the *heterogeneity* of peasant farms...[t]hey called this process "demographic differentiation", thus stressing that the chief cause of differences in farm size is the demographic processes of family growth as its age increases, and not social factors causing peasant farms to become capitalist and proletarianized, as we formerly supposed.'

Among the many criticisms made by Marxists was that Chayanov failed to situate peasant economy in relation to its national and international context, that he conflated middle peasants with kulaks, that smallholdings were unable to compete with large capitalist agribusiness units, and that the peasant family farm was in many instances itself differentiated endogenously in terms of ownership of the means of production. Insofar as his approach privileged the definition of value subjectively, as a function of needs, the Chayanovian model was regarded as no different from that of neoclassical economic theory. The survival of peasant economy was attributed by Kautsky not to an innate efficiency on its part – including thereby meeting familial subsistence requirements – as to its being a source of labour-power wanted by local capitalist enterprises.[14] Hence it was this external dynamic, and not any internal one (= 'self-exploitation'), that prevented the expropriation of the peasant family farm, and thus ensured its 'survival' (= economic reproduction) in contexts where it would otherwise have disappeared.

Evidence from Russia at that conjuncture suggests that cooperatives were not only well established but also operating along lines that were already capitalist.[15] Noting that just before the 1914–18 war small cooperative credit associations in Russia 'have especially facilitated the purchase of cattle and the lease of farm lands rural buildings', a report on the subject goes on to observe that 'certain large and especially prosperous [cooperatives] have at their disposal very large funds amounting to millions of rubles'.[16] About the way such units perpetuated an already unequal class structure in the Russian countryside, the same report indicates that cooperative membership was composed of 'more or less well-to-do farmers' who then availed themselves of its credit facilities in order to lend to poor peasants outside the system 'under conditions extremely burdensome for their debtors'.[17] In Siberia, where this kind of unit 'attracts to itself the households of the more prosperous peasants', there existed by 1907 some 270 cooperative societies with a combined membership of 52,000

---

14   Kautsky (1984).
15   Details about the history, the economic structure, and the social composition of agrarian
      cooperatives in European countries are set out in the United States Senate Commission
      (1913: 233ff.). Some 782 agrarian cooperatives had already been formed in Russia during
      the 1872–1877 period, providing short- and long-term loans for farm improvements.
16   United States Senate Commission (1913: 236).
17   According to the United States Senate Commission (1913: 237, 240), therefore, '[t]he zem-
      stvo boards of management...found that a large number of peasants in comfortable cir-
      cumstances, who had enough money to satisfy their personal requirements, borrowed
      from cooperative societies solely to lend in their turn to a third party and that under
      conditions extremely burdensome for their debtors.'

peasants.[18] Even Chayanov accepted that in Siberia cooperative forms grow 'rapidly' and not only 'soon break [their] link with export trading capital' but also appear 'on the London market' thereby 'frees itself from any influence of trading capital'.[19] Although Chayanov believed that, insofar as they enable the state to put into practice its plan, cooperatives 'might be the basis for a future socialist economic system', there are grounds for questioning this prognosis as too optimistic.[20]

That the path followed by a cooperative structure is capitalist not socialist, emerges also with regard to agrarian reform programmes in Third World nations during and after the 1960s development decade. Emphasized thereby are the kind of political and economic obstacles to worker empowerment which continue so long as private property, in the form of the peasant family farm, remains lodged inside the cooperative structure, as envisaged by Chayanov. Just such a pattern, underlining the contradiction between private/ public ownership, occurred in Peru, where the 1960s agrarian reform converted large estates owned by landlords into production cooperatives co-owned by ex-tenants and ex-sub-tenants, now peasant proprietors who were also members of the cooperative. A case-study of developments that happened during the mid-1970s within one such agrarian co-operative, located on the semi-tropical eastern slope of the Andes in the Province of La Convención, underlines the problematic nature of Chayanovian theory. That conjuncture witnessed two developments: first, the struggle between rich and poor peasants in producer cooperatives; and second, an unsuccessful attempt by state bureaucrats to prevent individual appropriation of commonly owned economic resources on the cooperative sector, a process that amounted to 'internal asset stripping' on the part of the peasant membership.[21]

Along with other means of production (tools, implements, seeds, irrigation) on the cooperative sector in question, land was parcellated and in effect privatized, livestock was slaughtered and consumed, as were crops grown on this sector. Rather than being sold for the benefit of the agrarian unit as a whole, assets were transferred from the cooperative sector co-owned by all its members to the peasant sector where members also owned individual holdings. This same process of appropriation extended also to the labour-power of cooperative members belonging to the poor peasant stratum, highlighting the

---

18   On the Siberian cooperative system, see United States Senate Commission (1913: 240ff.).
19   Chayanov (1966: 264).
20   Chayanov (1966: 265).
21   Further details about this particular case-study can be found elsewhere (Brass, 1999: Chapter 2; Brass, 2017: Chapter 15).

impact of class difference and struggle inside this agrarian unit. Because their personal labour-power was bonded by debt, therefore, poor peasants among the membership whose personal and family labour-power had been acquired by rich peasants from whom they had borrowed money were unable to meet the condition of membership by fulfilling the statutory work input on cooperative land. Expelled from membership, these same indebted poor peasants (and their kinfolk) were then redeployed by better-off peasants, and returned to the cooperative sector not as members but as agricultural labour. Better-off peasants benefitted from this process in a number of ways: not only did they profit from the peasant/cooperative sectoral wage differential, but their statutory work input (and continued membership conditions) were met, enabling them to consolidate their control over the cooperative sector itself.

Chayanov: The Political Case Against

Over the last two decades of the nineteenth century, economic crisis generated debate between Marxism and Populism about the efficacy of different kinds of rural property, together with their role in large or small agrarian units created as a result of future reform programmes.[22] Marxists argued that, as capitalism penetrated the countryside, petty commodity production fragmented into opposed class elements, consisting of three distinct strata: a rural bourgeoisie (composed of rich peasants), agricultural labourers (composed of poor peasants), and subsistence cultivators (composed of middle peasants) whose economic position was subject to constant erosion. This interpretation was opposed by populists such as Chayanov, who denied the existence of depeasantization, arguing instead that an homogeneous peasantry endured because the economic reproduction of the individual family farm was governed not by class but by its own demographic cycle. The significance of these diverging views lies in their respective political trajectories. Whereas for Marxism peasant differentiation set in motion class formation and struggle, making possible

---

22   This difference in political approach to agrarian reform is set out in the following table:

Theory	Landholdings taken from	Landholdings given to	Property relation
Marxism	Landlords and peasants	The State	Collective
Populism	Landlords	Peasants	Private/individual

a transition to socialism, populism led to no such outcome.[23] Much rather the opposite, in that an undifferentiated peasantry, deemed to be historically eternal, in many instances embodies the ethnic/cultural/national identity supportive of the political right.

Accordingly, more often than not throughout history peasants have given their support to nationalist and conservative political mobilizations.[24] Prior to the 1939–45 war, most peasant parties throughout Europe and Asia were strongly nationalist, and agrarian populist organizations generated much rural grassroots support for right wing or fascist movements. This was because for populism a 'pure' (or middle) peasantry engaged in smallholding cultivation within the context of an equally 'pure' village community (that is, unsullied by an external capitalism or socialism) was presented as embodying all the culturally-specific attributes – timeless/sacred 'natural' and ancient bonds such as ethnicity, language, religion, customs, dress, songs, traditions – that were constitutive of a 'pure' national identity. Much the same was true of Latin America at that same conjuncture, when similar views were held by José Carlos Mariátegui and Hildebrando Castro Pozo, whose formal position on the Peruvian left masked their populism.

What the latter had in common were golden age visions of the agrarian myth: on the basis of a shared epistemology, they subscribed to the view that the Spanish Conquest imposed an 'inauthentic' and 'foreign' (= European) feudal tenure structure on what each of them interpreted as being a materially self-sufficient and culturally 'authentic' indigenous Andean peasant community

---

23   Broadly speaking, Marxists have always doubted the revolutionary potential of a subsistence oriented middle peasantry, at best allocating to it a subordinate political role in a worker/peasant alliance. Lenin and Kautsky advocated merely the political neutralization of the peasantry, while Trotsky and Luxemburg regarded it as actively counterrevolutionary, maintaining that once they became proprietors, peasants would resist any further attempts to socialize the means of production.

24   In part, the affinity between populist and conservative ideology derives from a shared perception of the countryside and those who live/work there as the embodiment/upholders of national identity, culture, and tradition. Although obviously not all those who endorse the peasant family farm model of Chayanov are conservatives, his interpretation of rural society and its resistance to modernity tends to fit rather too neatly with non-progressive ideology. Among those whose pro-peasant views echoed those of Chayanov, therefore, was the rural sociologist Pitrim Sorokin (Kerblay, 1966a: xxv, note 2), whose undifferentiated concept of 'farmer-peasant' (Sorokin & Zimmerman, 1939: Chapter III) was no different from Chayanov's peasant labour farm. Not only was Sorokin a vehement opponent of Bolshevism but he also subscribed to 'the worst of the racial fallacies' of Gobineau (Harris, 1968: 103, 218). More recently, the pro-peasant-family views of Chayanov have been endorsed as a 'Third Way' alternative to Marxism by a conservative supporter of agrarianism (Carlson, 2007: Chapter 3).

that characterized the pre-Columbian era. More important was the fact that for Mariátegui and Castro Pozo this discourse also possessed a programmatic status: their 'socialism' entailed building on what each perceived as being a still-viable peasant economy, a residue from the golden age of Peru that had survived colonialism. Like their counterparts in Europe and Asia, therefore, theirs was a discourse-for/discourse against that structures *indigenismo*, populism and the agrarian myth.

Current populists who advocate repeasantization make a similar mistake, based on the same kind of political misrecognition. A case in point is the enthusiastic reception accorded by van der Ploeg to the historical novel, *Stepmother Earth* (1936), written by Theun de Vries.[25] Presented as a vindication of Chayanovian theory, the book is said to confirm the view that Marxists were unable to understand Dutch agricultural development in that era because they adhered too closely to the Leninist concept of peasants differentiated along class lines. The inference is that in the Netherlands this did not happen: much rather, it was rich/large farms that failed, while small/poor ones prospered, the opposite of what Lenin maintained would occur.[26] Having argued that it was peasant economy – the peasant family farm of Chayanov – which prevailed, van der Ploeg then contradicts this by outlining how capitalist penetration of the agrarian sector led to widespread depeasantisation, a process represented by him not as systemic but merely as a 'misfortune'.[27]

Contrary to the case made by van der Ploeg, therefore, what the novel by Theun de Vries shows is that capitalism did indeed penetrate the countryside in the manner Lenin said it would.[28] Lamenting that populism is too closely linked to fascism, van der Ploeg attempts to rescue it politically, as more closely linked to socialism.[29] He reports with indignation that the book by Theun de Vries was well-received by Nazis in the Netherlands, thereby failing to understand why the depiction of the rural in novel was praised by fascism as supportive of its own blood-and-soil ideology. In short, why – like Mariátegui

---

25   van der Ploeg (2021).

26   For references to large farms that quickly become unviable, see van der Ploeg (2021: 1129, 1130).

27   See van der Ploeg (2021: 1134), who describes the outcome as a 'squeeze on agriculture [which] relates with the slow but persistent generalization of capital relations'.

28   Identified by Theun de Vries are all the characteristics of capitalist competition: the effects of a price squeeze, whereby peasants were caught between increasing input costs and deceasing returns for output; similarly, peasant family members and/or kinsfolk either work as hired labour externally, or are exploited/overworked internally by the household head.

29   For the description of *Stepmother Earth* as 'a truly socialist novel', see van der Ploeg (2021: 1127).

and Castro Pozo – the *indigenista* approach of Theun de Vries was simply a nationalist struggle, not a socialist one.[30] Despite this, the book is said by van der Ploeg to contain a socialist programme, consisting of individual peasant proprietors and agrarian cooperatives. In short, not socialism but the populist agenda proposed by Chayanov.

II

As well as being a social scientist with an interest in the political economy of rural development, Chayanov also published numerous works on art, literature, and history. Described as 'a cultivated man', he travelled extensively throughout Europe, beginning with a visit to Lombardy in 1908 and ended with one to Berlin in 1928.[31] Letters written by him whilst in Italy and Germany reveal an anxiety concerning the political reception in the USSR of stories he had written anonymously.[32] Among them was *The Journey of My Brother Alexei to the Land of Peasant Utopia*, an account of time-travel from 1920s to 1980s Moscow, composed in 1920 about a fictional agrarian populist utopia and its dystopic socialist 'other'.[33] As presented by Chayanov, using the pseudonym

---

30   The views of Maríategui and Castro Pozo are invoked by van der Ploeg (2021: 1126, note 5), who observes merely that they were 'unorthodox'. Themes and discourse encountered in *Stepmother Earth* are in many ways no different from the ones found in Latin American *indigenista* novels, such as *El Indio* (1937) by Gregorio López y Fuentes, *Huasipungo* (1953) by Jorge Icaza, *Broad and Alien is the World* (1941) by Ciro Alegría, and *Llallipacha: Tiempo de Vencer* (1965) by Jesús Lara.

31   See Kerblay (1966a: xxvi).

32   These letters have been translated by Bourgholtzer (1999). That Chayanov wrote the stories anonymously, and – as his letters indicate – was anxious lest his identity as author became known, suggests the political symbolism outlined below (characters embodying antagonistic populist/socialist positions) cannot be regarded as accidental.

33   As with his other stories written by Chayanov at that period (see below), this one appears under the pseudonym Kremnev (1977). The central character in this narrative is Alexei Kremnev, a socialist living in the drab Soviet Russia of 1921, who is suddenly transported forward in time by sixty years to Moscow in 1984, where he is mistaken for an American visitor. Half a century on, he finds that socialism has collapsed, towns have been abolished, and Moscow is now a rural arcadia without either heavy industry or proletariat. Established as a result of peasant opposition to socialism, the labour-intensive agrarian economy of what has now become the Russian Peasant Republic is in the fiction of Chayanov based on the restoration of private property in the form of the peasant family farm, and the corresponding absence of planning and state intervention. Discovering that half a century earlier he himself was responsible for the supression of the peasant movement in Soviet Russia, and by implication the idyllic pastoral (= agrarian utopia) that Russia would have become had this not been done, Kremnev repents and rejects his socialism in favour of populism.

Ivan Kremnev, the contrast between the two conjunctures is absolute. The utopia of populism is depicted positively, as an harmonious rural place devoid of
strife, where small-scale producers (artisans, peasants) predominate, and from
which both capital and a proletariat have been banished. The dystopia is portrayed negatively, as urban context in which large-scale industrial production
generates conflict between capital and labour that leads to socialism.[34]

Significantly, in this fictional portrayal of Moscow as it would be in the mid-
1980s, Chayanov reproduces one of the central arguments made by agrarian
populists in Russia during the 1920s, namely that: 'Thanks to its fundamentally healthy nature, agriculture had avoided the bitter cup of capitalism and
[the ruling peasant regime of 1984] had no need to direct [its] developmental
process into that channel'.[35] Such a view contrasts with that of the Bolsheviks
in general and in particular Lenin, who argued that the Russian village community was not a bulwark against capitalism (as populists maintained) but
much rather had already been penetrated by this economic form, as a result of
which the peasantry was disintegrating along class lines. Much the same is true
of three other stories written by Chayanov at the same conjuncture: 'The Tale
of the Hairdresser's Mannequin' (1918); 'Venedictov, or The Memorable Events
of My Life' (1922); and 'The Venetian Mirror, or, The Extraordinary Adventures
of the Glass Man' (1922).[36] As will be seen below, in terms of symbolism each
one projects the same political dichotomy, based on a positive/negative opposition between populism and socialism.[37]

---

34   On the structure and symbolism of this utopic/dystopic opposition, see Brass (1996/1997).
35   Kremnev (1977:90).
36   All these stories by Chayanov are found in a single volume, translated from the Russian by
      Muireann Maguire (2013). They are: 'The Tale of the Hairdresser's Mannequin' (Maguire,
      2013: 35–65); 'Venedictov, or The Memorable Events of My Life' (Maguire, 2013: 66–88);
      and 'The Venetian Mirror or, The Extraordinary Adventures of the Glass Man' (Maguire,
      2013: 89–107). A number of other stories, written by him at around the same time, remain
      untranslated. These include 'The Deceivers' (1921), 'The Unusual but True Adventures of
      Count Fedor Mikhailovich Buturlin' (1924), and 'Julia, or Meetings at Novodevichii' (1928) –
      all listed in the volume edited by Thorner, Kerblay, and Smith (Chayanov, 1966: 292–93).
37   Although in her Introduction Maguire (2013: 13–21) notes the operation of an anti-Soviet
      ideology at work in the contributions, taking the form of a discourse-against in the
      Russian Gothic Tales, she does not consider the presence in these same narratives of a
      discourse-for. The latter is particularly important in the case of Chayanov since, as will be
      argued below, he was not merely content to project a critique of socialism but was intent
      additionally on confronting this with an alternative vision of what in his view ought to be.
      That is, an agrarian populist discourse-for. This, as has already been argued, structured his
      The Journey of My Brother Alexei to the Land of Peasant Utopia: below it is argued that the
      same discourse also informs the three stories by him considered here.

Undiscovered Country?

With its privileging of interrelated concepts like 'the uncanny', 'the unknowable', 'the irrational', and 'the supernatural', Gothic fiction can be seen as a part of the conservative reaction by Romanticism to the questions posed by Enlightenment discourse and the European (and American) revolutions over the eighteenth and nineteenth centuries. To ideas about progress, scientific reason, secularism, modernity, and egalitarianism championed by Enlightenment philosophy and political economy, therefore, Romanticism and its accompanying Gothic literary genre counterposed – and, indeed, asserted the historical immutability of – nature, tradition, hierarchy, religious and monarchical authority. While the Enlightenment attached importance to thinking, Romanticism by contrast emphasized the significance of feeling. The latter process was encapsulated in the term 'sublime', a heightened form of astonishment that overwhelmed the human senses, and thus corresponded to the victory of feeling (= irrationality) over thought (= rationality). As such, not only is it the basis of conservative philosophy, but according to Burke the sublime/feeling (= the instant and more *natural* reaction) prefigures – or 'anticipates' – the rational, and in this sense is said to be a more authentic response to something on the part of the individual subject who experiences it.[38]

In keeping with this approach, Gothic fiction can be seen to some degree as a bid to escape from the domain of rationality/science (= the known) back into the realm of superstition/mythology (= the unknown). This evasiveness notwithstanding, the alternative reality constructed by this literary genre, in the form of the supernatural, is itself a site where ancient and unresolved struggles about class in the material world are played out. In the case of the ghost stories written by M.R. James, for example, this involves the return – in the guise of a malevolent/hostile apparition – of an ancient power (monarchy, church, landowner) rooted in the soil of the nation, one that is impervious to scientific

---

38   The sublime, explained Burke (1808: 157–58, original emphasis), not only projects but subsumes all the other categories – horror, nature, religion – associated with feeling. As described by him, '[t]he passion caused by the great and sublime in *nature*, when those causes operate most powerfully, is astonishment; and astonishment is that state of the soul, in which all its motions are suspended, with some degree of horror. In this case the mind is so entirely filled with its object, that it cannot entertain any other, nor by consequence reason on that object which employs it. Hence arises the great power of the sublime, that, far from being produced by them, it anticipates our reasonings, and hurries us on by an irresistible force.'

or rational explanation.[39] As such, it is best left undisturbed: when this is not done, and an attempt is made to appropriate symbols or resources (a crown, treasure, or land), retribution follows swiftly. Just such a discourse, it will be seen below, informs the Gothic fiction of Chayanov, albeit with one important difference.

As crucial to an understanding of Chayanovian Gothic fiction is the role of the agrarian myth, an ideology which posits rural identity as an historically innate and enduring characteristic of society, based on a non-transcendent distinction between the urban sector and the countryside and their respective interests, organization, and populations.[40] Agrarian myth ideology is differentiated internally, giving rise to a set of binary oppositions: between landlord/ aristocratic (= 'from above') and peasant/plebeian (= 'from below') variants; and between pastoral (= harmonious/tranquil) and Darwinian (= 'red-in-tooth-and-claw') versions.[41] Common to them, however, is a shared view of land/nature as eternal/sacred, an ancient form of existence depicted in folk-lore/myth/legend that warn against efforts to change rural society. Although the Gothic tales of M.R. James and Chayanov correspond to the Darwinian

---

39 For a materialist analysis of the ghost stories by M.R. James (and others), see Brass (2014: Chapter 4).

40 As outlined elsewhere (Brass, 2014), agrarian myth discourse endorses small-scale economic activity (peasant family farm) and culture (religious/ethnic/national/regional/ village/kin identities), perceived as instinctive/'natural' because they are derived from nature. By contrast, it is antagonistic to large-scale economic activity (industry, finance capital, manufacturing, planning, collectivization, the city) together with its accompanying institutional effects (class, revolution, socialism, bureaucracy, the State).

41 Lest it be thought that pastoral/landlord/aristocratic versions of the agrarian myth are confined to pre-capitalist eras and Third World countries, the following is a lyrical account as seen by a present-day conservative with close ties to government and land-owning circles in the UK: 'I'm watching my farming neighbour...churn up his fields with his plough', writes Swire (2021: 276–77), '[i]n the hands of this experienced farmer the field is willing [and] has tolerated him and his family for generations...I wonder how [they] have kept their life so small and simple for so long; how they have managed to govern themselves against a tide of progress, to remain local, true to their soil? Theirs is the history of our island story. Now they belong to an extinction package devised by [the EEC, which is] trying to transform the peasantry into [its] own vision of a social model. And it was not only the people [the EEC] targeted but the land they worked and nurtured. This was the ambitious destruction created by [the Common Agricultural Policy] – the annihilation of everything we truly hold dear: hedgerows, flora, fauna, small family farms...' This combines all the tropes of conservative discourse: an aesthetic vision of the countryside, family farmers as backbone-of-the-nation, smallholding as eternal because opposed to progress. In short, a relay-in-statement whereby peasant = Nature = nation.

variant, those of the former constitute the landlord/aristocratic kind, whilst those of the latter fall into the peasant/plebeian category.

Journeys: Space, Time, Politics

Of the three stories by Chayanov, the first ('The Tale of the Hairdresser's Mannequin') commences with Vladimir, a Moscow architect, who – because he feels old – 'craved provincial naivity', and travels to the countryside outside Moscow.[42] There he finds and purchases two wax mannequins, based on the conjoined Hendrickson sisters, about whom he becomes obsessive. Journeying throughout Europe in search of further information on them, his travels take him to Venice, where he encounters the sisters themselves.[43] The latter are 'strikingly beautiful', and Vladimir falls in love with one of them who, giving birth to his daughter, subsequently dies, along with her sister and her infant daughter.[44] Unable to remain in 'the city which had entombed his happiness', Vladimir returns to Moscow, but after a year has passed again travels to Venice as 'he wished to breathe in, one last time, the warm rays of the Venetian sun, to hear the plash of oars on the night-time water of the canal ...'.[45] Upon seeing there a public display featuring 'the wax busts of the Hendrickson sisters', he collapses and dies.[46]

Set not in Venice at the start of the twentieth century but rather in Moscow and London a century earlier, the second story ('Venediktov, or The Memorable Events of My Life') is about 'an ordinary man', Bulgakov, who rescues a young woman from two malevolent pursuers: an evil spirit, Venediktov, and his master, the devil. Nastasya, the young woman, is controlled by the devil – described as 'diabolical ordinariness..,saturated with meaning and power' – but manages to escape from him and seeks refuge with Bulgakov.[47] However, the latter is forced to hand her over to Venediktov, who informs Bulgakov that as she is no longer controlled by the devil, '[her] soul is now free, the chains are cast off,

---

42 Maguire (2013: 38).
43 The description (Maguire, 2013: 51) of Vladimir arriving in Venice – 'a gondola was carrying him over the black waters of the canals of that great city of masks, ghostly mirrors, silent doges, Goldoni's heroes, Gozzi's characters, and the great Venetian painters' – is such that it suggests Chayanov himself did indeed visit the city.
44 Maguire (2013: 52ff.).
45 Maguire (2013: 62–63).
46 Maguire (2013: 64–65).
47 Maguire (2013: 70).

she loves me'.[48] Venediktov recounts how, when in England, he took part in a card game in 'the London demons' club', and 'had won human souls from the demons of London'.[49] Among his winnings is Nastasya, whom he then loses to a Prussian soldier, Seidlitz, 'who should never be mentioned after sundown'; the latter murders Venediktov, chases Bulgakov and Nastasya to Paris, where he is himself killed in a duel.[50] Bulgakov and Nastasya return to Moscow, where they marry and she keeps her own soul safe from demons.[51]

Venice is once again the context where the events of the third story originate ('The Venetian Mirror, or, The Extraordinary Adventures of the Glass Man'). It is the place in which the main protagonist, Aleksey, finds a mirror 'in cellars of a Venetian antiquary', and purchases this for his home in Moscow.[52] Back in Russia, however, he finds that the reflections in the mirror are different.[53] A doppelganger – a 'diabolical double' – emerges and consolidates on the other side of the glass: gradually, his own mirror image takes on a life of its own, not only struggling with Aleksey himself but also arousing the sexual desire of his partner Kate and then making love her.[54] Although the mirror shatters during this struggle, the mirror-man escapes to this side of the glass, and abducts Kate.[55] Pursuing his doppelganger to a dark house, Aleksey finally catches up with his 'other' image and succeeds in killing his double: on his return home, he finds Kate there, waiting for him.[56]

As well as being Gothic tales, these three stories are anchored in an idiom belonging to an equally long-standing form of popular culture: the Russian fable. Illustrative of the latter are the stories written and published by Ivan Krilof

---

48   Maguire (2013: 75).

49   Maguire (2013: 77ff.).

50   'That evening she told me', recounts Bulgakov (Maguire, 2013: 87), 'that on the night that would prove so fateful for him, a drunken Venediktov had received in his room the diabolical soul that refused to submit to him; he then lost Nastenka [= Nastasya] to Seidlitz at cards and perished attempting to wrest his IOU back from the Prussian by force.'

51   Maguire (2013: 86–87).

52   Maguire (2013: 89).

53   'Everything within the little house had been miraculously transformed,' writes Chayanov (Maguire, 2013: 91), 'as if invisible streams of liquid glass were flooding the rooms...The mirror's surface appeared to radiate a subtle, centuries-stored venom...'

54   Maguire (2013: 95). In the words of Chayanov (Maguire, 2013: 94–95, original emphasis), 'Aleksey was astonished by...the ghostly beings [in the mirror, and] their constant resistance to their "masters" and their desire to control the latter and force them to reflect *their* actions and thoughts...Aleksey grew convinced that his double was steadily strengthening his control over his earthly destiny.'

55   Maguire (2013: 96ff., 102).

56   Maguire (2013: 106–7).

at the start of the nineteenth century: all express a moral position, regarding what is thought by the author to be a desirable path and what happens when this is not followed. Like those of Chayanov at a later date, the fables of Krilof contain positive/negative characters and characterizations, endorsing action that meets with favour while admonishing that which invites disapproval. Like those of Chayanov, therefore, the stories of Krilof 'as a general rule, conveyed either a valuable warning or a wholesome reprimand'.[57] Implicit in Chayanov, but foregrounded by Krilof, is a discourse about rural society, and in particular the way peasants are oppressed. Broadly speaking, in the fables of Krilof peasants feature mainly as victims, taken advantage of by other, more cunning or more powerful agents in the Russian countryside (thieves, animals, bureaucrats, merchants). As in the stories of Chayanov, peasant economy/society is represented by Krilof as being under constant attack by 'others' who, for the most part, are not themselves petty commodity producers.[58]

Not the least important of the protagonists in the narratives of Chayanov is place: hence the significance attached to the city of Venice which, one way or another, features in two of the three stories. In the first, therefore, it is where Vladimir finally tracks down the conjoined sisters, and to which he returns after their death, there to find the wax images of them on public display. Absent from the second, the city is once again the setting for the third, the place in which the main character, Aleksey, finds the mirror in an antiquarian shop in Venice. Although old and equated symbolically with tradition, and indeed containing within itself aspects of the agrarian myth, Venice nevertheless represents the epitome of the urban.[59] As such, it is historically the locus both of finance and – in the way ship construction was organized in the Arsenale – of an early form of an industrial division of labour, each of which can be seen as a systemic enemy of peasant economy. Of significance is that, as presented in Gothic fiction, Venice is portrayed as doom-laden, a city in a state of decay/decline: this, too, reinforces the dichotomy structuring the neo-populist vision

---

57   Ralston (1869 x). On the themes structuring the folktale in Russia and elsewhere, see Lotman and Uspenskij (1984) and Propp (1968).

58   Just as in the stories of Chayanov, however, the oppressed in the tales of Krilof sometimes manage to turn tables on their oppressors, and thus emerge victorious from the preceding conflict. This folkloric trope – in which characters belonging to a subordinate category outwit more powerful opponents – also structures the stories by Jacob and Wilhelm Grimm (1948: 311–16) about Germany and by Joel Chandler Harris (1883; 1925) about the antebellum Southern plantation.

59   On the agrarian myth and Venice, see Chapter 7 above and also Brass (2014: Chapter 8; and 2018: 243–44).

of Chayanov – the fading away of the urban, and its replacement by a vibrant, eternal rurality.

Valuable Warnings, Wholesome Reprimands

The first of the three stories ('The Tale of the Hairdressers Mannequin') contains a brief reference to peasants and the agrarian situation in northern Italy, in which the main protagonist – the Moscow architect Vladimir – expresses his disdain for 'the dull, monotonous spectacle of agricultural labour and peasant culture'.[60] This negative opinion is in one sense unsurprising, since Chayanov put it in the mouth of an urban character from whom such views might be expected. In another sense, however, Chayanov is being ironic: indicating such issues are unimportant is exactly the opposite of what he believed to be the case. By attributing this disdain for agrarian issues to the urban Muscovite, moreover, it is possible that Chayanov was also inferentially making a critique of the Bolsheviks and their approach to the agrarian question.

Accordingly, the sisters and the wax mannequins based on them, together with the fact that the fate of one who becomes the lover of Vladimir affects the conjoined twin, all suggest the presence of an underlying theme. Namely, that they represent the linked but antagonistic politics of neo-populism and Bolshevism. Initially encountering the real conjoined sisters in Venice, and later their wax mannequins when he returns to the same city, the character of Vladimir brings to a head the contradiction between the sisters: by choosing one of them as his lover, therefore, he cannot but affect the situation (and life) of the other sister. That it is an urban Muscovite who makes this choice, and does so in Venice, which in the end leads to the death of both

---

60   Travelling away from Venice, therefore, Vladimir (Maguire, 2013: 61–62) initially describes what he sees in the countryside in a non-committal manner: 'This train seemed to him unusual. There were no foreigners on it. Stocky, sturdy tillers of the soil laughed and chatted loudly about superphosphates and Randall's disc harrows, complained about their agronomist...and swore loudly, spitting on the floor, about a breed of horned cattle... The train stopped in Piacenza, the agricultural centre of the Italian north. This was an unknown Italy: the stuff of the real nation, which no foreigner ever sees. Italians like to dream of a "third Rome". If the first was the Rome of antiquity and the second the Rome of the Popes, the third Rome will be a Rome of cooperative farms, perfected agriculture...' Subsequently, however, he gives vent to his contempt for all things agricultural: 'Vladimir M. had nothing to do with any of this, and he wandered gloomily through Piacenza and through the agricultural show, looking at fat, overfed bulls...Tiring of this monotonous spectacle of agricultural labour and peasant culture, Vladimir moved on to Pavia...'

TABLE 1   The Tale of the Hairdresser's Mannequin

Protagonist/Place	+/- Characterization	Political identity	+/- Outcome
Vladimir	-	-	-
Mannequin/Sister 1	-	Neo-populism	-
Mannequin/Sister 2	-	Bolshevism	-
Venice	-	urban	-
Moscow	-	urban	-

sisters, underlines the point Chayanov was keen to make: the contradiction triggered by representatives of the urban (= the Muscovite Vladimir, the city of Venice) privileges the socialist policies of the Bolsheviks (= one of the sisters) at the expense of peasant economy championed by neo-populists (= the other sister), the outcome of which in the opinion of Chayanov would result in the ruin of Russian agriculture. On his return to Venice, therefore, Vladimir is confronted with continuing symbolic evidence of the Bolshevism/populism antagonism (the two wax mannequins, still conjoined), as a result of which he dies, signalling that the opposition between these two views about peasant farming remain unresolved.

The characterization informing this and the other stories, in terms of negative (-) or positive (+) attributes, together with the political identity symbolized and the kind of resolution involved, is set out in Tables 1–3.

Confirmation of this Bolshevik/neo-populist subtext is found also in the second of the three stories by Chayanov ('Venediktov, or The Memorable Events of My Life'). Each of the main protagonists – the devil, Bulgakov, Nastasya, Venediktov, Seidlitz – possesses a recognizable political identity and agency. Just two of the four are depicted in positive terms. Hence the character Bulgakov, the authorial voice, is that of Chayanov, and represents the ideological desires/aspirations of neopopulism itself.[61] For her part, Nastasya represents the Russian people, the object of the desire felt by all the others who wish to possess her. For obvious reasons, the remaining three are portrayed negatively: the devil, who stands for the Czarist autocracy ('saturated with meaning and power'); Venediktov, because he symbolizes Bolshevism/

---

61   The narrator Bulgakov, we are informed by Chayanov (Maguire, 2013: 66), is 'an ordinary man, a Russian,' living 'for many years in [his] rural retreat'. A countryman at heart, in other words.

socialism; and Seidlitz, because he signifies German capitalism. In the opinion of Chayanov, therefore, each of them not only embodies all the undesirable characteristics that neopopulism opposes, but every one of the three is also engaged in a political struggle with it (= Bulgakov) for the soul of the Russian people (= Nastasya).

In this struggle, Nastasya (= the Russian people), controlled initially by the devil (= Czarist autocracy), escapes with the help of Bulgakov (= neopopulism), who in turn is compelled to surrender her to Venediktov (= Bolshevism/ socialism), whose claim is based on having won souls from London demons (= British capitalism). Venediktov (= Bolshevism/socialism) wrongly believes that Nastasya (= the Russian people) loves him, but loses her to Seidlitz (= German capitalism). By contrast, Bulgakov (= neopopulism) rescues Nastasya (= the Russian people) from the devil (= Czarist autocracy), then loses her twice, both to Venediktov (= Bolshevism/socialism), and subsequently to Seidlitz (= German capitalism). Eventually, however, Bulgakov regains and marries her: in symbolic terms, therefore, having successfully resisted Czarist autocracy, socialism and capitalism, the Russian people finally espouse neopopulism, the outcome desired by Chayanov. As the latter made clear elsewhere, the antagonism he felt towards Germany was based in part on the fact that industrial/ urban development there was responsible for the emergence and consolidation of the equally feared 'other' of capitalism: a large, well-organized working-class movement, resolved to bring about a socialist transition.[62]

Many of the same anxieties and concerns inform the third story by Chayanov ('The Venetian Mirror, or, The Extraordinary Adventures of the Glass Man'). Just as in the first, therefore, the city of Venice is a malign locus, the source of the item containing the negative 'other' image of the main character. Like the second tale, moreover, the role of the female (= Kate) is a passive one, destined to be fought over by rival male protagonists (Aleksey and his mirror image 'other'). Rather than the mirror in question reflecting an external reality inhabited by the gazing subject, it becomes instead an 'other' space within the mirror in which the onlooker (and his female partner) also possesses an 'other' and different identity.[63] This juxtaposition generates conflict between the two,

---

62 As explained by Kerblay (1966a: xlv) with reference to another story written pseudonymously by the same author in 1920 (Kremnev, 1977), for Chayanov a key historical issue was that 'it is within the gates of the German capitalist factory that socialism was born as the antithesis of capitalism.'

63 The theme of an image seen in a mirror (or in the case of Dorian Gray, a painting) that, disconcertingly, consists either of a malevolent spirit, of an altered reality, or of a person that is not oneself – usually involving an encounter by someone of another, different,

TABLE 2   Venediktov, or The Memorable Events of My Life

Protagonist/Place	+/- Characterization	Political identity	+/- Outcome
The Devil	-	Czarism	-
Bulgakov	+	Neo-populism	+
Nastasya	+	The Russian people	+
Venediktov	-	Bolshevism/ socialism	-
Seidlitz	-	German capitalism	-
Demons	-	British capitalism	-

as gazing subject and his (or her) double confront one another, the doppel-ganger attempting to convert the external reality and its subject into a copy of what occurs inside this 'other' space within the mirror.

In common with the second of the three stories, conflict between the protagonist and his 'other' on either side of the Venetian mirror can be seen – much as the conjoined sisters in the first story – as a proxy for the struggle in 1920s Russia involving the neopopulist vision supported by Chayanov and the Bolshevik one to which he was opposed. Hence the fear expressed by Aleksey – like Bulgakov in the second tale, the authorial voice – that he was being forced to become more like his 'other' inside the mirror, the former embodying neo-populism while the latter (like Venediktov) represents Bolshevism.[64] Each wants to possess the female in the story, Kate, who – again like her counterpart Nastasya in the second tale – represents the Russian people. Given the political

---

perhaps even truer, selfhood in the mirror, one that may eventually replace the spectator him/herself – is a narrative trope found in various forms of popular culture. It extends from *Alice Through the Looking Glass* (Carroll, 1872) and *The Picture of Dorian Gray* (Wilde, 1891) to films such as *Duck Soup* (1933), directed by Leo McCarey, containing the justly famous Marx Brothers mirror routine, the wicked Queen in Walt Disney's *Snow White* (1937), and the 'Haunted Mirror' section, directed by Robert Hamer, in the Ealing Studios film *Dead of Night* (1945).

64   'Bewitched by the strange mirror,' recounts Chayanov (Maguire, 2013: 92), 'Aleksey felt as though he had [like Kate] changed into someone else...Some dreadful force was pulling him closer and closer to the mirror...His mirror double had seized his right hand and forcefully tugged it under the surface of the mirror...their bodies fused, struggling...he was forced to copy each movement within the gradually settling interior of the Venetian mirror.'

TABLE 3   The Venetian Mirror, or The Extraordinary Adventures of the Glass Man

Protagonist/Place	+/- Characterization	Political identity	+/- Outcome
Aleksey	+	Neo-populism	+
Kate	+	The Russian people	+
Aleksey-in-mirror	-	Bolshevism	-
Kate-in-mirror	-	The Russian people	-
Venice	-	urban	-

views Chayanov held about this conflict, its resolution is in a sense predictable: Aleksey, who represents the 'good'/neopopulist viewpoint, overcomes the glass man inside the mirror, who signifies the 'bad'/Bolshevik approach, in the process destroying the mirror itself (= Venice/urban) and regaining the affection of Kate (= the Russian people).

Conclusion

The political importance of Chayanov transcends his own time and space, influencing as it has done – and continues to do – both the debate about rural development in Third World countries and – more broadly – resurgent agrarian populist interpretations circulating in academia and elsewhere. Less well known, but epistemologically as revealing of his politics, are his non-economic writings, particularly his contributions to the Gothic literary genre. Examined here, therefore, are three stories written pseudonymously by Chayanov, which – together with his dystopic novel – are structured by the same discourse.

All were composed over a short period just after the Bolsheviks took power in Russia and reveal as a sub-text the political divergence and concomitant struggle between neo-populist and Bolshevik versions of rural development. Insofar as Venice embodies a process of melancholic decay, not just physically but also economically, it symbolizes in these stories the decline both of urban society and of capitalism. Since each of the latter constitutes the 'other' of peasant economy, Venice as a city experiencing this twofold decomposition may well have been for Chayanov also a metaphor for the ultimate triumph of his neo-populist vision.

In economic terms, Chayanov promoted the idea of the peasant labour farm as an ever-present pan-historical category, the reproduction of which was – and is – determined endogenously: by the size of the household, the link between its producing/non-producing components, and the work intensity required to meet family subsistence requirements. Because smallholding agriculture survived despite exogenous systemic change, he maintained that development entailed no more than the modernization of petty commodity production as it already existed. Such an approach was criticized by Marxists, who pointed out that peasant economic activity was immune neither from capitalist penetration nor from class differentiation. Furthermore, the continuation of private property in the shape of smallholdings threatened to undermine agrarian reform programmes based on planning and collective ownership. In political terms, the peasant embodied a traditional form of cultural identity historically supportive of conservativism and nationalism.

This antimony between neo-populism and socialism, muted in his economic writings, emerges more strongly in his fiction, particularly the Gothic tales. The latter, in keeping with the discourse of a Romanticism combining opposition to modernity with a reassertion of the agrarian myth, structures the three stories examined here. Each is informed by the same dichotomies: a positive/negative depiction that corresponds both to populism/Bolshevism and to hero/villain. Cast as villains, therefore, are characters symbolizing all the negative forms of 'otherness' to which neo-populism is opposed: Czarism, German capitalism, British capitalism, socialism, and the urban. By contrast, the heroes in each narrative are engaged in a conflict with these same 'others' in order to rescue the Russian people from the forces of capitalism and socialism, thereby vindicating the neo-populist *weltanschauung*.

Foliage from the mosaic in Torcello.

FIGURE 6   Foliage (Torcello)
© ANNA LUISA BRASS

Conclusion

Better Worlds?

As used here, transition refers broadly to the way in which a politics is syn-thesized with antinomic elements, as a result ceasing to be recognizable as what it once was. As such, it covers a variety of issues in a range of contexts at different conjunctures, all of which entail a discursive movement – explicit or implicit – away from Marxist theory. This process also involves replacing the latter approach with non- or even anti-Marxist interpretations of the phenom-ena in question, extending from meanings attached to issues like racism, the industrial reserve army, modes of production, and unfree labour, to tourism and the trajectory of capitalism itself. For its part, silence – where and when relevant – encompasses an analogous set of phenomena, extending from what is dismissed, what is not addressed, to what is left out of a debate or narrative. One consequence has been that those who study the social sciences, especially political economy, are currently faced with what seems to be an unexplained contradiction: between the onward march of *laissez-faire* capitalism, together with its accompanying barbarism, and silence about opposing this by means of effecting a radical transition to socialism.

Seen from a Marxist perspective, this contradiction ought not to surprise, given that barbarism is a logical outcome of the transnational path (= globali-zation) followed by capital. A crucial effect of the latter is a process of multiple competition: between capitals, and between the latter and labour. The imple-mentation of *laissez-faire* policies in different countries results in the intensi-fication of class struggle, but now on a global scale, as employers in the same markets as their rivals attempt to gain competitive advantage by deploying ever-cheaper forms of labour. This search for monopoly, so as to dampen inter-capitalist competition, in turn generates an economic strategy that entails drawing on the industrial reserve where and when possible: in a labour process where existing workers have jobs that are permanent and secure, and labour is well-paid and unionized, capitalists seek to replace them with temporary, insecure, and less costly equivalents.

Such restructuring of capitalist production, involving as it does a combina-tion of workforce decomposition/recomposition, takes on a global form: either downsizing, outsourcing and relocation to contexts where labour-power is rel-atively inexpensive and unfree, or insourcing migrant workers from these same kinds of places. It is, in short, class struggle waged by employers ('from above'). Equally unsurprising is the 'from below' reaction to this kind of *laissez-faire* economic strategy, again one that manifests itself at a global level: fuelled by capital and its state, the outcome has been – and is – a rise of identity politics, consolidated in a mobilizing discourse that is populist, based not on class but on nationalist and racist ideology.

In metropolitan capitalist nations, an effect of outsourcing/relocation of manufacturing has been casualization/underemployment/unemployment, which in turn has had a deleterious impact on working class formation, organization and struggle. Where labour is concerned, the capitalist State has cut back or privatized welfare provision, depriving workers and their families of crucial elements of the social wage. For its part, capitalist growth has been effected not by an expansion in secure employment but by an intensification of labour and workforce 'flexibility', in the process dismantling work/welfare rights won by labour historically. Those expelled from permanent industrial jobs have sunk into the industrial reserve, where they compete with immigrants for insecure and low-paid jobs, replicating the pattern that used to be associated with Third World nations, but is now well established in the core economies of European capitalism. Inevitably, a result of this fragmentation/ restructuring of the labour process is that employers possess an enhanced form of control over their workers.

In the light of this development, the expectation would be that the structure and *raison d'etre* of the current barbarism – an inescapable outcome of a global *laissez faire* capitalist system – would invite a political response by leftists along Marxist lines, positing a transition to socialism as an outcome that is not just desirable but necessary. Instead, the call from many leftists is that the main hope of a challenge to the 'onward march of barbarism' lies in mobilizing déclassé elements (jobless youth, erstwhile industrial labour, women employed in sweatshops, undifferentiated peasants, and immigrants), without at the same time asking what kind of political programme – other than a return to a 'nicer'/'kinder' form of capitalism – would or could unite them. The danger is clear: the political consciousness that has emerged has little or nothing to do with either Marxism or socialism, being rather a populist discourse privileging non-class identities based on ethnicity and/or nationalism.

An obvious question raised by this contradiction – the lack of a sustained and specifically Marxist response to this a rampant *laissez-faire* capitalism – is how to account for such an absence, in effect a form of silence. On occasion this involves taking a radical Marxist analysis but attaching to it a non-Marxist outcome – a different and from a capitalist viewpoint a 'happy' ending: deradicalizing it politically, in other words. The logics of this theoretical and political silence, together with its systemic production and reproduction, can be traced partly to its institutional locus, and the role it plays as the driver of epistemological transition, among them debates about labour regime change and its connection to modes of production. Many leftists who entered academia encountered there a politically hostile intellectual environment, shed their Marxism and opted instead for a safer paradigm, the 'new' populist postmodernism. When this transition was analysed critically by those who remained Marxists, one of the most common responses has been silence, thereby avoiding political debate.

In part, the reasons for this silence stem from several interlinked causes. Of these, one of the most important – notwithstanding its seeming triviality – is methodological: not examining the analysis under scrutiny, a process which entails not just looking at a particular article or book but rather locating the latter both in the wider political context and the narrower ensemble of related analyses. As important are what might be termed externalities: the declining interest in and knowledge of Marxist theory, as it ceased to be fashionable and was replaced by postmodernism. These in turn have to be linked to internal causes: the exit of Marxism from the streets and its entry into the university system, in particular social science departments, as a result of which it ceased to be a guide to practice and became simply a topic for study.

Insofar as it was then deemed to be an obstacle to acceptance by academia, a Marxist approach was quickly discarded by those who held it; apostasy was justified intellectually by claims that it was no longer relevant to the political concerns of the real world. What replaced it was similarly misinterpreted, since those who endorsed varieties of identity politics, the focus of which was not on the disempowerment of class (as Marxists argued) but rather on the empowerment of non-class categories (ethnicity, nationality, religion), were unaware of the extent to which the new allegiances had their roots in conservative or reactionary discourse (nationalism, racism). Among the most problematic aspects of this transition, therefore, has been a return to a discourse about the innateness and non-transcendence of non-class identity, not least that of race.

For mid-nineteenth century reactionaries like Gobineau and Wagner, their exclusionary position was driven by culture, a racist/anti-semitic discourse informed conceptually by ideas about the 'other' not-belonging and never-belonging to the nation. In this discourse, therefore, 'otherness' embodied notions of difference amounting to 'strangeness', signalling in turn a non-transcendental ethnic/national identity that was – and could never be anything other than – 'not-us' and 'not-the-same'. Opposition to the 'other' expressed by plebeian components of twenty-first century metropolitan capitalist nations, is somewhat distinct: its exclusionary position vis-à-vis the 'other' is informed to some degree by livelihood considerations, and the concept of 'not-belonging' is accordingly linked more closely to the economy. In sharp contrast to the earlier views of Gobineau and Wagner, therefore, current antagonism projected onto 'otherness' is because its subject is nowadays very much 'like-us', possessing a 'sameness' which in economic terms licenses serious and sustained rivalry in the labour market.

Not only does the same concern about the 'other' becoming more 'like us' appear in narratives about travel, but analogous depictions of ethnic difference are found in accounts of journeys outside and within Europe. Thus, just before and after the 1939–45 war, travel narratives by Lévi-Strauss, Greene, and Bowles romanticized 'otherness', essentializing locals in places visited (Liberia, Brazil, the Sahel) as culturally pristine and unchanging. Modernity, progress and development, by contrast, were dismissed in these accounts as undesirable forms of 'civilization', 'Westernization', and 'Europeanization', to be rejected by these writers as inappropriate for the rural inhabitants of such contexts. Travel narratives of journeys within Europe during the post-war era contained analogous perceptions of local underdevelopment/impoverishment, viewed positively as evidence of cultural alterity. This is much the same kind of approach to 'otherness' as that which emerged subsequently as the 'cultural turn'.

Like much writing about travel, the Gothic fables of the Russian neo-populist Chayanov are opposed to urbanization, industrialization and modernity that underwrote the Bolshevism/populism antagonism. They also project an image of innate 'otherness', in his case the peasant/plebeian version of the agrarian myth, combining both the pastoral and the Darwinian variants. Crucially, therefore, the deployment of agrarian myth discourse as an alternative to capitalist development underwrites the reactionary views of Gobineau, Wagner, and Lawrence. The same discourse – a vital component of both populism and nationalism – extends from the ideology of the planter class in the antebellum American South, via Chayanovian fables in early twentieth century Russia, to those writing about travel and tourism from the late nineteenth century onwards. Accordingly, for travel writers like Greene and Bowles 'otherness' was looked upon favourably so long as its subject was found 'in its place': essentialized as pristine and unchanging subsistence producers inhabiting rural contexts situated in far off locations.

An exception is Lampedusa, whose account of European journeys not only reproduced agrarian myth discourse consistent with his own class position as an aristocratic landowner, but also confined his most vehement anti-semitism to members of the Jewish community who were poor. More broadly, as soon as hitherto pristine forms of 'otherness' become more 'like-us' – adopting traits/ practices in keeping with 'Westernization'/'civilization' – these subjects are described less favourably in such narratives, as no longer culturally 'authentic' but now 'like-us'. Whereas travel accounts of journeys outside Europe defend the 'other' against the encroachment of Western 'civilization', those about travel within Europe seek to protect the same Western 'civilization' from an equally undesirable – but different sort of – 'other': the mass tourist, or the plebeian from home.

Speaking very generally, and at the same time emphasizing that they are not mutually exclusive, it is possible to identify three stages in the way the 'otherness' of race is perceived. The first corresponds broadly to the pre-capitalist era long before the nineteenth century, when indigenous groups inhabiting far-off contexts were seen by Europeans as different, possessing their own customs and practices, quaint – inviting curiosity even, but not yet positioned on a hierarchy claiming to be about civilizational superiority/inferiority. With the consolidation of nationalism in Europe, and colonialism/imperialism abroad, the nineteenth century marked a transition in perceptions of 'otherness', as not just different but inferior, a perception that licensed and justified a discourse about the necessity of rule by 'higher' races.

As capitalism developed and went global throughout the twentieth century, however, the 'other' was recast ideologically yet again: seen no longer as a cultural inferior, but now much rather as an economic equal, and thus – when s/he migrated into the metropolitan capitalist heartlands – as a rival in labour market competition. A transition, in short, from a perception of the 'other' as merely 'different', via different-but-'inferior', to equal and a potential/actual rival in a labour market that was increasingly global. Consequently, as the 'other' has drawn ever closer to the self who inhabits and gains a livelihood in metropolitan capitalism, not only does the meaning of this identity change, but it is not the ethnic identity of the 'other' so much as the economic proximity in the same labour market that is increasingly viewed by the plebeian self as worrying. This seems to have been the issue in the Red Wall seats of the northern UK, where working class discourse about the meaning of immigration, and why this is perceived negatively, is framed largely in terms of its economic consequences for persons like themselves.

For this reason, the emphasis by inhabitants of such contexts that their opposition to immigration is based not on ethnic or national 'otherness' as on an economic dynamic coupling a lack of employment in their own areas with little or no possibility of moving south in search of better jobs. Hence the lament by Red Wallers about the loss of economic opportunity in general, and well-paying employment in particular, a situation attributed by them in part to the presence of immigrant workers undercutting wages and taking jobs. Significantly, the locus of this economic impact is perceived to be not so much in the Red Wall areas as in London, the capital being a place where either they

themselves or their children might otherwise have sought alternative positions. Hence the hostility expressed by working class Red Wallers towards
London and 'the South', since these areas represent for them economic opportunities (plus the livelihood prospects) that were no longer available to their
kind of people.

Accordingly, behind the racist ideology of separatism, both in the antebellum South and that of Brexiteers in the UK a century and a half later, together
with their respective nationalisms, lies a common issue: intensified labour
market competition generated by capitalist development from the nineteenth
century onwards. Thus the 'from above' defence of slavery by Southern planters
depicted unfree production relations as a benign form of refuge, a 'subsistence
guarantee' not available to free labour caught up in competition for employment that characterized the northern economy. Opposition to immigration on
the part of those advocating Brexit similarly presented withdrawal from the EU
as a method of eliminating labour market competition, an objective embodied
in the reassertion of sovereignty by 'taking back control of our borders'. Using
the same kind of language contrasting 'selfhood' with 'otherness', in each case
discourse formulated and reproduced 'from above' (planters, employers) was
aimed at and circulated among 'those below' (workers, tenants, peasants).

Planter discourse in the antebellum South emphasized the advantages
to non-plantation workers and tenants of keeping slaves on the plantation,
thereby preventing them from entering the labour market as rivals, competing
for employment with those already in it, north as well as south. Underscored
thereby is the populist element, since 'those below' at the lower end of the social
hierarchy (free workers, tenant farmers) are encouraged to make common
cause with those occupying different class positions (planters, capitalists), on
the grounds of a shared ethnic identity. In much the same way, conservatives
in the UK have been able to present Brexit as a means of avoiding intensified
labour market competition, by undertaking to exclude EU migrants: projected
thereby is an image of conservatism as possessing not just a common identity
with the existing working class, but also as a defender of its interests.

For their part, many of those on the political left in metropolitan capitalist
nations have, much like postmodern theory, appeared to blame opposition to
immigration by members of the working class simply on the innate racism
of the latter. This instead of contextualizing and historicizing the discourse
about the meaning of non-class identity: that is, the shift from viewing the
'other' as 'inferior', and thus incapable of competing with the self, to someone
who is able to enter the same labour market to compete as an equal. Marxism,
by contrast, has viewed such opposition rather differently, as being as much
a reaction to capitalism and its form of labour market competition involving

unfettered access to a globally expanding industrial reserve. Rather than being seen as innate, therefore, plebeian racism can be interpreted as a response fostered 'from above' as a divide-and-rule tactic used by capital and its representatives to play different components of the workforce (migrant/local, white/non-white) off against one another, so as to undermine or pre-empt the actual/potential development of political consciousness and solidarity based on class.

Questions linked to the expansion of the industrial reserve are compounded by the exploitative nature of the way in which such forms of labour-power are inserted into the labour market, contributing to the cost advantages enjoyed by capital, the levels of surplus extracted, and consequently the competitive pressure experienced by those already employed. During the post-war era, the connection between forms of labour-power that were unfree and capitalist accumulation was central to much debate about rural development. A crucial aspect of the ensuing discussion concerned the extent to which different relational forms constituted obstacles to economic development, and why. Central to these deliberations was the link between capitalism and modern forms of unfree labour (peonage, debt bondage, indenture, chattel slavery). From the 1960s to the 1980s, the dominant paradigm maintained that, as unfreedom and economic development were – and are – incompatible, accumulation in Third World contexts depended on the spread of free labour.

From the 1980s onwards, however, this claim was challenged and replaced by a Marxist interpretation based on the primacy of class struggle, which argued much rather for the acceptability to capitalists of production relations that are unfree, maintaining that employers were restructuring the labour process by replacing free workers with unfree equivalents, a procedure termed deproletarianisation. In a global economy where business had to become increasingly cost-conscious to remain competitive, enterprises reproduced, introduced, or reintroduced unfree relations in preference to free labour, a practice amounting to workforce decomposition/recomposition. Originally confined to discussions about Third World countries, the capitalism/unfreedom debate has shifted, and now includes developments in the labour regime of metropolitan capitalist nations. Somewhat predictably, decoupling and recoupling capitalism and unfreedom in this manner has procrustean effects. On encountering unfree production relations where they should not be, in the midst of capitalism, many of those who previously endorsed the incompatibility approach (capitalism ≠ unfreedom) experienced a certain amount of epistemological distress, resolved in different ways.

Thus, for example, Banaji simply redefined such relations as free wage labour, since for him coercion at the point of recruitment is sufficient for the production relation to be regarded as unfree, and where this is absent, he regards the relation as free. Hence his view that, outside of slavery, most forms of labour-power are free (= contract), a definition he shares with bourgeois economics. In siding with neoclassical economics on this issue, Banaji ignores the fact that for Marxism unfreedom is defined also by an inability to exit from the production relation: that is, to be free the owner of labour-power has to retain the ability to commodify this on an unconditional basis. This error on the part of Banaji is itself reinforced by his view – similarly problematic – that merchant capital is the dominant economic form that stretches from ancient society to the present-day, an argument that emerges clearly from his two most recent books. Other, seemingly unimportant details, bolster this view: his support not just of cliometric historiography (for which capitalism is similarly eternal) but also of Mommsen (who thought Rome was capitalist) against Marx (who didn't).

A result of having altered the meaning of what is studied by reconceptualizing it, Banaji finds himself on the wrong side of Marxism in virtually all questions of theory. This break extends from the characterization of production relations, especially the free/unfree labour distinction, via the privileging of trade over production and merchant capital over its industrial counterpart, the historical dynamic of economic development and/or decline, the dominant/subordinate forms of capital extant at particular historical conjunctures, to the occurrence or lack of systemic transition. Although these departures are presented as an endeavour to 'improve' or 'update' Marxism, it is hard to disguise the fact that over the years the approach of Banaji has had more in common with neoclassical economic theory than with Marxism, a point that emerges clearly with regard to the way he defines unfree labour. Contrary to what he claims is the case, Marx did indeed perceive labour-power as a commodity and freedom as a desirable object of working class struggle.

Of the many objections to his interpretation of modes of production and their form of transition, not the least important is methods. Throughout his books dealing with late antiquity, feudalism, and capitalism, there are many references to archaeological and other kinds of evidence which is never presented, let alone interrogated. In this he follows the tendency by those currently writing about late antiquity and feudalism to slap the label 'capitalist' on any and every form of economic activity at these periods, regardless of what such activity was or how typical and widespread its impact. It wasn't always like that (ancient history has in the past prided itself, rightly, on its rigour), and one suspects that, Banaji apart, the present trend among some classicists is in a large part down to a desire – perhaps even a requirement – to find 'new' developments or interpretations justifying academic relevance.

A similar transition has been effected by the 'new' populist postmodern analyses, which from the 1980s onwards privileged the non-economic identity of the subject, recasting peasant family farming as a form of cultural empowerment. Such approaches persisted in regarding petty commodity producers simply as cultural subjects, thereby ignoring the fact that large numbers of rural cultivators separated by capital from their means of labour were on an increasing scale joining the ranks of the global industrial reserve army. By not addressing the wider systemic logic – that of continued accumulation – advocates of non-class identity as empowering overlooked the implications of this process. What is missed by this focus on the cultural 'otherness', therefore, is the changed economic role of peasants: for the most part, they are no longer required as cultivators or consumers (as 1960s modernisation theory argued) but simply as providers of labour-power (the Marxist argument, elaborated by Kautsky). Because it does not advocate the transcendence of capitalism as a system and perceives empowerment simply in terms of re-establishing/protecting traditional rural culture, the 'new' populist postmodernism – unlike Marxism – is unable to address this problem.

Linked to this is an additional political difficulty facing 'multiculturalism', the central theoretical emplacement of the 'new' populist postmodernism. It fails to differentiate between two specific and – in terms of political economy – contradictory phenomena. Within the context of the nation, therefore, it argues uncontroversially for an egalitarianism covering all the different ethnic minorities, a position from which no socialist would dissent and one that Marxism wholeheartedly endorses. A problem, however, arises when the same concept – multiculturalism – is extended to cover the right of everyone to enter the labour market in same nation on the grounds simply of belonging to a different ethnicity. With this broadened meaning of the same concept, political economy generally and Marxism in particular, sees a difficulty.

Applying the term in this additional manner leads to a rather obvious predicament: this is because used in this way, it licenses an almost unconditional access by capital in the nation concerned to the industrial reserve army of labour, in the process undermining any socio-economic gains that might have been achieved hitherto by existing workers of whatever ethnicity, contributing thereby to the reproduction of the accumulation system. Evidence for this is that employers are not slow to avail themselves of this advantage, encouraging workers to replace their consciousness and struggle based on class with that based on ethnic or national identity: the well-tried 'from above' tactic of divide and rule.

Currently, this can be seen in the way the 'new' populist postmodernism tends to view the 'other' as an undifferentiated category wanting only cultural empowerment. The intellectual hegemony exercised by the 'cultural turn' has been facilitated not just by a renewed privileging of 'otherness' in academia, but also by the marginalization of Marxism, not least through the logics of silence. Among the more worrying developments of such a change is that, having displaced Marxism, non-Marxist approaches have failed to anticipate the reasons for and political effects of the impact on advanced capitalist economies of a burgeoning industrial reserve army, fuelling the rise of populism and the far right.

Finally, it is hard to avoid the baleful state of much social science discourse, particularly that concerned with the study of development. The latter has been – and remains – characterized by twisted trajectories and curious chronologies, at times conveying the impression that development theory is not just fragmented but purposeless. In a sense, indicting aspects of capitalism – almost a *de rigueur* default mode in the social sciences – is all too often accompanied by a desire not to transcend but to rescue this economic system. Saving accumulation in this manner paves the way epistemologically for the adoption of non-Marxist alternatives. Hence the common element seen all along this route: a double transition, away from Marxism and socialism, and towards populism and conservatism, a movement evident in most of the theoretical, methodological, and political shifts marking the trajectory under consideration.

Bibliography

Aitken, Ben, 2021, *The Gran Tour: Travels with my Elders*, London: Icon Books Ltd.

Althusser, Louis, and Etienne Balibar, 1970, *Reading Capital,* London: New Left Books.

Amis, Kingsley, 1965, *The James Bond Dossier*, London: Jonathan Cape.

Archetti, Eduardo P., and Svein Aass, 1978, 'Peasant Studies: An Overview', in Howard Newby (ed.), *International Perspectives in Rural Sociology*, New York: John Wiley & Sons.

Autonomia, 1980, Italy: Post-Political Politics, *Semiotext(e)*, Vol. III, No. 3.

Bailey, Hugh C., 1965, *Hinton Rowan Helper: Abolitionist Racist*, Montgomery, AL: University of Alabama Press.

Balfour, Arthur James, 1908, *Decadence (Henry Sidgwick Memorial Lecture)*, London: Cambridge University Press.

Banaji, Jairus, 1976, 'The Peasantry in the Feudal Mode of Production: Towards an Economic Model', *The Journal of Peasant Studies*, Vol. 3, No. 3.

Banaji, Jairus, 1977, 'Modes of Production in a Materialist Conception of History', *Capital & Class*, No. 3.

Banaji, Jairus, 1979, 'From the Commodity to Capital: Hegel's Dialectic in Marx's Capital', in Diane Elson (ed.), *Value: The Representation of Labour in Capitalism*, London: CSE Books.

Banaji, Jairus, 2001, *Agrarian Change in Late Antiquity: Gold, Labour, and Aristocratic Dominance*, Oxford: Oxford University Press.

Banaji, Jairus, 2003, 'The Fictions of Free Labour, Contract, Coercion, and So-called Unfree Labour', *Historical Materialism*, Vol. 11, No. 3.

Banaji, Jairus, 2010, *Theory as History*, Leiden: Brill.

Banaji, Jairus, 2018, *Exploring the Economy of Late Antiquity*, Cambridge: Cambridge University Press.

Banaji, Jairus, 2020, *A Brief History of Commercial Capitalism*, Chicago, IL: Haymarket Books.

Barber, John, 1981, *Soviet Historians in Crisis, 1928–1932.* London: The Macmillan Press Ltd.

Bardhan, Pranab (ed.), 1989, *Conversations between Economists and Anthropologists: Methodological Issues in Measuring Economic Change in Rural India*, Delhi: Oxford University Press.

Barrientos, Stephanie, 2019, *Gender and Work in Global Value Chains*, Cambridge: Cambridge University Press.

Barrientos, Stephanie, Uma Kothari, and Nicola Phillips, 2013, 'Dynamics of Unfree Labour in the Contemporary Global Economy', *Journal of Development Studies*, Vol. 49, No. 8.

Beidelman, T.O., 1959, *A Comparative Analysis of the Jajmani System*, Locust Valley, NY: Association for Asian Studies.

Belloc, Hilaire, 1922, *The Jews*, Boston & New York: Hough Mifflin Company.

Benjamin, Walter, 1979, *One-Way Street*, London: NLB.

Benjamin, Walter, 2007, *Archive: Images*, Texts, Signs, London: Verso.

Benjamin, Walter, 2014, *Radio Benjamin*, London: Verso.

Benjamin, Walter, 2016, *The Storyteller* (Translated and edited by Sam Dolbear, Esther Leslie, and Sebastian Truskolaski), London and New York: Verso.

Bernstein, Henry, 2018, 'The "peasant problem" in the Russian revolution(s), 1905–1929', *The Journal of Peasant Studies*, Vol. 45, Nos. 5–6.

Bernstein, Henry, 2021, 'Into the Field with Marx: Some Observations on Researching Class', in Alessandra Mezzadri (ed.). *Marx in the Field*, London: Anthem Press.

Biddiss, Michael D. (ed.), 1970, *Gobineau: Selected Political Writings (Roots of the Right – General Editor: George Steiner)*, London: Jonathan Cape.

Bierce, Ambrose, 1967, *The Enlarged Devil's Dictionary* (Researched and Edited by Ernest Jerome Hopkins; Preface by John Myers Myers), London: Victor Gollancz.

Bika, Zografia, 2007, 'A Survey of Academic Approaches to Agrarian Transformation in Post-war Greece,' *The Journal of Peasant Studies*, Vol. 34, No. 1.

Billig, Michael, 1978, *Fascists: A Social Psychological View of the National Front*, London: Academic Press.

Bloch, Maurice (ed.), 1975, *Marxist Analyses and Social Anthropology*, London: Malaby Press.

Blok, Anton, 1972, 'The Peasant and the Brigand: Social Banditry Reconsidered', *Comparative Studies in Society and History*, Vol. 14, No. 4.

Blok, Anton, 1988 [1974], *The Mafia of a Sicilian Village 1860–1960: A Study of Violent Peasant Entrepreneurs*, Cambridge: Polity.

Bloomfield, Paul, 1962, *L.P. Hartley*, London: Longmans Green & Co.

Bolton, Charles C., 1994, *Poor Whites of the Antebellum South*, Durham, NC: Duke University Press.

Bourgholtzer, Frank (ed.), 1999, *Aleksandr Chayanov and Russian Berlin*. London: Frank Cass Publishers.

Bowles, Paul, 1988 [1979], *Collected Stories 1939–1976* (Introduction by Gore Vidal), Santa Rosa, CA: Black Sparrow Press.

Bowles, Paul, 2006 [1963], *Their Heads are Green and Their Hands are Blue: Scenes from the Non-Christian World* (with an Introduction by Edmund White), New York: Harper Perennial.

Bowles, Paul, 2010, *Travels: Collected Writings*, 1950–93, London: Profile Books.

Brady, Frank, and Frederick A. Pottle (eds.), 1955, *Boswell on the Grand Tour: Italy, Corsica, and France 1765–1766*, London: William Heinemann Ltd.

Brass, Tom (ed.), 1995, *New Farmers' Movements in India*, London and Portland, OR: Frank Cass Publishers.

Brass, Tom (ed.), 2003, *Latin American Peasants*, London and Portland, OR: Frank Cass Publishers.

Brass, Tom, 1986, 'The Elementary Strictures of Kinship: Unfree Relations and the Production of Commodities', *Social Analysis*, No. 20.

Brass, Tom, 1996/1997, 'Popular Culture, Populist Fiction(s): The Agrarian Utopiates of A.V. Chayanov, Ignatius Donnelly and Frank Capra', *The Journal of Peasant Studies*, Vol. 24, Nos. 1&2.

Brass, Tom, 1997, 'Introduction: Free and Unfree Labour: The Debate Continues', in Tom Brass and Marcel van der Linden (eds.), *Free and Unfree Labour: The Debate Continues*, Bern: Peter Lang.

Brass, Tom, 1999, *Towards a Comparative Political Economy of Unfree Labour: Case Studies and Debates,* London: Frank Cass Publishers.

Brass, Tom, 2000, *Peasants, Populism and Postmodernism*, London: Frank Cass Publishers.

Brass, Tom, 2003a, 'Why Unfree Labour is Not "So-Called": The Fictions of Jairus Banaji', *The Journal of Peasant Studies*, Vol. 31, No. 1.

Brass, Tom, 2005, 'Late Antiquity as Early Capitalism?', *The Journal of Peasant Studies*, Vol. 32, No. 1.

Brass, Tom, 2007, 'Weapons of the Week, Weakness of the Weapons: Shifts and Stasis in Development Theory', *The Journal of Peasant Studies*, Vol. 34, No. 1.

Brass, Tom, 2011, *Labour Regime Change in the Twenty-First Century: Unfreedom, Capitalism and Primitive Accumulation*, Leiden: Brill.

Brass, Tom, 2012, 'Jairus Banaji's mode of production: Eviscerating Marxism, essentialising capitalism', *Journal of Contemporary Asia*, Vol. 42, No. 4.

Brass, Tom, 2014, *Class, Culture, and the Agrarian Myth*, Leiden: Brill.

Brass, Tom, 2014a, 'Debating Capitalist Dynamics and Unfree Labour: A Missing Link?', *The Journal of Development Studies*, Vol. 50, No. 4.

Brass, Tom, 2015, 'Peasants, Academics, Populists: Forward to the Past?', *Critique of Anthropology*, Vol. 35, No. 2.

Brass, Tom, 2017, *Labour Markets, Identities, Controversies*, Leiden: Brill.

Brass, Tom, 2018, *Revolution and Its Alternatives*, Leiden: Brill.

Brass, Tom, 2020, 'Is Agrarian Populism Progressive? Russia Then, India Now', *Critical Sociology*, Vol. 46, Nos. 7–8.

Brass, Tom, 2021, *Marxism Missing, Missing Marxism*. Leiden: Brill.

Brass, Tom, 2022, 'Twisted Trajectories, Curious Chronologies: Revisiting the Unfree Labour Debate', *Critical Sociology*, Vol. 48, No. 1.

Brass, Tom, 2022a, 'Marxism, Peasants, and the Cultural Turn: The Myth of a "Nice" Populism', in David Fasenfest (ed.), *Marx Matters*, Leiden: Brill.

Brass, Tom, and Marcel van der Linden (eds.), 1997, *Free and Unfree Labour: The Debate Continues,* Berne: Peter Lang, AG.

Breman, Jan, 1974, *Patronage and Exploitation: Changing Agrarian Relations in South Gujarat, India*, Berkeley, CA: University of California Press.

Breman, Jan, 1978, 'Seasonal Migration and Co-operative Capitalism: The Crushing of Cane and of Labour by the Sugar Factories of Bardoli, South Gujarat – Parts 1 and 2', *The Journal of Peasant Studies*, Volume 6, Nos. 1 and 2.

Breman, Jan, 1985, *Of Peasants, Migrants and Paupers: Rural Labour Circulation in Capitalist Production in West India*, Delhi: Oxford University Press.

Breman, Jan, 2013, *At Work in the Informal Economy of India: A Perspective from the Bottom Up*. Delhi: Oxford University Press.

Breman, Jan, 2019, *Capitalism, Inequality and Labour in India,* Cambridge: Cambridge University Press.

Brooks, Mel, 2021, *All About Me: My Remarkable Life in Show Business*, London: Century/ Penguin Random House.

Brown, Peter, 1971, *The World of Late Antiquity AD 150–750*, London: Thames and Hudson Ltd.

Brown, Peter, 1978, *The Making of Late Antiquity*, Cambridge, MA: Harvard University Press.

Bull, Anna, and Paul Corner. 1993. *From Peasant to Entrepreneur: The Survival of the Family Economy in Italy*. Oxford: Berg.

Burke, Edmund, 1808, *The Works of the Right Honourable Edmund Burke*, Vol. I, London: F.C. and J. Rivington, St. Paul's Church-Yard.

Byron, Robert, 1982 [1937], *The Road to Oxiana* (with a New Introduction by Paul Fussell), New York: Oxford University Press.

Byron, Robert, 1991, *Letters Home* (edited by Lucy Butler), London: John Murray.

Carlson, Allan C., 2007, *Third Ways*. Wilmington, DE: ISI Books.

Carroll, Lewis, 1872, *Alice Through the Looking Glass,* London: Macmillan.

Carstensen, Lisa, 2021, 'Unfree Labour. Migration and Racism: Towards an Analytical Framework', *Global Labour Journal*, Vol. 12, No. 1.

Casson, Lionel. 1994. *Travel in the Ancient World*. Baltimore, MD: The Johns Hopkins University Press.

Chandler Harris, Joel, 1883, *Uncle Remus*, London: George Routledge and Sons.

Chandler Harris, Joel, 1925, *Nights with Uncle Remus*, London: Chatto & Windus.

Channon, Henry 'Chips', 2021, *The Diaries: 1918–1938* (edited by Simon Heffer), London: Hutchinson.

Chayanov, A.V., 1991 [1926], *The Theory of Peasant Cooperatives*, London and New York: I.B. Tauris & Co. Ltd.

Chayanov. A. V., 1966 [1923] *The Theory of Peasant Economy* (edited by Daniel Thorner, Basile Kerblay, and R. E. F. Smith), Homewood, Illinois: Published for The American Economic Association by Richard D. Irwin, Inc.

Chesshyre, Tom, 2020, *Slow Trains to Venice: A 4,000-Mile Adventure Across Europe*, London: Summersdale Publishers Ltd.

Cole, John W., and Eric R. Wolf, 1974, *The Hidden Frontier: Ecology and Ethnicity in an Alpine Valley*, New York: Academic Press.

Cottrell, Leonard, 1960, *Enemy of Rome*, London: Evans Brothers Limited.

Cox, Terence M., 1979, *Rural Sociology in the Soviet Union*, New York: Holmes & Meier.

D'Eramo, Marco, 2013, 'Populism and the New Oligarchy', *New Left Review*, 82.

D'Eramo, Marco, 2021, *The World in a Selfie: An Inquiry into the Tourist Age*, London: Verso.

Damir-Geilsdorf, Sabine, Ulrike Lindner, Gersine Müller, Oliver Tappe, and Michael Zeuske (eds.), 2016, *Bonded Labour: Global and Comparative Perspectives*, Bielefeld: Transcript Verlag.

Danilov, V.P., 1988, *Rural Russia under the New Regime*, London: Hutchinson.

de Neve, Geert, 2005, *The Everyday Politics of Labour: Working Lives in India's Informal Economy*, Delhi: Social Science Press.

Debray, Régis, 2002, *Against Venice*, London: Pushkin Press.

Deutscher, Isaac, 1968, *The Non-Jewish Jew and other essays* (edited with an introduction by Tamara Deutscher), London: Oxford University Press.

Diskalkar, P.D., 1960, *Resurvey of a Deccan Village: Pimple Saudagar,* Bombay: Indian Society of Agricultural Economics.

Dobb, Maurice, 1955, 'Full Employment and Capitalism [1950]', in *On Economic Theory and Socialism*: Collected Papers, London: Routledge & Kegan Paul.

Dobb, Maurice, 1967, *Capitalism, Development and Planning*, London: Routledge and Kegan Paul.

Dummett, Jeremy, 2015, *Palermo: City of Kings*, London: I.B. Tauris & Co. Ltd.

Duncan, Kenneth, Ian Rutledge, and Colin Harding (eds.), 1977, *Land and Labour in Latin America*, Cambridge: Cambridge University Press.

Durrenburger, Paul E. (ed.), 1984, *Chayanov, Peasants, and Economic Anthropology*, London: Academic Press.

Ellen, R.F. (ed.), 1984, *Ethnographic Research*, London: Academic Press Limited.

Elliott, E.N. (ed.), 1860, *Cotton is King, and Pro-Slavery Arguments, Comprising the Writings of Hammond, Harper, Christy, Stringfellow, Hodge, Bledsoe, and Cartwright on this important subject.* Augusta, GA: Pritchard, Abbott & Loomis.

Ellis, Frank, 1988, *Peasant Economics*, Cambridge: Cambridge University Press.

Elsner, Jaś, and Joan-Pau Rubiés (eds.), 1999, *Voyages and Visions: Towards a Cultural History of Travel*, London: Reaktion Books.

Epstein, A.L. (ed.), 1967, *The Craft of Social Anthropology*, London: Tavistock Publications.

Eribon, Didier, 2018, *Returning to Reims*, London: Allen Lane/Penguin Random House.

Esterci, Neide, 1987, *Conflito no Araguaia: Peões e posseiros contra a grande empresa*, Petrópolis: Editora Vozes Ltda.

Evola, Julius, 2002, *Men Among the Ruins: Postwar Reflections of a Radical Traditionalist*, Rochester, VT: Inner Traditions.

Éwanjée-Épée, Félix Boggio, and Frédéric Monferrand, 2015, *Jairus Banaji: Towards a New Marxist Historiography*. http://www.historicalmaterialism.org/interviews/jairus-banaji-towards-a-new-marxist-historiography/.

Fielding, Nigel, 1981, *The National Front*, London: Routledge & Kegan Paul Ltd.

Fine, Ben, and Alfredo Saad-Filho (eds.), 2012, *The Elgar Companion to Marxist Economics*, Cheltenham, UK: Edward Elgar.

Firbank, Ronald, 1951, *Five Novels*, London: Gerald Duckworth & Co. Ltd.

Fite, Emerson David, 1968 [1909], *Social and Industrial Conditions in the North during the Civil War*, New York: Frederick Ungar Publishing Co.

Fitzhugh, George, 1960a [1854], 'Sociology for the South', in Harvey Wish (ed.). *Antebellum: Writings of George Fitzhugh and Hinton Rowan Helper on Slavery*. New York: G.F. Putnam's Sons.

Fitzhugh, George, 1960b [1857], *Cannibals All! or, Slaves Without Masters*. Cambridge, MA: The Belknap Press of Harvard University Press.

Fogel, Robert W., and Stanley M. Engerman, 1974, *Time on the Cross*: Volume I – The Economics of American Negro Slavery, London: Wildwood House.

Foucault, Michel, 1996, *Foucault Live: Collected Interviews, 1961–1984* (edited by Sylvère Lotringer), New York, NY: Semiotext(e).

Fox-Genovese, Elizabeth, and Eugene D. Genovese, 1983, *Fruits of Merchant Capital: Slavery and Bourgeois Property in the Rise and Expansion of Capitalism*, New York: Oxford University Press.

Fudge, Judy, 2019, '(Re)Conceptualising Unfree Labour: Local Labour Control Regimes and Constraints on Workers' Freedoms', *Global Labour Journal*, Vol. 10, No. 2.

Fukazawa, H., 1982, 'Agrarian Relations and Land Revenue: 2 – The Medieval Deccan and Maharashtra', in Tapan Raychaudhuri and Irfan Habib (eds.), *The Cambridge Economic History of India*, Volume I: c. 1200-c.1750, Cambridge: Cambridge University Press.

Genovese, Eugene D., 1968, *In Red and Black: Marxian Explorations in Southern and Afro-American History*, New York: Pantheon Books.

Genovese, Eugene D., 1969, *The World the Slaveholders Made: Two Essays in Interpretation*, New York: Pantheon Books.

Genovese, Eugene D., 1975, *Roll Jordan, Roll: The World the Slaves Made*, London: André Deutsch Limited.

Genovese, Eugene D., 1994, *The Southern Tradition: The Achievement and Limitations of an American Conservatism,* Cambridge, MA: Harvard University Press.

Gereffi, Gary, 2018, *Global Value Chains and Development: Redefining the Contours of 21st Century Capitalism*, Cambridge: Cambridge University Press.

Gereffi, Gary, John Humphrey, and Timothy Sturgeon, 2005, 'The governance of global value chains', *Review of International Political Economy*, Vol. 12, No. 1.

Gibbon, Peter, and Michael Neocosmos, 1985, 'Some Problems in the Political Economy of "African Socialism"', in Henry Bernstein and Bonnie K. Campbell (eds.),

Contradictions of Accumulation in Africa: Studies in Economy and State, Beverley Hills, CA: Sage Publications.

Ginsborg, Paul, 2003, *Italy and Its Discontents: Family, Civil Society, State, 1980–2001,* New York: Palgrave Macmillan.

Ginsborg, Paul, 2004, *Silvio Berlusconi: Television, Power and Patrimony,* London: Verso.

Ginsborg, Paul. 1990. *A History of Contemporary Italy: Society and Politics 1943–1988.* London: Penguin Books.

Glyn, Andrew, 2006, *Capitalism Unleashed,* Oxford: Oxford University Press.

Gobineau, Arthur de, 1915 [1854], *The Inequality of Human Races* (translated by Adrian Collins), London: William Heinemann.

Godelier, Maurice, 2018, *Claude Lévi-Strauss: A Critical Study of His Thought* (Translated by Nora Scott), London: Verso.

Godoy, Richard J., 1985, *Chioggia and the Villages of the Venetian lagoon: Studies in urban history,* Cambridge: Cambridge University Press.

Goldman, Albert, and Evert Sprinchorn (eds.), 1977, *Wagner on Music and Drama,* London: Victor Gollancz.

Góngora, Mario, 1975, *Studies in the Colonial History of Latin America,* Cambridge: Cambridge University Press.

Goodfellow, Maya, 2020, *Hostile Environment: How Immigrants Became Scapegoats,* London: Verso.

Goodman, David, and Michael Redclift, 1981, *From Peasant to Proletarian: Capitalist Development and Agrarian Transition,* Oxford: Basil Blackwell.

Graves, Robert, 1960 [1934], *I, Claudius,* Harmondsworth: Penguin Books.

Graves, Robert, 1961 [1934], *Claudius the God,* Harmondsworth: Penguin Books.

Green, Peter, 1953, *The Expanding Eye: A First Journey to the Mediterranean,* London: Dennis Dobson.

Green, Peter, 1957, *The Sword of Pleasure,* London: John Murray.

Green, Peter, 1972, *The Shadow of the Parthenon: Studies in Ancient History and Literature,* Berkeley, CA: University of California Press.

Green, Peter, 1989, *Classical Bearings: Interpreting Ancient History and Culture,* London: Thames and Hudson.

Green, Peter, 1993, *Alexander to Actium: The Hellenistic Age,* London: Thames & Hudson.

Greene, Graham, 1936, *Journey Without Maps,* New York: Doubleday, Doran & Company, Inc.

Grimm, Jacob and Wilhelm, 1948, *Complete Fairy Tales* (Introduction by Padraic Column, illustrated by Josef Scharl), London: Routledge & Kegan Paul.

Guha, Ranajit (ed.), (1982–89), *Subaltern Studies I–VI,* New Delhi: Oxford University Press.

Hamilton-Patterson, James, 2006, 'The End of Travel: Paradise, before the rest of us arrived', *Granta,* 94 (Summer).

Hardt, Michael, and Antonio Negri, 2000, *Empire*, Cambridge, MA: Harvard University Press.

Hardt, Michael, and Antonio Negri, 2005, *Multitude: War and Democracy in the Age of Empire*, London: Hamish Hamilton.

Harris, Marvin, 1968, *The Rise of Anthropological Theory*, London: Routledge & Kegan Paul.

Harrison, Mark, 1975, 'Chayanov and the Economics of the Russian Peasantry', *The Journal of Peasant Studies*, Vol. 2, No. 4.

Harrison, Mark, 1977, 'The Peasant Mode of Production in the Work of A.V. Chayanov', *The Journal of Peasant Studies*, Vol. 4, No. 4.

Harrison, Mark, 1979, 'Chayanov and the Marxists', *The Journal of Peasant Studies*, Vol. 7, No. 1.

Hartley, L.P., 1953, *The Go-Between*, London: Hamish Hamilton Ltd.

Hartley, L.P., 1958, *Eustace and Hilda: A Trilogy*, London: Putnam.

Helper, Hinton Rowan, 1860, *The Impending Crisis of the South: How to Meet It*, New York: A.B.Burdick, No. 145 Nassau Street.

Higham, Charles, 1970, *The Films of Orson Welles*, Berkeley, CA: University of California Press.

Hilferding, Rudolf, 1981 [1910] *Finance Capital: A Study of the Latest Phase of Capitalist Development.* London: Routledge & Kegan Paul.

Hilton, Rodney (ed.), 1976, *The Transition from Feudalism to Capitalism*, London: NLB.

Hilton, Rodney, 1985, *Class Conflict and the Crisis of Feudalism: Essays in Medieval Social History,* London: The Hambledon Press.

Hindess, Barry, and Paul Q. Hirst, 1975, *Pre-Capitalist Modes of Production*, London and Boston, MA: Routledge & Kegan Paul.

Hobsbawm, Eric J., 1969, *Bandits*, London: Weidenfeld and Nicolson.

Holland, Robert, 2018, *The Warm South: How the Mediterranean Shaped the British Imagination,* London and New Haven, CT: Yale University Press.

Horkheimer, Max, and Theodore W. Adorno, 1973 [1944], *Dialectic of Enlightenment* (translated by John Cumming), London: Allen Lane/Penguin Books Ltd.

Howe, Irving (ed.), 1964, *The Basic Writings of Trotsky*, London: Secker & Warburg.

Jagalpure, L.B., and K.D. Kale, 1938, *Sarola Kasar: Study of a Deccan Village in the Famine Zone*, Ahmednagar: R.B. Hiray.

Jasny, Naum, 1972, *Soviet Economists of the Twenties*, London: Cambridge University Press.

Juvenal [Decimus Junius Juvenalis], 2004 [c.100 AD], *The Sixteen Satires* (edited, translated, and introduced by Peter Green), London: Penguin Books.

Kautsky, Karl, 1984 [1894/95], 'The Competitive Capacity of Small-scale Enterprise in Agriculture', in Athar Hussain and Keith Tribe (eds.), *Paths of Development in Capitalist Agriculture*, London: Macmillan.

Keenagh, Peter, 1937, *Mosquito Coast: An Account of a Journey through the Jungles of Honduras*, London: Chatto & Windus.

Kelley, William D., 1866, *Speech of the Hon. William D. Kelley on Protection to American Labor, delivered in the House of Representatives, 31st January, 1866*. Washington, DC: Printed at the Congressional Globe Office.

Kenway, Emily, 2021, *The Truth about Modern Slavery*, London: Pluto Press.

Kerblay, Basile, 1966a, 'A.V. Chayanov: Life, Career, Works', in Chayanov. A. V., 1966 [1923] *The Theory of Peasant Economy* (edited by Daniel Thorner, Basile Kerblay, and R. E. F. Smith), Homewood, Illinois: Published for The American Economic Association by Richard D. Irwin, Inc.

Kerblay, Basile, 1966b, 'The Russian Peasant', in Michael Kaser (ed.), *Soviet Affairs* (St Anthony's Papers, Number 19), London: Oxford University Press.

Kerblay, Basile, 1971, 'Chayanov and the Theory of Peasant Economies', in Teodor Shanin (ed.). *Peasants and Peasant Societies*, London: Penguin Books.

Komlosy, Andrea, and Goran Musić (eds.), 2021, *Global Commodity Chains and Labor Relations*, Leiden: Brill.

Kosminsky, E.A., 1956, *Studies in the Agrarian History of England*, Oxford: Basil Blackwell.

Kremnev, Ivan (pseudonym of A.V. Chayanov), 1977 [1920], 'The Journey of my brother Alexei to the land of Peasant Utopia', in R.E.F. Smith (ed.). *The Russian Peasant 1920 and 1984*, London: Frank Cass & Co. Ltd.

Lampedusa, Giuseppe Tomasi di, 2007 [1958], *The Leopard* (translated from the Italian by Archibald Colquhoun), London: Vintage Books.

Lampedusa, Giuseppe Tomasi di, 2010, *Letters from London and Europe (1925–30)* (Edited with an Introduction by Gioacchino Lanza Tomasi; Translated by J.G. Nichols), Richmond, Surrey: Alma Books.

Lampedusa, Giuseppi [Tomasi] di, 1962, *Two Stories and a Memory* (Translated from the Italian by Archibald Colquhoun; Introduction by E.M. Forster), London: Collins and Harvill Press.

Latham, R.G., 1859, *Descriptive Ethnology (Vol. I: Eastern and Northern Asia – Europe; Vol. II: Europe, Africa, India)*, London: John van Voorst, Paternoster Row.

Lawrence, D.H., 1930, *Assorted Articles*, London: Martin Secker.

Lawrence, D.H., 1936, *Phoenix: The Posthumous Papers* (edited and introduced by Edward D. McDonald), London: William Heinemann Ltd.

Lawrence, D.H., 1948, 'Letter from Germany [1928]', in Pritchett, Victor Sawdon (ed.), 1948, *Turnstile One: A Literary Miscellany from The New Statesman and Nation*, London: Turnstile Press.

Lawrence, D.H., 1968, *Phoenix II: Uncollected, Unpublished and Other Prose Works* (Collected and Edited with an Introduction and Notes by Warren Roberts and Harry T. Moore), London: Heinemann.

LeBaron, Genevieve, 2021, 'Marx, the Chief, the Prisoner and the Refugee', in Alessandra Mezzadri (ed.). *Marx in the Field*, London: Anthem Press.

LeBaron, Genevieve, and Ellie Gore, 2020, 'Gender and Forced Labour: Understanding the Links in the Global Cocoa Supply Chains', *The Journal of Development Studies*, Vol. 56, No. 6.

Lenin, V.I. 1962 [1905], 'Preface to the Pamphlet Memorandum of the Police Department Superintendent Lopukhin', *Collected Works*, Vol. 8, Moscow: Foreign Languages Publishing House.

Lenin, V.I. 1964a [1900], 'The War in China', *Collected Works*, Vol. 4, Moscow: Foreign Languages Publishing House.

Lenin, V.I. 1964b [1903], 'Draft Resolution on the Place of the Bund in the Party', *Collected Works*, Vol. 6, Moscow: Foreign Languages Publishing House.

Lenin, V.I. 1964c [1913], 'Critical Remarks on the National Question', *Collected Works*, Vol. 20, Moscow: Foreign Languages Publishing House.

Lenin, V.I. 1965 [1919], 'Anti-Jewish Pogroms', *Collected Works*, Vol. 29, Moscow: Foreign Languages Publishing House.

Lenin, V.I. 1968 [1916], 'Notebooks on Imperialism', *Collected Works*, Vol. 39, Moscow: Foreign Languages Publishing House.

Lenin, V.I., 1963 [1898], 'The Heritage We Renounce', *Collected Works*, Volume 2, Moscow: Foreign Languages Publishing House.

Leon, Donna, 2021, *Transient Desires*, London: Penguin Books.

Lévi-Strauss, Claude, 1961, *A World on the Wane* (Translated by John Russell), London: Hutchinson & Co. Ltd.

Lévi-Strauss, Claude, 1966 [1962], *The Savage Mind*, London: Weidenfeld & Nicolson.

Lévi-Strauss, Claude, and Didier Eribon, 1991, *Conversations with Claude Lévi-Strauss* (Translated by Paula Wissing), London and Chicago, IL: The University of Chicago Press.

Lewis, Norman, 1953, *A Single Pilgrim*, London: Jonathan Cape.

Lewis, Norman, 1964, *The Honoured Society*, London: Collins.

Lewis, Norman, 1978, *Naples '44*, London: Collins.

Lewis, Norman, 1998, *The Happy Ant-Heap*, London: Jonathan Cape.

Lewis, Norman, 2016 [2000], *In Sicily*, London: Eland Publishing Ltd.

Lewis, Wyndham, 1939, *The Jews: Are They Human?* London: George Allen & Unwin Ltd.

Lichtenstein, Alex, 1996, *Twice the Work of Free Labor: The Political Economy of Convict Labor in the New South*, London: Verso.

Little, Peter D., and Michael J. Watts, 2022, 'The afterlife of living under contract, an epilogue', *Journal of Agrarian Change*, Vol. 22, Issue 1.

Lombardozzi, Lorena, 2021, 'From Marx's "Double Freedom" to "Degrees of Unfreedom": Methodological Insights from the Study of Uzbekistan's Agrarian Labour', in Alessandra Mezzadri (ed.). *Marx in the Field*, London: Anthem Press.

Long, Norman, and Ann Long (eds.), 1992, *Battlefields of Knowledge: The Interlocking of Theory and Practice in Social Research and Development*, London and New York: Routledge.

Lopreato, Joseph, 1967, *Peasants No More: Social Class and Social Change in an Underdeveloped Society*, San Francisco, CA: Chandler Publishing Company.

Lotman, Jurij, and Boris Urpenskij, 1984, *The Semiotics of Russian Culture*, Ann Arbor MI: University of Michigan Press.

Lukács, Georg, 1971 [1922], *History and Class Consciousness* (translated by Rodney Livingstone), London: The Merlin Press Ltd.

Lumley, Robert, 1990, *States of Emergency: Cultures of Revolt in Italy from 1968 to 1978*, London: Verso.

Macaulay, Rose, 1964, *Letters to a Sister* (Edited by Constance Babington-Smith), New York: Atheneum.

Macaulay, Rose, 2021 [1935] *Personal Pleasures: Essays on Enjoying Life*, Bath: Handheld Press.

MacClancy, Jeremy, 2002, 'Paradise Postponed: The Predicaments of Tourism', in Jeremy MacClancy (ed.), *Exotic No More: Anthropology on the Front Lines*, Chicago, IL: University of Chicago Press.

Maguire, Muireann, 2013, *Red Spectres: Russian Gothic Tales from the Twentieth Century*, New York, NY: The Overlook Press.

Maher, George, 2021, *Pugnare: Economic Success and Failure*, London: Kilnamanagh.

Mann, Harold H., 1967, 'Foreword to A Resurvey of a Deccan Village', in Daniel Thorner (ed.), *Harold H. Mann – The Social Framework of Agriculture: India, Middle East, England,* Bombay: Vora & Co.

Mann, Harold H., and N.V. Kanitkar, 1921, *Land and Labour in a Deccan Village*, London and Bombay: Oxford University Press.

Mannin, Ethel, 1975, *An Italian Journey*, London: The Travel Book Club.

Marquardt, Felix, 2021, *The New Nomads: How the Migration Revolution is Making the World a Better Place*, London & New York: Simon & Schuster.

Martin, Judith, 2007, *No Vulgar Hotel: The Desire and Pursuit of Venice*, New York: W.W. Norton & Co.

Martins, José de Souza, 1997, 'The Reappearance of Slavery and the Reproduction of Capital on the Brazilian Frontier', in Tom Brass and Marcel van der Linden (eds.), *Free and Unfree Labour: The Debate Continues*, Bern: Peter Lang AG.

Marx, Karl, 1972, *Theories of Surplus Value – Part III*, London: Lawrence and Wishart.

Marx, Karl, 1976, *Capital Volume 1*, Harmondsworth: Penguin Books.

Marx, Karl, 1978, *Capital Volume 2*, Harmondsworth: Penguin Books.

Marx, Karl, 1981, *Capital Volume 3*, Harmondsworth: Penguin Books.

Marx, Karl, 1985 [1866], 'Instructions for the Delegates of the Provisional General Council: The Different Questions', Karl Marx Frederick Engels *Collected Works*, Volume 20, London: Lawrence & Wishart.

Marx, Karl, 1986, 'Economic Manuscripts of 1857–58', Karl Marx Frederick Engels, *Collected Works*, Vol. 28, London: Lawrence & Wishart.

Marx, Karl, and Frederick Engels. 1934. *Correspondence 1846–1895*. London: Martin Lawrence Ltd.

Mattinson, Deborah, 2020, *Beyond the Red Wall*, London: Biteback Publishing Ltd.

McCusker, Brent, Paul O'Keefe, Phil O'Keefe, and Geoff O'Brian, 2013, 'Peasants, pastoralists and proletarians: Joining the debates on trajectories of agrarian change, livelihoods and land use', *Human Geography*, Volume 6, No. 3.

Meades, Jonathan, 2021, *Pedro and Ricky Come Again: Selected Writing 1988–2020*, London: Unbound.

Mencher, Joan P. (ed.), 1983, *Social Anthropology of Peasantry*, New Delhi: Somaiya Publications Pvt. Ltd.

Mezzadri, Alessandra (ed.), 2021, *Marx in the Field*, London: Anthem Press.

Mezzadri, Alessandra, 2021, 'Introduction: Marx's Field as Our Global Present', in Alessandra Mezzadri (ed.). *Marx in the Field*, London: Anthem Press.

Mezzadri, Alessandra, and Lulu Fan, 2018, '"Classes of Labour" at the Margins of Global Commodity Chains in India and China', *Development & Change*, Vol. 49, No. 4.

Miles, Robert, 1987, *Capitalism and Unfree Labour*, London: Tavistock Publications.

Miller, Jeffrey (ed.), 1994, *In Touch: The Letters of Paul Bowles*, London: HarperCollins Publisher.

Morand, Paul, 2002 [1971], *Venices,* London: Pushkin Press.

Morris, Jan, 2001, *Trieste and the Meaning of Nowhere*, London: Faber and Faber.

Morris, Jan, 2021, *Allegorizings*, London: Faber and Faber.

Mortimer, John, 1988, *Summer's Lease*, London: Penguin/Viking.

Mortimer, John, and Mortimer, Penelope, 1957, *With Love and Lizards*, London: Michael Joseph.

Moulier Boutang, Yann, 1998, *De l'esclavage au salariat: Économie historique du salariat bridé*. Paris: Presses Universitaires de France.

Moulier Boutang, Yann, 2018, 'Forms of Unfree Labor: Primitive Accumulation, History or Prehistory of Capitalism?', *Viewpoint Magazine*, 1 February.

Müller, Gersine, and Johanna Abel, 2016, 'Cultural Forms of Representation of "Coolies": Khal Torabully and his concept of Coolitude' in Damir-Geilsdorf, Sabine, Ulrike Lindner, Gersine Müller, Oliver Tappe, and Michael Zeuske (eds.), 2016, *Bonded Labour: Global and Comparative Perspectives*, Bielefeld: Transcript Verlag.

Natarajan, Nithya, Katherine Brickell, Laurie Parsons, 2021, 'Diffuse Drivers of Modern Slavery: From Microfinance to Unfree Labour in Cambodia', *Development and Change*, Vol. 52, No. 2.

Navrozov, Andrei, 2002, *Italian Carousel: Scenes of Internal Exile*, Oxted, Surrey: Hurtwood Press Limited.

Negri, Livio (ed.), 1990, *The Sheltering Sky: A Bernado Bertolucci Film based on the novel by Paul Bowles*, London: Scribners.

Newby, Eric, 1971, *Love and War in the Apennines*, London: Hodder & Stoughton Ltd.

Nieboer, H.J., 1910, *Slavery as an Industrial System*, The Hague: Martinus Nijhoff.

Novak, Paulo, 2021, 'Marx, the Chief, the Prisoner and the Refugee', in Alessandra Mezzadri (ed.).

Nove, Alec, 1990, 'The Return of Chayanov', in Mats Lundahl and Thommy Svensson (eds.), *Agrarian Society in History: Essays in Honour of Magnus Mörner*, London: Routledge.

Paulson, Beldon, 1966, *The Searchers: Conflict and Communism in an Italian Town*, Chicago, IL: Quadrangle Books.

Payne, Sebastian, 2021, *Broken Heartlands: A Journey through Labour's Lost England*, London: Macmillan.

Pegler, Lee, 2015, 'Peasant inclusion in global value chains: economic upgrading but social downgrading in labour processes?', *The Journal of Peasant Studies*, Vol. 42, No. 5.

Phillips, Ulrich Bonnell, 1918, *American Negro Slavery*, New York: D. Appleton & Company.

Phillips, Ulrich Bonnell, 1929, *Life and Labor in the Old South*, Boston, MA: Little, Brown, and Company.

Phillips, Ulrich Bonnell, 1939, *The Course of the South to Secession* (edited by E. Merton Coulter), New York: D. Appleton-Century Company Inc.

Prakash, Gyan (ed.), 1992, *The World of the Rural Labourer in Colonial India*, Delhi: Oxford University Press.

Prakash, Gyan, 1990a, *Bonded Histories: Genealogies of Labor Servitude in Colonial India*, Cambridge: Cambridge University Press.

Prakash, Gyan, 1990b, 'Bonded Labour in South Bihar: A Contestatory History,' in Sugata Bose (ed.), *South Asia and World Capitalism*, Delhi: Oxford University Press.

Prasad, Pradhan H., 1974, 'Limits to Investment Planning', in Ashok Mitra (ed.), *Economic Theory and Planning: Essays in Honour of A.K. Das Gupta*, Calcutta: Oxford University Press.

Prasad, Pradhan H., 1989, *Lopsided Growth: The Political Economy of Indian Development*, Bombay: Oxford University Press.

Pritchett, Victor Sawdon (ed.), 1948, *Turnstile One: A Literary Miscellany from The New Statesman and Nation*, London: Turnstile Press.

Propp, Vladímir, 1968, *The Morphology of the Folktale*, Austin TX: University of Texas Press.

Ralston, W.R.S. (ed.), 1869, Krilof and his Fables, London: Strahan and Co., Publishers.

Red Notes, 1978, Italy 1977–78: 'Living with an Earthquake', London: Red Notes.

Regalia, Ida, Marino Regini, and Emilio Reyneri, 1978, 'Labour Conflicts and Industrial Relations in Italy', in Colin Crouch and Alessandro Pizzorno (eds.), *The Resurgence of Class Conflict in Western Europe Since 1968: Volume 1* – National Studies, London: The Macmillan Press.

Rioux, Sébastien, Genevieve LeBaron, and Peter J. Verovšek, 2020, 'Capitalism and unfree labour: a review of Marxist perspectives on modern slavery', *Review of International Political Economy*, Vol. 27, No. 3.

Risley, Sir Herbert, 1908, *The People of India*, London: W. Thacker & Co.

Robb, James H., 1954, *Working Class Anti-Semite: A Psychological Study in a London Borough*, London: Tavistock Publications Ltd.

Rodinson, Maxime, 1974, *Islam and Capitalism* (Translated by Brian Pearce), London: Allen Lane, Penguin Books.

Rodríguez García, Magaly, 2016, 'On the Legal Boundaries of Coerced Labour', in Marcel van der Linden and Magaly Rodríguez García (eds.), *On Coerced Labour: Work and Compulsion after Chattel Slavery*, Leiden: Brill.

Rostow, W.W., 1960, *The Stages of Economic Growth: A Non-Communist Manifesto*, London: Cambridge University Press.

Rudra, Ashok, et al. 1978, *Studies in the Development of Capitalism in India*, Lahore: Vanguard Books.

Runciman, Steven, 1991, *A Traveller's Alphabet: Partial Memoirs*, New York: Thames & Hudson.

Russel, Robert Royal, 1923, 'Economic Aspects of Southern Sectionalism, 1840–1861', *University of Illinois Studies in the Social Sciences*, Vol. XI, No. 1.

Russell, Bertrand, 1956, *Portraits from Memory and other Essays*, London: George Allen & Unwin Ltd.

Sahlins, Marshall, 1972, *Stone Age Economics*, Chicago, IL: Aldine Atherton, Inc.

Said, Edward W., 2002, *Reflections on Exile and Other Essays*, Cambridge, MA: Harvard University Press.

Sartre, Jean-Paul, 1948, *Portrait of the Anti-Semite* (translated by Erik de Mauny), London: Secker & Warburg.

Satya, Laxman, 1997a, 'Colonial Sedentarisation and Subjugation: The Case of the Banjaras of Berar 1850–1900', *The Journal of Peasant Studies*, Vol. 24, No. 4.

Satya, Laxman, 1997b, *Cotton and Famine in Berar, 1850–1900*, New Delhi: Manohar.

Satya, Laxman, 2004, 'Balutedari as a System of Production, Distribution and Power in Eighteenth and Nineteenth Century Deccan', in A. Satyanarayana and P. Chenna Reddy (eds.), *Recent Trends in Historical Studies*, New Delhi: Research India Press.

Scott, James C., 1976, *The Moral Economy of the Peasant: Rebellion and Subsistence in Southeast Asia*, New Haven, CT: Yale University Press.

Scott, James C., 1985, *Weapons of the Weak: Everyday Forms of Peasant Resistance*, New Haven, CT: Yale University Press.

Serge, Victor, 1963, *Memoirs of a Revolutionary 1901–1941*, London: Oxford University Press.

Shah, Alpa, and Barbara Harriss-White, 2011, 'Resurrecting Scholarship on Agrarian Transformations', *Economic and Political Weekly*, Vol. XLVI, No. 39.

Shanin, Teodor (ed.), 1971, *Peasants and Peasant Societies*, London: Penguin Books.

Shanin, Teodor, 1972, *The Awkward Class: Political Sociology of Peasantry in a Developing Society – Russia 1910–1925*, London: Oxford University Press.

Shanin, Teodor, 1985, *Russia as a 'Developing Society' – The Roots of Otherness: Russia's Turn of Century, Volume 1*, London: Macmillan.

Shanin, Teodor, 1986, *Russia 1905–07, Revolution as a Moment of Truth – The Roots of Otherness: Russia's Turn of Century, Volume 2*, London: Macmillan.

Shanin, Teodor, 1990, *Defining Peasants*, Oxford: Basil Blackwell.

Silone, Ignazio, 1960 [1934], *Fontamara* (Translated from the Italian by Harvey Fergusson II, Foreword by Malcom Cowley), New York: Atheneum Publishers.

Slicher van Bath, Bernard Hendrik, 1963, *The Agrarian History of Western Europe, A.D. 500–1850*, London: Edward Arnold Publishers, Ltd.

Smiles, Samuel, 1877, *Self-Help; with illustrations of Conduct and Perseverance*, London: John Murray, Albemarle Street.

Smiles, Samuel, 1885, *Character*, London: John Murray, Albemarle Street.

Smiles, Samuel, 1888, *Thrift*, London: John Murray, Albemarle Street.

Smiles, Samuel, 1892, *Duty; with illustrations of Courage, Patience, & Endurance*, London: John Murray, Albemarle Street.

Smith, R.E.F. (ed.), 1977, *The Russian Peasant 1920 and 1984*, London: Frank Cass & Co. Ltd.

Smith, Valene L. (ed.), 1978, *Hosts and Guests: The Anthropology of Tourism*, Oxford: Basil Blackwell.

Sorokin, Pitrim, and Carle C. Zimmerman, 1939, *Principles of Rural-Urban Sociology*, New York: Henry Holt and Company.

Srinivas, M.N., A.M. Shah, and E.A. Ramaswamy (eds.), 1979, *The Fieldworker and the Field: Problems and Challenges in Sociological Investigation*, Delhi: Oxford University Press.

Stevano, Sara, 2021, 'Marx and the Poor's Nourishment: Diets in Contemporary Sub-Saharan Africa', in Alessandra Mezzadri (ed.). *Marx in the Field*, London: Anthem Press.

Sutch, Richard, 1975, 'The Treatment Received by American Slaves: A Critical Review of the Evidence Presented in Time on the Cross,' *Explorations in Economic History*, Vol. 12, No. 4.

Sweezy, Paul M., 1946, *The Theory of Capitalist Development: Principles of Marxian Political Economy*, London: Dennis Dobson Limited.

Swire, Sasha, 2021, *Diary of an MP's Wife*, London: Abacus.

Symonds, John Addington, 1884, *New Italian Sketches*, Leipzig: Bernhard Tauchnitz.

Symonds, Margaret, 1908 [1893], *Days Spent on a Doge's Farm*, London: T. Fisher Unwin.

Szerb, Antal, 2012 [1937], *Journey by Moonlight* (Translated from the Hungarian by Len Rix), London: Pushkin Press.

Szerb, Antal, 2014 [1936], *The Third Tower: Journeys in Italy* (Translated from the Hungarian by Len Rix), London: Pushkin Press.

Tadman, Michael, 1989, *Speculators and Slaves: Masters, Traders, and Slaves in the Old South*, Madison, WI: The University of Wisconsin Press.

Tappe, Oliver, and Ulrike Lindner, 2016, 'Global Variants of Bonded Labour', in Damir-Geilsdorf, Sabine, Ulrike Lindner, Gersine Müller, Oliver Tappe, and Michael Zeuske (eds.), 2016, *Bonded Labour: Global and Comparative Perspectives*, Bielefeld: Transcript Verlag.

Taussig, Michael, 1984, 'Culture of Terror – Space of Death: Roger Casement's Putumayo Report and the Explanation of Torture', *Comparative Studies in Society and History*, Vol. 26, No. 3.

Theroux, Paul, 2018, *Figures in a Landscape – People and Places: Essays 2001–2016*, London: Hamish Hamilton.

Thorner, Daniel, 1966, 'Chayanov's Concept of Peasant Economy', in Chayanov. A. V., 1966 [1923] *The Theory of Peasant Economy* (edited by Daniel Thorner, Basile Kerblay, and R. E. F. Smith), Homewood, Illinois: Published for The American Economic Association by Richard D. Irwin, Inc.

Thorner, Daniel, 1980, *The Shaping of Modern India*, New Delhi: Allied Publishers Private Limited.

Trotsky, Leon, 1930, *My Life*, London: Thornton Butterworth, Limited.

Trotsky, Leon, 1934, *The History of the Russian Revolution* (Translated by Max Eastman), London: Victor Gollancz Ltd.

Trotsky, Leon, 1962 [1928], *The Permanent Revolution*, London: New Park Publications.

Trotsky, Leon, 1964 [1937], 'Thermidor and Anti-Semitism', in Howe, Irving (ed.), 1964, *The Basic Writings of Trotsky*, London: Secker & Warburg.

Trotsky, Leon, 1972, *1905* (translated by Anya Bostock), London: Allen Lane The Penguin Press.

United States Senate Commission, 1913, *Agricultural Cooperation and Rural Credit in Europe*, Washington, DC: Government Printing Office.

van der Linden, Marcel, and Karl Heinz Roth (eds.), 2014, *Beyond Marx: Theorising the Global Labour Relations of the Twenty-First Century*. Leiden: Brill.

van der Ploeg, Jan Douwe, 2021, 'Stiefmoeder Aarde [Stepmother Earth] by Theun de Vries (1936)', *The Journal of Peasant Studies*, Vol. 48, No. 5.

van der Ploeg, Jan Dowe, 2013, *Peasants and the Art of Farming: A Chayanovian Manifesto*, Halifax, NS: Fernwood Publishing Co. Ltd.

van der Ploeg, Jan Dowe, 2017, 'The importance of peasant agriculture: a neglected truth', Address at Wageningen University, 26 January.

Verga, Giovanni, 1928, *Cavelleria Rusticana and Other Stories* (Translated and introduced by D.H. Lawrence), London: Jonathan Cape.

Verga, Giovanni, 1929, *Little Novels of Italy* (Translated by D.H. Lawrence), Oxford: Basil Blackwell.

Visconti, Luchino, 1970, *Two Screenplays: La Terra Trema, Senso* (Translated from the Italian by Judith Green), New York: The Orion Press.

Walbank, F.W., 1946, *The Decline of the Roman Empire in the West*, London: Cobbett Press (Past and Present Series: Studies in the History of Civilization).

Walicki, Andrzej, 1969, *The Controversy over Capitalism: Studies in the Philosophy of the Russian Populists*, Oxford: Clarendon Press.

Wallerstein, Immanuel, 1979, *The Capitalist World Economy*, Cambridge: Cambridge University Press.

Weiner, Myron (ed.), 1966, *Modernization: The Dynamics of Growth*, Washington, DC: Voice of America Lectures.

Westermark, Edward, 1906/1908, *The Origin and Development of the Moral Ideas* (2 volumes), London: Macmillan and Co., Limited.

Wharton, Clifton R. (ed.), 1970, *Subsistence Agriculture and Economic Development*, London: Frank Cass & Co. Ltd.

White, Caroline, 1980, *Patrons and Partisans: A Study of Politics in Two Southern Italian Comuni,* Cambridge University Press.

Whiteside, Andrew Gadding, 1975, *Austrian National Socialism before 1918*, The Hague: Martinus Nijhoff.

Wickham, Chris, 1985, 'The Uniqueness of the East', *The Journal of Peasant Studies*, Vol. 12, Nos. 2–3.

Wickham, Chris, 2021, 'How did the Feudal Economy Work? The Economic Logic of Medieval Societies', *Past and Present*, Vol. 251, Issue 1.

Wilde, Oscar, 1891, *The Picture of Dorian Gray*, London: Ward Locke & Co.

Winters, Ben H., 2016, *Underground Airlines*, London: Century/Random House.

Wish, Harvey (ed.), 1960, *Antebellum: Writings of George Fitzhugh and Hinton Rowan Helper on Slavery.* New York: G.F. Putnam's Sons.

Wish, Harvey, 1943, *George Fitzhugh, Propagandist of the Old South*, Baton Rouge, LA: Louisiana State University Press.

Wolpe, Harold (ed.), 1980, *The Articulation of Modes of Production*, London and Boston, MA: Routledge & Kegan Paul.

Wright, Adrian, 1996, *Foreign Country: The Life of L.P. Hartley*, London: Andre Deutsch.

Author Index

Subject Index